unCONVENTionAL WOMEN

Copyright 2001 by Marie Therese Gass
Printed in Canada

Short quotations from this book may be used in book reviews. Otherwise, no part of this book may be reproduced in any way without permission of the author and publishing company.

Permission to quote from Joseph V. Montville's Preface to Michael Henderson's book, **The Forgiveness Factor** (Grosvenor Books, 1996) is gratefully acknowledged.

Permission to reprint Will Liebo's essay "My First Grade School Year" is also gratefully acknowledged.

Publisher's Cataloging-in-Publication
provided by Quality Books, Inc.

    Unconventional women : 73 ex-nuns tell their stories /
   [compiled] by Marie Therese Gass. – 1st ed.
      p. cm.
      ISBN: 0-9651816-5-0

      1. Ex-nuns—United States—Biography. 2. Monastic
   and religious life of women--United States. 3. Catholic
   Church--Controversial literature. I. Gass, Marie
   Therese

   BX4668.2.U53 2001   271.9'0022
                             QBI01-200456

ISBN: 0-9651816-5-0

Layout, cover, design by MTG

Sieben Hill, PO Box 243, Clackamas OR 97015

unCONVENtional WOMEN

73 EX-NUNS TELL THEIR STORIES

Marie Therese Gass

Sieben Hill

dedication

to the 73 women who tell their stories here
to all former women religious
to good women everywhere
and
especially
to "Dorothy" (1917-1999)

UNCONVENTIONAL WOMEN

Table of Contents

Dedication...i
Table of Contents...ii
Note to the Reader...vii
Prologue..xi
Preface...xii
Introduction by Lillana Kopp, SFCC......................................xviv
Key to Participants' ages, years spent in convent..................xx

I Beginnings

What is this thing called Vocation?..3
Religion and family backgrounds of the participants...............6
The first steps...12
Schooling before entering the convent..................................16
The main reason we entered (hindsight)...............................17
Persons/things that Influenced our entering the convent.....19
Dowry, trousseau...32
Haircuts..34
The religious habit (clothing)...36

II Religious Life

Aspirancy, Postulancy, Novitiate...47
Juniorate (Temporary Professed), The Final Professed.......54
The Holy Rule..58
Meditation..62
Greeting phrase, Silence,..64
Required prayers, Rituals..68
Permissions, miscellaneous arrangements..........................71
Tea for the Benefactors..75
The Leaving process...77

III Good Things

Music, leisure, laughter, feastdays, humor...81

IV Suffering

Flagellation, other instruments of self-torture...93
Attitude toward Suffering in general..100
Chapter of Faults..108
Guilt, assigned/voluntary penances...116
Naivete and self-esteem..118

V The Refectory

Food, ambiance, rituals..123
Readings...128
Doing Martyrology...130

VI Health in the convent

Physical and mental health in general...139
Sleep, insomnia..152
On feeling of value..155
Control over one's life..157
What made nuns cry?..159
Cancer and other illnesses...161

VII Sexuality

Notes on sexuality, crushes..165
Friendships and Particular Friendships...166
On being Lesbian...172

Foreknowledge of sex..176
Sexual attractions in the convent..178
Having sex in the convent..184
Pregnancy, abortion..186
Bride of Christ, Jesus as teen idol..187

VIII The World as seen from the convent and vice versa

Knuckle-rapping nuns 195
Changing familial relationships...197
Contacts, the media, voting, advisory boards 200
My 1st Grade School Year 203
Education, careers, jobs, salaries...204
Relationship with the Pastor..210

IX Liabilities

Racism, Prejudice, Public Injustice..213
Tension, Fear, Use of Guilt..218
Dealing with personal Injustices, Unhappiness.......................227

X Peers

Social strata, gossip, rank...241
The convent elite..247
Personal Shunning...250

XI Leaving

Why I Don't Tell That I'm an Ex-Nun 263
The Leaving decision, process...264
Leaving in the 50s...266
Leaving in the 60s...269

Leaving in the 70s..286
Leaving in the 80s..300

XII Healing, Dreams

Healing and dreams...305
Advantages to having left the convent...309
Disadvantages to having left the convent..310
Blocked memories..313
First memories—bitter, sweet?..318
Satisfaction (hindsight)..325
Letters home..328
Early dating, relationships...329
Outsider reaction to ex-nuns..333
Meeting with other ex-nuns, nuns..338
Organized Convent Reunions...340

XIII Advice

Advice to the Pope...351
Advice to Catholics in America..356
Advice to those wishing to enter a convent..362
Would we encourage anyone to enter a convent today?..............................367

XIV Today's ex-nun and the Church

Treatment by the Church..371
Practicing Catholicism...373
Brands of American ex-nun Catholicism..377
Holding with the Pope's authority..379
The role of women in Church...382
Relative value of the religious Vocation...388
Sacraments and sacramentals today..391

God, Hell, angels, Mary, Immaculate Conception.....................397

XV Making It

Current statistics on Participants..............................407
On having been a women in the convent........................410
If things had been different, would we have stayed?..........416
Are we glad we were nuns?.....................................420
Are we happier now?..427
Convent values retained..431
Can you recognize an ex-nun on the street?..................438
On being Successful...441
On having worked the questionnaire...........................448

XVI Glossary

Brief descriptions of terms according to mid-1900s thinking............457

XVII Notes

The Questionnaire..479
Methodology..487
Charts, tables, other statistics................................493
Epilogue and Acknowledgments.................................499
About the Author...501

Note to the Reader

Welcome to our stories. unCONVENTional WOMEN relates the extraordinarily true and hitherto untold accounts of the lives of 73 U.S. Roman Catholic ex-nuns. This book is a telling of personal experiences; it is not a history book. The first woman participant in this project to enter a convent did so in 1933, and the last one left in 1985. Each of these women spent a part of the mid-1900s in convents, although there is a distinct difference between what happened in pre-Vatican II and post-Vatican II institutions (see Glossary, as well as numerous references throughout the text). For more on Vatican II and its meaning, read Jo Ann Kay McNamara's historical/sociological *Sisters in Arms*, Andrew Greeley's fictionized *White Smoke*, or any of the many fine books and articles on the subject.

The Glossary (Chapter XVI) is valuable to any reader, but particularly to those who are unfamiliar with older Catholic terms. Explanations of each entry are geared toward what was known/believed in the 50s. Take a quick peek at the glossary every time you meet a term you don't understand.

For the sake of brevity and uniformity, the terms "Nun" and "Sister" are used interchangeably, as are "Order" and "Community". We use "Ex-Nun" because it is shorter and more familiar to the reader than "Former Woman Religious". "Girl" is often used to refer to the candidate ready to enter the convent, because most of these ranged from 14-18 years old.

"All", "everyone" and other inclusive/exclusive terms in reference to mores outside the convent, refer to the usual standard, e.g., "No one dyed her hair purple in those days" does not mean that nowhere on the planet had any human being ever dyed her hair purple, but that generally no one did this, and that you would be hard pressed to find a purple-haired person on the streets.

The signed name at the end of a quotation is a pseudonym, though one or two women decided to use their real first names as their code names. Out of respect for their choices, the author has numbered duplicate names, e.g., JEAN-2, JEAN-3, rather than deny the participant her choice of name. The person with the pseudonym "Marie" is not the author. All convents, Superiors, states, Nun-names, and other identifying details have been changed. You may notice that some Latin names for flowers have been substituted for Sister-names. No incidents are fictitious.

The Key Page (before the text) lists the participant's pseudonym, the *age* at which she entered the convent, and the *years* she entered and left. This is important in order to understand why or how two persons from the same Order could have had two opposite experiences—as we have said, before Vatican II and after it were different worlds. Also, the early-teenager came with (and interpreted) experiences different from the 30-year old. The woman who spent most of her convent days under the old regime, has vastly different tales from the one who entered in the midst of the changes. Of course, the nun who was in the convent for 2 years has a different outlook than the one who was there for 40 years.

As often as possible, the exact words of the contributor are used. Other grammar preferences, elimination of repetition, and occasional inclusion of the question in the answer, are editorial changes. In no case has the original meaning or bent of the ex-nun's answer been tampered with.

No one thinks *exactly* the same as anyone else. For this reason, on Yes/No questions followed up by Why (or some other tangent), what the participant wrote was not changed, e.g., she may have answered Yes, then given a reason that I personally think goes with No. Her Yes/No answer would then be listed as Yes, and her explanation follows as it was written. It is not the author's place to change the answers.

Though there were 73 participants, not every question has 73 answers. Some women preferred not to answer certain questions; others gave two answers where one was asked for. In most cases, the number of ex-nuns who answered the question in any way, is listed.

In general, when no distinction is made, the stories/editorializing are done from the viewpoint of the mid-1900s. As much as possible, the ambiance of that time is laid out before the quotations, e.g., in those days, everything had to be "looked up" somewhere in order to be considered valid—basing knowledge on your own feelings or thoughts was not permissible. No one was allowed to trust her inner self, or even acknowledge it. Anything printed in a book was considered to be true. The *appearance* of things and situations was more important than what was *really* going on, and telling Catholic inner-workings (secrets) was both *verboten* and scandalous. It was common to obey for the sole reason that "the Church said so", and it was considered rude (and possibly dangerous to one's faith) to ask questions or expect explanations. Hell was a real place to which one could go in a second, if one died with mortal sin on one's soul. Priests interpreted the religion to the people; one did not make up one's own mind what the Bible was telling us. Negative and problematic things (e.g., racism) mostly were not spoken of. Most Caucasians associated only with other whites, and had no occasion to think about the rest of the world. Your parents and other adults were right and to be obeyed; the government was right, the Church was right, and above all, your Mother Superior was always right—she was the conduit for the Will of God to you.

As in real life, every category overlaps. E.g., the answer to a specific question could add more value to several chapters, not just one. So if you're looking for, say, Good Things in the convent, the chapter called Good Things is not the only place you'll find them.

unCONVENTional WOMEN is the non-glamorized version of convent life. Most ex-nuns felt the Church and laity did not care about them or why they left; now they are telling their stories. The accounts deal with issues and incidents that will touch you, make you angry or amused, or may even shock you. Reading about someone else's injustice may tap into your own feelings of having been unjustly treated. But you are an intelligent 21st century reader—you know how to get help when something happens that you cannot handle alone.

This book is best approached without pre-judgment. Listen, learn, and enrich your own life by reading the stories and comments of the courageous women who experienced life in U.S. convents in the mid-1900s.

❖❖❖

UNCONVENTIONAL WOMEN

Prologue

The first year I began working on unCONVENTional WOMEN, I developed an unusual physical problem: several times a day and during the night I would get violent uncontrollable dry heaves. I wasn't nauseated, just retching. These incidents would come on without warning, even in the dentist's chair. It was very embarrassing. The doctors checked all the usual places where cancer might have recurred, and two infectious disease specialists tried for a diagnosis along with several other doctors, but nobody could find the reason.

My primary physician had always held the theory that the body knows anniversaries, so I'd checked all the traumatic events in my life, but none of them seemed to match.

Then one day—it was near the end of June, I'm back in the doctor's office complaining again and hoping for some cure, and I'm saying, "I don't *need* an illness. My life is just fine. Why is this happening?"

He thinks of something. "What date did you leave the convent?"

"June 26th." I inhale quickly without meaning to.

"No, what year?"

"Year? I don't know. '64 or '63—1963, that was it." And right then my brain blanks out. I don't understand the connection between the convent and the retching. I haven't thought about the convent for years. And my brain refuses to compute the years since then.

"It's thirty years," he says softly. "1963 to 1993."

We are both silent.

The retching tapered off soon after that, no other cause ever having been found.

❖❖❖

Preface

Once upon a time there was a young girl who felt called by God to enter a convent. In her first years there, she memorized The Holy Rule and learned to observe the customs of the Order. She was surprised that life in the convent was not exactly the way it appeared to those on the outside. For example, the Rule of Silence was often difficult for her, because as a teenager, the girl loved to talk.

The girl stayed for 16 years in that Community. During that time, she met and became friends with some wonderful, inspiring women. She also had run-ins with nuns whose ideas conflicted with hers. She prayed every day and asked God to keep her Vocation safe, and to help her to do her jobs well.

But one day, after a long time of doubt, it became clear that the girl (now in a woman's body) needed to leave the convent in order to preserve her ideals and individuality. By then, she saw that there were many ways in the outside world that one could serve God through humanity. The girl left the convent and started her new life, which was lonely at first, because she had been told not to speak to the nun-friends she left behind.

Some days the girl was happy, so happy that she could walk in the sunshine and talk to everyone and make her own decisions about what to wear and how to live. Other days, the girl cried because she missed her friends, and she was still hurt from some things that had happened while she was a nun. The girl had a choice: to bury all the negative memories and concentrate on her new life, or to think things through and discuss them with a friend, a therapist, or with other ex-nuns.

While she was deciding what to do, a questionnaire became available for a survey project by another ex-nun. The girl decided to try filling in the answers, but soon discovered three things: 1) there was more than one line's worth that she wished to say about some subjects, 2) the questionnaire reminded her of some things she had tried to forget because they were painful, and 3) she was concerned that this material might be used to "prove" that ex-nuns were bad, or that the convent was bad, or that convent life was worthless.

The girl called the author of the project. "I have never told anyone that I am an ex-nun," she said. "When I entered the convent my parents disowned me, so when I left, I went to another state, and have never told anyone. What good will it do to write this down now?"

The author told her about using a pseudonym, and promised never to tell the girl's real name without her permission. She also told the girl about other ex-nuns who were too timid to tell their stories, but who could reach some healing by reading her story. So the girl, and 72 others like her, answered the questions, sent tapes, and typed many additional pages of information for the project.

This is their book.

Marie Therese Gass
March 11, 2000

INTRODUCTION

During the mid-20th Century, massive transitional forces were unleashed within the once rather changeless Catholic Church. Even previous to the Vatican II Council reforms, this earlier update movement began addressing many antiquated patterns within the Catholic Sisterhoods of vowed Women Religious--especially their highly authoritarian governance, patterns of exclusion "from the world", and their medieval dress styles. All of Catholic Christendom was impacted to some degree by trends toward modernism. But inevitably, the most rigid, highly structured and male-dominated patterns unique to Sisters, felt the tremors of the modernization transition most disruptively, when in the early 1950s, with no previous communication or cooperative input from world Sisters, Pope Pius XII issued two directives that would alter their lives significantly, and in some instances, traumatically.

The Pope's directives required Sisterhoods to accelerate the educational status of their members, and to eliminate out-dated rules and their traditional 16th century dress codes. The response of the Sisters in the United States was less than immediate and sometimes unexpectedly disruptive. For example, the fact that the younger Sisters were soon sent off to colleges and universities for degrees, tended to create age factions and status differences seldom experiences in former eras. This book by Marie Therese Gass may be the first to address this particular renewal issue as problematic. Her survey and interview methodology with 73 "ex-nuns" contributes to a forceful presentation of a negative effect of a positive step forward. Sisterhoods had been such closed-off, in-bred, exclusionary groups that even to this present period, negative aspects of religious life were seldom discussed and exposed to view outside the confines of the convent. Before 1965 when Phase II of the religious renewal process began in aftermath of Vatican II document publications, little had been researched and written about the ordinary travail and psychological tensions generated by the extremely structured and burearcratized lives of Sisters in their highly efficient institutions. At that time, for Religious Women to live without criticism or complaint was regarded as the height of virtue. Directives from Rome were especially honored without critique, and even thought of as the Word and Will of God on the Sisters' behalf.

But during the second phase of renewal, a significant turning point emerged. It represented no revolutionary uprising of Sisters, but rather a GREAT AWAKENING among those who had become theologians, psychologists, sociologists, philosophers, and experts in other fields of research and study relevant to Sisterhood Renewal and Religious Life development. These newly degreed scholars began to add their insights and voices to the Renewal Literature and Renewal Conferences which had previously been almost the exclusive domain of the clergy and Church hierarchy. The latter, though no doubt men of high intelligence and talent, were far less aware of some of the most important issues recognized by Women Religious as imperative for research and remediation. Consequently, a major characteristic of Phase II Renewal was that change initiatives became almost wholly Sister-generated. The forces triggering this unprecedented response from American Sisters were thought to have been the cumulative impact of the following:

1) Pope Pius XII's mandate for the acceleration of the education of Sisters to match the expertise of their professional peers

2) Vatican II's liberating influence, and in particular its call for the broad implementation of the social principles of subsidiarity and collegiality through the Church

3) The world-wide WOMEN'S MOVEMENT committed to the promotion of social justice in all spheres of human activity, and especially in the religious sphere where patriarchal clergy were exercising male dominance in churches, temples, and synagogues, and persistently diminishing the sacred rights of women by falsely claiming that women are innately inferior and created thusly by God.

A major characteristic of Phase II Renewal of Sisterhoods lay in the fact that American Sisters took over the leadership of their own renewal initiatives. The proliferating writings by dozens of highly qualified Sisters from various Religious Congregations helped to unite American Sisters into many new cooperating groups that bridged their former isolation from one another, and gave a new strength to their roles in the Church. American Sisters, once conditioned to rely only on the words of the clergy, now began to read the books and articles of other Sisters. Some were shocked and dismayed at the new frankness and openness of some writers, but most Sisters seemed elated, encouraged, and inspired by the new confidence and expertise Sisters were manifesting.

Renewal literature of the sixties does not speak of a Phase III of Renewal, but the titles of the collective writings of Sisters appeared to be announcing the Era of the NEW NUNS> Sister Mary Charles Borromeo, CSC, theologian and professor at Notre Dame University, edited with a group of other Sisters (each adding a chapter) the 1965 book on *The Changing Sisters*. This was followed by her publication of *The New Nuns* with others joining her again to address the issues of importance in the Renewal process.

In 1968, sociologist Sister Mary Audrey Kopp's *New Nuns: Collegial Christians* gave the reading public a bold presentation on the history of dominative authority in the Church, a person-diminishing pattern that Vatican II's principle of collegiality could remedy, if implemented. This mini-book, first presented as the opening paper of the 1967 American Catholic Sociological Society Conference, would likely have been condemned for reading by Catholics and especially by Sisters in pre-Vatican II days, but a new sense of freedom and frankness in the late sixties not only allowed, but promoted its reading and discussion at hundreds of Sister Conferences in the United States and Canada, making collegiality a top Renewal goal.

Also in 1968, Sister Mary Peter Traxler edited *New Works of New Nuns* with 17 Sisters contributing chapters describing their new types of service and ministry far beyond the traditional roles of Sisters. Another exciting contribution to the literature of the late 20th century was the 1985 publication edited by Sister Ann Patrick Ware, *Midwives of the Future: American Sisters Tell Their Stories*. This book had a purpose other than story-telling. It was published as a strategy planned by the National Coalition of American Nuns to help counter "ominous signs in the air", and the fact that in 1983, the Congregation of Religious and Secular Institutes in Rome had issued a document called *Essential Elements of Religious Life*. This was a regressive document, and if enforced, could set back the Renewal accomplishments of world Sisters. It seemed to Sisters that the Renewal mandated by one pope was being suppressed by a subsequent pope and men in Rome who had little real understanding of what motivated world Sisters to spend years of collaborative research and prayer to remedy. What many American Sisters feared as a result of the *Essential Elements* document in which they had no voice, came to pass. When their new constitutions were sent to Rome for approval, a cloud of frustration and despair enveloped many Sisterhoods whose most positive constitutional changes were struck out in Rome with red ink. The Sisters had embraced the Vatican II principles of subsidiarity and collegiality with alacrity and gratitude; the men of Rome seemingly had not considered those principles applicable to world Sisters whom they controlled. The results have been tragic and undoubtedly part of the current problem of Vocational dearth afflicting American Sisterhoods.

During the late 1950s and early 1960s American Sisterhoods had experienced an unprecedented growth spurt. Idealistic young women were genuinely interested in living lives of Christ-commitment and service to others through the traditional works of the Sisters. These young women were also expressing deep concern for their own personal maturation and spiritual development.

Consequently, by 1965, the Sister population in the United States peaked at 186,944. Such growth expansion forced many Sisterhoods to build additional facilities for the housing and education of new Postulants, Novices, and Junior Sisters. The Sister Formation Conference, a cooperative, inter-congregational enterprise initiated during the population peak period, had planned a detailed education curriculum and two colleges expressly for the formation of these new members. This splendid new Formation Program flourished a little over a decade and bottomed out for a number of reasons, one of which was a sudden drop in the Sister-population. Mysteriously in one sense, understandable in others, the Kennedy National Catholic Directly statistics showed an erosion in the Sisterhoods. By 1995 the peak statistic of 186,000 had slumped to 86,000----all that loss in a thirty-year period! Three major factors seemed to have been operative:

1) Natural Attrition, or the deaths of elderly members
2) An increased exodus of dissatisfied members

3) A greatly decreasing entrance rate for new candidates

This membership depletion has continued alarmingly into this new millenium with no prospects of abatement or reversal in sight. Many convents, Catholic schools, and social agencies have been forced to close or be staffed by secular workers. Most Sisterhoods have come upon hard times and their continuing visibility is problematic. The accounting firm of Arthur Anderson, Inc., has issued a statement on the financial status of American Religious every two yeaRS SINCE 1984. Their recent reporting shows a $7.9 billion shortage of retirement funds for Religious men, women, and priests.

Why this tragic depletion in a once-vibrant institution? Articles by members of the Catholic hierarchy have shown a certain evasiveness in sharing responsibility for a drastic drop in Church personnel and a concurrent dearth of new Vocations. They seem inclined to attribute the drop-offs to "the signs of the times", to the materialism and selfishness in a secXXX –preoccupied society that produces multitudes of self-centered, pleasure-seeking youths. There is certainly a modicum of truth in the above hypotheses, but do they fully cove the reality? This writer heartily disagrees with Rome's thesis and with the Sacred Congregation for Religious and Secular Institutes in its suppression of collegiality in the new constitutions of the NEW NUNS of America and throughout the world. As a research sociologist for 40 years, a traditional Sister for 30, and initiator of The Sisters for Christian Community—a non-canonical, collegial unity in its 30th year now, we have seen the SFCC become the fastest-growing Sisterhood in the Western world. The SFCC is composed mostly of "ex-nuns", dynamic spiritual women who, in conscience, left traditional Sisterhoods that had become bureaucratized, and which had incorporated into Religious Life all of the dysfunctional elements of bureaucracy. For many of over 1000 members welcomed into this collegial Community of the SFCC, the last straw that broke their resolution to remain traditional Sisters was the *Essential Elements* document and male suppression of collegiality in their new constitutions. Only a collegial community model of the spiritual life welcomes the voice of every member in decision-making for the common good. The voiceless women of the Church must be heard on an equal basis with men in a partnership relation, before true Church and Sisterhood renewal is achieved.

I am confident that those among the NEW CHRISTIANS who have honored the collegial ideal, will also warmly welcome and be enriched by the voices that will inform us in this new contribution to Renewal Literature. *UnCONVENTional WOMEN* has the power to RENEW our determination to continue working in every way possible, for the rebirth of collegial community in the new millenium Church. In respect for a passing culture pattern and a dying authoritarian institution, the voices of these 73 ex-nuns have been silent for too long. Christian Community needs their continuing input, and that of all its members.

Lillana Kopp, SFCC

June 15, 2000

KEY TO PSEUDONYMNS OF PARTICIPANTS, AGES ENTERED, YEARS SPENT IN THE CONVENT

PSEUDONYM	ENTERED AT	ENTERED	LEFT
Ann	18 yrs	1957	1969
Anne	18	1952	1979
Beverly	18	1964	1966
Caren	18	1958	1965
Carol	17	1955	1969
Carol-2	17	1959	1973
Carolyn	19	1960	1979
Casey	15	1960	1973
Cherry	20	1960	1973
Connie	18	1962	1969
Denise	14	1964	1971
Diane	17	1960	1984
Dolores	18	1953	1960
Donna	18	1963	1965
Doris	15	1956	1963
Dorothy	18?	1934	1954
Eileen	28	1952	1971
Eleanor	14	1952	1965
Elizabeth	16	1956	1967
Ellen	19	1955	1963
Ellen-2	27	1957	1974

Frances	16	1942	1968
Gayle	17	1957	1963
Gina	22	1955	1972
Grace	19	1948	1960
Helga	18	1952	1968
Holly	18	1954	1983
Jan	16	1956	1961
Jan-2	19	1946	1972
Jane	17	1962	1972
Janet	24	1960	1972
Janet K	17	1955	1972
Jann	17	1958	1970
Jean	18	1959	1981
Jean-2	19	1957	1969
Jean-3	18	1946	1967
Jessica	18	1958	1970
Josephine	18	1955	1957
Judy	18	1939	1972
Julia	18	1963	1973
Julia-2	19	1956	1963
Julianne	18	1949	1976
Kate	18	1959	1971
Kathleen	16	1956	1957
KT	18	1961	1969
Lilla	18	1946	1965
Lorena	19	1950	1971
Lorna	18	1955	1956
Louise	16	1954	1985
Mae	18	1962	1985
Margaret	15	1958	1977
Marie	18	1960	1985

Marietta	23	1957	1978
Martha	18	1958	1963
Mary	18	1943	1965
Mary S	17	1958	1981
Mary-2	18	1961	1974
Maxine	30	1955	1957
Mert	18	1959	1965
Muriel	18	1952	1977
Nancy	18	1951	1958
Nell	18	1953	1973
Otter	18	1963	1967
Priscilla	21	1933	1972
Rose	17	1953	1968
Sarah	18	1963	1977
Shirley	17	1957	1962
Suzanne	18	1959	1974
Theresa	18	1959	1970
Therese	17	1952	1969
Therese-2	17	1940	1966
Trace	18	1953	1959
Yvonne	18	1939	1969

Beginnings

religious & family background
immediate stimulus/influences to entering
previous schooling, dowry, trousseau, first steps
the religious habit (clothing), haircuts

What is this thing called "Vocation"?

Why did they, these intelligent young girls from varied backgrounds and families—why did they enter the closed-off convents of the 1900s? Why would any teenager (and most of them were that) in love with the good life want to leave her boyfriends and girlfriends, job and career opportunities? Whatever gave them the idea to become nuns? Why enter a convent?

First of all, in a convent, you could save the world. Young women of the first half of the century had the same yearnings to save the world as a lot of students today, but then there was no Peace Corps, no local or national organizations where high school or college graduates could do a stint at giving back, while they saw the world. Religious Orders, besides teaching Orders, were involved in missionary work, nursing, working with the poor. In a computerless world with far less individual monies and fewer prospects of travel, they were an organized way of being able to reach those who needed help.

Secondly, you had a Vocation. A female only entered the convent if she "had a Vocation" with a capital "V", spoken of with a slight pause before the word (e.g., Mom, how do you know if you have a * Vocation?). Vocation in Catholic circles *always* referred to the direct calling from God to an individual, an unrefusable request (we wouldn't call this an "order" since we were taught that God respected our free will) to spend her life in service to humankind according to a certain Religious Community's rules and direction.

One "knew one had a Vocation" if one felt drawn to the work of a specific Community or Order, or to the religious life in general (about which the lay person and pre-entrant knew maybe 2% in those days of secrecy). We, who in the 1950s were told not to question authority nor to follow our own ideas, were told to "listen" to someplace inside of us where the call would be heard. It was easy to think long enough about the possibility of a Vocation, then "know" one had one.

The other way a girl learned of her Vocation was: if a nun whose wisdom she feared or respected *told* her that she had a Vocation, then no doubt about it, she had one.

The girl would mull over the idea, speak to the Superior of the Order she felt most drawn to, and agree to enter for what was technically a trying-it-out period, though most entrants were as hesitant to leave after a month as if they'd stayed for years. To leave was not only humiliating (the entrant did not realize this coming in), but it had implications that the girl had failed or wasn't good enough. It also might lead others to suspect that one lacked good judgment or whatever other qualities one would have had to have had in order to "stay". I don't recall anyone of our group's leaving without floods of tears and much anguish, even though we were not allowed to speak to the person leaving, and merely watched surreptitiously as she was counseled in hallways or stairwells.

There was also the very real possibility in those days, that a girl who left, even in the early months, was *denying* her Vocation, a very serious thing indeed. While no one accused the girl of this aloud, she was spoken of in hushed tones with shakings of the head. "We don't *know* if she had a Vocation", a Superior told us solemnly when one of our group left. Was she mistaken in her calling? Could she possibly go to Hell for not having followed her Vocation? It wasn't possible for us to figure it out, but it gave us shivers, and we prayed all the harder—not that we would know IF we had a Vocation, but that our Vocations would be secure.

Religious Vocations, an honor and a privilege, came with heavy punishment for the girl who spurned the call. Many of us had been taught by priests and nuns that to refuse a Vocation would put us in danger of going to Hell. And Hell of the early 1900s was the real thing: eternal and unbearable fire and brimstone with torture from the devils themselves, who took out their revenge on lost souls since they were not able to get back at God Himself. From the guest mission priest who hollered about eternal punishment from the pulpit in parishes a couple of times a year, to our Superiors who spoke of it in hushed tones, we learned that there was no recourse from a Hell-sentence, and that if we didn't want to be in extreme pain and suffering for all eternity from the moment of our death, we should avoid anything that might land us in the fiery pit. Losing or denying your Vocation was one of those things.

Non-Catholics have objected: "Couldn't she just go to confession? Wasn't that supposed to remove all sins?" Confessed sins are forgiven under the following conditions: that the confessee was truly sorry, and that she had a firm purpose of amendment—in other words, if she righted the wrong, or went back to the convent (if allowed) after denying her Vocation, she might be forgiven, if not—who knew?

Today, in the 21st century when we respect our own intelligence and rarely do anything *just* because we are told to (without understanding the reasoning behind it), we are certain that girls/women can devote part of their lives to serving God through serving humanity, then leave and do something else, without any fear of Hell whatsoever. God is considered today (by most) to be more Love and Understanding than Wrath and Judgment.

From the mid-60s through at least the 80s, convents and their members were in flux. Individuals and individual thought emerged. Convent rules relaxed in most cases, and convent experiences differed greatly, one house from another, and all from those of previous years. For that reason, the Key to Participants chart is inserted before the first chapter. When you read of two diametrically opposed convent experiences, take a look as to which years are involved: it may help you to understand.

Religions and family backgrounds of the participants

The 73 women involved in this project were not all cradle-Catholics—one each were Methodist, Mormon, Episcopalian, and five were of various other unnamed Protestant denominations, although of course, all converted to Roman Catholicism before entering their convents. The rest came from Catholic families.

For 5 (out of 65 answers) women, religion before the convent played no part or an extremely small part in their lives; for 27, religion took a moderate standing; and for 33 participants, religion was very important in their pre-convent routines. "Practicing one's Catholic religion" in the mid-1900s consisted mostly of attending Mass on Sunday, going to confession and Communion at least once during the Easter season, and contributing to the collection plate. Attendance at Sunday Mass was required under pain of sin. Whether the "sin" part was a true tenant of Rome's written law is irrelevant; it was the common preaching at the time. Not going to Sunday Mass was listed as a sin in all of the Examination of Conscience booklets which Catholic children were given to jog their memories about which sins to confess in confession.

One could be a Catholic in good standing without attending the peripheral ceremonies offered during the year, however, the devout and those who were determined to work off their sin-debt took advantage of all of them. Not all girls/women who entered convents in the early- or mid-1900s had the strong and consistent habit of attending Novenas or First Friday and First Saturday Masses, Stations of the Cross, Benediction, or Our Lady of Perpetual Help Devotions.

Praying for Vocations and saying the Rosary were strongly encouraged, though not mandatory, and the lack of these prayers was not considered sinful. Public Rosaries were said by congregations in church, and are still said at funeral vigils and on Catholic radio programs. Whole worldwide crusades were mounted over the issues of praying for Vocations and saying the Rosary and rare was the

Catholic who did not at least own at least one rosary of her own. "The family that prays together, stays together" was a popular saying.

DID YOU PRAY THE ROSARY AS A FAMILY :
    YES: 34   OCCASIONALLY: 4   RARELY: 1
    NO: 30   NOT ANSWERED: 3

DID YOU PRAY FOR VOCATIONS:
    YES: 30
    NO: 39

DID YOU ATTEND SUNDAY MASS:
    YES: 67
    NO: 4

In the mid-1900s, reasons were rarely given for anything in the Church's teachings. For example, a number of answers to religion questions in the Baltimore Catechism said that such-and-such a thing was that way "Because the Church says so." The rationale behind the urgency of praying for Vocations ran something like this: God (who determined whether one had the highest Vocation--a calling to the priesthood or Sisterhood) calls many, but few listen and respond to their Vocation. Catholic congregations pray that those who have a Religious Vocation will recognize and accept their calling. In the first half of the 1900s as well as for all the years before that, priests and nuns were the official interpreters of God's word to the average lay person. Catholics are sometimes accused of not reading the Bible—well, that was the purpose of listening to sermons in church where the *priest* told the people how it was with them and God. The interpretations of individual Catholics had no standing. The individual Catholic would no more think of reading the Bible and interpreting it him/herself than of writing a letter to the Pope. Catholics were under the impression that they *needed* priests and nuns to guide them in finding God and thus to reach their universal goal of going to heaven. The general feeling and fear was that without enough priests and nuns, the whole religion would go down the tubes. Hence, the importance of prayers for Vocations.

That year all the nuns were praying for 50 candidates in that year's class (there were about 5000 nuns in the Order). It was for some anniversary. I think I entered at the height of the entrances. CHERRY

We had an old packing crate painted white and covered with special cloths, a statue of Mary, and it usually had a vase of flowers and some vigil candles on it. Every night we knelt in a straight row in front of this altar and prayed the rosary aloud together, sometimes said prayers for Vocations, then added our night prayers. Usually some younger child would get tired and lean, and whoever was next to them would push them back into place and a fight would erupt. Or one of the boys would go to sleep and get smacked upside the head. Rarely was there any major punishment for what went on while we were saying the rosary. Mom said it with us, and Dad did sometimes, but he worked 3 jobs and often was sleeping. DORIS

The Roman Catholic religion had many more diurnal rules than just not eating meat on Fridays. In order to receive Communion, one had to fast from all food and water from midnight. When the Host was raised during the Mass, one bowed one's head, and never stared at it. Scary stories were told in schools about children who looked at the Host and became blind, or who bit the wafer (you were supposed to let it eventually melt on your tongue) and had blood coming out of their mouths. Children attending Catholic schools had to attend Mass first every day. Catholic life was tricky and serious.

In the days of fasting (food and water) from midnight, I remember going to the water fountain in the morning at school to take a drink of water, all of a sudden remembering that it was a First Friday, feeling horrified, and spitting out the water. Not being sure it was all off my tongue, I decided to play it safe (you didn't fool around with going to hell) by not going to Communion, even though that would bring on more punishment and interrogation and dirty looks from the nun-teachers, could cause my siblings to tell on me, and sometimes earn me physical punishment from my parents. Definitely there was a lot of yelling about it. At Mass, nobody was allowed to do anything but sit, stand, and kneel straight, look straight ahead (except at the Consecration when we thought we'd be struck dead if we looked), be sure you were following on the correct page of your missal, answer the prayers aloud (when those days finally arrived), and be sure to go to Communion unless you wanted everybody to think you were in the state of mortal sin. I remember my brothers getting hit by my father in church; nobody even looked around. Once when I'd forgotten and drunk water again, I sweated it out all through the beginning of Mass, finally deciding that whispering it to my father right before Communion might save a scene when it came time to get in the line for receiving the Host. He was furious and did his terrifying yell-whisper back to me, harrumphing loudly every few seconds and giving me the evil eye. I thought I might wither up and die even before Communion or before whatever punishment awaited me when we got home. DORIS

In the 50s, it was still generally taught and believed that the Religious Vocation was the highest of all callings. Before entering the convent, all participants knew that their Vocation was a call from God for service to humanity, thus serving God. Only two women in the survey mentioned that they had "becoming a teacher" in mind as well.

Religious Vocation meant dedication. It did not mean doing something specific such as teaching, nursing, or missionary work. I saw it as a living of my religion. I suppose the best word is contemplation. JULIANNE

It was a call to the highest state on earth. GAYLE

Vocation was a call to give up all things and to be God's bride. LILLA

It was an honor and an obligation. JEAN-2

I entered this Order based on the illusion that they were nicer than the first one I had considered. I had met these nuns during a high school retreat, and a friend of mine had encouraged me to get acquainted with this Order. She, her cousin, and about a dozen others of us who graduated from high school in 1960 entered the Order then. It was a "groupie", "God has chosen you/us", and "we're all so special" type of thing. JUDY

Having been talked to about the importance of Vocations since they were little children, and nurtured in the thought by the nuns at Catholic school, girls in those days entered convents as early as age 14 (in this study). The most common age to enter was at the end of high school. Here and there, a candidate would have attended some college, actually have a degree or profession, or (like one woman in this group) have been in the military.

Fifty-nine of the 73 attended Catholic grade schools, some for all eight years and some for less. Fifty-five attended some Catholic high school. Only six women had not been in any Catholic school at all. Of those who were taught by the nuns, 40 entered that same Order.

The reason we moved to a Catholic school when I was in the 4th grade is that the parish that we belonged to had a priest who was strictly hellfire and damnation, as they used to say in those days, and they made my parents feel that if we stayed in public schools, that they would go to hell. So they felt obligated, even though it was very difficult financially to put us in the Catholic school. That's also why I went to a Catholic high school—because they felt they would go to hell. CHERRY

I admired several of the nuns in the Order that taught me, but hated enough of them not to want to enter that Community. JUDY

In grade school there were a couple of nuns I thought were nice, but more that I feared. One nun had a permanent frown pressed into her face from scowling and yelling at us. You never felt safe. For no reason at all, just anything out of the blue, you'd be the object of ridicule and punished. I remember shortly after I'd arrived from Canada, our third grade class was marching back to school from Mass when the girl in front of me in line rubbed her eye. The line was immediately stopped and the nun pulled that girl out and interrogated her loudly in front of us: Why was she doing that? Didn't she have good hygiene? And finally, the point of it all: If she truly had washed her face that morning and wasn't lying about it, why would she have to rub the sleep out of her eye? The girl cried and was pushed back into line. I felt that nun in particular was a vulture. Here again, I had no idea of the rules of the game, so I just stayed away from her. DORIS

At the time of entering the convent, 49 (of 70 who replied) participants lived with both birth parents, three with grandparents, seven with a single parent, and one was old enough to live by herself. Only two women had been adopted. Oldest children, youngest, and middle-child candidates were quite evenly divided. Two were the only children in their families. (See Chapter XVII: Notes: Charts, for more statistical information.)

The First Steps

The Aspirancy was the first possible step in becoming a nun. Not every Religious Community had an Aspirancy. And even when they did, some Orders did not make everyone who entered begin there; some entered as Postulants the way candidates had always entered before the Aspirancy experiment began. The Aspirancy program was a newish idea in the 50s. In it, girls (usually still in high school) would wear regular school uniforms (no makeup), live in a separate area from the nuns in the convent (under an nun-Aspirant Mistress) and be groomed for nunhood during the hours that they were not attending school. Aspirants were not allowed to speak to the other girls, even their best friends, except for absolutely necessary statements and polite answers or greetings. The 12 women in this project who spent time in the Aspirancy said their time there ranged from 5 months to 4 years. At the end of the Aspirancy period, a ceremony often marked entrance into the Postulancy.

For some Orders, Postulancy was the next step; for others, it was the first one. The Postulant's year-requirements were also flexible, often depending on the scheduled date of the "veil ceremony" or entrance into the Novitiate. In Orders that had a Postulancy, no girl was a Postulant for less than half a year. Postulants wore either partial habits (often with an elbow-length cape) or shorter nuns' habits with black stockings and shoes. Usually, Postulants wore nothing on their heads except when they went to chapel, when they wore black tulle or lace fold-up veils which they kept in their pockets. As in the regular nuns' habits, pockets were reached through an opening in the outer wool serge skirt. The pocket itself was sewn into the black chintz full-length half-slip, and was used instead of a purse. In some Communities, there was a separate Postulant Mistress and separate Postulants' quarters; in others, the Postulants were housed and trained in the Novitiate under the same Superior (Novice Mistress) as the Novices. Twenty-eight women in this survey spent a year in the Postulancy, and four spent two years there.

A bridal (often public) ceremony marked most entrances into the Novitiate. Most Orders used the term "Bride of Christ" and dressed the candidate in modest recycled wedding dress and veil for the ceremony to receive her habit. Then, while the ceremony for profession of vows went on without these bridal candidates, they were taken to another room where their hair was cut and they were helped dress in the habit of the Order, after which they marched back into the Chapel according to rank.

The Novitiate, or formation time, in most Orders included the first or canonical year, and the second year. The candidate was called a Novice for both years. Generally, she wore the Order's full habit, except for her veil, which was white (in Orders with usually black veils). However, black veils were always donned by Novices when they went out of the convent, e.g., to school, to the doctor, or when traveling. The canonical year was one of stricter isolation than any other. The canonical Novice did not attend school outside of the Novitiate, travel, or attend outside functions. Letters in the Novitiate were read coming and going, and it was not unheard of for a Novice to have to rewrite the monthly or yearly letter home in accordance with the wishes of the Novice Mistress or Community.

From the very first year in the convent, candidates were warned not to speak of convent rules or rituals or unpublic happenings with outsiders, including their families. Novitiate members often did the grunt work—cleaned more toilets, shucked more corn, worked more in the garden and laundry, than did older members of the Community. The word "formative" in describing those years, was taken literally. Public punishments or penances (see Chapter V: The Refectory) were common. In a few cases, the Novitiate was the first step for Community membership. No women in this survey served less than a year in the Novitiate; 15 served 1 ½ years; 32 for 2 years; seven for 2 ½ years; and two for 3 years.

At the end of the Novitiate, the case of each Novice came up for review with the Novice Mistress, the Superior General, and the Council. It was the consensus of these who decided whether the Novice should be allowed to take first (temporary, usually 1-3 years) vows, or not. Some who did not take vows were returned to the Novitiate to continue formation with another class, and others were sent home.

I was one of three people in my class who was subjected to being "held back"—I did not get to make first vows with my group in August, but had to wait until the following February. During the interviews, one of the five Council members asked me if I was every tense around the Novice Mistress. I was honest and said Yes, I was sometimes very tense around this extremely neurotic person. Of course, in those days we thought she was a saint and didn't recognize all the mental problems some of these women had. On the day when the list of acceptees was to be read and the special ceremony of acceptance was to be held, I was called into the Novice Mistress's office and told that I didn't make it. She claimed she had recommended our entire set for first vows, but the Council overrode her and held three of us back. One of those three later had a nervous breakdown, and the other left the Order later. JUDY

Those who were accepted for temporary vows took part in a (usually public) ceremony, recited their vows together, and from then on wore the full habit with black veil (different color, of course, for those with habits other than black). They were called Junior Professed or Temporary Professed ("Juniors", for short) and still lived in dormitories separate from the Final Professed. They took part in some of the mature Community's ceremonies, e.g., singing in the choir and Chapter of Faults, but were still in formation under the Juniorate Mistress. If the Temporary Professed nun was sent on Mission or away to school during this time, she would have her local Superior *and* the Juniorate Mistress to answer to. Except in certain cases on Mission and on "talking" feastdays, Junior Professed nuns were not allowed to speak to either Novitiate members (or members of the Aspirancy) or to Final Professed nuns. Some Orders had no Juniorate; others had Juniorates of varying years:

No Juniorate: 17
Substituted 3 yrs. on Mission: 1
6 months Juniorate: 1
1 year Juniorate: 9
2 to 3 ½ years Juniorate: 27
4 to 6 years Juniorate: 10

At the end of the Juniorate, when the nun's temporary vows were about to expire, she went through more interviews with the same groups (in some Orders—others didn't speak to the Juniors, just handed down their decision). A Temporary Professed nun could often renew her vows for a year at a time, but usually not beyond three years. At the end of the temporary period, she would either become a Final Professed nun (taking perpetual or permanent vows) or leave the convent. More nuns left the convent near this period than in any other single year.

After the Juniorate came Final Profession (if one passed the interviews). Another step, another ceremony. Final Professed nuns looked no different from Temporary Professed ones. They were now permitted (during non-silence times) to mingle with the entire Community except the Juniorate, Novitiate and younger members. Most things (seating in the Refectory and in Chapel, lining up to go anywhere, etc.) were still done in order of rank, and would be until some Communities changed that rule after Vatican II.

Schooling before entering the Convent

Fifty women in this project (ages 15-18) entered the convent after graduating from high school. A few were allowed to be Aspirants during their senior year. Some in convent-run schools were told that they could not take their last two years of high school together *without* entering the Aspirancy. Two entered convents after the 8th grade; two after the 9th, and two after the 11th. Twelve had 1 to 2 years of college first, two had their Bachelor degrees, and one had a Masters degree.

Women by the mid-1900s had begun to branch out into a few professions, but generally, those in high school in the 50s knew that if they went to college, they would most likely be either a teacher, a nurse, or a secretary, or they would take liberal arts courses until they "caught" a husband. A woman had to be quite astute, persistent, independent, and mature to forge ahead alone in any other professional career. Even should she receive a degree in, say, engineering—there were rarely places that hired females in those areas. Equal rights for women was not yet a cause.

Before entering the convent, only 9 of the participants (of the 62 that replied to this question) had no specific career in mind. Others:

                teaching: 25
                nursing: 7
                other medical: 7

The rest list accounting, law, history, art, theatre, secretary, social work, interpreter, and becoming a missionary as careers they were most interested in.

Thirty-four women say they became interested in teaching after entering the convent, 9 in the medical field, and the others in art, music, office work, law, or *"just being a sister"*.

❖❖❖

Looking back, do you feel any one reason caused you to enter the convent more than any other?

YES: 61
NO: 9

Six general categories emerged of reasons why these women (now think they) entered the convent:

1. Security:
   Need for security after parents died, escape from molestation: (4)
   Escape from sexuality, marriage, children: (5)
   Escape from home to peace: (1)

2. Education:
   Wanted to be a teacher, nurse, educated: (5)

3. Personal Influences:
   Comfortable with, liked by, recruited by nuns: (6)
   Please my parents, authority. Expected. Catholic upbringing.
   Esteemed position: (15)
   Knew someone there. (2)
   Talks with a friendly priest. (1)

4. Idealism:
   Wanted to be in a caring group of women searching for perfection: (5)
   Called by God: (8)
   Desire to spend my life serving God, Church, world. (10)
   Overwhelming gratitude for God's forgiveness. (1)
   Wanted more personal relationship with God. (2)
   Inspired by book by Thomas Merton: (1)

5. Adventure:
>   *Wanted to follow the hordes:* (1)
>   *Always have been a seeker.* (1)

6. Settlement or bargain with God:
>   *It was a way of being permanently good.* (2)
>   *Deal: cure my brother:* (1) *compensate for sinful sib:* (1),
>   *save family's souls:* (1)
>   *Convinced by nun it was either my Vocation or hell.* (2)
>   *I had no peace until I did finally enter.* (1)

Do you feel that you were influenced by anyone/anything to enter the convent?

We are all persuaded to do what we do by outside influences or by internalized effects of past influences. These are the bases for our thoughts, and ultimately, our decisions. What was sought here, though, was: Do you see a clear line between someone/something and your entering the convent? Did anything that you know of give you a push in that direction?

No one is impervious to sway. We also sometimes cannot recognize powers at the moment that they influence us. Nevertheless, conclusions were drawn:

Yes: 6
No: 20
Maybe: 2
Not answered: 44

A related question near the end of the survey asked: Do you feel that having a crush on a nun precipitated your entering? Results:

Yes: 11
No: 55
Maybe: 2

The ultimate reasons that Participants entered convents are varied, yet similar. Read on:

I was urged to enter by my senior religion teacher, who convinced me that if I really loved God, I could sacrifice. I was told that religious life was "nobler" than motherhood. I wanted to be the best I could be. I wanted to please God and my dad. I hoped that in the convent I would find peace, community, and friendship. THERESA

My parents did not understand at all what I was doing. My mother accepted by decision reluctantly--she didn't cut me out of her life. My father, on the other hand, was totally without understanding. And once he had taken a stand, he didn't know how to go back on it. So during the entire 7-year period I was in the convent, my father and I had no connection at all. Letters I would write to him would go unopened. The one time I was able to visit home, he found out I was coming and left. Again, I don't think it was out of anger or lack of love for me--it was just a total lack of understanding on his part. JULIA-2

I looked for peace, dedication, and love of God in the convent. My parents disowned me for ten years after I became a Catholic and joined the convent. They came around and things between us got better after that. ELLEN-2

I entered the community with a lot more maturity and experience than most. Religion during most of my life was Mass and confession once a year. I didn't get interested in [the convent] until I had graduated from high school. We had a parish priest that was very kind and I talked to him a lot. This is how I got interested in religious life. Religious life to me meant living in a community, pooling talents and resources to help other people. Unfortunately, this is not what it turned out to be; it turned out to be a very lonely existence. Although I did find my idea of a community before I left while living and working among another order of Sisters. GINA

Born in a little mining town, I was a child destined for much sorrow in my early life. My mother died when I was two. I was adopted by an uncle whom I adored and loved as my father. He died when I was eight. For three years I went from family to family because no one really wanted me. Finally, my brother and I were sent to an orphanage run by the order. This was the beginning of my faith.

My mother had had me baptized at three months, but I had not actually practiced the Catholic Faith, having gone to whatever church was in our neighborhood, including Lutheran, Congregationalist, Methodist, and several Four Gospel evangelical churches.

The sister who greeted me led me to the Chapel and explained that Jesus was there in the little golden house on the altar, and that whenever I felt the need to talk to Him, I would find that He was my best friend. I believed her utterly. Not too long after, I was on my knees praying with only the vigil light in the chapel when the light went out. I went crying to Father Henry, whose rooms were adjacent to the chapel. "Father, Father, God left the Church!" "Child, what makes you think that?" "I don't know what I did, but the light went out and God left." Well, Father turned on a light and showed me that the vigil light was just a big candle and the person who attended to it had not noticed it was almost burned out. He then replaced the light and assured me that God was there all the time and the candle was just a sign of His divine presence.

It was there in the Orphanage that I learned the Catechism and made my first confession and First Communion. I was there a little over a year and the practice of the faith became firmly established. I realized that no other faith satisfied me. I had loved the Bible stories and the singing in all the churches I attended, but in the Catholic Church as presented to me in that Orphanage, I felt at home and have never wavered since or sought solace in any other church. In the fall of my tenth year, my aunt took me to take care of my little "sister" (really my cousin) who was five years old. My aunt made it clear that the only reason she was taking me was to care for the child. I continued to go to Mass by myself and joined the choir wherever we lived. When my little "sister" was ten years old, she was baptized and I was her godmother. All through my high school years I felt I was being called to be a Sister. I didn't really date until my senior year, as I saw enough of boys during the day in public school. I also worked every night after school, which left little time for much else. When I made up my mind to enter the convent and told my three closest boy friends of my decision, I received three proposals of marriage. One wrote, one called, and the other drove over from a neighboring university to propose in person. But I convinced them that I was intent on pursuing my Vocation. My parents (aunt and her husband) were very much against this and would not help me in any way. In fact I was told that if I did enter, I could never come home again. The day that I entered in 1950, I knelt before the Blessed Sacrament in the convent chapel and prayed, "Here I am. I will stay until You send me away, no matter how difficult it is." It was almost prophetic as I look back on those words. Life was not hard for me in the postulate or novitiate as I was a naturally obedient and pliable person, having had to adapt to a number of different families in my early life. Whatever was required I did and believed it was God's will. Even when my aunt died and I was not allowed to attend her funeral, I believed it was the will of God and that He would bless my family if I stayed. LORENA

I was influenced to enter the convent by my school teacher (nun) who told me I had a vocation. I believed her because I wanted to. In the convent I hoped to fulfill God's will for me. My mother didn't like it; my dad did. OTTER

No one influenced me to enter--I wanted to do good, to help the poor through the convent. My parents were proud that I entered, but my relations with my siblings soon changed: I became a prima dona with the encouragement of the Church. SUZANNE

My father was active in his union and my mother was an outspoken feminist long before the word was used where we lived. Neither of them tolerated anything even resembling religious or racial prejudice. Early on I developed a need to defend the poor, the weak, and the underprivileged. If there had been a Peace Corps when I graduated from the academy, I might have joined it. I had an irresistible desire to dedicate myself but my opportunities were limited in our town in 1934. I had won a scholarship to college, but having been educated by the nuns and having admired their teaching skills, I had given some thought to joining their ranks if they'd have me. On the other hand, the Depression had set in, so I thought perhaps I should look for a job to help out financially at home. Then one of the teachers urged me to follow my Vocation to the nunnery. When I said I might wait a year, she told me I just didn't have the courage. The fiery crusader in me responded to the challenge. Many of the nuns were good at putting pressure on us. They took great pride in their "catches", symbolically stringing them up for the order. My mother served a meal like a last one before my "execution", everything I liked, the day I left for the convent. From the entrée to the dessert it dropped into me like so many underripe crab apples. I felt unworthy. DOROTHY

Chapter I: Beginnings

The Superior of the nuns who taught me persuaded me that God had sent me to this order for a reason. It seemed logical. I wanted to find a way to "grow up" as well as a means of dedicating myself to a worthy cause. SARAH

You bet I was persuaded. We had moved to another school in my 8th grade and the nun-principal acted like she liked me somewhat, but I shied back when she told me that she had a gift from God to be able to tell if a girl had a Vocation, and I had one, period. I was shocked. I was in love with a handsome boy, his family knew mine somewhat, we went to ballgames and dances at the public high school with his older brother--I was having too good a time. But my fear of hell (what would happen to me if I didn't follow a true Vocation) was so great that I hung around this nun as much as possible, trying to talk her out of this notion. She kept it up, and within two years it dawned on me that I was wasting my time unless I wanted to go to hell, so I gave up and got it over with. I expected to have peace and time for myself in the convent. My mother worked hard, but she was often pregnant or sick and my dad was working 3 jobs, so somebody had to run the farm. We had no hired hands. My jobs were milking the cow, separating the milk and getting it ready for pickup, killing the chickens, driving the flatbed and helping toss up the hay bales, plus a lot of regular little jobs like collecting the eggs, feeding the rabbits and chickens and cows, overseeing what the little kids did at home and in the berry patch, etc. Even though I knew we had no money, and there was little choice about who did what, I was tired of having to do so much. I mused that a peripheral reward for entering the convent might be instant prestige from donning the religious habit. Since I felt I didn't really count except for the jobs I did, this would make me a real person. I also thought being a nun would precipitate me into an adult life, my life, not one run by someone else. (Stop laughing!) Mainly, I wanted rest from fighting the notion of having a Vocation. And I counted on the promise that God would love me specially, since outside of my boyfriend, I thought nobody did at the moment. In the convent, I also might have more friends. Some nuns had told me I was a "catch", so maybe there would be others in the convent who liked me. Up to that point, I wasn't allowed to associate with anyone non-Catholic, not even to go on a buggy ride with the neighbors (girls & boys). I was not allowed to date anyone non-Catholic, but didn't know any Catholic boys my age because I went to an all-girls school. I don't remember having any classmates stay overnight. I was too busy with schoolwork, commuting 1 1/2 hours one way to school (the nuns had given me a scholarship), farm chores, and operetta rehearsals to make good friends. I remember one night I had fallen asleep over my Latin homework when my mother came upstairs and put her hand on my arm, saying she was worried because I had so much to do. I was flabbergasted. Neither she nor dad had ever even hinted that they were concerned about my welfare--it was usually, well, why isn't this or that job done yet. What I wanted was friends who would care about me as a person. I was good at helping others, at serving humanity. "Think of others first" was sort of a family preaching. I figured I'd had so much practice that I could do good works in the convent and it would automatically make me feel great.. By the end of my second year in high school, I'd had a couple of conferences with the Superior General of that order and been offered a chance (rare in those days) to finish high school at the end of my junior year--if I entered the convent in the charter group of Aspirants. These were girls who lived in the convent under the direction of a nun, but attended class as usual sans makeup or jewelry. Aspirants were forbidden to take part in the "funner" parts of high school, such as dances, dating, parties. They were also asked not to speak to the other high school girls except for civilities like "Good morning" or necessities like "What page did she say?" I had no idea what cutting myself off from my friends in plain sight would feel like. At that time of my life, my parents and I shared few personal thoughts and it was awkward when I asked for permission to enter the convent. First I got them both alone in their bedroom with the door shut against sibling noise. I told them about the early graduation and they seemed pleased. It was not easy to please my father. "There's one condition, I said, proceeding to describe the Aspirancy program. "But would you want to do that? my mother asked. "Yes," I nodded, "I have a Vocation." As good Catholic parents they could say nothing against that, though they conferred alone for a while. Soon they held several meetings with the Superior General, the gist of which was that they were trying to blame my favorite teacher for talking me into going to the convent. I was so angry that they would attack someone I cared about, a gentle soul who had never talked me into anything, that I fought all the harder for my right to enter. They gave their permission then. I was fifteen when I entered the convent. My siblings didn't say much--they were pretty young and this was just one more unexplained thing in their lives. They just went where they were pointed, did as they were told, and didn't question anything for fear of the razor strop. They came to the long entering ceremony, but were tired and bored. My parents said the usual "We're proud of you" that I got when I excelled in anything, plus some pious things, and my mother wiped away a tear. I thought their only protest would be based on the hardship of replacing me as a worker. Nothing led me to believe they didn't want me to enter otherwise. About 30 years later, after my parents had died, I learned from an aunt that they--my mother especially, had not wanted me to enter the convent at all. I was in shock. For all we'd been preached to about the wonder and importance of being called to a Religious Vocation, I thought they would have wanted me to go. Since I felt I had no choice but to enter the convent or go to hell, I'd at least held out hope that by entering the convent I could earn real respect and a place of honor in my parents' eyes. If I'd had the slightest inkling that my mother wanted me at home, really wanted me--I would have cancelled my plans in an instant. That would have been the sign from God of my draft deferment. I began to cry. "Why didn't they tell me?" I sobbed over and over. "Why didn't they tell me?" DORIS

    My mother gently persuaded me to enter, saying, "One child should be given to God." In the convent I hoped to find security, education, and companionship. My parents and siblings were proud of me when I entered. KATHLEEN

    What I hoped to find in religious life was a purposefulness and a sense of community. Although I had, off and on, planned to join the convent since I was 11 or 12, I recognized at the same time that there were aspects which were repugnant to me, principally the "standardization". For a few months as a child I was in a boarding school and suspected the convent was very much like that. And so it was. ANNE

    My mother never made married life seem like anything great. Religion was a major force in her life and therefore in ours. Religious Vocations were a special gift. I think she wanted all of us to go to convents and seminaries and most of us did. When I was a junior in high school my parents were offered a half scholarship for me at the boarding school my sister went to. I thought it was their hope that I would go to the same community as my sister and I did. I did not talk about any of this with my brothers and sisters. MERT

A nun persuaded me to enter by her constant "private" conferences. She was fostering vocations and gave me special attention. I entered because it was my "duty" to do the "best" thing. Mom wanted me to wait a year, then the priest delivered a sermon against her. She was furious and humiliated. My brothers and sisters were against it and tried to get me to leave the whole 12 years. My 3-year old sister cried and called for me at night. JANN

Persuaded? No. Encouraged, yes. The nuns kept those of us who were smitten busy doing activities such as making prizes for CCD and serving at tea for the cloistered sisters. I was a very sensitive, impressionable child, and when my oldest sister went to live with my father after the divorce (I was 4) and twin sisters left when I was 6, I was quite alone. Grandmother came to live with us to raise me because Mama held down two jobs. Then Grandma was killed in an accident when I was eleven. The shock was traumatic---Mama told me years later that the doctor said he had never seen such deep shock in a child at someone's death. When I was a 9th grader, my mother divorced my stepfather and I convinced her to let me live with my sister at the airforce base. At once point the question of my typing skills arose in public school and the Principal became insulting to my sister, who then angrily told him she would enroll me in parochial school. He retorted, "What's the matter? Is she a juvenile delinquent?" And so I came into the mystical awesome world of Catholicism. I had attended whatever Sunday school was near us. Adults in my family had strong religious convictions, but I never knew which denomination they espoused until this past year when I was going through old family effects. From the moment I stepped into that church, I was in the home for which I had been searching all my life. I didn't ask my parents' permission to become a Catholic, but informed the parish priest that if a child could legally choose which parent she would live with at age 14, then I most certainly could choose my own religion. Besides, my sister who was Catholic would see to it that I never faltered in my faith. Wonder of wonders---he baptized me and I sewed a little white dress for myself and made my First Holy Communion the next Sunday. I literally left my mother in Bullock's department store less than a month after my 18th birthday in 1949 with a note pinned to a package with a bobby pin telling her that I loved her dearly but that I had to leave to give myself to God. I then rushed home to grab some clothing, a few cherished snapshots, and went to meet the

Provincial of the order who was waiting for me at the church. So, was I persuaded? "Persuade" is not the right word. I had strong convictions and nuns helped to nurture those convictions. We all know our Lord's words concerning those who leave father, mother, and brethren for his sake. I remember kneeling in the quietness of a Gothic church and "giving" to Him the 13 children that I had always said I wanted, if He would only have me to be His Bride Forever. LILLA

By entering the convent, I hoped to find a way of "being good" all the time. Because of the separation from my siblings we were much more distant. I didn't see them and I didn't know what was happening to them. I also became part of a mysterious group. THERESE

In retrospect I realize how influenced I was to enter the community. When I graduated from high school in 1961, I had made plans to attend a business school. Our parish priest had asked me to teach second grade. I didn't want to, but he persisted and I relented. What I found out ten years later from one of the nuns who was assigned to teach religious vacation school in our small town, was that this priest had said to the nuns about me, "I've got one here for you and if you don't get her now, you never will." So naturally, the Sisters were very kind to me: they let me eat meals with them (unheard of then), talked to me about having a Vocation, complimented me on being such a good teacher, and on and on. Needless to say, I was overwhelmed and flattered by their compliments and in the short span of time when they came to town and left (two weeks) I had decided to enter the convent. My parents felt I would be taken care of in a safe environment. I was the oldest of their children, and they seemed to have no reservations about going to a way of life completely foreign to them. My mother's comment was kind of strange: "Your grandmother will be pleased." In those days, having a religious Vocation was considered a special blessing from God for the family. Because of this "God factor" I was hesitant to leave for the ensuing 14 years, even though I wanted to. MARY-2

I was influenced to enter by St. Therese of Lisieux, by her autobiography, <u>The Little Flower of Jesus</u>. I wanted to love God as she did. At the age of 16, I was converted as a result of her book. THERESE-2

Nobody directly persuaded me to enter, but from the time I was in religion class at about 9 years old or so, very much was made of the superior calling of the religious life. People who got married or remained single were inferior to anyone who was in religious life. Naturally, I wanted to be the best, so that's what happened. But nobody specifically talked me into it. When I was in high school there weren't many options open to women and I had never really thought of a career. I know it sounds kind of silly, but there were no guidance counselors. There was nothing--a woman could be married or a secretary or a nurse or something like that--or a teacher, but those options were never presented to me in any formal way, and other options were not presented either. What I know now is (and I didn't know it then) that my parents had saved a college fund for me and that they expected that I would go to college, but they never told me that. And when I said well, I'd enter the community, I didn't say to them (because our communications were poor) because I want the higher, the best way. They were just sort of silent. I didn't know really how they felt. I didn't know that they had a college fund for me. When I was entering, I didn't think of teaching, though ours was a teaching order. CAROL

My parents were very sad at my entering, and opposed it. After I entered, I was encouraged to be rigid and distant with them. My parents mentioned that I was "holier-than-thou". CASEY

My Vocation was so much a part of my being from the time I was very small that no one really had to persuade me. However, as I matured and entered the last two years of high school, I began to question the timing. My mother was not well and my parents were having serious financial problems. I went through a period of months when I had to decide whether I would enter right out of high school or wait a year, work and help my parents out. My mother helped me work through my decision. Other Sisters influenced me far more by their listening, understanding, and acceptance. Most of them were excellent teachers, really dedicated to their professional lives as well as their religious lives. Several tried to dissuade me from entering, not so much by the spoken word, but by conveying to me that I was too emotionally immature. In some ways it was very true. My parents were happy that I entered the convent, though I found out later that my mother could not bring herself to clear my bedroom of my clothes. We had become very close during my high school years. My oldest brother and I were very close. He was in the seminary, so naturally he was very supportive. I'm not sure my other siblings realized what it was all about, except that my two older sister thought I should have either waited or not entered at all. JULIANNE

I believe I was encouraged, not persuaded to enter the convent. Everyone seemed to be saying that I had a Vocation. I felt free to choose this, and hoped to find peace, involvement with teaching, and good people there. My parents and siblings were sad to see me go. DIANE

My parents had thrown such an absolute fit when my older sister wished to go into a convent, so I knew that it would be difficult. It was a royal battle and ended up in my being totally ostracized. My mother carried on and made life a perfect hell, I believe, for all of my brothers and sisters after me because, to this day, there are gigantic and deep rifts and we mostly don't talk to each other. I would be willing to, but they don't. I really don't know what my parents told my siblings during the time I was gone. My parental relationship when I entered the convent is a book in itself. It totally tore up the family. My entering the convent had made our family totally dysfunctional. CHERRY

I decided on my own to enter. The decision just popped into my head while I was in a car with the boyfriend I had been dating for several months. It was while we were "necking" in 50s parlance, that I blurted that I wanted to enter the convent. I had not given this any thought prior to this. Of course, the fear of adolescent sexuality is obvious now, but I thought my motives had more to do with sacrifice for my father who was an atheist. After I left religious life, a therapist came up with this (without my telling her about my getting sexually aroused for perhaps the first time) as one of my reasons for entering religious life. She based it on the fact that my father was a womanizer and on typical adolescent reactions to taboos. I thought that in the convent I would be doing good for others. I envisioned a more direct caring for people. JEAN-2

A nun music teacher thought I had a Vocation and would make a good music teacher besides. We had conversations in which she built up the prestige of the Community. I practiced the harp there on weekends and would see the Sisters going to prayers. I was convinced I would find charity and love, not fault-finding and humiliation. My mother seemed happy about my entering, but because we were told to leave the "World", I kept my feelings to myself and distanced myself from my family. JEAN-3

My third grade teacher belonged to the order I entered. I was a Mormon at the time and she was the first nun in my life. My teachers seemed to treat me as if they knew I had a vocation. I was a baptized Catholic at 15 (after waiting for permission since the 3rd grade) and very caught up in devotion. I hoped the convent would be love, peace, joy, and fun. My Catholic stepfather was glad that I entered; my mother disowned me the whole time I was in the convent (7 years) and only started to become a little interested when I said I was getting out. CAREN

I was told from grade school on by nuns and a couple of priests that I probably had a Vocation. I was the oldest of six children; our family didn't have much money. Though I was valedictorian of the 8th grade and my senior class, I was never encouraged or talked to by anyone at school or at home about planning for college. I think I chose to enter partly as a way to get a college education and I did think I would make a good teacher. Didn't ever consider such things as "lawyer". I remember a priest that I admired a great deal (who has since left his order to marry) saying that women should be teachers or nurses. This would have been in 1955-6. I had a romantic liaison with a priest who was also an alcoholic--lots of hugging and kissing (dry) in the period of six months or so before I entered the convent. This caused me some trauma after entering and being cut off from this "friendship". I was physically and emotionally deprived by my parents all through childhood and this priest considered himself a counselor of some sort and was trying to "help" me overcome some of my inhibitions. Since I was the organist at the church, we had many opportunities to be alone. The only "counseling" I got regarding this traumatic relationship was through an old priest in the confessional during the novitiate. JUDY

From all I could tell, everyone accepted my decision (to enter the convent) neutrally. There had been brothers and sisters before me going out on their own, and I don't think I made any waves. Our pastor dragged his feet in writing the letter of recommendation to the Provincial Superior---I think he thought I might change my mind. I'm not certain now, but I do think I just expected to go there and get perfect and die young. I think some measure of safety from a night-prowling brother entered into it, too. I don't recall getting encouragement from anyone, though in snapshots of the ceremony, my parents looked proud. TRACE

I was persuaded to enter the convent by my parents and teachers, probably because I was a "pleaser" and not very assertive, they were constantly telling me what a good nun I'd make. I went for happiness and satisfaction. KATE

We prayed the family rosary, we prayed for vocations. My mother always prayed that God would bless our family with a vocation to the priesthood. Vocation meant a call from God, a definite desire to serve God, something you would never turn down, and if you had [a Vocation] you were considered to be so privileged. I was the oldest and the responsible daughter and I took that definitely to heart and entered the convent. My mother particularly was proud of me; my father was proud, too, but he didn't want it to happen as strongly as my mother did. And they really did consider this such an honor to have a daughter in the convent. I think the secret is that my mother would have gone to a convent herself. Going to the convent was something I really wanted to do. I wanted to be a teacher like the nuns and wanted to live this life that they had told us about and have this wonderful community, have the sense of identity as a strong woman role model which in those days didn't exist very much outside in any other realm. MARGARET

My geometry (nun) teacher spoke to me of spiritual things and convinced me to enter the convent. My spirit of faith made me believe I was ready to sacrifice my personal pleasures for God. My mother objected, but my father thought it was okay. I hoped to serve others through the convent. YVONNE

I had no idea what to expect in the convent, but as an orphan, I felt like I might like to belong to the family of the church. MAXINE

❖❖❖

Dowry, trousseau

Forty-two of the 65 who answered this question say that the convents they entered required dowries. For 5 of the 65, the dowry was waived. Five more could not remember a dowry. Eighteen were not asked for a dowry. In some Orders, dowries were paid only by the "choir Sisters" (those who would go to school, teach or nurse, etc.) and not by the "lay Sisters" (housekeepers and cooks).

I was more or less disowned by my family, but not completely. It was all one-way communication. Once in a while would my mother allow someone to come and see me—my grandmother came a few times. I didn't realize that she had paid money to anybody until when I left, I was asked what I wanted done with the dowry (it was $500). And I said, Well, I have no dowry so there's nothing to give to me. And they said, Yes, you do. So the dowry was returned to me. Looking back, I believe that my grandmother must have been the one to pay. I know of no one else that gave them any money. CHERRY

I was supposed to pay a dowry, but I arranged to bring the bare minimum. I felt that they were going to have my service for a lifetime, and I wanted to spend the money that I made the summer before my entrance on my family—I had planned a special time alone with each family member. I think I ended up bringing $50 to the convent. MARTIIA

It was common for parents to pay medical and dental bills, at least until final vows. Dowry money was often put in an account and held until the nun either left the convent or died, though in one case it was reported that the woman's U.S. bonds had immediately been cashed in. Of course, no nuns before Vatican II received personal salaries. And *no one* in this study said they received their dowry back plus the interest that accrued. Two participants say they were told that their dowry would go into an escrow account, but the lack of contracts or signatures make that actuality doubtful. In many communities during the 1900s and even in some today (which operate uncertified private Catholic schools), nothing was paid into Social Security for working nun-teachers and nun medical personnel, so the only money that the leaving nun had to start out her life, was the returned dowry (see Chapter XI: Leaving). In 1999, one ex-nun in this group of participants told us by phone that her former Order had paid up past Social Security payments—even for its nuns who had left the convent, and that she was now able to collect something in her retired years. This is true justice in action.

Two women said their dowries were $2000 each, and one paid $1000. Other than that, the most common amount for a dowry was $500, although in some convents there seemed to be a sliding scale based on ability to pay. Other Orders charged fees in addition to the dowry, e.g., room and board (paid per year), investiture fee, profession fee, incidentals fee, etc.

"Trousseau" conjures up hand embroidered dish towels, silk beddings, etc., placed in one's "hope chest", plus a last-minute flurry of clothes-buying before one's wedding. The convent trousseau was completely basic and practical, consisting usually of a trunk or simple suitcases, certain described items of clothing, e.g., *white drawers or bloomers of knee length*, stockings, nightwear, apron and robe, incidentals such as shoe polish, gloves, towels, soap, umbrella, etc.–usually required in black. Some listed the girl's Postulant and Novitiate clothing, plus material for making further clothes. The candidate brought her own required prayerbooks (or paid for them at the convent), stationery supplies, etc. One order's list asked that the candidate *not* bring shampoo, nail clippers, razor, hand lotion or powders of any kind, anything scented or gilt edged (e.g., the New Testament), or even handkerchiefs that had hemstitching or edging on them.

Some candidates were given "going-away" showers by their friends who used the trousseau list as a guideline for gifts. There were generally 50 items to choose from on the trousseau list--some quite specific in description, e.g., one description of a black apron designated the material to be used, type of neckline, height of collar, length and width of sleeves and cuffs, distance from the floor, type of pockets, etc. Other items were easily bought at any department store.

❖❖❖

Haircuts

For some reason, the mystery of it perhaps, the lay public had always been inordinately curious about nuns' hair, particularly about how much of it they had left under their headgear. Rumors that nuns shaved their heads were more intriguing in the days before one could walk down the street and meet men, women, teens, or even children boldly walking about with shaved heads—and drawing few stares. These days, if it is one's choice to go bald, it's basically no one else's business. But in the mid-1900s before widespread chemotherapy or shaved heads as a fashion statement, one kept one's hair. To shave one's head on purpose was nearly unthinkable. So to imagine nuns with shaved heads was doubly titillating—the mystery of what their heads were like under all that white stuff, added to the shock factor of possible head-shaving.

To answer the question about haircuts: only 6 (of the 63 who replied) shaved their heads, and some of these did not do it regularly. It would have been possible to wear long hair under the coif, and some nuns did grow their hair out when they knew they were going to leave the convent, but long hair only added to the uncomfortableness of held-in heat from the entire ensemble. It was easier to cut one's hair quite short, often shaving a bit up the back or in front of the ears so that wispy bits of hair did not work their way out and make children point and giggle: "Look—Sister's got hair!"

Hair was originally cut by another nun, but some Sisters regularly cut their own. One's hair wasn't seen by anyone else except sometimes a doctor or nurse. Some nuns who did the job better than others were prevailed upon to be the "house barber". Silence was the rule even during haircuts, preferences indicated by hand signals and pantomime, though the younger nuns often broke out in giggling. Forty-two out of 65 said they had a choice as to length. Eight didn't like the short cut or were upset by it.

The haircut was a strong experience for me even though my hair was not beautiful in many ways. The shortness affected me, as it was meant to—this worldly sign of our being a woman of the world was cut off just like a butch haircut. It was very humiliating for me as my hair was a sense of pride for me. We had no choice about the length, and it was cut in silence. You could tell it was a hard thing for our whole group. MARGARET.

I was very upset and cried at the time. ELEANOR

Thirty-six accepted short haircuts as *okay, no big deal, a part of joining the convent,* and six said they *liked* their hair short. Most, whether they liked it or not, realized the practicality of wearing their short hair under the layers of headgear.

The Religious Habit

This may be the last century when the medieval religious habit as we know it, is worn at all. In the beginning, this garb blended in with what the populace wore, but by the mid-1900s it was getting a little ridiculous to wear yards of wool serge during the summer. So in the 60s, after Vatican II, Religious Communities began to incorporate slight changes, e.g., replacing the wool serge with lighter fabrics for summer or hot climates, abbreviating the starched headdress, and shortening the veil. Once these changes began, the habit was destined to disappear altogether, since there was no longer any real reason to wear it, and many reasons not to. Communities did not decide to modify habits because of any requests from the lay public; most habit-decisions were done in-house by the Council or with the recommendations of a specially appointed committee. It seemed, even at the beginning of the changes, more difficult for the lay person to accept a difference in nuns' clothing, than it was for the nuns. Persons on the Internet today who rant about "nuns taking off their habits and so now they get the disrespect they deserve" seem enigmatic. Why should they care? One theory is that so much fantasy and holy myth had been invested in the habited nun, that some persons just did not want to accept the fact that nuns are quite ordinary people who happen to feel called to a different mission than the lay person. Wearing or not wearing a habit does not change the person involved. Many nuns of today have shed the old habits, and dress like the conservative populace, signifying their dedication by a cross on a neck chain, or by some other simple sign. Because a number of (especially older) nuns who had worn the same habits for many years, became anxious at the changes, most communities allowed their nuns who felt uncomfortable in street clothes, to continue wearing the old habit or some modification of it.

The habit set us apart as Brides of Christ and made me feel very special to be among those chosen. The lay people highly respected the habit. LILLA

Chapter I: Beginnings

Habits in the mid-1900s came in several colors, the most common being black. There were also Orders who wore grey, blue, brown or white, or combinations of a color with black or white. A few wore touches of red, for example, in a woven ribbon-like piece that hung down from the side belting.

There were differences in each Order's habit, most noticeably in the headgear. All habits, however, had some basic things in common: most were shoe-length wool wide-pleated skirts sewn onto buttoned or hooked bodices that had wide sleeves. Over this was worn the scapular--another long (front and back) straight piece, wide enough to cover the shoulders, with a neck hole and buttoned keyhole slit at the back. Some Communities wore circular capes instead of, or besides the scapular.

Once a year the skirt and bodice were separated and the skirt cleaned and pressed by its wearer. I don't know how many yards there were, but the yardage was re-pleated by a formula so as to keep its proportions and to even out the wear. Something like turning a mattress, I suppose, back to front and up to down. A black felt-like edging was sewn to the skirt's hem to minimize abrasion. It was inside and barely showed, but was effective. I'd guess at least 20-25 years of wear could be gotten out of the skirt before it even got thin. TRACE

It was awfully hot and I couldn't figure out how people wore things like this when it would make you sweat—I couldn't understand how you could keep clean. Except that we wore this thing they called a chemise underneath it, made out of muslin. And we all knew why they made us bring I-don't-know-how-many yards of muslin—that was so that they could keep making more of these chemises, which we wore underneath, and could change. But you really couldn't change your dress or wash the thing—you couldn't dry it. Some of us later figured out how to make them so that the top unhooked from the skirt, and we were able to launder the tops. That was kind of neat, because by the 60s people were more aware of being clean. CHERRY

The habit had yards of serge in the skirt, very heavy, got dirty and stayed dirty. I think we washed the skirt portion twice a year. It required ripping apart and re-sewing it to the vest part. Hours and hours were spent on ironing and fixing habits. JUDY

In the earlier years, neckwear, headwear, and the veil stiffeners (veil boards) were made of cotton, the veil boards and collars being heavily starched. Later, heavy celluloid collars and headbands (sometimes called "bandeaux") were utilized in some Orders, because they were more easily cleanable and did not require the hours of laborious starching. Celluloid yellowed, however, and had to be replaced periodically. From the standpoint of the wearer, celluloid was a detriment since it held in the heat to quite a degree.

It was common practice to cover every bit of the hair with a coif (coiffe) or wimple. Some headcoverings were like caps and fastened under the chin. Others were like folded fabric sewn together at the bottom with a chin-gusset. One put one's face through the hole, pulled the coif back tightly, then safety-pinned it shut at several points from the back crown of the head to the neck. The bottom of this coif was covered by the collar(s)—some wore shoulder-wide collars, and others, pleated shorter ones that also covered the hair. No matter the shape, a second collar like the priest's white collar could be worn above the main collar piece.

The headband (bandeau) was usually starched cotton and went over the forehead back on both sides and fastened at the back of the head. Some veils (sewn with much finger-pricking onto veil boards) were pinned to the coif and/or headband in the front and sides with wicked long black quilting pins. Others had different ties, pins, or attachments to keep the headpiece from blowing away in the wind. A few Orders wore hat-variations, like the Flying Nun from television. There were Orders that had as a part of their headdress, what the public referred to as "blinders", starched white fabric all around the face under the veil. Some of these "blinders" as well as the wider starched veil boards inhibited good driving, but they were great for the privacy of the wearer.

It was all very uncomfortable, especially the stiffness of the collar and the tight and hot headgear. HELGA

The habits were not and uncomfortable, but I found cleanliness the biggest problem. We took the habits apart and washed them once a year--otherwise they got worn almost every day. As for headgear— driving a car, the starched sides of the veil were a hazard. To this day, I will not wear anything on my head. GINA

Commonly, Orders wore stiffly woven belts over the habit but under the scapular. Other Communities wore leather belts or cords around the waist, knotted or not (3 knots represented the 3 vows), and hanging down the sides or not. Many wore, sewn or hooked to their belts, oversized Rosaries made of wood or large seeds with metal links and a crucifix. The rustling of this Rosary served as an early-warning system for hundreds of schoolchildren.

Black stockings (cotton at first) and "sensible" black laced up shoes with a (then-called) cuban heel (wide, an inch or two high) were usual. Since most habits were worn before the invention of common tights, the stockings were held up either by garter belts, or they were rolled just below the knee and kept in place with rubber bands. Half-galoshes were common for rainy seasons.

A long black chintz half-slip (lightly-gathered)with deep side pockets big enough to store many items (these took the place of a purse) was buttoned over the longish unbleached cotton chemise, an upper body undergarment used to protect the habit from perspiration, and also utilized in some Orders as a modesty garment during bathing. The sexy knit silk chemise of today bears no resemblance to the nun-of-that-time's pullover short-sleeved woven garment. In the late 50s, before the lightening of habit fabrics, some underarm dress shields (a new product then) were distributed to nuns with special needs. In some Orders, the saddle-bag type pockets were hung separately from a belt at the waist.

The serviceable black underskirt had 2 capacious pockets—I know one Sister carried 3 regular-sized books in her pockets—must have felt strange, but didn't show much. TRACE

Especially younger nuns wore the common full cotton panties found in the back of the lingerie department (included in the trousseau-- the list of items she was to bring with her to the convent); others wore either cotton bloomers, or a sort of shorts held up with either elastic or a cord. Sanitary needs were answered with birds-eye weave cotton cloths folded and pinned in place. One hand-washed one's own cloths, then dried them and put them into the common laundry. By the late 50s, the common thick sanitary pads and belts of the time were admitted—but at first, only if parents bought them. Tampons were smuggled in and passed around before they were formally allowed. Some nuns were told that the use of these was sinful. Cotton bras were worn in the beginning, if brought as a part of the candidate's trousseau. Later, the choice of wearing a brassiere became optional, and communities stocked those items regularly. Of course, every single item of clothing had to be nametagged.

Ah, underwear. Instead of bloomers or underpants, DRAWERS. These were two separate overlapped enclosures, joined at the top to a tunnel waistband containing long drawstrings. There was no bottom to the drawers. When using the toilet, one spread the overlaps apart and sat down. The strings had only to be tied in the morning and untied at night. Drawers, which were of an extremely sturdy cotton, lay nearly flat for mangle-ironing. I tried one time to make myself a sanitary belt. I don't know how much sewing time I spent on this contraption, but when I'd finally finished it and tried to wear it, I discovered that I'd not allowed for the elastic to stretch, and so could not get into the thing. So much for holy poverty! Another time I made a black underskirt, but put the pockets on wrong; the wearer would have to have been a kangaroo. Note: I was briefly on the sewing crew. TRACE

When I entered, we were discouraged from wearing bras. The bodice was supposed to be worn very tight and take the place of a bra. I conformed for several years, but finally asked to wear a bra. By then, I realized that not wearing one had permanently affected the muscle tone in my breasts. I was given permission without any problems. JULIANNE

We wore mannish boxers and t-shirts with a scarf to disguise breasts. CASEY

Underwear was ugly convent issue. We never got to fit a bra—were allowed to have them by mail order only. ROSE

Nightwear issue consisted of two weights of white pioneer-style long-sleeved floor-length nightgowns: flannel, and lightweight cotton. White cotton caps that tied under the chin covered the hair. Slippers were sometimes available even if not originally brought by the candidate. A black wrap-bathrobe of rayon or lighter cotton was to be worn whenever the nun walked outside of her cell at night, say, to use the bathroom. In later years, other nuns besides the Novitiate members who brought their pyjamas with them when they came, could wear these also.

There were several peripheral wearables in most Communities, e.g., sleeves. Short and elasticized at the top like the old printers' sleeves, these were worn from wrist to above the elbow under the wide wool sleeves of the habit. One was not "dressed" without them. They came in two weights—a cotton for winter, and a gauzy nylon for summer. Gloves or mittens were either knit by the nun or bought by her parents. Same with shawls. Many a newcomer's first "recreation hour" project was crocheting herself a warm shawl with the yarn and crochet hook provided by her family. In the early days, nuns (especially the Final Professed) were given long heavy wool cloaks (mantles), fine for keeping out the cold during lengthy outdoor funeral processions or traveling. Those without cloaks wore their shawls—which were essentially useless in the bitter wind.

For dirty work, some Orders lifted the front hem of the skirt and, holding it to the waist, safety-pinned the skirt hem in back. Some wore aprons—the regular bib-style gathered skirt ones, and a few substituted "cobbler" or "Dutch" pullover aprons (with wide sleeves) for their outer habits.

The washing of undergarments and headpinnings was done at the Motherhouse in the central laundry by Novitiate members and a few assigned Professed Sisters. One picked up one's cleaned items at a pigeonhole that had one's name on it. Slips were often handwashed and line-dried. The wool serge habit (one had the use of two or three) was taken apart at the seams once a year, spotcleaned, brushed for lint and dirt, and each piece handwashed by the individual nun, then ironed and sewn back together again. Habits and undergarments, like everything else in the convent, were not owned by the nun, but belonged to the Community. When speaking of these items, the politically correct (and firmly ordered) way was to say: *Our* chemise. *Our* habit. Not: *My* chemise or *my* habit.

Forty-nine out of 59 who answered the question, agreed that, when wearing the habit for the first time, they were treated differently by the public. While 18 used words like *trapped, hemmed in, restricted, confined, cumbersome, closed off,* and *uncomfortable* to describe how they physically felt in the habit, no one called it a joy to wear, or said it was light and easy. What they did focus on was their state of mind when they put on the habit. They said they were *proud, respected, felt special and protected, regal, graceful, dignified, marvelous, important, good/great,* and like they *belonged.* Though a few said that wearing the habit made them feel *stripped of individuality, invisible, stiff, different,* and even *ugly.*

Most definitely, yes—wearing the habit gave us a lot more respect and honor. It was embarrassing sometimes, but you could always count on the respect. It made me feel like someone in a play, like somebody else who didn't have any problems, who was dignified and respected no matter who I was. DORIS

Senior citizens gave me their seats on public buses—I hated that. THERESA

Twelve out of the 50 who answered this question, listed physical health problems that developed as a direct result of wearing the habit. A lot of the problems were heat and skin-related: *cradle cap, hair fell out, allergies to wool and celluloid, prickly heat, throat permanently scarred from the coif.* A number of women acquired a sort of "swimmer's ear" from the coif.

Outside of sores under my chin from the gusset on the coif, I developed chronic ear infections for which I infrequently received cortizone. The doctor and the infirmarian (a 76-year old nurse who had entered after her mother died) were both angry that we had to wear headgear that kept the moist air in and caused itching and rash in the ears. DORIS

Changes in the habits and the wearing of street clothes eliminated new cases of these problems. Only 20 of the 59 who answered this question, said their habits were modernized in any way before 1965. Any change at all, whether a shortened veil, less headgear, or a lighter weight dress—precipitated the beginning of the end. Once the wearing of the habit was openly questioned and it was realized that the original reason for wearing a habit had changed, combined with the permission from Rome (Vatican II) to actually make changes, habits disappeared in many Orders in a very few years. Though it is a sign of the new thinking also, that Orders permitted those individuals who felt more comfortable in any stage of the habit, continue to wear them.

We were given a choice regarding the type of wool serge in our habits. There were two weights, one of which was very light. I preferred the heavy wool

because the habit fit better, but the difference in weight was as much as six pounds. The last heavy one I wore weighed ten pounds. The first change in habit style was a shortening of the skirt about ten inches, and the introduction of a headdress which enabled us, when driving, to remove the starched band that extended around our faces. There was some concern about peripheral vision. JULIANNE

Only 22 out of 66 respondents said they discussed wanting habit changes with their superiors. Sixteen talked about habit changes with lay friends, and 35 with other nuns who were not their Superiors.

It was a hot topic and controversy always came between all those who wanted the change and those who didn't. TRACE

During dinner at a local convent, while I was waiting table on the Provincial Superior, she expressly told me I was <u>disloyal</u> to discuss habit change. I was very much influenced by my aunt who was in the St. Paul province, and <u>way</u> ahead of Los Angeles liturgically and ecumenically. After that blast from the Provincial, I never spoke of habit changes other than with my aunt and my immediate family. I knew some local nun had "told on me". HOLLY

I was one of the ones asked to model the new shortened veil, and when I entered the Community Room, Sr. Rugosa announced that I looked "awful" and "scandalous". I couldn't figure out why. Later I asked one of the older nuns what made it look so bad, and she said that Sr. R was just angry because the new veil made me look pretty, and that wasn't what nuns were all about. DORIS

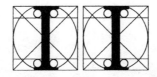

Religious Life

overview: Aspirancy, Postulancy, Novitiate
The Temporary and Final Professed Nuns
Permissions, The Holy Rule
meditation, silence, prayer
rituals, the Leaving Process

Chapter II: Religious Life

Overview: Aspirancy, Postulancy, Novitiate

NOTE: Many subjects touched upon here, are revisited in detail elsewhere in the book.

Nuns in the mid-1900s, as they are now, were on the lookout for new members. Some likely prospects (intelligent, productive, malleable) were given "scholarships" to Order-operated high schools; others groomed by either much attention and a few by fear/fate, e.g., a nun's saying to a young girl: "I can tell when a girl has a Vocation, I can see that you have a Vocation, and we all know that anyone who ignores her Call from God goes to Hell." On the other hand, a number of nuns became acquainted with the Order through the recommendation of a priest- or nun-friend, or because of the Motherhouse's proximity to the candidate's home or school. In any case, the candidate's main reason for entering was to do good works for God, humanity, and in fulfillment of her Vocation. Visits between the candidate and the Order's top Superior were scheduled, then the candidate was generally discussed by some Community committee before being formally admitted. Interviews and/or discussion of the candidate by the Order's Superior and its Council would recur before each move to another level in the convent.

Since most of the candidates before 1960 were still teenagers (down to 14 years old), parental consent was necessary for entrance into the convent. Older candidates signed themselves in. A "trousseau" list of items, plus a dowry and sometimes other fees, were paid. The date of entry was set; the candidate's business and goodbyes were taken care of, and the girl/woman arrived at the convent.

Some started in the Aspirancy, (see also Chapter I: Beginnings) especially those who were still in high school. Aspirants lived in the convent separately from the other nuns, and were seen to by an Aspirant Mistress. In the hours that they were not attending classes, Aspirants were being trained in convent mores and introduced to prayer. Aspirants wore the regulation school uniform, no makeup, and did not associate with the other students except academically. One stayed in the Aspirancy for as long as the Mother General deemed necessary before moving on to the next step.

The Postulancy, not less than 6 months, was also available for seniors in high school. Some Orders began their process with this step. The Postulant either lived in the Novitiate and was directed by the same Novice Mistress, or lived in separate quarters with a Postulant Mistress. She wore an abbreviated habit, often a cape instead of a scapular, no permanent veil, and began her indoctrination into the ways of this particular convent, outside of school hours. Postulants were sometimes excused from the harsher realities of convent life, e.g., Chapter of Faults, but did take part in public Refectory penances. A "Bride of Christ" ceremony marked her entrance into the next level.

At this point, the candidate received her "nun name". The idea was to lose the old self and begin anew. In some Orders, the candidate was allowed to submit several names, from which the Council might or might not choose her new name. Often, until the priest actually called her by her new name during the ceremony, the new nun would be in suspense. Many nuns were named after male saints, or the candidate submitted names of the males in her family. The women in this survey were not asked questions about their nun names, and many chose not to share what that name was.

The white-veiled Novice's first (of usually two years) year was called "canonical" and consisted of strong formation in the Community under the tutelage of a Novice Mistress. A "ranking" was given her at this point. Nuns who entered before her, held higher rank. In her own class, the ranking was decided by the Council. Rank determined who went first through a doorway, who sat where at any function, etc. No outside trips or schooling except in-house theology classes and many instruction sessions on The Rule of the Order were allowed during the canonical year. The second year Novice put on her (for public only) black veil and attended school, usually college, or was sent directly into the classroom, mission kitchen, or medical facility to work. She still underwent formation by the Novice Mistress, and in most cases, lived at the Motherhouse. Another ceremony marked the end of the Novitiate. Novices did not speak to anyone outside of the Novitiate except on rare feastday celebrations.

Chapter II: Religious Life

It was not unusual for nuns of other Communities, say, where the Novices attended college, to do their bit to keep Novices humble, regardless of the fact that they were from different Orders.

I was the only nun in my Life Drawing class, and when we had live nude models, especially men, I would see the faces of the rest of my group (nuns) outside pressed up against the windows. Though I had been praised as having artistic talent for years, the teacher took every opportunity to show and tell my mistakes as if they proved how personally inadequate a human being I was, as if I should have known all this before I came to class, and was deliberately doing it another way. When I mentioned how difficult this situation was to another nun of our Order, she said, Well, you've got to expect that when you're a Novice. At one point that first semester, I had surgery, and when I returned, the class was doing charcoal still lifes. I had never even handled charcoal and had no idea where to begin. When I asked the instructor, she said loudly that if I chose to be away from class during the instruction (she knew I'd been in the hospital), I'd have to figure it out for myself. No matter how I tried to sneak instructions out of her when she was near, she refused to speak to me on that subject, nor did she let me ask any of the other students (Novices were not to speak to anyone), so I started an abstract, cubistic still life—I'd always wanted to try cubism. The instructor had her hands full shushing the girls who raved about my piece. On the way out that day, one girl offered me $20 for the art, and the teacher blew up, saying loudly how unworth anything this picture was, what bad taste I had (it was a chair and a plant—how bad could that be?), how this line and that line was wrong, etc. I smuggled it out to my parents, and it now hangs in my house years later, a piece that typifies my first independence, and that art-wise, isn't all that bad. DORIS

If humiliation was the "bread and butter" of the Novitiate member, doing the majority of the heavy convent housekeeping was the very air they breathed. Taking wax off floors and putting new wax back on those same floors, brushing each wooden stair on hands and knees, taking down each venetian blind and hauling it to a cleaning area before wiping it, helping prepare food in the kitchen then serving it at meals, growing and picking the strawberries before canning them—these were parts of the daily life of a Postulant or Novice.

In our Novitiate we were all lumped together—it was a small Community, and Novitiate meant all the candidates from the Aspirants and Postulants to the Novices. We did everything from all the hard labor jobs—cleaning, outdoor yard work, serving tables and the Community, and the canning. It was hard work. We were a very hard working group of people. After you were a senior Sister and got older and older, you had less of those chores to do. MARGARET

Most often I went to summer school, but one summer I helped at the mangle in the Motherhouse laundry, and also did a lot of canning of pears. There was always an emphasis on cleanliness and obsessive dusting and cleaning of bathrooms. JEAN-2

Until I left (8 years) my main assigned job was to clean toilets. I never got the dusting jobs. They insisted that the job be done by a certain time before we left for work in the morning, and with the nuns going in and out to use the stalls, I nearly threw up every morning. Once in a while after studying extra or being away, I'd forget a toilet area, and I'd awake in the night with a start, in terror that I was going to "get it" for not cleaning the toilet. DORIS

I worked mostly in the kitchen and laundry, but one summer I cleaned 47 toilets a day in the nursing home. ELIZABETH

In the earlier years when Motherhouses still had nun cooks, members of the Novitiate were assigned on a rotating basis to help prepare and serve the food. Forty-three (of the 59 who answered) said they worked in the kitchen. Most of the work was done in silence.

No talk, huge pots and pans, getting very greasy and messy in those awful hot habits. JANN

The Sister in charge of Kitchen would tell everyone of my mistakes and make fun of me. If I was serving at the head table, she would tell all of the Sisters my mistakes and laugh at me. There were times when I thought her goal was to make me cry—and she did. MERT

I spent quite a bit of time in the Diet Kitchen, which meant getting trays ready for the infirmary Sisters. We also took our turn serving tables, cleaning up, and washing dishes. I didn't mind these duties as it gave us a chance to relax and we did talk, even though we weren't supposed to. MARY-2

Regardless of how tedious peeling vegetables and washing dishes was, I enjoyed it because the Kitchen Sisters were so sweet. They smiled and winked and patted us on the shoulders when we couldn't talk. They looked into our eyes as if we were really there. I loved them. DORIS

Kitchen duty in the Novitiate was a very unpleasant experience because the sole Sister in charge was extremely overworked. She was responsible for putting out three meals a day for 250 people, 365 days a year, once a year for two days provide chicken dinner for the hundreds that attended our annual festival fund raiser, and received little recognition for this work. She had to rely on green Novitiate help-- on a rotating basis, besides. But as young persons, all we saw was this very nervous, angry, demanding woman who seemed to demean us at every turn. I dreaded any interaction with her. Luckily, one of our Novices had been a professional cook, and shielded me by assigning me to the pots and pans or to the cellar to peel potatoes. THERESE-2

After the steady of stream of exiting nuns began, many mission houses no longer had Cook Sisters, and the teaching or nursing nuns often took turns cooking.

Usually we had a rather fair distribution of household tasks, but once our Superior burdened a young nun with the full responsibility of the kitchen in addition to her teaching. Even that wasn't as bad as the fact that the Superior took it upon herself to play God and humiliated this sensitive young person with frequent scoldings. On one occasion I found her sorting apples in the basement cellar with tears running down her cheeks—the scolding had been over letting some of the apples spoil. We became friends that day when I helped her realize that the Superior was not God, that she was an ordinary human woman like ourselves, and that sometimes she saw things in a distorted way, putting emphasis on picayune matters and making mistakes in her judgment. That little nun still credits me with helping her get through one of the most trying years of her life. THERESE-2

After my first profession of vows, our Sisters staffed the seminary students and priests' kitchen. We worked hard. The rules about not speaking to seminarians were very strict. Casual conversations were to be reported to the Superior. EILEEN

I rotated working in the kitchen during the Novitiate and also volunteered to cook one day a week in the girls' kitchen once I was a Professed nun, in order to relieve the Sister who had that job. MARTHA

A common task of Novices during their canonical year, was to learn the Order's Rules from the little black Community Rulebook. The injunctions in this book had been either written by the founders or modified by later formal Chapters (conventions). The Rules could include larger issues like limiting the entrants to virgins (the Communities who did this usually asked, but didn't check physically), or smaller things like demanding that Sisters stopped speaking in mid-word at the "first sound" of the end-of-recreation bell (buzzer). A Community's Rules theoretically applied to everyone from the Mother General on down through the ranks to the newest aspirant.

Mostly, the lower ranks (Aspirants, Postulants, and Novices) could not expect to be granted Rule exceptions. Practically speaking, any already-careered woman who entered (there were two in our class) was given all sorts of exemptions, though not publicly or on paper. In general, the 30-40 year old nuns in our Community took the most freedoms, asked for and granted, or just taken. Certain members went to spa outings, had wine parties during Grande Silence, talked to each other on unnecessary issues, kissed and hugged in front of beginners who were told not to touch each other, and sometimes donned civilian clothes to meet and drive away with lay friends in the middle of the night. They were allowed to rest when they felt like it, though others needed at least the note of the infirmarian, skip prayers (no one checked on them as did the Novice Mistress), and visit lay persons with impunity. Novices were not allowed these things; nothing in the book spoke of the Rules being lifted for age or assertiveness, but they were. As a

Novice who mentioned these disparities, I was accused of jealousy and given a penance for my sin. DORIS

Juniorate (Temporary Professed), The Final Professed

The Temporary Professed nun wore the same habit and black veil (or other color equivalent, if the Order's habit was not black) as the Final Professed. She requested and was allowed to take vows for 1-3 years, then to renew them one year at a time for a couple of years. Generally, if a nun couldn't decide whether she <u>certainly</u> wished to take her final vows after 5 years of Temporary Vows, she was counseled to leave the convent. Temporarily Professed nuns had their own Superior, the Juniorate Mistress. While their formation at this point was more sparse and sporadic, especially since the nuns were most certainly by now involved in the Community's work and perhaps residing at a mission house, they were still overseen by the Juniorate Mistress.

Twenty-one out of the 60 who answered the question, said Yes, there was a social strata for unpleasant jobs among Professed nuns. Thirty-one said No, not to their knowledge, and eight could not recall.

Superiors did not do them. K.T.

Youngest members did the most unpleasant jobs. THERESE

In many ways it was fair, but there was definitely social strata, people who were unfairly excused, and those who were unfairly burdened by their own goodness of heart or lack of intelligence with jobs that they really didn't want to have. MARGARET

Assigned chores the participants (60 responses) liked the best were:
sacristan, cleaning chapel – 18
cleaning, housekeeping – 10
garden, farm, picking fruit – 9
kitchen, canning – 8
They liked these chores the least:
cleaning, housekeeping – 29

kitchen, canning – 11
garden, farm, picking fruit – 5

Other unliked jobs were: *scrubbing floors with steel wool, serving the priest, working in the print shop, waxing 5 flights of stairs, dusting something that didn't need dusting, emptying cloth sanitary napkins into a large container, stripping wax off the floor and waxing it again.*

As for occupations, 21 (of the 60 that answered) worked at boarding schools, 5 in hospitals, 3 in nursing homes, 2 in orphanages and baby homes, 2 in court-ordered residences, 2 in kitchens, and the rest taught elementary school, high school, and college.

❖

Final Vows made the nun a full-fledged member of the Community. (Also see Chapter: Liabilities.) Outside of what they felt at going through a public (with lay persons present) or private (in front of the Community only) vow ceremony, each nun experienced strong emotions at moving on to the next step. Many, but not all, were delighted to do so. The participants who answered this question (What did you feel as you moved on to each stage of vows?) gave one or more answers. (Twelve did not respond.) They said, I felt:

fulfilled, wonderful, privileged, elated, proud, glad, happy, eager: (22)
confident, relieved, grateful, successful: (8)
accepted, passed, ready, okay, content, I'd just got by, made it, some liberation: (12)
committed, responsible, serious: (6)

ambivalent: (3)

confused, doubtful, agonized: (6)
hopeless: (1)

I made vows because I couldn't get out of it. The last ones, I said the words, but in my mind, I said I didn't mean them. JEAN-3

I felt more and more committed and yet more and more hopeless that I wasn't ever going to be able to leave because it seemed like I was stuck there. It was like a marriage to me—those final vows especially—that was a life commitment. MARGARET

The vows were to the Pope, not God: he could release me. BEVERLY

Our vows were solemn; there was no way out. ANN

We were told that it was bond between God and us. And how can you break that? Man cannot intervene and break the bond. Even later, if we should leave, the bond would still be there, and if we were at fault, guilty, then we would go to hell, I was certain. CHERRY

Vows were made to God at this time, so no one knew if you could ever get released. GAYLE

Temporary vows were temporary; final vows were final. But dispensations could be granted. NELL

Since I had been trying to leave ever since I was a postulant, the closer I got to final vows, the more panicked I got. I just didn't want to be there. It wasn't the loving community I had hoped for, but I didn't know how to get out of it without going to hell. DORIS

I didn't want to make last vows. By the time I was there 7 years, I realized that I did not want to go on because I knew by then that I only felt alive when I had a close friend to share with and love. Also because I found the daily _fear_—of teaching, of Superiors, of criticism by older nuns, of my own inadequacy, such a constant drain on my energy and vitality. Yet I was imprisoned by my conviction that, hate it as I did, this was God's Will for me. And, never having held a job, I didn't know if I could make it in the world by myself. THERESE-2

Final Professed nuns were not allowed to speak to those still in formation (Aspirants, Postulants, Novices, Juniors) unless it was a free day (feastday where permission to talk had been given). The Final Professed nun still walked and sat in chapel or Refectory in rank, as she expected to for her entire convent life. (Some Orders eliminated "rank" by the 1980-90s.)

The Holy Rule

The nun was now fully immersed in the work of the Community. Her immediate Superior was in-house; her ultimate Superior, the Provincial Superior (in larger Orders), then the Mother General of the Order. In between, other officially appointed nuns had say in various areas of her life, e.g., the Directress of Studies, who decided and arranged everything having to do with schooling and careers, the Directress of Music (if she were a music teacher), etc.

Superiors always had the final say, with no appeal, no matter if the Superior was the Mother General or your Novice mistress. They never used language that would lead you to believe the process might be democratic or flexible, or even take into account an individual's personal background or problems. Superiors spoke, and underlings literally bowed and obeyed. Mostly there was no gripe about that because theoretically you knew when you entered that that would be the case, even if you never _really_ imagined it would, or thought it through. DORIS

Two participants say they "discussed" a rule with their Superior; 26 actively protested at least one rule, and 38 say they never protested rules.

When studying for my Masters alone at a secular college, I went veil-less. CASEY

I protested all the bitsy rules. In the summers of 1965-6, as a result of Vatican II, we had a Provincial meeting with delegates from every convent. I was elected to represent some 20 Sisters. Our study group discussed obedience. I was chosen to record and report to the assembled conference all the rules our group thought should be changed or abrogated. The Provincial took umbrage at my report and "put me down" verbally. But after I left the convent, all those rules were changed. THERESE-2

I never protested a rule because we were taught that even if something seemed wrong to us, the Superior represented God's Will and we would do right if we obeyed her. LILLA

According to the Ordo (rules for liturgy), we did not have to have Benediction every day during Lent, so, as sacristan, I didn't set up for it in chapel (local convent). The Superior went wild. I "fell on my knees" as I was supposed to when getting reprimanded, but I knew I was right and she just screamed and screamed at me. I didn't feel contrite, but right. (See also Chapter IX: Liabilities.) HOLLY

The ordinary rules, I didn't protest. My first questioning of authority happened when I was a Junior Professed, and I helped another nun (who suffered severe back pain) put on her shoes and stockings in the mornings. The Juniorate Mistress questioned what I was doing, and said I shouldn't be taking so much time at it. I spoke up then and explained, then kept on doing it. Another time years later, I refused to be moved to another teaching assignment in another city because I felt it was unjust. So I told the Provincial I would wait two weeks and speak with her successor, which I did. CAROLYN

Once I asked the Mother General from Rome, how a nun could be appointed a Postulant Mistress when she was so unjust. She replied that she was hearing from everyone that "we need young blood" and that the good outweighed the bad. When I asked about Sisters who were blatantly mean and flaunted the rules, I was told that the good-tempered Sisters had been called upon to put up with it because the others were incorrigible, and that God would bless the good especially. LILLA

From 1967-77, nuns in our Order were allowed to keep articles of clothing given to them by their parents, but not money given for the same. I felt the rule was unfair, that it had nothing to do with the real spirit of poverty, and I kept the money. SARAH

I came from a very authoritarian family. I didn't question rules of authority until many years later. THERESA

After vows, my parents offered to pay for contact lenses for me, but the Provincial Superior said that was not appropriate because it was not prescribed or doctor-recommended—it was just an option. When I protested, I was told it was vanity that lay behind this desire. My mother particularly found it difficult that, whenever she gave me gifts, they were put into the general supply—that was discouraging and disheartening for her. K.T.

When the Vatican II changes began, there were pockets of us in the Community—just as there were in other Orders all over the United States—protesting and asking for change. Earlier, I never questioned the rules. What happened was that over a period of about 10 years, I started to question my sexuality and every other rule in the convent. The rules that I questioned, I would not follow. This made me feel really guilty at first—practically like a "mortal sin" feeling, but eventually I changed so that I felt it was the rule that was wrong, and not me. Generally, I questioned myself right out of the convent and out of the Catholic Church. I continue to be a creative thinker—someone who does not take anything for granted just because I am told it. MARGARET.

This is what happened when I had philosophical differences with authority: I felt a call to medicine almost as early as a call to a spiritual relationship with God. I entered a congregation of nurses and teachers. I was told to teach—tossed in a sea of 55 third graders with no help, no practice teaching, and told that God would provide. He didn't. (This should have rung a warning bell.) The 5 years I taught school, I had no class discipline and no will to have power over them. I wanted for them the freedom I wanted for myself. Because of my intelligence, my failure was judged to be willful. My distinction that my wanting to be in medicine didn't rule out the fact that I was willing to try my best to be a better teacher—that was not appreciated. I was the only one in my group held back from making final vows, and told that I was proud and needed to learn humility. ELLEN

I chose to join them and the rules were their rules, so I guess it was shut up, put up, or get out. TRACE

I was too scared of disobeying and being sent home. MARY-2

I do not think many individuals ever took this Superior on, but I felt I had to take a stand in order to survive. I guess I intimidated her, for once she told me I was exactly like my mother. I told her I was grateful for that. It was not a good period in my life. I made mistakes too, but I feel strongly that the environment within the community was very unhealthy emotionally for many of us. In some cases I chose to continue following the rule, but in others, I simply let them slide. They were historically unsound and some of them placed me under even more time constraints—something just had to give. GAYLE

After the first incidents, when I asked if it were possible that we could have a variation of a rule and was told, No, I stopped asking. DORIS

Meditation

Convent life on mission was modeled as much as possible on that of the Motherhouse, given the exceptions necessary to do the outside work of the Community. Each Order had its own versions of everything, though generally, all Orders were similar in basic rules, customs, etc. The day began for most active Communities, on mission or at the Motherhouse, no later (and sometimes earlier) than 5 a.m. when the nun would rise at the sound of a bell, dress quickly, and within half an hour, be in Chapel for morning meditation. Meditation was done *en masse*, though on an individual basis. This was followed by chanting or silent reading of the Holy Office, and by daily Mass, at which point the nuns were often joined by lay members of the congregation. Mass was followed by a silent breakfast, then work of the day.

All the participants (69) who answered the question, said their Communities had group meditation every morning. Nine *liked* or *loved* meditation, 6 *hated it* or *found it extremely difficult*, and 22 said it was *okay, good, or fine*. Forty-one said they *often* slept during meditation, and others *sometimes slept* or *frequently fought sleep*. Thirty-three women said that falling asleep made them feel *guilty, frustrated, embarrassed,* and *foolish*. Five said that falling asleep didn't bother them or make them feel guilty. *So what?* said one. *I wish I could sleep away the convent years,* said another. One participant pointed out: *The brain waves for meditation and for sleep are close.*

I tried to meditate, but my mind wandered a lot. JULIA

We were never given instruction in how to meditate. All it was, was thinking about something we had read. GINA

During most of the first years, my zombie years, I became rather bored with it and felt I wasted a lot of time meditating. I couldn't keep my mind on anything, but I do think now, looking back, that it was the habit of setting aside that time that carried through my life up until today. MARGARET.

I liked meditation. We were to stand up if we were in danger of falling asleep. Supposedly, that was a public penance, but I welcomed the change of position. I couldn't meditate very well, though, standing up. TRACE

It made me feel inadequate. I never felt I knew how to do it. It was never clear to me just what it was all about. It was not supposed to be an intellectual experience, but I did learn a great a deal about Christ, his teachings, and something about our relationship. Those hours of meditation made me more profoundly appreciative of the contemplative aspects of life, its beauty, its subtlety, its power. There was a strong tension in me between the community's priority, teaching, and what I believed was primary, that is, prayer. Because I could not live in this dichotomy, I finally chose to leave. JULIANNE

Meditation was not well taught—we were basically told to read a line and think about it. As a young teen, I never got enough sleep anyway, and at 5 a.m. I'd spend an hour trying to meditate, jerk myself awake, feel guilty and worry about disobeying the rule to meditate, doze off again, feel guilty, etc. It was miserable. It was many years after I left the convent before I learned to meditate. DORIS

Well, I didn't know if I was up to being as good as the rest of the nuns in meditation, but the sleepiness got to the point where after a while, I couldn't do anything about it. CHERRY

Meditation brought a discipline into my life that I had not known before. To become quiet and allow God to work in me, to open myself, to spend prime time with God's word or with great writing. JANET

It took about 5 years before I ever developed a style of meditating that was appropriate to me. I have no idea if it helped me or not. DOROTHY

It helped me take a long range view of my life, and calmed me. THERESE

❖❖❖

Greeting Phrase, the Holy Rule of Silence

Communities generally had a special greeting phrase: whenever one passed another nun of the same Order (though not in public), the youngest in rank would say the first half of the greeting, and the older nun would respond. Five women did not answer the question about the Community greeting, and eleven did not remember if their Order had one. Greetings used by the others were:

First person: Praised be Jesus Christ.
Second person: Now and for all eternity.

other variations of Praised be Jesus Christ, including the Latin:
   Laudetur Jesus Christus.

Glory be to Jesus and Mary.
Praised be Jesus and Mary.
God be with you.
Blessings. (also in Latin)

In the very same Order, 12 nuns said they had an official greeting and 6 said they did not. This is easily explained by the fact that, starting with the Vatican II changes, some Orders gradually dropped their greeting phrase, especially when their rules of silence changed. Nuns who entered later were not introduced to it.

The Rule in the mid-1900s was still daily silence (except when it was necessary to speak and on permission-to-talk feastdays), though nuns who attended or taught school, especially college, became so used to using their voices that they often lingered in conversations with the laity or each other before leaving school. After school there was usually a short time for preparation of the next day's classes, plus for doing whatever household cleaning task one had been assigned for the month. Then dinner (silent, except for feastdays), a half hour to an hour of "recreation" (see Chapter III: Good Things, for the recreation rules), night prayers, and bedtime about 9:30 p.m.

There was a period of recreation after the noon meal and the evening meal, about 30-45 minutes. If one was working in the diet kitchen or elsewhere doing one's "charge" (assigned job), or if one were the youngest in rank in a mission house, then one might get only a few minutes of recreation or none at all. Recreation was taken in the Community Room. While I was doing my student teaching, I may have gotten up to 10 minutes of recreation total. In Seattle, I got perhaps 5 minutes each evening—not enough to re-pleat my skirt, but maybe enough to see if I had mail, though the time was too short to read it. TRACE

Grande Silence prevailed from after recreation in the evening until after breakfast the next morning. Breaking Grande Silence was a more grevious act than speaking during daily silence. Even those who tended to ignore The Rule of Silence frequently, wrote notes during Grande Silence, rather than speak.

Besides observing silence in general, each Community had certain rooms where it was forbidden to speak, notably the Refectory(except during "talking" meals), bathrooms, and dorm. To speak, even necessarily, to someone in one of those rooms, both parties were to step outside into the hall, or at least, into the doorway.

Oh, silence—that was such a hard one for me, even though I was such a good little conformist and did most of the things I was supposed to in those early years. Silence was hard for me because I was an extroverted woman and needed to express myself and discover myself through self-expression. It was one of the healthiest things for me that I broke the rule of silence (sometimes a lot), or I would have shut myself down totally. I didn't feel guilty enough about that, but speaking was a lifeline for me; I've always had to process by communicating and could not stop myself from doing it. MARGARET

I valued the peacefulness and quiet of the convent, especially after the turbulence of my growing up years at home. Later, I found that silence gave me freedom from listening to mindless chatter, especially at breakfast. ANNE

There were times when I appreciated the quiet to read and study, but I never saw the point of so much silence. It seemed an unnecessary struggle. JEAN-2

I was already an introvert and understood and respected the need for time alone and "peace and quiet", but to tell the truth, I thought the silence rule was silly. I never could understand how speaking to another person could harm me or make me less of a person. SARAH

I really thought we were saving souls by keeping silence. MARY-2

Wonderful. NANCY   *An albatross.* LORNA

It was a very sacred obligation. LORENA

Four women did not answer this question. Seven said they liked keeping silence, and 25 said it was *okay, fine,* or that they *accepted it.* Twenty-seven thought it *difficult,* and *didn't like it.* Nine said that that much silence was *dumb, stupid, silly, handicapping,* and that they *hated it.*

Part of the problem with silence was the ban on speaking to the laity, except during meetings or emergencies. One ex-nun told the author she considered that inhuman, and went right on speaking/listening to the boarders who needed to speak to her. For this she and others of like mind, were constantly reprimanded and given public penances (see Chapter V: The Refectory).

Not only were we not supposed to converse with any of the girls with which we attended college, but even worse, we were not allowed to explain to them why we were ignoring them! DORIS

Superiors who were human, figured you had enough sense to talk to the laity. But my first superior took over all outside interactions and kept the rest of us "within the wall". This meant that Sisters who were there before that Superior came, and who had lay friends, had to stop talking to them with no explanations given. One young Sister (age 22) became <u>very</u> depressed because of this and other oppression by the Superior. ROSE

For us, it came down to common sense—unless we were working only with Sisters, we were permitted to speak to each other and to any one else, students and lay persons. JULIANNE

If one was caught or reported breaking "separation" silence with the laity, this is what happened: 2 ignored it; 2 felt guilty; 5 obeyed the rule, so it was not an issue; 13 said it was not an issue in any case; 15 received reprimands and/or public penance, and 1 was sent home. Thirty-four women declined to answer this question.

Required prayers, Rituals

What each nun was supposed to fulfill each day on her own, was: her job, her prayers (group prayer, 15 minutes of spiritual reading, plus the Rosary and individually-said parts of the Office,), and her housecleaning job. Fifty-five out of 70 participants who answered, said they were required to say the Rosary daily; 12 answered No, they were not, and the rest could not recall. Twenty-seven said they felt guilty when they stopped saying the daily Rosary; 5 admit outright lying about whether they said it, and several who quit said no one ever asked them if they were still praying the Rosary, so they said nothing about it one way or the other

Gosh, in those early years it was part of a daily process. Of course I remember being bored to death as we went through the routine. In some ways I felt I was lying about saying it, sitting there fingering the beads, not thinking at all about what I was doing, daydreaming. MARGARET.

I said it, but often grudgingly. If my mind didn't drift off, I'd get to thinking about something in Jesus' life, say, and forget all about getting from one bead to the next. I've always preferred prayer to prayers. TRACE

For many years I said the Rosary daily, then with overwork and study, I abbreviated it. I just didn't have the stamina to do everything, nor the interest or drive to keep up every single prayer. The Rosary was the one thing that just didn't seem as important as spontaneous praying during the day or the work I was doing. I felt that the Divine Office was better suited to the modern Sister, and certainly gave as much opportunity to praise God and Our Lady as saying the Rosary did. Repeating the same words over and over never seemed valuable to me. DORIS

Fifty-two of the 69 who answered, said they were required to pray the Office daily, and 2 said they prayed it only on weekends.

Until Vatican II, we chanted the Little Office daily in the Novitiate, and on weekends thereafter, except during retreats when we chanted it daily. After Vatican II, the Divine Office replaced some of our daily prayers. JULIANNE

It was only towards the very end when I became discouraged and abbreviated the Office. I tried to tell myself it was the same as saying the whole thing, but I felt guilty about it. CAREN

I liked the antiphonal chant very much and liked the psalms much better than Mass or the Rosary. JEAN-2

The last year I simply could not do all that was required of me—being principal of the school as well as full time 8th grade teacher, doing the sewing for all the nuns of the school and day home, my share of the housework, being choir director and organist—it reached the point where I just gave up, saying Matins and Lauds alone, or the Rosary in their place. At first, I confessed it in the confessional, but what was the use when I couldn't get it all in regardless? No use telling the Superior—she was plainly cruel and would only chastise me and make my life more difficult. Sometimes those "lost prayers" still bother me. My reasoning tells me it is all right, but I still feel a horrendous amount of guilt, yet I don't pray extra Rosaries to make it up and I don't know why. I think that perhaps I'll do it this year so that it will be gone at last. LILLA

Outside of the above, nuns had other obligations to various groups and committees, organizations with which they worked, parents of the students they taught, etc. Each nun was also responsible for cleaning her own outfit, for getting her laundry done, and for doing the weekly assigned chore (which usually took up most of Saturday), such as working in the garden or laundry, or picking peaches for canning.

Once a month (once a year, in some Orders), Visiting hour was held for (mostly) families. In some Orders, one daytime visit was allowed with one's family (within driving distance) at their home, once a year.

No eating in front of seculars was permitted in the old days. Silent meals were taken in the Refectory (at the Motherhouse) or dining room while a reader read from pre-approved edifying material (see Chapter V: The Refectory). Eating was done at meals only, except on feastdays when there might be snacks such as popcorn or chocolates (gifts from the laity) available. Feastdays had different rules: the Superior usually (though not always) declared the day a "talk" day, which meant that outside of squeezing in one's prayer schedule on one's own, visiting or playing tennis or folk dancing was the order of the day. Feastdays often ended with a family-type movie, and if the film ran into Grande Silence time a bit, and the Superior decided it was all right to finish seeing the movie anyway, no speaking was allowed during the last part of it, or afterwards.

Once a week there was held an in-house community Chapter of Faults (see Chapter IV: Suffering)—a public confession of sorts, though private confession for actual sins was available weekly, sometimes daily.

Once every five years or so, a general meeting called "Chapter" (no relation to the Chapter of Faults) was held during which Final Professed nuns discussed changes in the Order, convent issues, and elected a new Mother General and Council. Chapter goings on (outside of the results) were not discussed with the younger nuns who did not attend.

Letters to family and (usually by permission) to others were written on Sundays once a month or less frequently, depending on the Order. Letters were left open, and incoming mail had the envelopes slit: some were read, in the Novitiate, especially. Phone calls were allowed by special permission, in cases of emergency.

Permissions, miscellaneous arrangements

Everything in the convent depended upon permissions. Lines of nuns would queue up in front of the Superior's door waiting to ask permission to get a single aspirin, more soap, thread, another pen or a glass of milk outside of meals, to read a book, walk outside, take a bath, to throw away old underwear or shoelaces, to write a letter, and on other occasions, to speak, go to the bathroom, or to just leave the room.

My aunt, a nun, told me to bring bras to the convent even though it didn't say so on the list. My friend asked me for my extra ones, so I went to my trunk and got them for her. That very day, the Postulant Mistress gave a whole lecture to the group on "You never go to your trunk without permission". HOLLY

You had to ask for everything—soap, toothpaste, toothbrush. You had to bring in stockings to show that they were darned to the point that you were darning the darns. LILLA

At some point, in some Orders, group permissions were given for insignificant things, much like General Absolution in the later years.

Each evening just before night prayer, the presiding Sister would face the Community, hands in her sleeves, bow, and say, "You may continue your occupations, Sisters. You have your permissions." The community would return the bow. That took care of that. If you weren't there, you tracked down the presiding Sister and got your daily permissions the same way. TRACE

Then there was "presumed permission", when there was no time or Superior available and one had to make a minor decision, such as, to use a typewriter or leave a note to someone. These presumed permissions were to be reported to the Superior after the fact.

Turning in gifts or supplies sent from home, or asking permission to use them (even stationery and stamps) was usual. Everything you received, even if your parents had bought it specially for you, was considered as belonging to the Community. Sometimes you did not physically touch the gift except to hand it to the Superior, who would either recycle it into the Community, or, if it were a particularly nice object, save it as a future gift for "The Benefactors".

Stationery or candy gotten at Christmas was turned in. We were supposed to write home at intervals, so maybe we'd be allowed to keep the stationery. Outside of a store, I'd never seen so many boxes of chocolates as I did there. I got the rockiest stomachache of my life on my first Christmas there. I had no idea candy could do that. When had I ever had a chance to find out? I learned great respect for overindulgence! Unwitting gluttony in a house of poverty—have a good laugh at me! TRACE

Years after I had left, it dawned on me that I ought to have a right to the flute (bought specially by my then-indigent parents) and my ring which, like many nuns', had been made of my grandparents' wedding rings melted together. I inquired about the ring from the current Superior of the Order, who said that she got requests like that all the time, and that the rings were constantly recycled and mine could be anywhere. She asked if I could identify it, since there were a few left in the box. Well, since we had not been allowed to own anything, and had been told that whatever we were given by others belonged to the Community, of course the ring had no personal markings. For that same reason (no personal ownership), I hadn't considered fighting for it when I left. DORIS

Asking permissions brought up these emotional reactions among the then-nuns:

It was stressful. BEVERLY
So anxious, that maybe I didn't need the item. JEAN
I felt somewhat humiliated. ELIZABETH
It made me feel adolescent, like a child. CONNIE, ELEANOR, GAYLE, JEAN-2, SARAH
Frustrated, annoyed—it was a bother. EILEEN, ANN, ANNE

Frustrated, resentful, and childish. DONNA, SARAH, THERESA
I felt like a dumb kid. MARY
Small, like my judgment wasn't good. KATE
Stupid, ridiculous, silly, but it was the rule. MAE, ELLEN-2, JANET K, DORIS, MARY S, DENISE
Restricted, subservient, dependent, controlled. DOLORES, CASEY, CAROL-2 MARIETTA, MERT, ROSE, LORENA
I was a legalist for a long time, so I asked permission. JULIANNE
I had to try to play the silly game to be honest with God. ELLEN
I was glad to surrender my will. JOSEPHINE
It got easier each time. JEAN-3
I accepted it as a part of religious life. SUZANNE
It was fine! NELL, DIANE

Reading material was limited up to the late 50s, to: spiritual reading, theology, the Bible and whatever other religious books a particular Order specifically pushed for daily reading, the Missal (during Mass), and books directly related to one's classes. Especially before final vows, reading anything else was cause for rebuke, and possibly, public penance.

Certain nuns were designated drivers. In some Communities, it took the equivalent of an act of Congress to get permission to learn to drive. In others, not. The Community car (more cars at the Motherhouse) was never touched without express permission of the Superior, who held the keys.

Punishments, penances, and public humiliation were a common part of daily life (see Chapter V: The Refectory). One walked with one's eyes cast down so as not to distract oneself or others from contemplation, though some few nuns could be counted on for a quick smile or wink.

Shunning was not a regular punishment in the convent, as it is in some religions. However, in some individual convents, shunning was applied both to women as nuns in this survey, and to some ex-nuns who spoke to the author, but chose not to make their stories public (see Chapter X: Peers and Social Strata).

Sleeping arrangements were almost always curtained dormitories for the younger nuns, and private/semi-private rooms for those of higher rank. One respondent to these questions said that in her Order, an older nun was paired with a younger one in the double rooms. Bathrooms were institution-style, down the hall. Rarely (except for Superiors) were there rooms with adjoining bathrooms. Every cell (space) or room had a twin bed, a small chest of drawers or nightstand, hook or shared closet area, and sometimes, a chair. In some Communities before Vatican II, it was expressly forbidden to go to one's sleeping area outside of official retirement time (not much was kept there except clothes, anyway). Permission to lie down during the day was not given without much evidence of illness.

I can remember being so very exhausted at one point, and begging for a few moments of lie-down on a Sunday afternoon. The Superior (I was a Junior by then) said, No, absolutely not. We don't go to our cells in the daytime. I never did understand why. DORIS

Visitation (referred to by various names in different Communities) occurred once a year. This was when the Mother General spent 5-15 minutes with each nun, asking her if she had any complaints. It was easy to "accidentally" get treated differently after a nun brought up an issue. Many nuns said they were Fine, thank you, and tried to deal with things on their own (see Chapter XI: Leaving).

As a young sister I was sent to a house that was known for its bitchy nuns and they left me there for 15 years. I stuck it out thinking it had to get better—it didn't. I was only in one place where I was reasonably happy, and that was only for 2 years out of 20, so I'm glad I left. MARY

Visitation went something like this: Superior General: How are you? Nun: "Fine." SG: "Any problems?" Nun: "No, not really." This was where you told about any difficulties within the mission—if you did not expect repercussions after the SG left. Silly me—of course there weren't any repercussions. The mission's Superior just happened to get a little sharper with you and said "No" to your next hundred requests. Nuns of her peer group whispered together and glanced at you, but had nothing to say to you except terse answers to direct public questions. So when asked, "Any problems?" the answer was often: "No." DORIS

❖❖❖

Tea for the Benefactors

Periodically, grand teas were given by the hierarchy for Benefactors--persons who had made large donations to the convent and were therefore held in high esteem (though most of us rarely heard their names). I remember being recruited as a very new postulant to assist at one of these very formal functions--someone had thought it might be cute to let the "babies" serve. A handful of us were apprised of the assignment in the cloakroom just a few moments before we were to begin. Though I had been a lead in the play every year and had even danced on stage, I still considered myself a "farm girl" and had never in my life been in a formal social situation; the very thought put me into severe panic. Add to that the fact that I was barely sixteen and like any teenager, self-conscious--I worried that I wouldn't know what to do, that I'd be out there by myself, everybody would be watching me, and my body would be frozen. My hair rose at the thought of walking into a group of society-wise people sitting around on chairs staring at us as we precariously negotiated the floor with hot liquids in tiny cups. About a third of that proper group was made up of nuns from the hierarchy and elite of our Order, most of whom were strangers to me. There was almost no smiling going on between these nuns and us postulants--we were in the Novitiate, you know. I panicked. "I--I can't do it," I said, wishing I weren't so country-hardy and could faint on demand. The Superior glared at me and said, hovering too near, "Yes! You! Can! And you will!" I was sunk. Maybe it would be short--no, they said "a few hours." Maybe I could get someone else to take my place--"No!" said the Superior. I tried to explain how scared I was, how inadequate and potentially klutzy--but she would have none of it. The last thing she said was, "Put on a smile and get to work." As if these were stage directions, I pasted a toothy smile on my white face, leaving only my eyes working since I had to find out where I was walking and what to carry. A thin, timorous hope arose: maybe I could learn to do this. I immediately squelched the thoughts that clamored to deny that possibility. It won't be that bad, it won't be that bad, I ached to convince myself. Until I walked into the room. A long table with elegant damask cloth and silver service, arrangements of pastel flowers, pale candles, and gold-touched dishes such as I had never seen, surrounded by a momentarily silent circle of strangers staring at the "babies"--I went into something like shock. My eyes glazed over. I would look at something and it would not register in my brain what the item was or what it was used for. An order from my Superior was an order, though my body was barely doing lip-service to my own commands. My hands shook and jerked and the cups rattled loudly in their saucers. I would pick out a destination, e.g., a group of three nuns by the window, order my feet to walk there, order my mouth to ask if they wished tea or coffee, and keeping that unchanging plastic smile below my frantic eyes, order myself to back away, turn, and go back to the large table. When I took the teapot around it was even more difficult because they all spoke softly and I couldn't read lips unless I looked at them, but we had been told to keep our eyes down, which I took literally. My body was wooden ice, yet I shook. It was ever more difficult to execute the next command from my head. Then in one group of unsmiling nuns, someone dropped something--could it have been me? I remember using one of the extra napkins I carried, and hearing one of the nuns say I should get a small cloth with water. Small cloth with water?!!! Where in my newly restricted unfamiliar world would that come from? My panic level rose higher. They were giving me more instructions, but I don't remember them. "Yes, Sister," I said through my clenched teeth, ordering my body to back away, to start walking toward the table. One of the nuns behind me said, "Did she hear us?" "Yes," the second. "I don't know--is she ill?" and so on. Tears obscured my vision as I tried to keep my trembling body upright. At that moment I made the risky decision to disobey—a survival decision it was--regardless of what I knew would come from that, so I kept walking past the table and out the door, back to the cloakroom next door where I hid and sobbed as quietly as possible. I knew now I'd been right, that I could never learn to do this--or perhaps many other things. I was a failure this early in my career, and worse, a disobedient failure. At one point I heard the Superior asking about me. Then she came to the cloakroom door. "Go back to the Novitiate," she said sternly and that was it. The incident--my shame--was never spoken of again. The good part was that I was never again asked to serve at another tea. DORIS

❖❖❖

Leaving process

When a nun before the 1960s (and some places, even later) decided to leave the convent, she told her Superior and if she was still under vows, a dispensation from Rome or the local Bishop was applied for. (Some Orders answered to Rome, and others, to the Archdiocese, depending on how they were approved of in the first place.). Before Vatican II, many Communities insisted that the leaving nun not tell anyone of her plans, so there was no closure, no goodbyes to friends, no wishes of good luck. The nun who was leaving was smuggled out by the Community in the night or during early morning prayer. There was no announcement, merely an empty place in chapel at her rank level; the other nuns were told to move up a notch. No one was allowed to discuss the leaving (see Chapter XI: Leaving). Nuns left for a number of reasons—regardless of the opinions touted in articles written by some men that surmise that the women just needed sex. In one nationally known article, the male author was not an ex-nun, nor did he research the article by speaking to ex-nuns—he spoke to nuns (Superiors) still in the convent, some of whom, in this author's opinion, still haven't the faintest clue as to why so many nuns left. (See also Chapter I: Beginnings, "Reunions".)

After having ushered the woman out of the convent secretly, a number of Orders refused to let the ex-nun communicate with any of her friends still at the convent. This, plus some bad feeling as to how ex-nuns had been treated (see examples throughout this book, as well as in the Leaving chapter), put up walls between the nuns and ex-nuns, and it was not unusual for one to pretend not to see the other, should they pass in a mall. When one ex-nun of the ones in this survey married a few years after she left the convent, her nemesis in the convent said to her, "It sure took you long enough, didn't it?" It took years after Vatican II before any Orders or Archdioceses had any sort of counseling or debriefing or aids to the ex-nun's transition. Or acknowledgment of the feelings of loss experienced by her convent friends. (For examples and details, see Chapter XI: Leaving.)

We had a hard time. I had honestly believed that becoming a nun was the way to be a saint. The Church strikes me as being completely oblivious to us ex-nuns. DOROTHY

Regardless of screening processes, there were as many types of nun personalities as there are on the outside, including those climbing the social ladder, the kind and the bitter, the naïve and the wise, the mentally ill, etc. There were lesbians as well as heterosexuals, the kind and the mean, the humble and snobs. The public's assumptions and view of nuns was highly cleansed and tinged with myth and assumption. One phrase an ex-nun used was "street angels, convent devils".

I think at the time we entered (50s), we were sort of new-fashioned girls entering an old-fashioned convent. They were constantly putting us down—we were supposed to feel bad, look bad. In general, they tried to "break" us, all in the name of sanctity or formation. I've heard that now the few that enter can even do good work, teach, help, etc. instead of that medieval crap we went through. ELIZABETH

Control is what it was all about. GINA

I just didn't fit the mold. You've got to change or croak—internally or externally, and of the two, externally is easier, believe me. JULIA

Of course there were positive things as well in the Religious Life (see Chapter III: Good Things, as well as other narratives throughout this book).

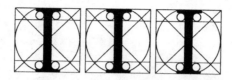

good things

happiness in the convent
leisure, recreation, hobbies
laughter and convent humor
music, choir, chant

Chapter III: Good Things

Music, leisure, laughter, feastdays, humor

Five categories of advantages to having been in the convent were mentioned in the answers to the questionnaire.: the safety of being in a convent, getting one's education, the wonderful mentors and friends one associated with, the excitement of ceremony—especially the taking of vows, and certainly not least: music.

In hindsight, the convent seemed a safe place where one could do good and be good. JEAN

The convent was a comparatively secure place to spend one's teen years. In the mid-1900s, mass school shootings were unheard of, (unfortunately) girls who got pregnant were immediately expelled from school and not thought of again, and the whole problem of "boys" was theoretically eliminated by having religious community-run girls' boarding and day schools. On the outside there was a goodly amount of drinking and smoking among teens, and smoking did sneak in among the girl boarders, but other drugs were rare and hardly known about outside the circles of their immediate users. No alcoholism, tobacco, or drug addiction issues were brought up spontaneously by those in the survey (as other issues were); neither did the author include questions about drinking (outside of wine), drugs, or smoking (or race-car driving or married love and other issues unimportant to this particular survey), considering that questions on those subjects might draw only blanks. It was so far removed from her reality to think of an addicted nun that the author never even looked for one. However, all things are possible. The fact remains that as a rule, young ladies who spent their teens in convents in those days were sheltered from many of the pitfalls of the outside world.

Another advantage, being able to get a college education, was mentioned frequently with gratitude (in answers to various other questions). The majority of girls (as they were called in those days) who entered the convent had finished high school, even some of the 15-year olds. Although in some communities candidates began college right away, others gave their second-year novices a year of schooling before sending them out to the missions to teach. Some did not even get that year before hitting the classrooms (see Chapter VIII on Schooling as well as *Knuckle-Rapping Nuns*). And some few nuns (especially those whose orders ran the colleges) earned several degrees during their convent stay. Regardless of how much education they got, nuns and ex-nuns were properly grateful. Getting an education was no small feat then as now. It was a fine thing.

In the category of good-things-that-are-exciting-and-stay-with-you-forever, was the meeting of some excellent women who became our friends and mentors—some of whom are still strong friends. The support and love of these women kept many a nun going through the hard times and gave her special joy and delight on feastdays when it was permitted to speak and play. These nuns are spoken of frequently throughout other answers, and especially in the answer to the question: Are You Glad You Were A Nun? (Chapter XV: Making It), and will not be repeated here.

One question: *What Did You Feel As You Moved On To Each New Stage Of Vows*, produced 19 enthusiastic answers categorizing that ceremony and transition as a very positive thing. These ex-nuns did not give explanatory sentences, but used words like: *in awe, glad, proud, happy, excited, eager, wonderful,* and *ecstatic*. (For a description of the ceremony and a discussion of the rest of the answers, see Chapter V: Religious Life.)

By far, music was the listed as the best advantage. (The negatives about convent music are discussed in Chapter V.) Rehearsal in the choir loft of an empty chapel added a quality akin to what singing into a karioke microphone does nowadays. Singing touched souls. *I loved to sing*, said many.

I had a good voice, I loved to sing, and my spirit soared. LILLA

Loved it! We were blessed with really fine choir directors. We sang the great motets and chant of our Catholic tradition and did it uncommonly well. To this day when we get together, we get out the old books and sing. JANET

Because music was such a major part of my life, I remember it being a very good outlet. We would often even sing during recreation time—that was one of my favorite recreations. I was one of the exuberant ones, enthusiastic about all of the singing, harmonizing, and folk singing we would do during the day. It was a major part of my life and I miss that still. I miss having the degree of community with music now in my life. MARGARET

What I liked most was the sound of the voices and pipe organ echoing through the empty chapel during rehearsals. I loved the polyphonic singing and most of the chant. And nothing will ever match the stupendous directing by one wonderful little nun from San Francisco. DORIS

To me, it was the best channel for prayer. It was also very creative—to be a part of a unified whole where everything and everyone merged into a beautiful completion. I have sung in choirs since I left, and I miss not having the opportunity at this time in my life. JULIANNE

It was spiritually stirring. I dearly loved all aspects of the music. ELLEN

Besides singing, a few nuns played orchestral and band instruments. (As of the 1950s, guitar was not yet mentioned in the music curriculum of most colleges.)
Private leisure time was not a part of any nun's schedule, especially before Vatican II. "Recreation" referred to the hour (or half-hour) after dinner and was a time for verbal socializing (on an equal scale—no small groups going off by themselves). Hobbies seemed to play little part in the mid-century nun's life.
You must be joking! There was no time for hobbies. THERESE
Embroidery (usually on items to be given as gifts from the community), crocheting or knitting shawls, simple leatherwork or rosary-making, small watercolors and calligraphy, as well as darning socks were allowable and frequent occupations during community recreation. Reading was not. After Vatican II changes, recreation no longer necessarily consisted of the entire group in one room. Tennis doubles and volleyball were allowed, as was flower gardening and newly introduced crafts that required more space.
On special feastdays, the rules changed: speaking was often allowed for most of the day, and outside of one's assigned daily chores and regular chapel

prayer times, visiting and playing sports, playing cards and swimming (if the convent had a pool), board games, folk dancing and movies—generally anything done in a group of 3 or more, was permitted. In the later days, watching certain television programs in a group was also allowed.

On "talking" feastdays ("*congé*" in French Communities), younger nuns were allowed to associate with and speak to the final professed sisters. This was a big deal. Most young nuns entered a specific community knowing and admiring a final professed nun—whom they were forbidden to see or speak to except on these feastdays. In fact, when asked, What Made You Happiest?—of the 73 participants, 37 gave answers that involved talking feastday activities, and 16 more specified the music, walks, and sports that were done during talking/sharing days. (Seven did not reply to the question.) Of the rest, the largest categories about what made the nuns happiest were: school (9), ceremonies (3), and prayer (3). Note that school, whether in teaching or learning, also involved interaction with other human beings.

As to which years in their convent experience were the happiest, the largest category named was: the Novitiate (26). Most ex-nuns, while in the Novitiate, were convinced that the convent was where they ought to be.

I think when I look back on it, that the first couple of years, the Postulancy and the Novitiate were the happiest years in the sense that I was doing something that I had dreamed of for quite a long time and really wanted to do, and I remember being particularly struck by the orderliness of the life. Part of my personality liked routine and order, and I was there with people I got to know and love. I think I was really happy those years and I really did feel that this was where God wanted me, and that I was doing what God wanted me to do. K.T.

Seven women said their last years were happiest, and thirteen declined to choose.

They were asked: Did You Laugh A Lot in the Convent? and 48 answered, Yes. Very few elaborated, though in an earlier question about humor, a number said they laughed as a release of tension. One said, *I was criticized a great deal for laughing too much. CAROL*

Chapter III: Good Things

I think I laughed a lot in the convent. Those years—it was my young life. We did a lot of laughing, and during it, were saved as a group as we went through all the weird things we had to do in the Novitiate. Some of the more adventuresome or the more self-confident would make up jokes about what we had to do, and that was a life saver in many ways. MARGARET.

There was a lot of tension about perfection and doing things right, and so humor was really our main release from dealing with that stress. There were some people in our group who were quite funny and did humorous things. K.T.

Outside, you learn to laugh at yourself in all kinds of situations. Inside, it's too serious. LILLA

Due to the artificial structure of convent life, more things were absurd. ANN

Relief from tension, though somewhat childish, was the essence of convent humor. JEAN

Nuns had their own humor with no relation to the outside world, e.g., joking about chasing a bat in chapel during Grande Silence, about how people wore their habits, about the short haircuts, washable sanitary napkins, or mispronouncing words while reading to the refectory crowd.

I thought that we had been reduced to juveniles because our world was so small and picky. Since we were treated like 10-year olds, we soon acted like them. MARY-2

Most of the humor was innocent and simple. Have you ever heard a 1st grade teacher share her experiences about what some of her students said or did? Or have you ever been in a group that spontaneously built an opera based on doing Saturday housework? JULIANNE

On special feast days there was open cloister—any Sisters could visit with Novitiate members for the afternoon. Thursday afternoons we went for long

rambling walks with our Novice Mistress. At a resting point, we'd sit on the rocks or lie on the grass and gobble up the box of chocolates the Mistress of Novices had brought along. Once we had a costume party—I don't remember for what. One Sister came wearing many manila envelopes stapled over brown paper—she was Joan of Arc wearing a coat of mail! The nun who used to do the flourishing floor kissing played Liberace. TRACE

When asked, Did your Superiors often have a sense of humor?, 26 out of 66 respondents said *Yes*; 18 said *Some did* or *Sometimes*; 4 said *Rarely*, and 18 flat out said, *No.*

Our Mistress of Novices had a good sense of humor. She had a playful quality. Most Superiors, however, did not. MARTHA

One Superior had a level head and a good sense of humor, but she was only there a couple of months. DORIS

The relationship was very vertical, so opportunity for humorous interchanges was very limited. JULIA

Superiors were rather a stuffy lot, with a few exceptions. JESSICA

They were self-serving old blisters. We were afraid of them. CAREN

They were great women for the most part. NELL

They weren't human. HOLLY

Western Superiors had an excellent sense of humor; Eastern Superiors did not. DENISE

You could joke about your own defects, but God help you if you mentioned theirs. ELEANOR

Chapter III: Good Things

A Superior I had in Spokane could see humor in so many situations. She loved the students and shared the many responses she got when correcting a very young student for coming in late or not being where he/she was supposed to be. She also enjoyed the humor of the Sisters, and when she laughed, one couldn't help but join in. I had other Superiors like her, but she stands out as the very first to free me from my solemnity. Another thing that I appreciated in Superiors was when, for no reason at all, a serious situation became funny, and they just let it ride. That often broke the tension and brought things back into perspective. JULIANNE

Of those nuns in the latter half of the century who were allowed to watch TV shows during recreation or on feastdays (25 from this study), the programs they were given permission for most often included: the news, Fulton Sheen, Perry Mason, Lawrence Welk, I Love Lucy, Ed Sullivan, and educational documentaries or shows on art or music.

Only 12 women said that the shows were their choice. One of these added: *I remember when we were watching a ballet. The superior turned it off in the middle because she did not think it was necessary for us to see men dressed in the tight pants they wore for the performances.*

Movies were shown on feastdays, almost always only a few times a year.

I remember that in the pre-Vatican II days we really looked forward to movies—two or three a year—that we were able to view in the community together. They were a reel to reel type thing, and were always like The Sound of Music, etc. MARGARET

We had movies about every two weeks except in Lent and Advent, because I was missioned in North Hollywood and lots of the parents of our children worked for the studios. I often "gave up" seeing movies as a form of "being holy". THERESE

Some ludicrous incidents that seemed hilarious in the convent, seem tragic or unfunny now, and vice versa. As in all enclosed situations, "you had to be there". Here are a few examples:

It was the feast of Our Lady of the Seven Sorrows and they had every multiple of seven you could imagine on the candelabras. It was my first year there and my night to lock up. I blew out the candle so hard that all the wax poured down my habit and it was Grande Silence and I couldn't talk. So this other nun came along and was getting all worked up, but she helped me iron the wax out of the habit. JEAN

We were told to fold our hands at all times when we entered chapel. I came in, hands folded, and felt the string holding my underpants giving way, but I kept my hands folded and walked on till they dropped to the floor. Then I glanced up at the Superior, who nodded slightly, so I picked them up and walked out. MARY

I have many funny memories: climbing a scaffolding and getting caught, literally polishing the waxed floor by the seat of my pants, smoking in the baggage room, falling asleep during prayers—these are funny stories. JULIA-2

In the Novitiate during Chapter of Faults, as a novice knelt down to ask for comments, a cow that had gotten loose mooed loudly. The Novice Mistress looked like she was about to laugh out loud, and sent us to our beds. CAROLYN

A nun who fell asleep during Mass, fell out into the aisle, so she faked a "faint", though her face was red instead of white. She was helped out of chapel by some of the laypersons there. As a nun, I thought this story terribly funny—not so much now. DORIS

I was caught on the elevator (and reported) without my veil. It was pretty scary until I found there wasn't much repercussion. CASEY

After a group gathering at the Provincial House, drivers were needed to take nuns returning to Seattle and Spokane to the bus depot. I hadn't been "chosen" as one of the drivers, but wanted to drive so badly that I volunteered and said I knew where the bus depot in Portland was. LIE! I didn't know and barely made the bus because I ended up out in the industrial section of town. No one ever knew that I didn't know where the depot was because I never told a soul! MARY-2

Chapter III: Good Things

 The day of our first profession of vows ceremony was a long day and we had Bishop Sheen as a guest because his secretary was in our set (class). We sat in order of profession, the Reverend Mother and the assistants at the top and the rest of us down the sides according to rank. They told me that I was to sit where the flowers were. I kept looking for what looked like the end of the table and I could not find it, but I found a spot near the inside of the circle. All during the feastday dinner we got to talk and the Reverend Mother kept asking me Who was the third priest on the left? And I said I didn't know. Then she'd ask Who was the fourth priest? and I didn't know—partly because I was from the West Coast and everyone else was from the East Coast. It was a closed ceremony and parents couldn't come—priests were the only ones who could come. This took place on a Friday, so we had fish and spinach and—I don't know, something else. And hot peach pie. And I threw up. I was in the center of the room and I slouched the whole dinner. So I said, Excuse me, Reverend Mother, and walked out. It was terrible in so many ways, but it was like, so funny—the perfect thing to do for all that stuff. JEAN

SUFFERING

attitude toward suffering in general
flagellation, other instruments of self-torture
naivete, self esteem, guilt
assigned & voluntary penances/punishments,
Chapter of Faults

Flagellation and other instruments of self-torture

Flagellation, the whipping of oneself with a rope called "the discipline", was a practice prevalent in monasteries and convents from before Medieval times to Vatican II. After Vatican II-influenced changes were adopted, many Orders/Communities discontinued any such practices. Though at times in history, erotic elements have been ascribed to it, flagellation of the mid-1900s was a serious act done to tame the body. The official reason was "mortification of the flesh", literally, dying to oneself. Why? "In order to live through Christ", said the Church. It was one of those phrases that seems to have escaped logic: though some ascetics/hermits choose to deny themselves, many people of all persuasions are able to maintain their goodness without grinding themselves into nothing, or, specifically, whipping themselves on the back with knotted cords. Conversely, whipping oneself does nothing by or of itself to produce goodness or sanctity, and it may do some harm.

Flagellation was not introduced until the candidate was a firm member of the Novitiate, usually after the optional Aspirancy and the Postulancy. Since the sleeping accommodations of these two groups were not mingled with those of other Novitiate members, and since (in every case here) flagellation was performed in the evening during Great Silence time, Aspirants and Postulants would most likely not notice it at all.

The usual instrument of flagellation, called "the discipline", was made of knotted cords about the thickness of a pencil strung together into a small bunch. It was hard in texture, as if starched, and could be made to smart easily. Some Orders used it as is and some dipped it in wax for greater efficacy. The whipping, generally done in semi-privacy (though everyone did it at the same moment), was timed either by a bell or by prayers said in common. No one was to speak of it, generally, but then, not many felt inclined to. Ditto for the question in this series, where few elucidations were offered.

Did your Order practice flagellation?

Yes: 34
No: 31
in earlier times: 5

Our Mistress of Novices showed us a hairshirt and passed it around for our inspection. I suppose it chiefly had novelty value for us. My impression was and is that keeping the rule well is sufficient discipline. I personally know one person who practiced flagellation and probably still does, and of another who, with permission, practiced tougher discipline. TRACE

We were never given the option of it. MARIE

I was told that all the nuns did it at the same time—certainly they did so in our dormitory. Though after I left the convent, I spoke to some who had whacked their beds instead. DORIS

It was one of the penances we did for faults like staring across the choir at someone else while we chanted the Divine Office. Sometimes we chose our penance, and other times were given it. MARGARET

Who practiced it and how often was it done?

Who practiced flagellation" answers fell into three categories, depending on the customs of that particular Order:

1. Novitiate members only—usually excepting Postulants and Aspirants.
2. Everyone in the community except Aspirants and Postulants.
3. Individuals who received specific permission to do so.

The frequency of flagellation varied. Most were in these categories:
1. Every other day, except Sundays and feastdays.
2. 1–3 times a week.

3. Once a month.
4. Rarely.

Was flagellation done in community?

We were in our cells, doors open, kneeling by the bed and praying aloud together. MERT

On "discipline" (flagellation) nights, we knelt inside our cell doorways or in a private corner. During the proscribed time of flagellation, we prayed aloud as a group. It was up to the individual how hard she hit herself. LILLA

It was always done at night during Grande Silence, right after the "lights out" bell. We were given a moment to stand up and get our disciplines (whips) out of their drawstring pouches, then one bell rang and all you heard was the sound of whipping until the next bell rang. Not very long, probably a couple of minutes, but some days it seemed like a very long time. DORIS

Flagellation in our community was very private. JULIANNE

Over half of those from communities who practiced flagellation, stated that it was carefully regulated. In fewer than half of the ex-nuns polled, it was optional.

They said in the beginning that flagellation was optional (we were strongly urged to do it). An older novice in our dorm reported everything to the Novice Mistress, and one day, someone who didn't do it was called into the office for a "talk". After that, it was spoken of something that you just did. I thought that if I was going to be a nun and this was part of it, I would have to do it. Besides, I was too timid to not do it. DORIS

A few of the 73 say they spoke of flagellation among themselves, especially in the later years. Two say they joked about it. In mid-century however, most discussion of the subject was forbidden as well as distasteful, especially outside of

Novitiate formation classes. Of course, it was never mentioned to lay persons. Reasons for not discussing it/feelings about it follow:

    I was afraid to talk about it, told not to. It was bizarre, but I didn't want to allow myself to think that. JEAN

    We weren't supposed to tell. I didn't like it. JULIA, DORIS

    I thought it was sick and neurotic—didn't do it very often as a novice. FRANCES

    That it had a place. It was personal prayer. NELL

    I thought it dumb, stupid. MARY, CONNIE, HOLLY, MARTHA

    It was kind of weird. ELLEN, JANET K, CONNIE

    It was unmentionable, embarrassing, private. DONNA, CASEY, MAE, LORENA, MARTHA

    Big secret! MERT, CAREN, HOLLY

    It wasn't important. THERESE-2

    I thought it peculiar. JESSICA

    We didn't question things in those days. CASEY, ELIZABETH

    It wasn't common and it seemed masochistic. THERESA

    It was crazy and absolutely ridiculous. I didn't tell because it was weird, that's why. KATHLEEN

    Okay, but I didn't overdo it. ELEANOR

Chapter IV: Suffering

I thought it was foolish. HELGA

Too bizarre and of questionable value to me then. JEAN-2

Very strange. Funny: Once a chain caught on the screening curtain and pulled it over the head of a Sister. Everyone started to giggle. MAE

I think there was a silent understanding that it was so rare that others would not understand. I cannot specifically remember speaking about it at a later time. Maybe in my early fervor I classified it as a saintly act, though I certainly was not attracted to it. At later times, I had questions about its purpose and effect on one's health. JULIANNE

I patiently tried to be diligent about using it. LILLA

It was silly. DENISE.

Public confessions and penances like kissing the floor made me feel I had to participate. LORNA

Hated it—I'm not a masochist. DONNA

These practices had deep spiritual origins and mortification advantages. YVONNE

I used to wonder if the others were as half-hearted about flagellation as I was. Our Novice Mistress de-emphasized it. I believe that she thought it excessive, so while we were taught to respect it, I doubt any of us Novices ever raised one welt among us. MARTHA

What other instruments of self-torture were used?

Bracelet with pokey things, worn on the upper arm (when I was a Novice) for a few hours. (1)

Chains. Worn above the knee monthly. (2)

Ropes. (1)

Small flagellation instruments with four or five 6" points. (1)

Waxing the discipline cords and knots to increase the pain. (2)

A whip with nails and sharp endings. (1)

Having to kneel on our finger knuckles nightly while praying 3 Our Fathers, Hail Marys, and Glory Bes for chastity. (1)

Overwhelmingly, the participants said they were either not aware of any additional practices of self-torture, said the use of such was "not encouraged", answered "No" to the question, or simply left it blank. One who had not experienced anything but the "discipline" seemed to take umbrage at the very question: *It was a convent, not an insane asylum!* Another commented:

At one point in my ascetic period, I knotted some cords and tied them tightly around my waist over a prickly burlap sack that I wore next to my skin. My Novice Mistress had approved of it, though she never mentioned it again or asked me how it was going after giving me permission. After about 8-10 months, I couldn't see that this had made me more saintly, so I cut off the cord and threw away the burlap.

However, allowing for the fact that there are 21 orders represented here, and that many of them did not have "individuals only" self-discipline practices in the early days, it is logical to conclude that more participants than those who shared in the Questionnaire, knew about these customs. It is unlikely that only one person in a particular community was given a manufactured "bracelet", for example. Or that others in the same communities as those who waxed their disciplines, never heard of the practice. It is more likely that some of those who were nuns before Vatican II were acquainted with such things, that they may have blocked them out or forgotten them for some other reason. It happens to be embarrassing to look back and think that we cooperated in some things. But maybe, just maybe, these good women simply didn't feel like talking about it—that is their right, and this author respects it.

Suffering in general

Suffering in a convent? Even suffering caused by nuns? Convent women are like people anywhere. Nowhere do they pass through a magical screen on their journey from the outside to the cloister. Nuns are usually ordinary human beings who feel called by God to serve him through service to humanity, be that teaching, nursing, counseling, or praying for those in the World. It follows that the population of each convent contains persons of all types, including those who cause suffering to others (see Chapter IX, Liabilities). Suffering in convents, as in the rest of the World, is also caused by illness, weather, disasters, death, and disappointment. So, did the nuns of mid-century 1900s suffer? Yes, of course they did. All or most of the time? Not usually (there were rare cases).

The point of the questions on Suffering was to find out what the women religious did with that pain—what their attitudes were toward it. Did anything make it better or worse? Were they happy to suffer, or did they avoid it? In Roman Catholic Church history, some canonized saints sought out suffering and were indeed, happy to bear it. Reasons that they and Church members today accept or even seek suffering are: 1) Emulation: St. X suffered greatly and so cleansed her soul and went to heaven, therefore, if I suffer greatly, the same will happen to me. 2) The universal sin-cleansing theory: Everyone in the world sins (does wrong) and some die with sin on their souls (serious sin sends one to hell, the Church teaches). Sin comes with a price tag, a certain amount of punishment attached in order to erase the sin. We can "make up for" or atone for some of that punishment due to our own and others' sins, by suffering. 3) Closeness to Christ: because Christ suffered on the cross for the sins of mankind, we can become close to Him by suffering in the right frame of mind. And closeness to God (Christ, Jesus) is what it's all about—what we do to attain eternal happiness after we die.

This is not what everyone believes—not even every Roman Catholic today. But in the mid 1900s, these beliefs were pretty universally accepted unquestioningly.

Were you encouraged to suffer silently for Jesus' sake?

>Yes: 56
>No: 9
>Not answered: 8

Always. I was told that suffering was a good thing—so said the nuns, the Church, my parents, and my religion. I was told to seek suffering. DORIS

Oh yes, very much so. I had to agree. KATHLEEN

We were definitely encouraged to suffer silently for Jesus' sake. MARGARET

I didn't go out of my way to suffer; I had enough handed me. Silent suffering was considered holy. I got the impression that the sick Sisters of the Infirmary were special because of their suffering. TRACE

Did you agree that suffering was a good thing?

>YES: 35
>NO: 24
>>Don't remember: 2
>>Didn't answer: 12

"Somewhat." LOUISE
"Limited yes." MURIEL
"Up to a point." BEVERLY

If it was necessary suffering. NANCY

Suffering would make us holier and better for Jesus, you know. MARGARET

In the beginning, I thought suffering was a way to some closer to Christ. Later, I thought it was specious. THERESE

In my younger years, I believed this completely. JULIANNE

No, I think I never believed that suffering was redemptive. I suppose I did not really suffer anything until my mother's death. The detachment we were supposed to cultivate regarding our parents seemed cruel and very wrong at that time. In the same vein, suffering this grief did not seem to have any merit for its own sake. I realized that grief was entirely natural and unavoidable, but not good for its own sake. JEAN-2

Did you go out of your way to suffer?

YES: 13
NO: 52
Didn't answer: 8

I went out of my way to fast, kneel, volunteer, etc. THERESE

I was able to "offer up" the constant pain I had, and I tried very hard not to complain about other things that were hard. I guess I did extra things that others did not want to do because of this motivation. However, I had enough suffering on a daily basis without doing anything more than what the community required. JULIANNE

I never went out of my way to suffer, and I kind of felt guilty about that, but I really didn't like to suffer, though it was considered virtuous to find bigger ways to deny ourselves. I didn't like to do it—I didn't have what I consider enough self control to do it, although it was a major act of self denial and lack of self acknowledgment just to be there for so many years, especially during those times when we were treated in many ways as non-persons. MARGARET

Yes, by using the hairshirt and by voluntary penances. DORIS

I did not go out of my way to seek suffering; I already had had that training at home: my mother tended to be a "victim" and I learned that attitude from her early in life. The convent merely perpetuated that attitude. SARAH

Was going out of your way to suffer considered virtuous?

YES: 31
NO: 15
Didn't answer: 25

Yes, but it made me want to say, hey, I'm worth something, too. KATHLEEN

I thought at the time that I was being virtuous by not complaining about the headaches and not taking medicine for a long time. However, that may also have been partially motivated by the fact that I would have had to ask permission for every two aspirins I needed. JULIANNE

Were you ever told that Jesus was all and you were nothing?

YES: 31
NO: 26
Don't remember: 3
Didn't answer: 13

We were taught that philosophy pretty strongly in those pre-Vatican years, and I guess I agreed with it. MARGARET

Retreat Masters of the "hell and damnation" school went on about this: "We are vile worms" bit. TRACE

We were taught that we must die to self so that Jesus could become our "all". We were not told that we were nothing. LILLA

How did this make you feel?

Like nothing, a non-person. MARY-2, SUZANNE
Humiliated, but I tried to believe it. ELIZABETH
Humble. CAREN, LORENA
Worthless. DONNA
Small. ROSE
Inadequate. JAN-2
Always a nobody. Just what they wanted. ELEANOR

I didn't believe it, knew it wasn't true. DENISE, DIANE, JULIANNE
Misinformed. It was just words. ELLEN, MAE
Didn't give it much thought. JULIA, SARAH

I accepted it, believed it. HOLLY, MERT
I felt it didn't matter if I hurt or developed or was happy. Yet I wanted to be happier than I was. DORIS

It's what you were used to hearing, but you learn to take their talk with more than a grain of salt. Well, I am nothing—but not that nothing. We really are nothings, but that's a wonderful thing so that God can show up better, but that's not how it was presented. It even reads weird on paper. TRACE

Did you feel you were being brainwashed?

YES: 29
NO: 30

Chapter IV: Suffering

Don't remember: 1
Not till later: 9

Not at first—in later years I fought it mentally. CASEY

I remember Cardinal Mindzenty's being brainwashed—so no, I don't think I felt I was being brainwashed. I think being immersed/saturated/enveloped by what the community was trying to get you to be was what you'd come for, so why fight it? TRACE

Not then. I did think that a lot of what we were told about Vocations and winning brownie points for heaven was foolish, and I realized we were kept isolated from outside viewpoints. However, I did not connect this with the word or concept of brainwashing until I left, when I most certainly realized that it was. JEAN-2

At the time of final vows, one of the Sisters stated that she had rejected a great deal of what we had been told because she thought we were being brainwashed. I know that this comment surprised me. I guess I believed that the individuals teaching us believed firmly in what they were saying. JULIANNE

Did that frighten you?

YES: 11
NO: 16
Don't know/remember: 1

I "drank" it all in. ELIZABETH

This is one reason I was asked to delay vows—I think they realized I could not be brainwashed. GINA

I probably should have been frightened. JULIA

I was disgusted with myself that I fell for it. ELLEN

I did not believe in Catholic education and wrote a paper on it. FRANCES

Were you told that you deserved to suffer?

YES: 14
NO: 31
Question not included in first questionnaires: 13
Didn't answer: 15

Did you believe that you deserved to suffer?

YES: 8
NO: 7
Question not included in first questionnaires: 13
Didn't answer: 45

I silently rejected some things and I believe I kept fairly mentally healthy. Some rules in the Novitiate were almost childish, meaningless, and not for adults, but I obeyed them. EILEEN

We tried to understand suffering. NELL

Christ wants us to be happy. MARY

I only realized that I had become brain dead later—you notice I don't remember a lot. JANN

I probably believed it because of the purgatory theology taught at home and school before the convent. MERT

I always felt important and worthwhile. JANET K

Chapter IV: Suffering

We had little choice. JAN-2

I thought I was a great sinner. LORENA

I was never told that. I had enough to endure without having that told to me. JEAN-3

Through our suffering we could help others as members of the Mystical Body of Christ. From the beginning when we were introduced gradually to the customs and rules, I was aware of what we now call brainwashing, but perceived it as always striving to reach the next step, the next goal—striving to please and to be deemed worthy and acceptable. And later, always striving to overcome faults, to become more perfect. The brainwashing was a growth in mind-set towards unquestioning blind obedience to become less to self and more towards worthiness, in order to be one with Jesus. Any material attachments were imperfections of our vow of poverty. LILLA

By the end of my 8th year, I finally gave up—I'd tried as hard as I could to suffer for God and to be faithful to my vocation, and I finally gave up trying to reconcile God's love and suffering. I wrote to the Provincial before I left and said I had thought over her theory of suffering and the story of St. Bernadette. My conclusion was that the system that made St. Bernadette suffer so that she could be a saint, required other people to be awful. Surely there had to be a way to come up with a better system where everyone could be holy and no one had to be cruel. I told her that being treated cruelly had made her cruel, and that I didn't want to grow up and be like that, sooo—goodbye. ELLEN

Chapter of Faults: the Ritual

The Chapter of Faults, or "Chapter", as it was called in daily jargon, was a public confession of sorts. The difference between Chapter and confession in the box (chapel or church confessional) was that one told sins, serious matter, in confession, and that Chapter was, like its title, reserved for faults. As in everything in life, however, there was overlap, e.g., being angry with someone could be construed as the sin of anger, as well as the fault of "failing in charity towards my neighbor".

Chapters during the Novitiate (again often excluding the Aspirants and Postulants) were usually in-house. The Professed nuns (often including Juniors) had their own Chapters.

For beginners especially, the solemnity of the occasion sometimes caused an eruption of muffled giggles when a peer would say anything even reminding one of a funny incident. Nuns entered the chapter room in rank, eyes cast down, completely silent, with hands folded under the scapular or tucked into their opposite sleeves. After everyone was seated, the Superior would begin with a prayer. Then individual nuns would rise from their chairs and accuse themselves before everyone of certain faults or infractions of The Rule (*Je m'accuse*, in French Orders), after which the Superior could ask if anyone else accused that nun of yet other faults. There was no arguing—if someone accused you, you stood accused, and you bowed your head to accept your penance. Penances to be performed could be to recite certain prayers, or a personal act of reparation such as an apology and doing something for the offended person, but often the penances given involved public humiliation in their performance, usually in the refectory (see Chapter V, Refectory) during meal time.

Chapter was not a subject for discussion except in Novitiate formation classes. Some Chapters were held in the dark or dimly lit room, but most were not. Though the Sisters faced each other, it was expected that they keep "custody of the eyes", that is, eyes cast down.

Did you have Chapter of Faults?

Three participants did not answer and two said they don't recall. Every one of the other 68 ex-nuns said Yes, we had Chapter of Faults.

We had Chapter of Faults every two weeks for external faults, not sins, e.g., having an untidy desk, not applying yourself. JEAN

The Superior sat at the head of two rows of Sisters facing each other. Individually, Sisters stood and recited rules violations. EILEEN

We all met in the Refectory in silence. There was some prayer first, then we had to shut our eyes in our seats. If we were guilty when something was criticized, we were to kneel. DONNA

The Sisters would file in in rank—anybody who was in your convent, and sit facing each other on sides of an aisle (usually 3-4 rows on each side). We had a sermon by the Superior who was sitting at the head of the aisle facing the Sisters, and she would say, "You may begin your accusations," and beginning with the youngest in rank, we'd take turns getting up, going to the middle of the aisle, and accuse ourselves of failing in poverty, (I never heard about chastity) or obedience, or whatever. Then you would say, "Sister, would you please have the charity to tell me my faults." That was horrible. The reason it was so awful was that you went out later and you had to just pretend that none of this had ever happened. That they hadn't told you—that they hadn't made critical remarks about you. There was one thing: you were never allowed to talk about it. It made you feel terrible. Also, if you didn't criticize a sister, then later you were told that that was part of being in the convent and you had to do that. And then also, you had to come back and work with these people and you never knew—Gosh, I remember one Sister told me that she thought I was using too much water in the shower—she has to have some other things to think about. And anyway, that emphasizes the absolute pettiness of all of this stuff, too. It was pretty ridiculous, and also, I think, harmful. The most positive thing that I got out of the experience of being in the convent was feeling and appreciating the value of community. And that Chapter of Faults—I think really just destroyed it all. I'm not going to discuss it, but certainly it was counterproductive. CAROL

Everyone was expected to make comments about others. MURIEL

During Chapter, we had to acknowledge at least three faults. LILLA

We definitely had Chapter of Faults. Once a week the Community would gather and file into the room in serious, somber silence, line up in rows facing one direction and the Mother Prioress. The Novices would have to lie prostrate and be first to (together) acknowledge faults to God and the community. Then we would all stand and recite individually. MARGARET

Each nun would have to kneel in front and receive "comments or observations of faults" and then ask for prayers. CAREN

Any Sister who had witnessed an infraction could remark on it (limited to three per person). JULIA-2

It was hilarious to hear what people said. JANE

One at a time by rank, Sisters came forward and knelt in front of the Superior accusing themselves of, e.g., lack of religious decorum by running on the stairs. Then they would ask, "Sister, will you have the charity to tell me my faults." Usually two or three Sisters, sometimes more, would stand, and in order of rank, mention a lapse that they'd seen, e.g., Sister seems often to fail in silence of action by slamming doors." If you'd been next to say the same thing, you sat down. If you'd had something different to say you said it. This seemed gently done, consistently. We were all under the same rules. Once in a great while, no one had anything to say to the kneeling Sister. Usually then, the presiding Sister would comment, again, kindly. The Sister next in rank would be standing behind the kneeling one waiting to take her place, so that there were never gaps of waiting. When the Postulants were done, a few words were said to them and they were dismissed. I was impressed when, finally wearing the black habit, I saw that the Mistress of Novices, the Superior, and Provincial Superior, and further, the Superior

Chapter IV: Sufferering

General each had a Sister whose responsibility it was to point out to her her external infractions of the rule. Only once did I hear a Sister mention something that was a matter for confession. Mother Superior stopped her immediately but gently, and told her so. I think Chapter was a great leveler, a good reality check. It might have been devastating, but I never found it so. TRACE

It was very controlled, not really unpleasant. BEVERLY

We knelt in community in the dark with veils over our faces and confessed faults like being too noisy while eating. MARY S

Every other Friday night we each knelt in front of the Novice Mistress and confessed a fault, then any of the other 60-90 Novitiate members could stand up and tell us our faults. This was probably the most psychologically damaging process in the Novitiate/Juniorate. It was unhealthy psychologically and built up much resentment among the Sisters. SARAH

You knelt and said, Sister, I humbly beg penance for being late to prayers— or for breaking silence, or breaking a dish. LORENA

Everyone filed into the dark recreation room, sat down, and each person took turns. The Chapter of Faults was perhaps the most rugged and horrible experience of the convent for me. This little exercise let me know that I wasn't perfect and that people looked for picky things to tell you. You heard the squeak of chairs as Sisters stood up to tell you things like: Sister walks too slow (or fast), Sister doesn't hold the door for people behind her, Sister eats too slow (or fast), etc. Being of a serious nature, I took all of this to heart. Now I look back and realize how STUPIE it was and how brainwashed we had become to buy this and actually go through it time after time. MARY-2

Only observable behavior was repeated, i.e., loud talking, disturbances, wasting something. And no motives could be implied. CAROLYN

Kneel on the floor. Others would say your most picayune faults that got on their nerves. Unhelpful. GAYLE

Chapter is one of the things I blocked out of my memory when I left, only remembering it when someone brought it up this year. Feelings connected with it are still very strong, however. We were told about the process some weeks before we participated and were left with frightening thoughts, but those were nothing compared to the terror I experienced upon actually going through the ceremonial. There was heavy, heavy silence--even the shoes of all of the nuns from the entire convent filing into the room didn't make more than a soft shushing sound. I tried to take comfort in the fact that everyone's eyes would be case down, till I glanced up and saw several older nuns looking right at me. I became more and more full of panic and anxiety as I listened to others recite their faults and be accused of faults by others. When my turn came, my voice sounded like it belonged to someone else reciting the lines I had memorized in case my regular brain wouldn't function due to my terror of the moment. I don't remember what I said, what anyone accused me of, or the penance that was given. The only other emotion I remember was great relief as we all filed out of the room afterwards. DORIS

The Sisters sat in two or more rows of chairs in the position of a gauntlet.... JULIANNE

Our chairs were lined up, eyes lowered as Mother Superior noted deviations from the rule. She didn't name names, but when you recognized yourself, you got up from the chair and kissed the floor. Mother Superior might then give you a penance, and when she released you, you would again kiss the floor. You always kept your eyes lowered during this time. There were certain Superiors who, I heard, could/would "mop up the floor" with the Sisters, but I rarely experienced that kind of treatment. MARTHA

In our community, the Chapter of Faults was held on Fridays during my Novitiate and Juniorate, which covered the years from 1960-1965.... K.T.

How did you feel participating in Chapter of Faults?

Not much. FRANCES

I thought it humorous. CONNIE

Humiliated. JANN, THERESA, MARY-2, KATHLEEN

Humiliated: slight infractions took on proportions of mortal sins. ELIZABETH

Humiliated and petty. KATE

Frightened in early years; it promoted pettiness. JAN-2

Frightened—I never spoke out against anyone and this was commented on, so I had to at least once. JULIA-2

Didn't want to listen or participate. ROSE

Embarrassed. SHIRLEY, JAN, THERESE-2, THERESE

It was embarrassing, childish. GAYLE

Not good; sort of like trying to figure out what to say like a little kid's first confession. JULIA

I hated it. EILEEN, CAREN, LOUISE, ANNE, MARIE, SUZANNE, MARTHA, JOSEPHINE,

Hated it; very humiliating. HELGA, JANE

Hated it. Accepted it as a growth option. THERESA

Hated it, feared it. It was humiliating. CASEY

Hated having to tell on myself—I was already in enough trouble, but I was honest, so to be honest with God I just got in more trouble. ELLEN

Hated it. Chapter of Faults made me feel trivialized and demeaned. It was evident that some nuns were unaware of motivations of less than kindly intent in making their accusations. When this happened, I started not taking the ritual seriously and generally tuned it out until next week. JEAN-2

Icky-picky. MARIETTA

Another demeaning program. DONNA

Awful—I hated it. MARY S

Terrible. DIANE

That it was a delicate thing and should not be misused. NELL

It could be very embarrassing. I remember it as a humbling, ego-reducing experience, and I didn't need it as my ego was already reduced. It was not a fun thing, but you just did it. It was a part of what everyone just did. MARGARET

Mixed feelings, a cleansed feeling afterward. I think I took most of it as it was intended. It was serious business, but rather a penance than a punishment. TRACE

Okay. PRISCILLA

It was something we had to do. HOLLY

Uncomfortable. DOLORES

It was like confession, humbling. LORENA

A good time to be healed. YVONNE

I hated it with a passion. Even thinking about it today makes me sick to my stomach. It was appalling, degrading, and encouraged the Sisters to spy and pass judgment on each other. It was a far cry from my understanding of Christian love. As a Novice, I obediently accepted it, but was always terrified when we had to go through it. JULIANNE

It was a very difficult experience, and was extremely humiliating for people who got several accusations. We always dreaded it and were relieved when one was over. I remember it as being humiliating and not anything I would ever want to participate in again because it was so public and it seemed especially that the people who were extroverts like me, often got more reprimands than the really quiet serious nun types. So there were some real problems with it. THERESE-2

Guilt, Assigned/Voluntary Penances

There will always be those who say that a consequential penance, i.e., a nun gets caught running on the stairs and is given a penance because of it—that that is not a punishment. That no one was punished in convents; only given <u>penances</u> to make them holy. Others maintain that penances are done voluntarily; punishments are not. In the convent, both types of penance/punishments were in use. Voluntary penances looked exactly like assigned ones externally. Usually, only the nun and her Superior knew whether she had asked for this penance in order to humiliate herself by appearing guilty (and thus create suffering which would bring her closer to God). Which subterfuge, technically, can be said to be a type of pride (the bad kind, the 50s kind), anyway. Most public penances were performed in the Refectory and are explained in that chapter.

Guilt was another story. Guilt was the mainstay of control in the mid 1900s everywhere. Watch a movie and see the prisoner cry because he feels guilty about hurting his mother's feelings. Classrooms were controlled by standing students in the corner (making them feel guilty) or by other public humiliation, such as knuckle-rapping. Convents were no different. The underlying purpose of the Chapter of Faults was to feel guilty enough to bring one's guilty deed into the open (by self-accusation), then to be made publicly guilty of whatever one was accused of by others, besides.

Some religious Vocations were begun out of guilt when the mission priest or pastor insisted that "one child be given to God" in each family. Novitiate control was often by guilt and fear: If you do such-and-such, you will lose your Vocation, therefore becoming guilty of grevious sin. And we all knew the consequences of that. Guilt was the oil in the cogs of organized religion's machinery.

Guilt presupposes the existence of conscience.

The Catholic Church left nothing to chance in conscience formation. Whole booklets listed sins of every category, sins that were to be confessed and atoned for, therefore, sins (actions) for which one should feel guilty. Sins were grouped under the specific Commandment (of the 10) which they "broke", and under the 7 Deadly Sins (Pride, Avarice, Lust, Anger, Gluttony, Envy, Sloth). Lay adults were persuaded that Catholic school education was best (regardless of any lack of equipment or certified teachers), and their children who attended these schools were lectured daily on morality and guilt. The convent had all this, plus The Holy Rule specific to each nun's Order, Community "customs" and "discretions" (lesser directives not mentioned in the Order's constitution), plus any command given by one's superior. Infractions of any sort were to produce guilt, remorse, penance, then a waiting period until the next infraction, when the circle began again.

Life was one great round of suffering in atonement for sin, whether one sought out suffering, or was sent on mission with someone who caused it. The nun's attitude towards suffering must be that she never complain and that she accept what she was given in life, for Jesus' sake.

Naivete and Lack of Self-Esteem

Naïve: unsophisticated, unsuspecting, simple, ingenuous, inexperienced, unseasoned, unworldly, trusting, gullible, immature—do these words describe the way you would like to be seen by the world? Naivete, an embarrassing form of suffering, was a redundant hammer upon the personality of the early 1900s nun: as a fully grown woman teaching in a classroom without having the education to do so; being forbidden to read the newspaper or anything else without permission; being taken to vote without even knowing who is running against the person whose name you were told to copy down; never listening to the news, let alone anything else on radio (or later, television); not being allowed to receive letters from friends or to write often or without censorship (one nun with a large family was only allowed to write 12 letters a year, which meant she couldn't even get around her whole family once during that time)—how was such a woman to "fit in" when she left the convent? "Naïve" as used to describe her is an understatement.

Going back to the convent---lay persons in the mid-1900s presumed (not without cause) that, by virtue of wearing the habit, nuns automatically knew what to say in difficult situations. Also that they had a direct line to God: "My sister-in-law just died, Reverend Sister, please won't you say something to my grieving brother?" The truth was that few nuns were trained in counseling or social work, unless that was their specific career (see Chapter VII, The World, on schooling). Though most nuns showed caring and kindness to seculars, their lack of training/education plus the chronic lack of self-esteem (from public humiliations, from being taught they were nothing, and from being dependent upon having to ask for permission for every little thing—Mother Mistress, may I please get some thread to mend my stockings some more?)—and you have women who on the one hand, were interiorly frightened of new "outside" experiences and on the other, concerned about giving the manditorily correct convent image. In many cases, they were left with no choice but to fake it. Hence the ubiquitous knuckle-rapping nun who, in desperation, reverted to the discipline of her own upbringing. They also became quotation-spouting persons: God wants you to do this, God wants you to do that? Did God tell them directly? No.

When I was first disguised as a nun (I was only a novice, but it was custom to wear the black veil in public), I was barely 17. What did I know about life? Nothing. But all around me other nuns were throwing God wantses and God willses about because that seemed to be what the public and the convent wanted and expected, so I took a deep breath and plunged in, scattering aphorisms all over the place, not infrequently relating my style loosely to the work of Thomas Aquinas or whichever Catholic theologian I happened to be reading at the moment.

Not wishing to disappoint anyone, least of all myself in this "turning into a nun" process, I played the role, but felt fake inside and worried that I'd be found out for the naive child I truly was. After I left the convent, I was so used to feeling that way (i.e., if anyone really got to know me they'd know how inadequate I was) that it took nearly 30 years and a lot of therapy for me to discern the substantial about who I really was and where I was going.

After my parents died, I discovered a huge envelope of my "God wills" letters written to the family in my early nun days, and I almost threw up in embarrassment. Those letters in the manila envelope—it's a wonder my brothers and sisters didn't hate me more. As for my parents, I wonder if they weren't caught in a tight situation: on the one hand, they'd encouraged us each to pray for a Vocation. Then when I got one (?) they didn't dare speak against it. And worse for them, I had become one of the "God wills"-spouting persons which they may or may not have formerly respected. Certainly, since they knew me, they had every reason to believe that this willful daughter who was now preaching to them was on absolutely no direct line to anywhere. But they couldn't say anything about that without denying the validity and value of the Holy Vocation. What was either of us to do? DORIS (See more in Chapter XII: Healing.)

It was this very confusion about self, plus their ingenuousness which kept women in convents malleable, controllable before Vatican II came along giving them ideas of individual rights. Those women who had entered in their teens and left in the early years before reform, had remained emotionally immature—one of the most difficult things to cope with upon leaving, next to the ignorance of many very basic operations in the outside world. Worse, to begin with, some did not know that they did not know, until being brought up short by some painful experience that set them face to face with their own naivete. A confidence-breaker, to say the least. Naivete to this extent was suffering. As for support, these courageous women who followed their consciences and left their convents had been cut off from contact with outside friends while they were nuns, and in leaving were been admonished not to speak to anyone back in the convent, so literally, they had to find their own bootstraps before they could pull themselves up by them, the whole process greatly slowed by this baggage of gullibility which they carried with them from their incarceration (see Chapter XI, Leaving).

Nor was the mere learning of the World's "ropes" enough—the ingrainedness of this naivete and the years lost in growing to maturity still leave their marks after 30-40 years. While being a trusting person may be nice, it is not practical in today's world. Trusting everyone comes from the habit of trying to see the good in every human being—and these days, a little of that goes a long way.

the refectory

food, ambiance, rituals
readings
Doing Martyrology
other Refectory penances

The Refectory: Food, Ambiance, Ritual

"Refectory" was the name of the room now most often called the dining room. In the Motherhouse or on large missions, it was a cavernous hall, often on the basement level, with painted or linoleum-covered cement floor and rows of long tables either set end to end in groups of two or three, or set singly. Often these tables had small drawers on both sides and the ends, in which were kept a plate, bowl, cup, utensils, and the week's napkin. Meals were served family-style in the earliest days, cooked by the kitchen Sisters and their Novitiate helpers, and distributed from carts by that week's designated serving Sisters, usually Novitiate members. Starting in the 60s, cafeteria lines were set up and food services were utilized, partly owing to a shortage of nuns.

In those days up to and including the 50s, the Refectory was a silent room except when the main Superior gave permission to speak during a feastday meal. In that case, the moment the after-meal prayers were over, there was no more speaking in the Refectory, even if permission had been given to speak the entire day. The Refectory was a silent room where one ate and performed public penances. If a nun wished to say something else, she would step outside the door into the hallway. In communities that forbade speaking in hallways, a nearby doorway would do.

In the mornings there were prayers in chapel before breakfast, and the single line of nuns (by order of rank—highest first) to enter the Refectory wound silently from the chapel all the way down the stairs. In many convents, the Superior greeted each nun at the door (for at least one meal). Did she smile and make eye contact or slap the Sister on the back, saying, How're you doing? No, of course not. No eye contact. No smiling. A hand stuck out and a word from the Superior, e.g., Benedicite (Latin for "blessings" or "bless you"), and a reply from the nun: Deo gratias ("thanks be to God). The nun entered the Refectory doors and stood by her place at the table, eyes cast down, took her place setting out of the drawer, and arranged it upon the table. When everyone was in, the Superior went to her own place at the table (someone else had arranged her place setting ahead of time) and began the prayer. Then all the nuns sat down very quietly. In the Refectory, if a nun made "unnecessary noise" like clinking her fork on a dish, or scraping her chair on the floor, she immediately knelt and kissed the floor. Should a new Postulant hesitate, wondering if she had made a loud enough clink to qualify, a surreptitious glance at the Superior would clear up the matter immediately.

The Superior stared at me until I finally kissed the floor. DORIS

Food was passed around each table or set of tables in the serving bowls. Postulants had been told in the very beginning to take something of everything, but to leave enough for each person at that table. One did not make a habit of leaving food on one's plate. When nearly everyone was served, the reader (seated before a microphone at a podium at the far end of the room) began reading. Several books were read from and continued from day to day, e.g., a classical theology tome like Thomas Aquinas or the *Imitation of Christ*, a modern theological reading, and lastly the Martyrology, which listed the saints who were murdered for their faith on this day, citing some of their good deeds and describing their killings in great detail, e.g., And after they tied St. X to a stake and cut off her nose and ears, she said, You can't hurt me because God is with me, so they took a red hot pincers and tore off her breasts, pouring hot oil on them at the same time.

At a certain point, large metal dishpans were brought into the room and dishes were quietly washed and dried at the table, then put away in the drawers. When all was finished, the final prayer was said and nuns processed, again in rank, from the room.

All guests and priests (except three cases from the later years) were served in the guest dining room, a tastefully decorated area near the parlors. Guest food differed from that of the nuns; it was made by a special cook and served by professed nuns with elegant manners. One ex-nun in this survey said this was *good hospitality,* and thirteen said it was *okay, fine, no problem.* Eight felt *resentful, discriminated against, angry, unfair,* and *I wished I could have some.* (Others did not answer.)

Guests were not allowed in our refectory until after Vatican II. Resident priests had their own dining room and were fed extremely well. I thought this uncalled for. Religious Communities were known for spoiling the clergy, and many of the clergy took real advantage of it. JULIANNE

It didn't seem right to me then or now that the priest ate so high on the hog. He certainly didn't, that I saw, practice what he preached. TRACE

The Sisters who cooked, in some orders, were called "lay Sisters", and had a ranking less than that of the teaching nuns. In other orders, they were just treated that way by some. In small missions without designated cooks, the Sisters took turns preparing meals. Outsiders were hired to cook especially in the second half of the century, with food services providing for the larger or school-connected institutions.

Most of the cooks did not want to go into cooking, but they didn't have the dowry, so they were told to. Very few people chose to cook. One nun protested the assignment, and she was related to another elder nun, so she got out of it. I didn't. Every time we heard of another cook leaving, we looked at each other. We told them, Until you start letting us choose our fields, you're going to lose more of us. ELEANOR

I loved the two cook Sisters at the motherhouse—they seemed to be the only ones who would touch you while you worked (a pat on the back) or risk smiling at you. You could do limited talking while you helped in the kitchen, supposedly related to the preparation of food, but the cook Sisters told funny stories about malfunctioning machines or mistakes in the kitchen. They winked at you when you passed them in the hall if nobody else was around, and always had a twinkle in their eyes. DORIS

There seemed to be a perverse custom in one province to assign as cooks those sisters who _really_ hated to cook. They were the most hateful group of women and the food that they turned out was almost unpalatable. There was one Sister who tried her best to get Mother Superior to "fire" her by cooking horrible food. Unfortunately, it was a battle that the Superior won—we lost. Example: Sister used to cook the fattest mutton and serve it floating in its own grease—when we didn't eat it, she would make casseroles out of it all week long. We used to wait for those meatless Fridays! MARTHA

Nine of the participants in this project referred to the food as: *starchy, horrible, poor, C-, plain, institutional, working class,* or *bland.* Sixteen said it was *okay, fair, not bad, decent, respectable,* and *some good.* Thirty-three considered the food *fine, mostly good, good, quite good,* or *very good,* and five called it: *great* and *excellent.*

The food was better than in my own home. THERESA

I grew up in a poor large family and was not a fussy eater. SARAH

The food was great and there was plenty of it. On Tuesdays, laundry day, breakfast was heftier, e.g., hot prunes, hot rice cereal, toast, cheddar cheese, and milk. TRACE

Food in the first half of the 1900s was basic and wholesome, though quite loaded with fat compared to the 90s. Junk food was not generally seen in the convents, at least before 1960, though giant cookies, puddings, and pies were the norm. Forty-one respondents said they remember certain foods being served on certain days (in the larger houses), e.g., spaghetti on Tuesdays. Other common dishes were: meatballs, mashed potatoes, gravy, roasts, overboiled vegetables (in the style of the day) with sauces or butter, homemade bread, and ice cream. In general, every nun ate the same food, although 7 of the women said their Superiors had special food, and one mentioned discrimination: *Nuns who said they were sick and asked for steak—you had to give it to them. But the poor ones with no dowry in the infirmary—they got what was left.*

Sometimes food served was influenced by donations. Once a company gave us cases of peanut butter that was going rancid. For a month we had peanut butter at least three ways every meal, from sauce on meat to cookies and pies. The rancid taste made me sick, and it took over 20 years before I could eat peanut butter again. DORIS

Chapter V: The Refectory

In the Novitiate we had above average institutional food—always plenty and varied. The congregation wanted us healthy. In the smaller houses, the food was better because it was prepared in smaller portions. The college and high school missions used food services. JANET

Having come from a very poor family, I found the food in almost every situation very good. It was plentiful, balanced, and well-prepared in most cases. I had no complaints. If anything, we had too much. Regular dishes on certain days depended upon where one was living. In the Novitiate, lay sisters did the cooking with assistance of Postulants and Novices. In the smaller convents, the Sisters took turns. JULIANNE

Without exception, there was silence in the refectories before Vatican II (not one No answer). Twenty-five remembered there being a penance for clinking a dish, half of these listing: Kissing the floor. Ten of the 25 said that made them feel *embarrassed, not great, pissed, hated it, humiliated, small, belittled, put down, resentful, uneasy.* Words like "stupid" and "silly" were used to describe the penance. Five persons said it was *no big deal, that it was part of the training, a silent "pardon me". I thought it would help me become humble at the time,* said one.

We didn't go in for punishment. CAROLYN

Eating between meals in the early years was forbidden. The kitchen had no snack foods lying about, and permission had to be gotten for everything. However, some nuns who might have had more sense than to obey rules that were not good for their individual (young and growing) bodies, would sneak down to the kitchen at night for bread and jam.

Fasting, in the Church ritual sense, was the rule at certain times of the Church year for those over 21 years old and younger than 65 years, provided they were not ill. One main meal was allowed (no snacking even for lay people), and the other two meals must not equal that one main meal. Of course, the trick was to have a huge main meal, then fasting was not so hard on the body. On fasting days, enough food was served in the convent that the younger Community members could still eat a full meal each time. ❖❖❖

The Refectory: Readings

Fifty-three out of the 64 who answered the question, said that at one time they were Readers in the Refectory.

We each had to read. In the Novitiate, it was difficult because a Sister was assigned to correct each reader if she mispronounced any word. However, after my initial fear, I really enjoyed reading and often volunteered to do it. JULIANNE

It may seem strange to readers of the 21st century that nuns were fearful or nervous about reading from the podium unless they remember that in the mid-1900s, teenagers (as most of the novices were) were quite timid. Every other kid you knew did not have a garage band or an Internet site. Students were not encouraged to speak up in class, and certainly not to disagree with the teacher. One did not seek publicity. The whole idea of life, especially in the convent, was to blend, blend, blend. Also, Novitiate members knew they were on trial; a Council would decide at the end of their formation period if they were to be admitted into the Community or not. It was easy to feel that every movement, every reading, was being judged. Travel and exposure to many peoples was not as common as it is now. The author's last year of high school, several seniors took the train 4 hours north to Seattle to attend a conference, and that was a very big deal--they were celebrities around the school for weeks, people crowding to get near them in the halls and hear what train travel or a different city was like. To sit alone in front of a large number of silent, unsmiling nuns and read aloud was not a mere thing, though those who got used to it, generally liked it.

There were very few things in the convent that we had any control over. The speed and inflection of my voice was one thing I could control. Besides, I had been in plays and loved speaking with a microphone. It was one of the few things I

was certain I could do well. It gave me a sense of power that I didn't get from any other job. DORIS

The choosing of readers was often left up to the Novice Mistress, as most of the readers came from the Novitiate, although some professed nuns were always available to fill in. Two women complained that only certain people were chosen, as if it were an exclusive thing. *Like I was too stupid,* said one. One hated it; 15 said it was okay, no big deal; 15 were (at least in the beginning) *frightened, embarrassed, anxious, fearful, scared, nervous,* and 16 loved it. Although:

When I was on mission with only two other nuns, I thought it was stupid. JANN

Overwhelmingly, the material was chosen by Superiors; readers merely read. Ten participants remembered times when the readings conflicted with what they were told by their Superiors. Then:

Blind obedience covered all conflicts. LILLA

We giggled. ELEANOR

We laughed about it. GAYLE

We ended up having a wonderful, intellectual, spiritual exchange over the matter. This was after Vatican II. The strength of the women in that Community in the presence of such an emotional upheaval was, in the long run, a power that I will never forget. JULIANNE

The reading of that book was stopped. HOLLY

I kept my mouth shut and cried in private. CAREN

By Vatican II, nobody agreed with anyone. ELLEN

❖ ❖ ❖

The Refectory: Martyrology

Though technically, Martyrology refers to the book of dead saints whose feastdays were commemorated by the reading of the details of their demises at the end of dinner, the phrase "to do Martyrology" also referred to public penances in some Convents, penances that were performed during the reading of the Martyrology while everyone was finished eating and washing dishes or just sitting there.

The actual readings were mostly accepted as: *okay, same old stuff, didn't make an impression*, and: *They didn't always make sense.* (FRANCES) To some, they were: *curious, out of date, strange,* yet not anything disturbing, although six thought them *gory, grisly, grotesque.*

We knew that things in the past were different. JANET K

I didn't think about it; it was just one of those things that happened. JEAN

Forty-five out of the 61 who answered the question, spoke of public penances performed during mealtime in the refectory. Because the silence and many rules created tension among the newbies, there were times when giggles rose to the surface, though every effort had to be made to stifle them. Everything was a potential trigger: mistakes or double meanings in the readings, klutziness, spilled or dropped things, a bird flying in the window. Then what?

We were corrected and we had to kneel and ask for a penance. MAE, MERT

Reprimanded by the superior. JOSEPHINE, HELGA, SHIRLEY, JEAN-2, JANET K, THERESA, JAN-2,

I was punished. CONNIE

Nothing. ANNE, MURIEL, DOLORES, EILEEN, YVONNE, NELL, CAROL-2, DENISE.

We got "the look". LORNA, JANE, DORIS, HOLLY, ROSE, LOUISE, MARIE, JULIA-2, ANN, ELLEN, JESSICA

(After everybody laughed) usually nothing. Sometimes the Superior granted talking. LORENA, GAYLE, ELLEN-2, MARIETTA

Attitudes toward public penances changed with the times, though not all convent revised their customs in the same year. A later entrant says:

We were never singled out except at Chapter of Faults. These (public) penances were chosen by the individual and found acceptable by the community, which did not aim to humiliate. We were encouraged to live in charity, to work hard, to be the best teachers we could be, to strive to be great women of the church. We were not there to be trounced upon. We were not taught that the body was bad—the body was a gift. Our talents were a gift. Our Vocation was a gift. The congregation was there to help us become the women God intended, not to beat out the evil, the weakness. My Superiors looked for the good and concentrated on that. JANET

"Doing Martyrology" meant performing some public penance while the Martyrology was being read, a penance often assigned in the Novitiate, but performed also by final professed Sisters. Martyrology was either assigned by a Superior for some infraction, or done voluntarily by the individual (with the consent of the Superior) as a humbling action, since no one else would know if that nun had done something she shouldn't or if she were just "building character". The length of the Martyrology reading varied from day to day; it was rarely brief. In one convent, during the short pause after the last theology reading, nuns who were involved would walk to the front near the podium and kneel. They would remain there, hands hidden, head bowed, until the reading of the Martyrology was over. Sometimes they would hold out their arms to the sides during the penance, or prostrate on the floor with arms out.

Kneeling for Martyrology was scary. Reading at the microphone didn't bother me—it was a sort of performance, but even eating in the Refectory--I felt that everyone was listening to every mouthful I swallowed in that silent room. I managed to avoid being assigned Martyrology, but even as a Postulant was badgered by the Novice mistress about volunteering for it so that people would think I had done something bad anyway. Finally, I gave in. The whole night before, I was frantic, fantasizing what it would be like. When it finally came time to go to that meal, I could hardly walk without jerking, I felt so frightened. What if I tripped on my habit when I got down or up? What if they all stared at me? What if they thought I was wicked? I was 15, and could hardly eat. When they announced the Martyrology, I tucked my hands under my cape (as modesty ruled) and walked with my head bowed to the front of the reader's stand. My face was red and my heart was pounding in my ears, but the room was absolutely silent. I knelt down in a wobbly fashion and bowed my head while they read. I didn't hear a single line. After a while, it occurred to me that the actual kneeling wasn't so bad—the only person who could see your face was the reader. But then I had to get up, face everyone, and go back to my place at the table as if nothing had happened. By then, I needed some tension release and was tempted to laugh, but a glance at the Novice Mistress's frown helped sober me. This was done to help accumulate grace—good points with God, in order to expiate our sins (we were told often how sinful we were) and the sins of others. DORIS

One Novitiate member got the giggles during her Martyrology, shaking and finally snorting with laughter and running out the door behind the podium. For that, she got *two* Martyrologies—during which she also broke out laughing so hard that she had to get up off her knees and run out the laundry door again. The Novice Mistress finally realized that giving her "Martyrology" was counterproductive, so she assigned the Postulant to cleaning toilets.

Each Order/Community had its own variations of Refectory penance. Some penances lasted the entire meal.

Sometimes you had to eat on your knees with a veil down over your face.
MARY S

Chapter V: The Refectory

We were encouraged to occasionally take our plate, silver, and napkin from the table, place it on the floor where it was not in the way, and eat the meal kneeling. When a Sister did this, she would bring her plate and kneel by the presiding Sister, requesting her to place food on the plate. Any Sister at any meal was encouraged to do this. If a Sister came late or dropped a utensil or distracted others in any way, she was expected to kneel and kiss the floor. Also, in the light of humility, a Sister could kneel and kiss the feet of several of the Sisters while they were standing waiting for Grace to be said before the meal. Kneeling with arms extended in the form of a cross while the Sisters filed into the Refectory was a common practice. JULIANNE, also GAYLE, SARAH, JAN-2, THERESA, , MARY-2, SUZANNE, JANET, HELGA, JAN-2, DIANE, GINA, KATE, PRISCILLA, ELLEN-2, MARIETTA, JESSICA, JULIA-2, LILLA, CAROLYN, TRACE

One novice had to carry in part of a sink she broke. ELLEN

Another penance was to kneel at the door and ask the other nuns for prayers. BEVERLY, JANET, THERESA, NELL, SUZANNE, DIANE

There was a mixture of nuns doing penances at various points in our meals and nobody considered it a horrible thing. If you broke silence at night by dropping, e.g., a hanger, you had to hold up the hanger the next morning at breakfast for a series of 5 Our Fathers, Hail Marys, and Glory Bes, upraising your hands and holding the hanger while the rest of the community ate. MARGARET

Before you went in, you asked for penance, saying it by formula while you kissed the feet of the nuns, climbing around underneath the table and trying not to get kicked in the face. My biggest memory was being afraid I wouldn't do it right—you know, that I'd trip over somebody's habit or land in somebody's food. JEAN

We didn't really think of it as a humiliation—the weekly recitation of a fault or kissing the floor—except when we broke something. <u>Then</u> we had to wear a piece of the broken thing. Our fear and constant mental joke was that one of us might break a toilet seat and have to wear that! MARTHA

What merited these public penances? Breaking silence, breaking minor rules, breaking anything. Coming in late. Making a noise. Breach of manners. Disobedience. Doing something stupid. Running in the hall. Not putting hands under the scapular. Arbitrary penance assignments from a Novice Mistress.

Being human and honest. ELLEN

When I broke Grande Silence by commenting to another nun on our way to the dormitory at night, how beautiful the snowflakes looked in the rare storm. SARAH

Reactions during the penance (How did you feel?) were: *embarrassed, worthless, ashamed, scared, frightened, humiliated, resentful, uncomfortable, nervous, self-conscious, (that it was) unfair.* Also: *humble, silly, virtuous.*

I was glad that I had the discipline to do it. NELL

It was just part of the package, expected. MARY-2, GAYLE

Everyone did it sometime, so it was accepted. THERESA

The first few times doing these penances was very hard. I was extremely self-conscious. In time, I was able to do them easily, but I never really liked it and did not really see the purpose of it except that I was being obedient. Our Superiors checked up on us as young people to be sure we did them occasionally. I experienced certain satisfaction that I had fulfilled an obligation—not a very high religious purpose, was it? JULIANNE

Performing voluntary Refectory penances had the stated goal of bringing the soul closer to perfection. What some ex-nuns have discovered decades later (and what some are still denying) is a free-floating shame or guilt. In the first place, we would always fail when we tried to be perfect—no one of us is perfect—we aren't even sure what "perfect" is, though we were encouraged to be so in the convent. We would have been better off accepting ourselves and the world around us. For now, this means accepting that we bought into the penance thing, that it is over, and that we are now healing.

health

physical and mental issues
sleep, insomnia
control over one's life, feeling of value
depression
cancer and other illnesses

Chapter VI: Health

Physical and Mental Health in the Convent

What could be healthier than the rosy-cheecked giggly young Novices one sees in movies, the energetic Flying Nun, or even the serene singing nuns in Sound of Music? In the real world of the mid-1900s, it was common for nuns (and even for some lay persons) *not* to have regular medical—or even dental, checkups. Psychiatry/psychology was looked upon as a service only for the obviously mentally ill. No one that you knew of ever asked, "How's your life going these days?"—and expected an answer other than "Fine."

One of the things that was upsetting to me was the attitude of people toward those who were sick. It was to simply ignore them. It was not okay to be sick. So that, for example, there were no medicine cupboards, no adhesive strips, no colds medicine—nothing available to you; like I say, it was just ignored. It was pretty hard. CAROL

If anyone took pills, we never saw it. Vitamins were unheard of. At one point in the Novitiate it was decided that we Novices give blood to the American Red Cross. We put on our better habits and (public) black veils, and were driven to the building in vans. It turned out that a number of us were anemic and could not contribute. But we could not anticipate the fury of our Novice Mistress, who ranted and yelled as though it were our fault and she were exempt from the Rule of Silence. Basic nutrition was not taught in those days, and we had been told that we had to eat everything put before us, which we did. Some of us dared to discuss this very briefly at a later time, but we never could figure out how it was our fault. In those days, we were still under the impression that whatever the Superiors did was right and beyond question. DORIS

Although each Order had its own mores regarding medical issues, in this area as in all others, Orders had customs in common. Before 1960, the process for obtaining a medical appointment involved convincing the Superior of the need (often by repeated complaints), then going with an assigned nun-companion to whatever doctor offered services without fee or at a reduced rate to convent members. Even those whose parents paid their nun-daughters' medical bills (and most did in the early years) were not allowed to visit their regular family doctor. HMOs were not yet on the scene, so the final say on who was consulted (and when) lay, as everything else, with the Superior. There was no public access in the convent to things like aspirin or band adhesives or peroxide. If you needed something like that, you stood in line and asked the Superior if you could ask the Infirmarian for it. That took a while, so for minor things, one mostly did without.

We would go to Mother Superior, kneel, and beg for the "Love of God" to see a doctor. She would decide, and if necessary, make the appointment. MERT

We would ask the Superior if we could consult the infirmarian nurse. An appointment followed if it seemed warranted/necessary. EILEEN

I only remember being at the appointments, not making them. The dentist's office was over the laundry. He gave me Novocain once, and I either fainted or nearly did. The next thing I knew he had my head down low and back in the chair, and my feet up and out the window. And he said, Well, we won't do that again. Once while I was a Novice, I had foot surgery (an office procedure) and had been told to take the bus home including walking 2 blocks. I remember the look of disbelief on the nurse's face when I told her. I couldn't get my shoe on, so they devised a "boot". Another time on mission I had an impacted wisdom tooth, which the dentist felt unqualified to remove. My Superior didn't want to take me to a specialist and told the dentist she was confident in him. He dug it out, but it became infected. I had that same Superior for 6 years. (See Chapter IX: Liabilities.) A young Sister (27 years old) died in that house because she was misdiagnosed by a quack doctor (he didn't charge nuns). The Superior made her feel like a hypochondriac; she was told she only had arthritis. She died of a heart problem. TRACE

Chapter VI: Health

  I had such difficulty walking that I was bedridden for a couple of weeks before I was allowed to see a doctor. Then the Superior had a nun drive me at night to a chiropractor--just dropped me off with no companion. I was shocked to be left in this dark building with no one but the male chiropractor, and me in less than half of my clothes. Luckily, he was an honest man, and in a very few minutes figured out that I had a cyst on my spine, and told me to get dressed, after which we spent the rest of the time (waiting for my ride back) looking at similar cysts in his medical books and discussing what the surgery would do for me. DORIS

  (In the 60s and 70s) there was yearly teeth cleaning by a dentist who came to the convent. SARAH

Some Orders insisted that the companion be right there during all of the visit, even if it was a proctology exam.

  Having the companion nun there embarrassed me more than the medical people. CAREN

  Being required to wear only a part of the habit in medical situations was sometimes humiliating.

  I had few medical appointments, but because we mended our black cotton stockings and underwear--our undershirts were worn until they were threadbare--we looked pretty shabby underneath our habits, and that was kind of embarrassing. MARGARET.

  When I was a novice, a dentist roughly folded back my headdress to work on my teeth, and he would not give me a moment to replace it with a bandeaux and simple cap. JULIANNE

  As a Novice in the city hospital, I had to wear my chemise, drawers, and headgear (except collars and veil), so I looked pretty odd with all those safety pins sticking out. There was a steady stream of nurses coming in to see the "17-year old nun". I felt like a freak.

Another time I was taken to a large clinic and dropped off without a companion. I don't remember how I was supposed to get home. They took me into an examining room and told me to take off my habit and wait for the doctor. It was not uncommon to have to wait a long time, since most of our appointments were "worked into" the regular schedule, so I didn't start worrying until I had been sitting on the examining table in my slip, chemise, and coif for over an hour. The next half hour was agony as I debated what to do. In those years in the convent, you didn't investigate things, you just shut up and waited, so that's what I did. Then the door opened and a man in a suit and badge walked in followed by a very well-dressed group, the Board of something-or-other on a tour. They all stared at me and were perfectly silent. I looked at them, then away. After some long seconds, the man asked what I was doing there. He might also have wondered <u>what</u> I was, dressed like that. I said I'd had an appointment and was still waiting. He and the group mumbled among themselves and stared at me for at least another minute. I wished I could faint or die. Then they left, and the man with the badge popped his head back in to say that he would get a doctor. After another half hour, a doctor arrived, did a cursory 5-minute exam, and said they'd "watch" things. He said nothing about the whole clinic's having gone home and left me there alone. It was the most humiliating scene of my life. DORIS

Eight of the participants were aware, as nuns in the formation years, that their parents were paying their medical bills. Fifty-four said they didn't think their parents were billed. At least two (of the eight) found out about the payments only after they left the convent.

When I was in the process of leaving, I expected to get back about $950 from the Community—a $500 dowry plus $450 from the sale of some bonds I had inherited. Well, what I got back was $400 with an itemized bill for dental and other things. I had no idea. CAROL

Thirty-one of the 68 who replied to the question, said counseling by a psychologist or psychiatrist was available in the convent. Two said it might have been, but they weren't aware of it. Nine weren't sure if it was or not, and 27 said No, counseling was not available. Eleven of the 31 said such counseling was easy to get, and three "guessed so". Seventeen said No, counseling was not easy to get. One said, *I never dared ask.*

> *I was told I would have to wait 1 or 2 years to make final vows, but not told why. I didn't know how to improve, as I didn't know what I was doing "wrong". Then I was told by the Mother General that I had total physical exhaustion and, six months later, was assigned a counselor. When he asked for a meeting with her to discuss <u>why</u> I was being held back, she refused to see him or let me see him any longer. I cried one whole night and ended up in the hospital.* ELIZABETH.

> *Before 1969, counseling help was rarely available; I know of only one or two nuns who went to see a psychiatrist during the Novitiate.* SARAH.

> *Things had to be pretty bad first.* KATE

> *This kind of counseling was not readily available. And when I was depressed, I didn't realize how sick I was, or that I needed help, because I was very, very conforming and non-aggressive and all that. I would cry at night and not know why, or go to talk to my Superior and not know what was wrong. I do know that I had unhappiness, because I was a "non-person" who didn't even know why I was unhappy. So I would feel guilty about it. One Superior would listen to me once in a while, and that probably helped. But what helped the most—because I was a person who did have to talk about and talk through things—was a network of friends within the Community, all of us having problems. I realize now that that was a support group.* MARGARET.

> *I was miserable enough that I doubt everyone's talking about it would have deterred me from asking for counseling, though when I'd finally "had it" and asked the Superior if I might see somebody, I think she thought it an odd request. But about 2 weeks later, a Retreatmaster was there to see me. As I recall, the interview was brief and unsatisfying. He laughed and said I was too young (age 23) to worry. His manner made me angry.* TRACE

> *One's compliance with the Rule was vital; one's mental health of no concern. The feeling was that you had to be a basket case and specifically ordered to*

get counseling, before you could. The only persons I ever knew who went to psychological counseling were semi-avoided. While no details were available as to what actually went on during the sessions, there were wise noddings of the head with a jerk in the direction of the accused, and several "you know"s, rolling of eyes, etc. What worrying adolescent in her right mind would choose that, when the whole idea of Community was to blend.

My first year on mission, I drew a superior who had a permanent frown stenciled on her face. Nothing I did was right. Though I had my black veil and should not have been fair game as the Novices were, I had been yanked out of college to teach, had all my college notes and concert sheet music (I did not play by ear) taken away without warning so that I couldn't hand-copy them first (copy machines hadn't yet made the scene) or even copy the titles to give to my parents in the hope that I could play those pieces again. I had been forbidden to use anything I had learned "away" in preparation for my Music Ed degree, and was told: You will teach only the things and ways we've always taught. Yet I was refused permission to consult or observe any traditional music teacher to discover what those ways were. One child and I were the only ones singing in church that first Sunday (my not having been notified that this was a children's choir Mass, or even that there should be a children's choir), and the songs the organist played were too high for my second-alto voice. It was very embarrassing to be the new music teacher in that situation. My music projects were cancelled under often humiliating circumstances. An older nun who was younger in rank than I and who was described as "sweet" by my Superior, was given my good assignments, and publicly took over my nearly completed projects as if I were incompetent. This nun in private was less than civil to me, yet was praised by my Superior as someone I ought to emulate. I was roundly criticized (read: yelled at) for complaining to my Superior about these things, and told I ought to be grateful for what I had. The beautifully-done 3-part thanksgiving song that I had taught the talented 7th grade students to sing for graduation was eliminated by my Superior a couple of days before the occasion because "we don't sing in harmony", and I was made to use an unpracticed hackneyed hymn in its place. I felt completely isolated. I gave private piano lessons while the other nuns' laughter came to me from the recreation room. The Superior and her peers were a crowd I feared; none of them ever made overtures to speak to me, even when speaking was allowed. I felt unloved, unwanted, inadequate, put-upon, and a total failure. Thirty years later this same Superior said to me (in a crowd of that Community) that Didn't I remember the good times?—as when she asked me to do a 3-kings bulletin board and it was spectacular? As if that ought to erase all the bad parts. When women began asking to consult me in parlor (a surprise to me—I knew nothing, but I could listen), I was told to push them away, that we (some of us, it seemed) had to adhere to the rule about not speaking unnecessarily to outsiders. In the warm summer, I was chided for developing a rash from a harsh deodorant, and in my naivete, racked my brain to figure out how this was my fault. It was sometimes all I could do to get through a public occasion without weeping aloud, yet I was never offered counseling, nor did it enter my mind that I belonged in the small much-discussed group of ostensibly weird nuns who "needed it". I believed that any therapist would report directly to my Superior anyway, so what would be the use of that? I felt trapped, and often heard myself speaking in a cheery voice several notes higher than my own. There seemed to be no end to the ways in which I could be humiliated, ways not apparent to any outsider beyond the convent porch. I was continually being "surprised", i.e., in my desperate need to belong, my naivete held full reign, and every single time the rug was pulled out front under me, I found that I had not expected it at all—again. I was barely 20 going on the same innocent 15 that I had been upon entering, and I hadn't the vaguest idea that people outside of prisons, let alone Christians—and especially nuns, would treat me this way. Were it not for a sympathetic confessor who told me I was normal and good, I might have died from grief in that miserable year. DORIS

Though I was told by doctors that my extreme fatigue was stress-related, no one ever suggested that I get psychological help until four years (1962) before I left. My friend who was seeing a Jesuit psychologist, saw me break down after an altercation with another nun, and insisted I take her appointment to see this priest while he was in town. With that, I entered a whole new world. Yet it still took years before I felt sufficiently grounded in my own being to make my decision to leave. THERESE-2

It is my strong belief and experience that gossip and speculation in the Community about this matter was rampant, and was not curtailed by the Superiors. I dreaded criticism, but I do think that I <u>would</u> have sought professional counseling if I really believed I needed it. JULIANNE

I didn't see a counselor until later when it was accepted. DIANE

It was a time of such incredible fear and tension about making the right moves—I probably thought at that time that asking for professional counseling would be a little bit off base, and I might lose my Vocation. JEAN

I did not ask for counseling, but had one very interesting experience related to it. When my headaches became so severe that I had to give up teaching for six months, the physician to whom I was sent advised my Superior (by letter) that I should receive psychiatric treatment. His reason? He could not find a medication that helped me, because my body would not physically tolerate them. He was also known to believe that all religious women were hypochondriacs. I agreed to go to the counselor, but I was angry with the physician for not discussing it with me, and even angrier with my Superior for agreeing with him and presenting the case to the Provincial Superior, at which point I was called in for consultation. The Provincial said she would arrange the appointments, but that she really did not believe I needed them. I never went. Sisters continued to be sent to that same physician. I did request and receive spiritual counseling prior to my leaving the Community, but that was in the 1970s. JULIANNE

Seventeen out of 51 who replied to the question, said they asked for professional counseling: 34 did not. Twenty-one declined to answer the question. In some Communities, certain nuns were listed as counselors—whether they actually had training and credentials, was not stated. Twelve of the 17 who asked for counseling, considered the experience "satisfactory".

Quite a few of the Sisters were counselors; they were accessible and honest. EILEEN

The counselor was totally non-directive. I got heart palpitations from anxiety. JANN

The Superior and the Confessor were deemed sufficient in the counseling category. LILLA

Counseling helped me see that I was normal, that life in the convent was not. ANN

The counselor made light of my trouble. TRACE

Counseling was by someone I could not respect: a nun who smoked and wore perfume. BEVERLY

I was happy with the counseling because I was encouraged to "be myself" and was helped to see that many of the (sexual) feelings I had were normal. SARAH

In the state hospital, they were incompetent. My doctor was an Asian woman who spoke in broken English. I met one good psychiatrist, a priest. He said I was sane, mentally sound, and the best proof of it was that I survived it all. LORENA.

I was ready for counseling—needed the support. DIANE

The counselor put me in group therapy with lay people, and I did not want to reveal my problems to them. JEAN-3

If you said anything to the counselor about some of the convent rules, he would stick up for the convent, and act like that was too bad that you couldn't understand or handle it. It was your problem. You didn't get anywhere. They were always right—the Superior was always right, no matter what. ELEANOR

Of course a proportion of the nuns would be ill, just like the lay population. CASEY

Fifty-four out of the 69 ex-nuns who answered this question, said that Yes, there were known mentally ill nuns at their convents. Eleven answered No, and 4 weren't certain or had no knowledge of mentally ill nuns at that time. How were they dealt with? Eleven mentioned medical treatment. Nine more say that they were treated *well, gently, very kindly, respectfully,* and *with compassion.* Others said:

>They were treated with kid gloves or disdain. Tolerated. LILLA, JAN-2, THERESE-2

>It was hushed. Secret. Private. Ignored behavior. HOLLY, ELIZABETH, SHIRLEY, JANN

>That was really amazing—people just kind of skirted the issue. This one nun who was known to walk around naked sometimes—not much reference was made except in hushed tones, but you knew the mental illness was there. Poor communication skills there again—it was indirect non-handling of the poor person who was going through this. Another nun (who'd had a lobotomy, the story went) would just start talking to people and saying exactly what she thought of them, and people just generally took that from her and didn't confront her. I think in some ways she got by with a lot that might have even been part of a game. But the fact is, we didn't deal with that at all in any kind of reality. People suffered from her, too, in the non-confrontive way we dealt with those problems. MARGARET

>How were they dealt with? Not well. Sent home or to the state hospital. I myself went into a physical depression because of a near diabetic state. I underwent 24 electric shock treatments. A doctor later said it was uncalled for, barbaric, and that I could sue the Community for neglect and the hospital for malpractice. He also advised against it. I had no desire to. LORENA

>If anyone had any kind of problems, they disappeared. We knew they had to go home—it was considered somewhat shameful. Interaction was so limited that if there were any mentally ill nuns left there, I was unaware of it. BEVERLY

>One Sister—I don't know where she came from or whatever happened to her—was really psychotic. And people just ignored her, didn't interfere much. She was in the Infirmary at the Provincial House. She would stand up in the middle of a

meal and unwrap her napkin and start swatting imaginary flies. Or cut up her mattress with a scissors or knives because she wanted to let the snakes out of there. And there were funny things that she did, too, like in a big crowd one time in the choir, she pushed her way through and she just kind of looked at me and said, Allow my virginal body to pass. I thought that was pretty funny.

We were all under stress. One shy Sister, a real sweetie-pie, asked to see a psychiatrist, and of course, you always have to have a companion, so they gave her one. Now the companion couldn't drive, so they assigned a driver. Then the driver had to have a companion, and that happened to be me. I don't know how I got chosen, but there I was. So there ended up to be four of us taking this woman to her first appointment with a psychiatrist—it was terrible. She went to pieces in the car. As we got closer and closer—and I think looking back, that she directed us to the wrong place because she didn't want us to know where she was going, and we never did find the place, and never did find the doctor, and she had a complete breakdown right then, right in the car. It was awful.

At the same time there was this mentally ill music teacher who was also colorful and vicious, and who had power over the Superior (who was really a very weak woman). She would lock all the doors so that we couldn't play any music or do anything. It was really crazy. And nobody ever acknowledged that she was sick. CAROL

There were different kinds of mentally ill nuns: overbearing, explosive, simpletons, glowering, demanding, etc. LILLA

They were sick and yet overlooked. JANET K

There was an Infirmary at the Motherhouse where these individuals went if they were serious cases. Some of them were relatively harmless so they lived in various mission houses and contributed what they could. There was a certain distance between such an individual and the other Sisters. In many cases, I was touched by the gentleness shown them by some, but in general, I think there was a fear of the unknown on the part of the nuns, so these Sisters were often shunned. But what was even worse, there was a great deal of spoken criticism about them as if they were responsible and could get over it if they tried.

.The ones that I knew showed hypochondriacal tendencies. And they were will, both physically and mentally. On the other hand, they were harmless. I found that if I listened to them, it eased their stress. Others were senile. I worked in the Infirmary for over a year after being ill myself. I was around these individuals and learned to love them for their simplicity. Some of the things they did made me laugh. And I got along with them. Yes, I was afraid of them and frustrated because of all the time that they could demand. But I was really grateful for this experience when my tension problems were interpreted by some in the community as being mental. I began to understand them a little better. JULIANNE

Some received help, others did not. HELGA

One who was schizophrenic began yelling. I was afraid of her because she was acting so bizarrely. She was hospitalized, and I later went to see her. THERESE

They were like zombies. JANE

Usually they were depressed. LORENA

Each was different. GAYLE

There was one lovely Sister who was always cheerful and kind. I had little dealings with her because I worked in a separate building, but she had the reputation of being very easy to get along with. One day I passed her in the hallway and she looked terrible to me. I stopped and asked her if she were okay. With tears in her eyes, she told me that she had been undergoing shock treatments and that she couldn't remember the simplest things. I felt so helpless. I've never been able to forget this Sister. MARTHA

As Novices, we were told that a certain nun was mentally ill. She mostly worked alone at menial tasks and I never saw her at celebratory gatherings. Some evenings she would race down the basement ramp to the kitchen, her arms outstretched, veil and habit flapping, yell-screaming. I feared going near her, because I didn't know how to act around her, and nobody had told us anything *about that. Looking back, she was probably just letting off steam, and may have been more healthy for it than we were. DORIS*

Perchance to Sleep

To those who sleep well, insomnia is a mere word. To those who dread getting into their beds each night because they know it means hours of tossing about, waking often and not being able to get back to sleep easily, having their best sleep begin about a half hour before the alarm, then rising day after day not feeling rested—insomnia is as disturbing as a nightmare. To those in mid-1900s convents who, because of work schedules and because of rules that excluded naps, not sleeping well was a major contributor to a lack of well-being. Not sleeping well and not complaining are two different things.

Sixty-three out of 64 answers stated that the participants did not complain <u>often</u> about insomnia. Several qualified their statements:

No, I didn't complain often about insomnia, but I frequently lost sleep because of headaches, for which I received medical care and medication. JULIANNE

We worked so hard and rarely could get 8 hours of sleep. JANN

Restorative sleep was an unknown or ignored term. I slept so little some nights and was so tired during the days that I finally mentioned it to the Novice Mistress, asking her what I could do. She stared hard at me and said firmly, You're in bed lying down, aren't you? You have your eyes closed, don't you? That's all that's necessary. Her tone said, Don't bring this up again. DORIS

I am a night person and we had to go to bed by 9:30 p.m. I complained, but nothing was changed. CAROL-2

Sixteen out of 67 women answered Yes to: Did you have recurring dreams/nightmares in the convent? Forty said No, and eleven could not recall.

Chapter VI: Health

I had dreams of suffocating. I think I was suffocating emotionally. CONNIE

We had many deaths in my early years, and bodies were laid out in the parlors—I think this is what did it. ELIZABETH

I dreamed I was trying to escape, or having bad experiences with the Novice Mistress. I still have these dreams occasionally. DONNA

I did dream that the place was burning down and I was running for my life. KATHLEEN

I still dream about having to be the cantor, leading Office. I can't sing. MARY S

Just before I left, I was in a cage without a habit, and others were on the outside with habits on. The door was open—my choice. Mice were in the highway and in an automobile with no driver. HOLLY

I dreamed of walking to the edge of a roof and jumping off. THERESE-2

Of a tornado that would almost get me! MARTHA

I dreamed of standing before a rack of beautiful clothes. I put them on, but my eyes wouldn't focus in the mirror. CASEY

I often dreamed of unruly classes and sometimes of terrible monstrous people. LORENA

The last year—of escaping from that situation at that convent. NANCY

As to the question: What did you think the dreams meant? *Inner turmoil, stress, frustration, unhappiness,* they said. Also:

I think it meant that I didn't belong there regardless of what I was told. DONNA

I did not know then that dreams had meaning. MERT

It meant that I just didn't like it anymore and I wanted the place to burn down. KATHLEEN

That I wanted to be free to do my own things. JANET K

That I felt I was not in control. HOLLY

I was unable to conceive of myself as a non-nun. CASEY

On Feeling of Value

There is a difference between "being valuable" and "feeling valuable" in Community. To the question: To what degree/ how did you feel valuable in your convent years? 16 said they did not feel valuable as a person, 30 said they felt valuable only as/primarily because they were good teachers or workers, and 12 said they *felt valuable, were valuable, gave it my best, was confident in my talents, had inner peace, and thought I was fulfilling a need in the Church* or *I was making a contribution.*

My talents were liabilities. ELLEN

Self-esteem really suffered during those years after Novitiate. The time spent working felt good and valuable, but success bred jealousy and harsh treatment from some Superiors. MARTHA

I liked teaching—my students made me feel of value. I'm sure I got positive feedback from other nuns and Superiors, but I recall nothing of that. JEAN-2

At times in the beginning when I still had outsider status, I felt needed for some of the skills I had developed. Later even that didn't matter. Can't say that I ever felt "valuable" unless it was that very short period (days) between being told I was chosen to go away to study, and finding out that a lot of older nuns were jealous and hated me. DORIS

I came to the Community with a fairly stable self-image. But during most of my religious life, I felt overlooked, felt that I was considered second class. I knew I was a good teacher, even though I really never wanted to teach, but I knew this primarily because my students told me, not my Superiors. If I had not made an issue of it, I doubt the Community would have allowed me to go on for a Masters Degree. One Provincial Superior stated that they did not think I had the health for it. Yet I had the health to teach day after day with severe headaches, and to carry my full share of other responsibilities. And when they did agree, not one person responsible for educational direction even talked to me about choice of fields. Possible options, future trends were not even offered for consideration. I was really in limbo. JULIANNE

Didn't feel valuable. Outside of one experience during meditation, I don't think I ever felt valuable in the convent. JANE

I didn't--always had to work too hard and do things I was not prepared for. I taught six years without being taught how to write a lesson plan. JANN

I know I was a valuable person and an excellent teacher, a person with friends inside and out.
LOUISE

Feeling valuable to the Community—I didn't. I felt like the younger nuns were always under suspicion and not trusted. I also never felt that my talents were tapped, that what I most had to offer was used. When I think of myself now, I know I am a very creative thinker, and a person who is a change agent. Of course that was not appreciated in our Community, and many of us who played that role are now gone. MARGARET

Who is running my life?

Did you ever (during convent years) want more control over your own life?

Forty-eight of 64 women who answered this question said Yes, I wanted more control over my life. Ten said No, and seven were undecided, or they qualified their answers.

I got what I needed. FRANCES

Not really more control, just more understanding. LILLA

Oh, yes—I wanted desperately to go to graduate school. I wanted very much to stay in a place more than a year, to put down some roots. JEAN-2

I felt physically incapable of going on in year 11. ELIZABETH

I was told by the Novice Mistress that it was wrong even to <u>want</u> control over my own life, so I tried not to think about it. DORIS

I was perhaps too accepting of the lack of control over my own situation. I remained for 10 years in a position where I was advanced to supervisor of the office. But it was while I was in the Philippines living in a Filipino barrio that I felt the most freedom and lack of being controlled by others. EILEEN

Lack of control over my own life was one of the main reasons I left. JEAN-3

I left because I wanted to be free and responsible to my own conscience. DOROTHY

I wanted more control over my life when I became mature enough to realize that I needed it. THERESE-2

What made you cry in the convent?

Eight women participants said they seldom cried during their convent years. Ten cried at deaths, *falling out with a friend, tiredness, sadness at seeing suffering or injustice (1), at being given sad news, during movies (1), etc.,* and one *cried for joy* at her naming ceremony. One ex-nun said she had no idea what made her cry, nor did she remember what made her happy in the convent. Of the 68 responses to this question, some listed several things that made them cry. Most answers fell into two categories: Loneliness (33) and Poor treatment by others (27).

Loneliness, no feedback or encouragement. MERT

Loneliness and unkindness. GRACE

Friends who snubbed me, the vow of obedience when I was not allowed to attend college. SHIRLEY

Humiliation and severe scoldings. CAREN

Being deeply moved by things I read, the wisdom of an old nun, the liturgy. MAXINE

Many things—I was idealistic and sensitive, and I felt treated unfairly. MARY S

Frustrations, dehumanizing in the Novitiate and during student teaching years. I went into hysterics and had to be sedated when I received word that my mother had died. I was so overcome by grief, and I appreciated and loved my mother very much. JEAN-2

Being systematically shunned. Having my music taken away. Being accused of fostering a PF when I had no idea what that meant. Having the priest yell at me when he dropped the Host at Communion. Being lonely. DORIS

I did not cry much, but the times I did was from loneliness or when I was feeling sorry for me. I cried at some funerals, especially when one of my closest friends died. Expression of emotion was, as I saw it, not "permissible", or it was considered a weakness. JULIANNE

I cried when they said they were kicking me out of the convent. DENISE

Have you had cancer since leaving the convent?

Of the 69 participants who answered this question in 1993-4, twelve had had cancer by then. Seven of the 12 had had breast cancer by that year. Other cancers listed were: ovarian, thyroid, colon, uterine, and cervical.

Some health professionals consider all disease to be stress-related; others say few-to-none are. Most people's opinions on this matter fall somewhere between the two extremes. The participants in this project were asked if they had other stress-related diseases besides cancer. Twenty-five out of the 49 who answered this question say Yes, they have other stress-related diseases besides cancer; 24 say they have not. The diseases they listed are:

allergies
alopacia
anxiety
arthritis
asthma
auto-immune diseases
bipolar disorder
depression
diabetes
diabetic-related diseases
esophageal reflux
fibromyalgia
headaches
heart bypass
heart palpitations
hemorrhaging pancreas
hiatal hernia
high blood pressure
high cholesterol

hip bursitis
hypertension
hyperthyroid
insomnia
irritable colon
lupus
migraines
muscle tensions
pneumonia
rheumatic arthritis
sarcoidosis
stomach problems
stomach ulcers
tension headaches
TMJ
ulcerative colitis
ulcers

VII
sexuality

love, like, lesbianism, heterosexuality
sex, pregnancy, abortion
sleep: dorms, private rooms,
friends, PFs, confidants, mentors
Bride of Christ, Jesus as teen idol

NOTES: Sexuality

To repeat: this s not a scientifically engendered survey; it does not represent the average population of convents then or now. These numbers are based solely on responses of 73 ex-nuns. Of these, if one says she became pregnant as a nun, it does not follow that 1 out of every 73 nuns gets pregnant. It only means the 1 of the 73 women *who answered these questions* became pregnant while in the convent. The real average may be more or less. In a place where women were ordered about, told to hide their own bodies in the bath with cotton tent chemises, a surprising number (or not—depending on your point of view) undressed for men or for each other. Of those who did not, many of the 50s nuns yearned for love and/or sex, having been recruited, overtly or subconsciously, into seclusion while they were still in their teens. It would be surprising if they did *not* occasionally think of or wish for sex—they were still human beings, after all.

The convent was not a good place to spend a normal adolescence. Regardless of rules, the seeking *spirit* of the young squeezed out from the restrictive and binding rules and produced unnatural emotional effects, which were later passed along by repressed individuals to the children whose knuckles they rapped. This author recalls convent debates about whether 'twas better to accept candidates for religious communities from the already educated and mature, or whether to get them while they're young and *mold them* (this term was often used) the way a community chose. Remember that even in the World outside the convent, these were the days of routinely sanctioned "breaking of kids' spirits"--for their own good, of course.

Do you now feel that having a crush on a nun precipitated your entering?

YES: 11
NO: 55
MAYBE: 2
NOT ANSWERED: 5

Were you encouraged to develop friendships in the community? Or not? Why?

What about Particular Friendships?

With regard to the above questions, pre-Vatican II convent life (roughly, before the 60s) was like a film negative of the after years. *Before*, it was commanded that there be no particular friendships. Officially, individual relationships were frowned upon.

We were to love our neighbor, meaning even the cantankerous nun next to us. Nobody asked us who we liked. It was important to hide those likes, or risk being accused of having a Particular Friendship.

After a religious community incorporated the directives from Vatican II, nuns were not only allowed, but encouraged to become close friends with the public as well as with their own community members. This was as disconcerting as the no-meat-on-Friday issue. If eating meat on Friday in 1949 had been objectively sinful, how could it be all right to eat meat on Fridays in 1969? Most Catholics, especially nuns, who had been under the impression that Church and convent rules were grounded in unchanging Universal Truths, were asking: What is it all based on? Notably for the nun who began her community life in the last years of the old regime, rules about the convent's allowable relationships were confusing.

Novices were told not to touch each other, though being young and playful, they sought out reasons to place a hand for a few seconds on another's arm now and then. Hugging or kissing (as women do nowadays) was definitely verboten--no question.

Up to the 60s, warnings were issued about a "seriously bad practice" known as the Particular Friendship or PF (see glossary). In those years, to establish any new friendship at all was a feat since regular obedience to the everpresent Rule of Silence forbade chatting outside of the proscribed half-hour recreation period. It also demanded that one "keep custody of the eyes", that is, no frivolous eye contact in passing.

Keeping my eyes cast humbly down for so many years---well, it was hard to look up again, even in my wedding photos. After my first job interview for a stewardess position, they said I didn't make enough eye contact. That was when I finally realized that I had a right to look up, and that the rest of the world did it all the time.

From morning till night every single day except special feastdays, one was to speak only in case of necessity. In crossing paths with another nun in any convent or non-public place, one would give the first half of the community greeting, such as: "Praise the Lord." The second sister would reply, "Now and forever." There was to be no laughter or (God forbid!) touching, or even smiling--nothing that could not be construed as a most temporary respite from the state of constant prayer which each nun was to continue in her heart.

Every convent without exception preached that each nun love her fellow nuns equally and that she shun the practice of PFs. Punishment for failing to do this, for even appearing to pay more attention to a single individual, was frequently swift and severe: sometimes a warning first, often public penance, but surely and quickly separate assignments to different missions.

Sex was not spoken of publicly in the 50s, not in the family or school and certainly not on radio or television. Movies were primarily declared "objectionable" or "condemned" by the powerful Legion of Decency for their degree of overt sex ranging from a little cleavage to scenes much milder than today's television fare. The priest assigned to give the "sex talk" to a local seventh/eighth grade girls' group said only: Now remember, it's always the girls's fault. Period. And the accompanying nun said nothing.

Novitiates in those years were full of young, idealistic, naive teenage girls who had not the vaguest idea *why* it was supposed to be so gravely wrong to like one person more than someone else.

Reasons given to them were:

PFs are the road to Hell.
With a PF, you could lose your Vocation.
Your friend is Jesus; you don't need more.
PFs are not healthy.
Some people are not "good" for you, especially a PF.
It is too "exclusive" for a religious community.
It conflicts with treating everyone equally.
PFs distract one from the search for God.
They damage the community.
They are a danger to the spirit of Chastity, which was "death to self and affection towards others in order to become more pure of heart and acceptable to Jesus".

"Be a friend to all, but not to anyone in particular" was one convent's directive. "Seldom one; never two, always three or more" was another's.

Not a word was said about lesbianism, though it was on everyone's mind. Most of the participants in this project speak of being warned about PFs in such a way that they understood the implication. In the same way that illicit sex was considered by the Church in the 50s to be one of the worst sins, PFs were the most feared possibility in the convent. This, even though the fact was that in those days, many nuns, especially those without worldly experience, knew what lesbianism really was.

"Fear of lesbianism" is mentioned recurrently in the written answers to this question cluster. Some people were afraid of "catching it" or of *"turning into a lesbian"* by associating with one.

Young nuns in their formative years (during pre-Vatican II days) were warned many times, albeit vaguely, about the potential perils resident in individual relationships. The older nuns were rigid in their condemnation of its dangers. A lot of guilt was generated in mid-century convents surrounding this subject.

If you had a PF, you would lose your Vocation. There was much internal guilt---God would come and take your Vocation away. So you worried much.

And yet, strangely and unfairly, besides those who worried that they *might be* attracted to particular friends, and those who were falsely accused and punished for PFs, there were the "teflon elite" who kissed and hugged each other publicly with impunity.

I was never accused of having a particular friendship even though I did fall in love with a woman and had a definite fullblown lesbian affair with her. I guess it was because it was so common: everybody at the time this was happening was seeing it happen in the community a lot. I did get approached the year before I left when I was having an affair with a lay woman, but it made me angry because the person who approached me was having an affair also, and I felt it was hypocritical, so we had a blowup.

And: *People knew I had one after the other, but nothing was ever said---to my face, at least.*

Prevention took the form of musical missions:
It was a practice in our community to send the young sisters to a different convent every year for the first seven years, lest they form undue attachments. After that it was 2 or 3 years in each place, and finally 5 years in the parish from which I entered.

This whole set of questions rakes some wounds in its discussion of personal and difficult things, and not surprisingly, some of the participants did not answer each question. Yet nearly a third of the total number of the group tell of being accused of having a Particular Friendship. A number of these women hadn't the vaguest idea of what they were being accused, though they were punished anyway.

The process was usually this: someone reported you, or a rumor reached your Superior. She called you and possibly the other nun in, and warned or lectured you. You were both sent to different missions, or infrequently, told to "watch it". Nuns were so afraid of being accused (some fearing loss of Vocation and therefore, Hell), that they generally complied reactively.

I didn't understand it, but cut that party dead thereafter.

I was forbidden to talk to her again.

I just ended it then.

My friend and I were dumbfounded—we had been friends in high school. We still are friends, and we aren't lesbians.

I was separated from that person and told not to associate with her.

Within half an hour we were both in tears in the Provincial's office. She never mentioned lesbianism (no one did) or the crying lack of affection available in the Novitiate to hitherto normal 16 year olds, but promised to separate us for life, starting with our being sent to different states. That decision spiraled into serious relationship side effects as well as a nervous breakdown for my friend and leaving the convent for me.

I tried to conform, but repeatedly got close to an individual and got called on the carpet for it. It placed both of us under great tension and frequently destroyed the friendship.

I was given a public penance and isolation.

I was reprimanded several times in private. I didn't understand why talking to someone would lead to something bad.

I believe it (the session with the Superior) played a role in destroying our friendship.

I was lectured on the subject and was not allowed to sit with or be with her.

I was accused by a jealous contemporary who had no friends and couldn't relate to friendship.

I was told by two superiors to stay away from a couple of my friends.

In my first months as a Postulant, a friend with whom I had shared slumber parties in high school was extremely upset and had cried for nights in our 5-person dorm. She slept several beds away from me, but one particular night she brought her pillow over during Grande Silence and motioned that she needed to speak to me. We lay on the narrow bed like little kids—I was 15 and she was 16, while she cupped her hands around my ear and whispered a sentence, then I answered her in kind. After an hour or so, she calmed down and fell asleep, and I, thinking nothing of it, fell asleep too. In the pre-dawn, our curtains were ripped open by the Superior who had been informed by one of the nuns in our dorm that we were sleeping together! Well, we were, but....

And so on.

Are you lesbian?

This question: Are you lesbian? had the highest number of responses in the entire survey. Only one person did not reply at all—most likely because she was not using the questionnaire as a guide for any answers.

So, out of 72 women participants, seven—nearly one out of ten--say they are lesbian. (Remember, these statistics apply only to persons who chose to participate in this book, not to the entire ex-nun population of the United States.) Not all are living openly gay lives now, which is one reason why the author is not even using identifying code names for this chapter.

Some lesbians in this project had sexual relationships with women who were not nuns—this while they themselves were in the convent. No one said specifically in her explanation that the person she was with *was* a nun. And some ex-nuns said that they knew they were lesbian then, but stayed celibate during their convent years.

I totally denied that I was lesbian in the convent, even though I had two lesbian affairs there. I had relationships with two women, but not with any nuns. I am openly gay now after 10 years of marriage, so am much happier about myself and who I am right now.

We only kissed—I don't know if they were gay or not—closeness then was just kissing. I now have a relationship with an ex-nun who is gay, but I am not openly gay.

Yes, I am a lesbian, and yes, I did know that while I was in the convent. I have known that since I was nine years old. I did not have a sexual relationship in the convent—the nun that I slept with every single night for a year—we didn't have sex, I just slept with her. Do I have relationships with gay nuns now? No. Am I openly gay? Yes. Special problems for the lesbian nun are that first of all, it isn't okay according to the Church to be lesbian. And second of all, you're locked in there with all these--for the most part—really good women, and it's hard to, uh-- And another thing, this is the part that really got me, was that they kept telling you to love one another, but when you did, it was not okay. And so it was really very, very confusing. I never felt that being a lesbian was wrong, but apparently other people did, and that was so confusing for me. And pretty hard.

It was like I had been trying to force myself into a puzzle with all the pieces going one way, and then one day I turned them all over and they made sense and I knew I needed to leave the convent. I had been attracted to several nuns, one of whom would come to visit and we would stay up late at night and share on emotional levels. All these relationships were not okay—at least, they would end.

The lesbian nun didn't exist! It was gossip about being with some nun.

I had 3 lesbian friends whom I loved dearly, yet I had no physical/sex attraction. This was a big factor in my leaving. Since I found I could not live without love, I left to seek it outside.

I think the convent was a good place for lesbians. Many of my friends managed to live together (by the time I left) and maintain a lesbian relationship while under no suspicion from the outside.

Being lesbian in the convent is a constant heartache, wanting to be with her, finding a place to be intimate, keeping it a secret, and wondering why love has to be denied.

The problem is that the Catholic Church is so prejudiced and judgmental. Many of my friends are gays and lesbians.

I don't know what special problems lesbian nuns had, but they sure worried the older nuns if you ever hugged them or touched their hand if you were lonesome!

One thing I cannot get out of my mind is that because of my emotional immaturity and inability to resolve my expressing love, I was probably thought of by my community as being gay. In fact, I would not be surprised if that is why my Provincial Superior recommended that I leave. It bothers me somewhat, but I can understand why someone might have thought that. I have not even thought of wanting same-sex relationships since the day I left the community. Having said this, I would add that the lesbian sister would have to face a great deal of rejection and isolation.

There were many sexually frustrated nuns in the convent. I was often approached and it made life difficult. I'm not sure the nuns were really lesbian, just frustrated.

Most older nuns didn't have a clue about what a Particular Friendship really was.

Looking back, I knew some lesbians, but I didn't know they were lesbian at the time. In the West we were so rule conscious we could not have been gay. I learned what "lesbian" was when I was 35 years old.

I always wanted to have a relationship with a man, which my mother refused to let me have. I had deep feelings for other nuns because I was never allowed to have any of those feelings while growing up.

Although I am not lesbian, I had the doubtful privilege of sharing a house with two women who later declared themselves to be so, even bragged about it openly. During the time I lived with them, they made my life miserable. But it gave me some time to look at the issue. The person who later flaunted the fact to the administration was a very immature, selfish person, and also a liar. In looking at that situation as well as others where I saw Particular Friendships, I had to wonder and still do, about the extent of lesbianism in religious life. Many of the people whom I saw as totally dependent upon another religious woman, seemed simply to need one other person to rely on. My overall impression is that, while some lesbianism does exist in the convent, what is more prevalent is people who are not strong enough to live a truly spiritual life without a partner. They need to be married. When I entered, numbers were flocking to religious life, and I believe many were for the wrong reasons. The true nature of asceticism was not understood. Which is why I believe that there is room for both married and unmarried clergy in the Catholic Church.

The same vow of celibacy holds for lesbians.

I don't think there's more problem for a lesbian nun than there would be for any other woman except that I feel that the lesbian nun who chooses not to live her celibacy—it's easier for her to do that in the convent. Also, in the convent, you can escape the knowledge of yourself longer.

So there you have it: Yes, there were lesbians in the convent, both active and inactive sexually. There was a great fear of lesbianism in the days before Vatican II and probably still some afterwards. Many nuns, starting their religious life in their mid-teens, were dying for affection and were of an age where crushes on both sexes were common, so it is not surprising that they felt drawn toward another nun or lay person who gave them attention and respect. Having a crush when you're a teenager doesn't mean you're lesbian. Lesbian nuns were misunderstood in ways different from the misunderstanding that other nuns experienced. And, being a nun does not make you lesbian.

Did you know what the sex act involved when you entered the convent? How did you find out?

Forty-two women said, Yes, I knew what it was all about before I entered the convent; 13 said they did not. As for how they came by this knowledge--by these answers we can gauge the outside influences on the girl/woman of those years. Besides those who did not specify or declined to reply, each respondant's answer fit into one of seven categories:

Home (parents, married siblings): 17

Friends, cousins, lovers, the grapevine: 15

Class (high school, college, Novitiate, Juniorate): 14

Books (including medical books, a Red Cross book, the dictionary) and pamphlets: 12

Husbands and lovers after leaving the convent: 6

Priest (either a class or individual talk): 3

Military (experience): 1

Eleven women replied that they knew *something*, *"vaguely"*, *"not completely"*, *"theoretically"*.

I had a fairly good idea, found out later I was fuzzy on some of the details.

And one remarked:

It's only a theory until you fall in love with someone.

Other comments:

We were instructed by a young priest when we were seniors. It was an appalling, embarrassing experience.

I was 28 and a virgin who'd had many boyfriends.

I was sexually abused at the age of 10.

As a postulant, I read the dictionary selectively until I got the idea of what was going on.

We had the weirdest sex instructions ever—the Novice Mistress told us it was a mortal sin if our sex organs moved!

My mother gave me a book about periods and babies, which explained it briefly. I understood that you put up with it and only did it for children.

Did you ever want to have sex with anyone while you were still a nun? What stopped you?

Almost as many participants in this project declined to answer this question as answered "Yes". Four specify the vow of chastity as being their reason for not having sex, one mentions fear of pregnancy, and others speak of conscience and commitment. One honest woman says that she and her friends were afraid of getting caught, two speak of their wall of naivete and immaturity, and one wanted to have sex:

--with no one in particular. I just wanted to have sex.

Of the No answers, only these explanations are given:

I could not have gone to communion. I would have left first.

I completely repressed all sexual desire as sinful.

I was committed to Jesus and to celibacy. The thought never did occur to me.

I just wanted hugs. Most of the time there was a lack of reciprocation.

I didn't even know what sex was.

Were you sexually attracted to priests or lay persons? What happened?

Of the women who answered (seven did not), the responses were almost evenly divided: 35 said Yes and 31 said No.

YES, I WAS ATTRACTED:

Usually I'd get a crush on a good-looking or dynamic retreatmaster (for the 15-day retreats). I'd make an occasion to talk to him privately about something, sigh about him a few times, then he'd leave and I'd forget his name.

I just thought about him.

I embarrassed myself by communicating silently.

I was attracted to a young woman at the college. It was short-lived; I was still quite young.

I was attracted to a young man. What did I do? I hid in the chapel.

When I was attracted, I "sublimated" the feeling. (see Glossary)

I kept it quiet.

I stopped it at first then later got involved with a lay person.

In the middle of those 20 years I fell madly, passionately, and unexpectedly in love with a woman who was a lay mother. It led eventually to a passionate love affair that was a breakthrough for me as far as waking me up in many avenues of my life—spiritually, sexually—every way.

What did I do? I left the convent and got married. (2)

Just daydreamed. (2)

Fantasized. (2)

We wrote notes.

I sighed hopelessly and got all flustered.

I was definitely attracted to priests while I was a sister. I worked in a business office with priest and brothers for 10 years. In the early times it bothered me a lot. After I mentioned it in confession to a wise priest—he said attraction was natural and a gift (not a sin), he said I simply had to make up my mind about my priorities and my vows, my commitment, and make my choice. It was very freeing. My husband and I are now still in contact with one of the priests for whom I worked.

I was able to remain professional.

We just talked about it. (2)

I had a relationship.

We were friends. (3)

I did nothing. (5)

NO, I WAS NOT ATTRACTED TO ANY PRIEST OR LAY PERSON:

We saw only one priest and he was very unattractive.

No, but I winked at a young priest once.

Were you sexually attracted to any other nun?
What did you do about it?
Why do you think you felt this way?

Were young women in convents supposed to be more secure in their sexual orientation than those on the outside? Spending their teenage years, hormones raging, in silence with other women, reaching out sometimes for forbidden affection, briefly wondering: What was that? then moving on with their lives as women—this is the picture the questionnaire answers give.

Only 24 participants said they felt sexually attracted to another nun in their convent years (8 declined to answer). In hindsight, had "sexual attraction" been more finely defined in the question, there might have been more—or fewer responses of this kind. One's personal interpretation of the phrase "sexually attracted to" colors one's answer. Forty-one said no, they did not experience sexual attraction to another nun. Yet if you put the "yes" explanations and the "no" explanations together, they both say mostly the same thing: we were lonely, young, and wanted affection. Read on:

YES, I FELT SEXUALLY ATTRACTED TO OTHER NUNS. Here's the story:

There were no males around and as a younger nun, I was infatuated. I needed friendship.

I think it was hormones.

I did not now how to handle my emotions of love. I struggled especially with the fact that we are gifted with a body that is capable of expressing profound love in a physical way. However, I did have two experiences where we engaged in sexual behavior. Both of these individuals are still friends of mine. The first one was in great need of support and love. I am not certain, but I think she is a latent lesbian who has not come to grips with it. The second is, perhaps, the closest friend I will ever have. In both of these relationships, there is now absolutely none of the sexual behavior we shared when we were in the community. I feel strongly that the environment was for some of us emotionally unhealthy.

I repressed it and naturally, felt confused.

There were no men. I had a couple of sexual relationships, but mostly we were just good friends.

I let her know my feelings. I think it was because I was refused requests to leave for some years, and I wanted to marry.

I was infatuated by a novice.

I was attracted because I was young and she was caring toward me. I spent time with her.

It was just a crush. We didn't do anything.

I knew I was lesbian.

It was loneliness.

She was beautiful and had a great sense of humor, so I sought her company.

I had crushes on other nuns; I was a late lesbian and didn't know it at all. I didn't do anything about those crushes on my teachers and older nun, just admired them from afar, and didn't know why I felt that way about it. I had had crushes on boys before I went to the convent, so I felt there was something bad or wrong about me if I felt that about nun, so I tried not to think about it.

It seemed strange—I did nothing, but was on guard.

Chapter VII: Sexuality

Finally I acted out sensually, when the nun reciprocated my attraction. I am bisexual and was truly in love.

I liked women and tried to be in their company more.

Because I am a lesbian, I tried to spend time with her.

There was no one else around but nuns.

She had a powerful personality. I got over it. It's part of being human.

Reason: the absence of men. We developed a close friendship, but didn't analyze it.

I was frustrated and lonely. We had close relations.

It was natural, though I thought the reason was that I was gay.

ONLY TWO NO'S OFFERED ANY EXPLANATION:

I was a virgin then, and didn't think I was supposed to do it.

All most of us wanted was some caring and personal attention—which we never got. I wanted affection. We, young teenagers who were not allowed to speak to each other or to older persons most of the time, who were not allowed to touch each other or even sit by the same person twice in a row during the short recreation period, were starved for affection. I desperately wanted someone to love me. Once I hugged my girlfriend from high school and as a result, was reported to the Mother Superior and lectured. I tried to hug my last superior once after a weepy talk session right before I left the convent, but was pushed away, though this person was famous in the community for hugging and kissing her special friend in public, so it's not like she was generally opposed to touching. That was it—two memorable occasions in all those years.

❖ ❖ ❖

Did you have sex with anyone while you were in the convent?
Did anyone else find out?
How did you feel afterwards? What happened as a result?

O ne could argue that if nuns followed the rules perfectly, there would have been no sex or desire in the convent--but there also would have been no human beings there. To be attracted, to want to be loved, to want sex—these are and were parts of being human, no matter how much they were denied by rule. Neither did the fact that rules existed mean that all avenues were blocked; once one decided to operate outside the lines, there were endless opportunities. For example, outside of those who met their secular friends at night, the rest of the convent was silent and asleep from 9:30 pm on. Nowadays we *expect* people to do what they want. Well, some of them did just that in the mid-1900s.

Eleven women did not answer the question: DID YOU HAVE SEX IN THE CONVENT?

Fifty-four women said, *No, I did not.*

I hardly knew what sex was, said one.

Snuggling only, said another.

It felt wonderful and no one else found out.

One who answered NO, gave this explication: *No one else found out, but I felt guilty and we stopped seeing each other.*

Eight women responded yes to the question: DID YOU HAVE SEX IN THE CONVENT?

Once—I confessed it and felt guilty. Then I decided to leave.

I felt guilty afterwards. Nothing happened as a result.

Afterwards I was supported.

Sex, but not intercourse. It was with a male good friend. I don't know if anyone found out, but nothing happened.

Yes—it was wonderful. No one else found out so I had more.

After, I felt very loved. I left the convent a year later and married.

While still in the convent, I had sex with a woman for quite a while in secret, in a mad passionate love affair. Then I had another woman after her who tried to push the first woman out of my life. This was towards the end of my years in the convent. First when I started having sex or even feeling sexual, I felt extremely guiltridden and had a lot of struggle. I tried to shut this off like an alcoholic and not to have anything to do with this anymore, but it was a major struggle, and I think my good self came to the rescue. There were other women at the same time having struggles in the convent, too. It was the time of the sexual revolution in the 60s and 70s and nuns everywhere were being liberated and struggling. Many of the nuns in my convent were falling in love with each other and with priests, so those of us who had a network of being able to share our struggles with one another were better off. I also did a lot of reading of the liberal theologians of the time, so it was an avenue of growth for me as well as great pain and struggle.

Did you become pregnant while in the convent? What was said or done?

One woman tells of her convent pregnancy; *a peer helped with the abortion.*

Five do not answer the question.

The rest say NO, and one adds:

> But I remember one sister who—she was in the infirmary, supposedly pregnant, with a pregnant-looking abdomen, but who knows? There was an awful lot of gossip, and who really knows whether she was pregnant or not? She could have had a tumor—that's what they said it was, and I prefer to believe the best.

Chapter VII: Sexuality

What did you think "Bride of Christ" meant?
Were you encouraged to fall in love with Jesus
as if He were a teen idol?

There have been acrimonious debates over the term "Bride of Christ". Once used everywhere, often in its full implied meaning (especially before Vatican II), in today's hindsight, "Bride of Christ" smacks of fantasy and pretending, reminding one of the few nun superiors who went over the line of reasonableness and talked love-starved candidates into *not* leaving by suggesting Jesus as an invisible boyfriend and the candidate as His true and secret bride. Regardless of the fact that many of the teen-children who came to convents in droves in the 50s knew little about the sex act beyond its correct biology, this same type of Superior encouraged them to satisfy their desires mentally, to sigh and be loved in their imaginations. Fortunately, there were many other superiors who did *not* preach this philosophy. Yet, in spite of its overtones, use of the term "Bride of Christ", now mostly used understood metaphorically, still lingers realistically in some places.

Both these questions are related in that candidates for the Religious Sisterhood who believed the second (Jesus as teen idol), usually were romantically attached to the term of the first (Bride of Christ). The reverse is not true.

Most of the participants were able to answer No to the question: WERE YOU ENCOURAGED TO FALL IN LOVE WITH JESUS AS IF HE WERE A TEEN IDOL? *Glad I escaped that at least,* said one. The idea of a lonely teen's being told to imagine Jesus as her boyfriend was disgusting to some:

That is sick!

I can't imagine buying such a presentation.

It didn't seem right.

Sounds sick to me!

That seems strange now.

Others considered the concept normal:

It seemed okay because He is our God and worthy of my love.

I felt okay about it.

I was married to Jesus. I didn't know anything else.

Those who had the infamous superior, tried to accept what they were told in the spirit of obedience, yet thought the idea confusing:

We were encouraged to think of Jesus as a wonderful idol and to give him all our love. I really tried to do that, but for most of those years, Jesus was not real to me—you know, I couldn't feel him or see him. I had a hard time with that. He wasn't somebody that personal, although I really gave it a try. I think I felt that I wasn't quite as holy as other people who seemed to have a direct line in that. I didn't share the fact that I didn't ever feel that, though, because I thought there was something wrong with me.

My Novice Mistress and retreatmaster insisted I think of Jesus as the teenage boy in my life. I was hesitant because, even though I was dying to love and be loved by someone, I realized that if I accepted this theory, I would be making up fantasies. Then if my relationship with Jesus was made up, what else was? Was any of this real or worthwhile? I was 15 years old.

As for the first question: WHAT DID YOU THINK "BRIDE OF CHRIST" MEANT? responses came in five categories, the second-largest of which held answers couched in romantic or pseudo-marriage terms:

It meant being the Beloved of Our Lord.

That Jesus was my special lover and friend.

That I was married to Jesus forever.

That I was His own, submissive.

I was His love slave.

He was my main love.

Jesus was my husband.

That Christ was my significant other.

Bride of Christ was what it meant literally, but it was never realized.

It meant we were the earthly brides of Jesus in the same way that others marry, except there was no physical touching or sex, not even in thought.

The next-largest group of replies (after "romantic") was service-related and spoke no-nonsensically of being dedicated to doing the work of Christ and the Church.

One person said she was: *A handmade (sic) of Jesus.*

Five considered "Bride of Christ" to be *a kind of jargon for "nun"*, or vow- and celibacy-related.

Three used the word "mystical" to describe the relationship of a nun with her God:
I had a mystical bond.

It was a mystical calling.

I believed that there was a mystical union between Christ and religious in that all of one's heart, time, and energy were spent in loving service. It did have a romantic slant to it, but being a virgin raised in a home where sexuality was not explained, my awareness of sexuality's ultimate expression was mirrored in the 50s movies, i.e., "The Kiss". I just figured I'd be a "kiss-less" bride!

Twenty participants did not reply to the question at all, two hadn't heard of it, and 5 called it an "old fashioned" term. The greatest number of answers were those including the words "special" and/or "chosen", e.g.:

I was His special servant and love

I was spiritually chosen to be close to God.

I had a special connection to Christ.

Christ chose me to serve him.

I was special.

I was chosen.

Christ had called me to stay very close to Him. I was special in His heart and He wanted me to group in His image in order to save my soul and help others to save their souls.

I was finally special for my connection with Jesus.

Everybody wants to be special to someone--that is completely normal. But when one's "specialness" is a tied to a decision involving hopes, dreams, and religious beliefs, e.g., a Vocation—which later turns out not to be in one's interests, does that sense of being "special" still reside in one's heart as she leaves the religious community? Most likely automatically and not right away. Because being a nun was such a deeply dedicated and religious determination, it commonly took tremendous effort and time for most ex-nuns to regroup their lives and personal resources after giving up the calling. To discover who they were and where they were going. (More in Chapter XI: Leaving). The whole concept of becoming the Bride of Christ, of having this relationship with Jesus, was the crux of being a nun in the first place. And who ever heard of divorcing Christ? Unless the marriage wasn't a real marriage in the first place—which would fall in line with the Catholic Church's view of divorce, namely, "annulment". But if the ex-nun *wasn't* married to Christ all those years, then what was she? And who was she when she left? These questions haunted the women who left convents, particularly in mid-century.

VIIII

THE WORLD
AS SEEN FROM THE CONVENT
AND VICE VERSA

convent's view, the public's view: then, now
school, degree, career
PR, newspapers, media, voting, advisory boards,
relatives, visitors,
pastoral relationships

Chapter VIII: The World As Seen From the Convent

Those Ubiquitous Knuckle-Rapping Nuns

Some years ago, this author, using a pseudonym—wisely, as it turned out, stated on an Internet message board (for Ethics and Values) that she was writing a book about ex-nuns, then posed this question: Did you know any nuns in the 50s, and what did you think of them— great, awful, or something in-between? The resulting hate-mail sent to her personally was shocking. How dare you write about God's women, wrote one. You have no right to spread scandal, said another. God will punish you for meddling where you do not belong, said one message. Notably, the majority of the letters mentioned The Nun Who Rapped My Knuckles in school. Some people were still angry about it, some bemused, others questioning as to how this knuckle-rapping came about. Risking still more verbal abuse, the author then asked the same message board specifically about knuckle-rapping theories. No one-fits-all reasons were suggested, so she spent the next two years querying nuns, ex-nuns, former students, priests who counseled nuns, psychologists, and anyone who would answer: Why do you think nuns rapped their students' knuckles up to the mid 1900s?

After much discussion and sifting through the possibilities suggested, the author offers this theory: Whether the public knew it or not, a goodly number of nuns in the mid-1900s and earlier were thrown into classrooms with no introduction, little or no training in the subject matter (no college degrees), and absolutely none on how to handle kids or what to expect. Then they were required to come up with impossible products, e.g., a chorus performance for some occasion in short order with only pieces of classtime to work at it. Many who had entered the convents as early as 14 years of age, found themselves in a few years assigned to teach a packed room of wiggly children who itched to test their distraction skills. These young nuns were unprepared academically, psychologically, and emotionally for the experience. In too many Orders, nuns in uncertified schools stayed there for years without getting their degrees. These women were concerned and often anxious about failing—not so much in state tests and gradings (there wasn't as much of that then), but in controlling the children, in having a quiet class—that counted for a lot in those days. It was upon making no waves that the teacher's reputation with the public and her Superior was built. Since these nuns knew nothing about the handling of large groups of children, many simply reverted, as did parents of children, to the way they themselves had been raised, i.e., "spare the rod and spoil the child". Spanking children was common at home and in school. Public schools used wooden paddles into the 60s. Wooden dowels called pointers sat on every chalkboard tray, and rulers were plentiful. It was easy to pick up one of these and rap the offending student on the knuckles, thereby psychologically and symbolically whipping the entire class into shape. After a while rapping knuckles became a habit, a tradition—it was accepted as well as common to rap a kid's knuckles. Many did it, expected it, and no one considered it "out of line". The possibility of harming the child or of his family's bringing a lawsuit against anyone was not even a concept, let alone a threat.

It is a historical fact that knuckle-rapping did happen, even often: denying that it existed will not make that fact go away. But the bottom line is, of course, that knuckle-rapping was not a good thing then, either, and merely theorizing about its origin does not excuse it. The author has heard of nuns who in this day have apologized for they way they treated their students in those days. Fear did strange things then as now.

Part of the reason that knuckle-rapping seems so foreign today, is that we in the early 21st century think of students (and everyone) on an individual, human basis. Not so, then. We consider each other's feelings and question where students' actions are coming from. As teachers, we have traded corporal punishment for reason and persuasion. We try to engineer change, to let it emerge from the student rather than forcing it upon him/her. Those of us who went to school or taught during the 1950s or earlier, remember the ambiance then; it was light years from today.

❖❖❖

Chapter VIII: The World As Seen From the Convent

Changing relationships: family

The families of new nuns understood as little about the convent as did the nuns themselves before entering. They knew what the habit looked like, that the candidate would most likely wear no veil during the Postulancy and a white veil during the Novitiate. They knew that there were Superiors who directed things, that the candidate might go to school and follow the order's occupation, e.g., teaching. They suspected that in the beginning, at least, the nuns slept in dorms and that they were silent part of the time. That they prayed in chapel.

As a rule, neither the families nor entering candidate knew that the new nun would not be telling what went on in the convent—this was strictly forbidden. Or that any gift she was given belonged to the community and she might never see it again—the individual owned nothing. Some families were irritated at the Postulant's referring to "our" umbrella, and even "our" habit—which she was wearing at the time. Neither families nor candidates had a clue about public humiliation/penances or flagellation/hairshirts or The Chapter of Faults. Increasingly, their lives diverged in spite of the monthly (at most) visiting hour.

How are you? Fine.   And you? Fine.

Then some smalltalk about siblings' football game or dance with a few meagre contributions by the nun such as: I helped in the garden this week. The lettuce is already coming up. Nothing personal, nothing that would normally bond a family together. Even if the young girl had previously been close to her family, she could not say, "I'm so lonely, Mom. Sister Chrysanthemum doesn't like me and she's always making me do Martyrology." By now, even their everyday vocabularies had changed.

All but 7 of those who answered this question: DID YOUR RELATIONSHIPS WITH PARENTS/SIBLINGS CHANGE AFTER ENTERING?

remarked on the convent policy of little contact or communication. A few lived too far (Alaska) for families to visit at all. *"I became part of a mysterious group,"* said one ex-nun. *"We were allowed to write only twice a year—Christmas and Easter,"* said another. Several had been disowned by their parents. *"We were told we had to leave the World, so I tried to distance myself,"* was another comment. Also, the convent changed the candidate by encouraging them to be *"rigid and distant, holier than usual."*

I hurt so much from the parting. My parents seemed to be heartbroken. I found it difficult enough to be treating them as outsiders as far as I was concerned, but when I had to tell them I couldn't even call them on the telephone, that I could never return to see them even if they were too ill to come to see me on the designated day-- I'd struggle with the inflexibility and dare I say inhumanity, of the rules. I was not permitted to offer my parents a glass of cold water on a sweltering day, nor a cup of hot tea when the temperature was forty below zero. I wanted to be kind to them, but it seemed impossible. I was determined to go on in this life I had chosen, urged on by this nun who said I had no courage. I was enough of an optimist to believe that things would improve with time. Perhaps the rules would bend or I would become more supple. DOROTHY

When I entered the convent, I was told we could not discuss our pasts. We were not to divulge our surnames or specifics about ourselves or our families. We were never to discuss friends or be allowed to communicate with them. We knew that correspondence with our families was only tolerated, as evidenced by the censoring of our letters home and the reading of the letters sent to us by our families. How could we be other than stilted with our loved ones when their influence and importance to us was daily being "weeded out" of us under the label of "worldliness"? I now cringe at the memories of myself seated, prim and proper, with hands—regulation-style—under the scapular as my loving Italian-American family tried to be at home with me. I, who was once the most demonstrative member of the family, now this stiff "nun". How bewildered they must have been! MARTHA

My family all admired me and I became this distant person, this model nun type of thing. It separated us and I had less and less meaningful contact with them.

Chapter VIII: The World As Seen From the Convent

The relationship became superficial and often falsely spiritual after that for many years. When I did come home, I was the token nun and everybody treated me like "the nun", so I didn't have any real relationships with the rest of my family for many years. It was most encouraged that that distance happened. Then my sister and I got together and discussed when I started having my crisis in religious life and she was having hers in her married life. We reconnected again and to this day she is my close soul-sister. But the rest of my family—it's been a hard relationship to reestablish because they never knew me beyond those young years. I am not a person to them, not a real person anymore. MARGARET

I remember not telling them or anyone about washing dishes at the table after meals. It seemed like a bizarre way to handle all the dirty dishes. We were told not to tell anyone about this. I probably did not say anything about the Chapter of Faults, either. JEAN-2

We weren't allowed to say much of anything about rules, and certainly not happenings except general stuff like making posters for feast days. So I mostly had on a frozen smile, waited out the time (as I'm sure they did) and went back to my other life for another month. DORIS

Once I had a severe sinus infection. The Superior finally took me to a "free" doctor who suctioned out current infected mucous. This went on for 6 weeks—every week I got suctioned. I couldn't breathe, sleep, or function. Finally I told the doctor that my mother was coming the next week and she would not understand why I was not well after suffering so long. He gave me an antibiotic and I was well by the time she got there. ROSE

Contact with the world:
news, radio & TV, books & magazines
voting, advisory boards

In all early-century Novitiates as well as a number of final professed groups, to read anything besides what was needed for class, one had to have specific permission from one's Superior. Books, magazines, newspapers, radio, and television were non-existent in many Novitiates. So how did history teachers survive? Several participants stated that the Superiors, old retired nuns, and history teachers were the only ones allowed to watch or listen to the news. It was presumed that other teachers would have no need of news of the world.

Of course, it must be remembered that in the mid-1900s there were no learning or science channels, no courses were taught on television (and there were no personal computers at all). Contrary to the PR about the "superior education in Catholic schools", most nuns knew very little about the real world or were capable of preparing students for making a living. In the days that they had attended college (if they did at all), it was considered best to have a liberal arts major. Few nuns specialized in any particular area of knowledge, e.g., physics or rocket science (although a nun-scientist was one of the first to examine the moon rocks). To learn merely for the sake of getting a job was beneath the dignity of "Real Education".

What about voting? In some communities where nuns voted, lists were posted of the "best" persons to vote for, according to someone(s) on the advisory board. Complete lists of the candidates and issues were not available. If asked to name those on the advisory board, most non-administrative nuns could not. Everything was passed down through the Superior, and there were no occasions when the lower-strata nun met or spoke to the advisors at all.

Twenty-eight answered Yes to the question: DID YOUR COMMUNITY HAVE ADVISORS, 23 said No, and 15 said they did not know for sure.

Chapter VIII: The World As Seen From the Convent

Financial and legal advisors met with the Council a few times a year, but not in the midst of the convent group—usually in the guest rooms. Those below the level of Superior had no need to know of their goings-on.

One thing the advisors did in our convent, at least, was to give us a list of whom to vote for. Neither they nor the Superiors said, You must vote for these people, but since we were not allowed to read newspapers or watch or listen to the news, the names on that short list were the only candidates' names we ever heard until we entered the polling box. Who else could we vote for? A few years after I left the convent, I was invited to represent women who had left the order in a panel on stage in front of the community. I brought up this voting list, stating my opinion that everyone had a right to choose her own candidates. So I was shunned during the break and from that point on—really, imagine, you go to pick up a cup of tea and everyone scatters as if you had the plague. Not even any eye contact. One nun my age who later left, passed me and spoke through her teeth, saying she was glad I'd brought it up, but that she couldn't be seen speaking to me after that. At the end I went to thank the Mother General for inviting me, and she turned her back on me without a word. Her Council members around her neither smiled nor spoke. I nearly broke into tears on the spot. It frustrated me to think that their meanness still bothered me even when I lived away from them. DORIS

Retreatmasters and the assigned chaplain were available to give advice in spiritual matters, but in the years after a Community started accepting suggested changes as a result of the hopes brought about by Vatican II, psychologists, counselors, and communications facilitators were also invited to give workshops to Community members.

Before drastic changes took effect, while most communities had banned newspapers, magazines, radio, and television from those in the formative years, a few older nuns took over the one black and white televisions and watched Lawrence Welk and game shows during recreation with special permission. Afterwards, it all loosened up.

We had to get permission for every book, but that permission was available. I left the Novitiate firmly believing that the only books I could read were spiritual ones. My Superior in Spokane introduced me to fiction. From that time one, I have read as much as I can. JULIANNE

So far as I know, the only place I saw a newspaper was in Seattle, and I believe the reading of newspapers or news magazines was restricted to Superiors and history teachers. I neither watched nor listened to the news. Part of me didn't want to anyway, but I believe it was strongly discouraged. TRACE

I am not ashamed to say that I took advantage of reading in college: if we were to read about a certain period of history, I also read biographies of persons from that time and some books that were written then. What I was supposed to read on my own only, were spiritual books—traditional, of course--none of that modern religious stuff! DORIS

One ex-nun who asked not to be quoted by name, told of her first day on mission in the early 1960s when she was sent by the Superior to the front hall to pick up the mail. She did so, and added the rolled-up newspaper to the stack, whereupon the Assistant Superior began yelling at her about not touching the newspaper, and made her set it down again. I wasn't reading it, the nun said, and the woman replied that the ban also extended to *touching* the newspaper without permission

In the later years of the century, as now, more Communities left reading, television, and gathering voter information to the discretion of the individual nun. Education was available in every area, and mingling with other students and lay persons encouraged.

My 1st Grade School Year

In my first grade school year I had a teacher named Sister Maryan. You see she was a nun and she was raised by the old Roman Cahtholic disapline. Witch in my opinion isn't the best for 1st graders. Even back then I had herendous behavior problems. I hadn't gotton my work done the day before and I was sent inside for my resess. I didn't really understand the concept of staying in so I went outside, she saw me and started chasing me. I thought it was a game. But, boy I'll tell you that nun could run. I ran up the plays structer with her fallowing. The bad part was that she broke her arm.

Education, Career, Jobs, Salaries

Generally, many nuns in the first half of the 1900s were not degreed. (See Charts: Jobs held before entering.) As soon as possible, they were put to work in classrooms or hospitals. Some finished their degrees later; others did not. Almost universally, however, during their canonical year (first year in the Novitiate wearing the white veil and full habit), Novices were not allowed to attend school except for theology classes taught in the Novitiate, either by a nun (academically qualified or not) or by a guest priest.

We were given weekly theology classes (non-credit) by either a Passionist priest (God help us!) or a Jesuit scholastic (thank you, God!). MARTHA

Even if they took no other college courses, nuns (especially during the formative years) were still able to audit theology classes taught (for credit or not) at the Motherhouse. Two ex-nuns who say they took no theology courses at all in the convent, 11 did not answer the question, and 6 say they don't remember, but most of the others who answered the question, completed several-to-many theology classes, the credit courses being taught by visiting nuns or priests from a variety of universities.

I had 28 theology extension course credits taught at the motherhouse by various people from a number of colleges. Not only did these courses not count for any degree, but it was embarrassing to list how many colleges I had "attended". DORIS

Five participants in this project did not attend a single college class during their convent years. Whether college courses were taken off or on the Motherhouse grounds (some Communities had their own colleges), all the others attended at least one college class during their convent years.

Chapter VIII: The World As Seen From the Convent

It appeared that those who had degrees came into the convent with them. Because we were a semi-cloistered congregation, none of us left the cloister except for medical appointments during the Novitiate. We were, however, given weekly classes (non-credit) by the one and only Sister who had a PhD. MARTHA

If my parents had paid the dowry, I think they would have let me study nursing. If you had money or a degree, you were one great person and got to have any expensive food or trips you wanted. But if you were a nobody, you got told so and couldn't even learn to drive a car. ELEANOR

Especially before the 1960s, when it was common to staff elementary school and high school classrooms with nuns who had either no college education, or very little of it, the nuns involved (and the state department) were told that they were "temporary" teachers; some remained that way until they left the convent many years later. Even today there are state-unaccredited Catholic schools staffed by non-certified personnel, who do not pay into retirement funds or Social Security—even for the degreed lay teachers who work there. Many mid-century nuns who staffed the classrooms during the day, took their college courses in weekend workshops and during the summer. Today, in most Communities, degreed education is considered a necessity.

When I left in 1965 after 20 years in the convent, I still needed 24 semester units for my Bachelor's degree. A Jesuit priest persuaded the Dean of a college in L.A. to let MARY (23 years in the convent) and me finish our requirements in our city, yet receive our degrees from the college in L.A. The Dean was removed in August of that year—I hope it wasn't because she helped us. LILLA

I attended college for many years on and off, but we were allowed to teach on a temporary certificate and get our training over the years that we taught. So between that and the fact that I was sent to various colleges during that time, it took me a little more than 8 years to get my bachelor's degree. MARGARET

At the end of my convent years when I went to leave, the Directress of Studies and the Mother General said the equivalent of Oh, my, she's been here 8 years and we haven't had her graduate yet—that looks bad. So they called the local college (run by another Order) and asked if they had a degree for the credits I had, and they said yes. But when I applied to the state (I had already been hired and was in the first week of teaching in another city), they refused to issue me a teaching certificate, saying that I needed 6 more weeks of student teaching. (I had already been teaching in the classroom for 3 years, and the college had verbally agreed that they would count that for student teaching.) So I had to write out checks from my salary to pay for a substitute teacher while I observed a French class (I was teaching general subjects in 7th grade) for 6 weeks in yet another school (run by yet another Order) where they did not let me teach except for one hour the day the college Supervisor was present. DORIS

Over half the women who answered the question (35 out of 63), had no say in choosing their college majors, minors, or colleges. Before Vatican II, most nuns had no say in many schooling decisions.

We were not allowed to pick our courses or majors/minors, let alone our colleges. I remember as a freshman (second year Novice), several of were sent to college on the first day of class with no papers or information, and merely told to see the Registrar. Our Community had given us the car, assigned the driver, given us black veils for the occasion and notebooks—so it's not like we were imagining that we were college students. Turned out, the Directress of Studies in our Community had neither registered us nor sent any information to the Registrar, who belonged to another Order. The Registrar chewed us out in the hallway in public for not having papers, but we simply weren't allowed to have the information; there was nothing we could do about it. We didn't even know our assigned majors. It was really embarrassing, all the girls passing by and watching us get lectured. DORIS

Twelve (out of 63 who answered) said their parents paid for their schooling, though most nuns were under the impression at the time that the nuns paid those bills since convents got free and reduced rates from the other religious Orders which ran the colleges. School supplies were paid for by the convents, except for some extras like a French dictionary (specifically mentioned). One ex-nun experienced an incident involving supplies. In her Community, the procedure was to put in a written request with the Directress of Studies, and the necessary class materials would be obtained.

One of the requirements for my design class was a little envelope of transparencies, available at any art store downtown, but I was neither allowed to buy them, nor to ask my parents for them, and the Directress kept putting off getting them. Every day in my college design class, the nun-instructor would harass me for not having the transparencies. I was the only nun in a room full of girls, but she knew I was a Novice (we wore regular black veils in public), and it was traditional to "build character" in Novices by giving them a hard time--even those not of the same Community. Not one of the few girls in my class with the same problem was treated as I was. Finally one day the teacher really blew, and I dripped a few tears on my work during the latter part of the period. She ordered me to stay after class, then shouted, "Just what do you expect me to do with you?" I was trying to speak, but my throat had this huge blockage from my trying not to cry. "What would you do if you were me?" she asked loudly. I remember that the door behind me into the hall was open, and I wondered how many persons were listening to this. For some reason, my courage rose and I said, "If I were in your place, I would try to understand." I re-explained the situation, which she sloughed off before she dismissed me. That night I struggled again as I stood before the Directress of Studies and again begged for the transparencies. She was irritated because I had asked her so many times, and was in no way impressed with the urgency of the situation. She said she'd get them when she got them, period. I again asked for permission to ask my folks to pick them up, but was refused. Though the instructor didn't yell at me as much or as loudly after that, it still took more than a week before I finally received the transparencies. DORIS

In the convents themselves, the daily Rule of Silence applied, more pervasively before Vatican II changes than afterwards. But for nuns who attended college during those early years, the general directive was to answer when spoken to, participate in class discussions, but not talk to instructors or college students outside of cases of necessity. Special permission from the Superior was needed in many Communities to study with anyone either in or out of the convent. Of the 55 who answered the question: Were you given enough time to study while you were attending college, 19 said No. Reasons given were:

We were always praying. JANE

Religious duties superseded. JAN, LOUISE, THERESE

Too busy doing dumb things! MARY

Too much prayer and manual labor. JANN

More important to pray and clean than to study. MERT

Regular early retiring time. KATE

I also taught full time and had to do papers. HOLLY, JULIANNE, THERESE-2

Between all the prayers and chores and regulated bedtime, studying wasn't considered important. One night in all those years I was allowed to stay up "late" doing a term paper, and I wildly worked on it without express permission until 3 a.m. We studied on the way to school (thank goodness I was quick and wasn't the driver). The evening before one set of final exams, we were told to spend our time cleaning the chapel. DORIS

About not speaking to other students on campus:

It fit logically in with "separation from the World". ANN

If I needed to talk or wanted to talk to someone, I did. My philosophy became: The only way to get a rule changed was to continually break it. GINA, DIANE

I always broke the rule ("breaking cloister") and was upset when I got in trouble. JANE, K.T.

Chapter VIII: The World As Seen From the Convent

That was a stupid, narrow regulation. CASEY   *It was dumb.* OTTER

It was as if the students could "contaminate" us. SARAH

I would have liked to get to know other students. NELL, DORIS

It was awful—we knew a lot of the girls and felt isolated from them. JAN-2, SARAH, MAE, LORNA, JEAN-2

It felt awkward. Strange. Embarrassing. Difficult. JULIA-2, CAROL, MARY S, CAROLYN, MARY-2

This was most difficult since friends from high school also attended that college. I accepted it as part of the sacrifice. THERESA

Fewer schools were teaching Latin in the 50s and 60s than in earlier years, yet 15 of the participants still took Latin in college. Twenty-one studied French at some point, six Spanish, five German, and one each Russian and Tagalog. Of all these, only 3 completed enough foreign languages courses to count as a minor. Some took the courses as a *requirement for a degree*, one because she *entered a French Order*, and one studied Spanish before she became an *instructor in the Philippines*.

Among many Catholics who lived through the mid-1900s, it was common knowledge that nuns worked for no salary. Whatever small sum was paid to the Community (and it was small, since the parish provided housing), was divided between the Motherhouse and the mission and used for necessities. In the 1970s and later, nuns procured their own jobs, not necessarily in their Order's schools, and different arrangements were made about salaries depending on the Order, and on whether the nun paid for her own housing.

(See also Chapter XVII: Notes, for chart about pre-convent jobs)

❖❖❖

Nuns' relationships with the Pastor

Though this was not a question in the survey, several nuns offered their opinions verbally. All agreed that it was unjust that the priest be considered the final word and head of the school, when he usually had no experience or degree in education, whereas even the un-degreed nuns had plenty of experience. No one in those days mentioned the "women and glass ceiling" thing, but it was implied. Women did not and do not care for men who try to rule their lives.

In spite of the resentment about his being top administrator, some nuns had personal relationships with priests, as they did with other persons (see Chapter VII: Sexuality). Most of those nuns without interest in the pastors, looked the other way.

On my first mission, I was shocked that the Superior was so witty and sweet to the Pastor until the door barely closed behind him, upon which she and others of her rank criticized and complained loudly about what they had a few moments ago praised. What bothered me most about this Jekyll-Hyde behavior was not knowing exactly what I was getting into, since obviously, one couldn't tell by the words/actions that were going on. DORIS

IX
LIABILITIES

treatment in convent by superiors
vocation doubts, threats of loss
tension, fear, sadness,
injustices, prejudice, racism

Racism, Prejudice, Injustice

In the mid-1900s before the phrase "civil rights" became everyday language, life on the surface was peaceful: whites had all the rights, and nobody talked about the rest of the people. It was also that way in the convent—the subject of rights (the nuns themselves had none, to speak of), treatment of ethnic minorities, or even interest in anything but mainstream white culture—these were non-issues. Looking back at possible racism in those years, it would be unfair to categorize one's referring to an African-American person as a "Negro", as politically incorrect or disrespectful. "Negro" in those days *was* a respectful term; "politically correct" was coined in the late 1900s. Even some folk who considered themselves respectful of blacks, called them "niggers" (a term they had grown up taking for granted)—though in a polite tone of voice. Americans were just not as careful or cognizant 50 years ago of the potential hurt in the terms they were used to. Prejudices were more easily passed on through generations without re-examination. When called on a disrespectful term, one's genuine reaction was likely to be: Who, me? What did I say? I've heard that all my life, from my parents and their parents. Why is it wrong all of a sudden?

For these reasons, it was complicated for the participants in this project to look back and identify racism or prejudice. Either things were going smoothly, or they weren't—terms themselves had nothing to do with it. The one criterion for prejudice was a disrespectful, putting-down attitude toward anyone. Nuns were supposed to be, above all, Christ-like, accepting and loving every human being regardless of color. However, they, like the rest of mankind, were also imperfect creatures. Most nuns in this survey had (by 1950) never had occasion to meet or speak to anyone of another race, had been raised with commonly accepted prejudicial and judgmental racial stereotyped attitudes, and were less aware that these were wrong then, than are those of us who lived through the borning of the Civil Rights Movement, attended anti-discrimination lectures and rallies, and most of all, deal daily with human beings of many ethnic groups.

Eighteen women said they noticed racism in their Orders at that time; 48 said they did not—although some qualified their answers with the fact that their convent and most of their schools were only one race—white.

The one example of racial prejudice was a nun who called little black children "dirty little niggers". LILLA

In the early 60s, the high school in which I was a teacher drew students from all over the city, surrounding towns, and the suburbs. There were no Blacks. The Administration decided to set up scholarships to help integrate the school. Three Black students were admitted that year. I couldn't believe how some of the teachers treated them. They set grades for them before they even taught them, they singled them out in class for misconduct, they ridiculed them in front of other students. The Vice-Principal, while carrying on a friendly chat with some seniors who were out of uniform, physically grabbed one of the Black students by the arm and scolded her for not wearing her uniform. We had a real challenge to face when that student set a fire on the stage in the auditorium. JULIANNE

The racism I felt in the Community was primarily associated with old style attitudes by the establishment. In 1965 I worked with our Sisters teaching at an inner city school, and was very happy with these progressive women. There was more racism taking place at our school in Africa. ANNE

The only racism I knew of was a fellow teacher (in her 70s) who did not want to teach "those niggers", as she called them. This was in 1957. I happily took her mixed race and black children into my classroom. I think those were the first black children I'd seen. To me, "nigger babies" were a licorice color. I was more familiar with Indians, having seen them in their beautiful buckskin garments when I was small. TRACE

Racism made me furious. PRISCILLA

Racism was too much tolerated in those days. School boundaries were gerrymandered to keep blacks out of certain high schools. ELLEN

Chapter IX: Liabilities

I was aware of it, and it made me ashamed. SUZANNE

It was embarrassing. HELGA

I purposely taught tolerance to the students in our high school. THERESE

We had our first "Negro" novice—she had to have a waiver to be admitted. DONNA

When I was at the Indian Mission, some thought I was an Indian and treated me inferiorly. At the end of the year, I told them I was just a white Wyoming girl. LORENA

The kinds of prejudice most practiced resulted from meanness, not ignorance. Those put down were (according to the participants in this project) of "lower" occupations, other religions, a lesser economic class, did not come from the country of the Order's origin, were not of the "elite" nun class (see Chapter V: Peers), were married (a "lesser" Vocation) lay persons, the less-educated, homeless, or had illnesses and lack of social skills. Even those lower in rank on the same mission, were, on occasion, treated poorly for that reason alone.

There was this superior attitude that Catholics belonged to the "one, true church" and others were heretics. JEAN-2

Catholics were superior. CAROL-2

Prejudice was against non-Catholics or more "lax" nuns. CASEY

There was a prejudice against anyone who disobeyed Church law. DORIS

I'm not aware of any prejudices of that time except those fostered by the R.C. Church, e.g., there was only one way to go to heaven—elitism. GAYLE

The laity was considered spiritually inferior by implication; nuns had the highest calling. BEVERLY

Prejudice? Only against lay people and other religious Orders. ANN

Our Order was world-wide and pretty tolerant. EILEEN

The lowest in rank were treated poorly, especially on mission. ELIZABETH

Lay Sisters, trained to do the cooking and housekeeping, were not educated. These Sisters really were in a sub-class, looked down on by some. I certainly did not agree that they should be treated differently, but there were actually some rules and practices which we were to follow, which set them apart. JULIANNE

Prejudice? Looking down on the cook Sisters. CONNIE

I don't remember any—maybe the treatment of the non-teaching Sisters as second class citizens. JULIA

There was prejudice against blacks, Hawaiians, and Mexicans. THERESE

Against the shiftless poor. LORENA

Three said they bought into the prejudice, one said she did *"at that time"*. Five said they remember no prejudice in their Community, and 12 said they were unsure. Fifty women did not answer the two questions about agreeing with and practicing prejudice.

I thought acting prejudiced was stupid, especially when one was to obey just for the kicks of the Superior. MARY

It made me feel rotten and angry. ELLEN

I did nothing—I was in no position to do anything about anything. DONNA

Chapter IX: Liabilities

I went along with the program. ANN

It was unChrist-like, and I tried to counteract it. LORENA

I felt prejudiced against, myself—I was always struggling with grades. DIANE

The family that I thought I would find in the convent was not there most of the time. I wrote poetry and essays, and inspired students to write for a magazine— this was an outlet for my need to change the world. They wrote against racism and every kind of prejudice, but I could not share with them the injustices that were meted out to me. DOROTHY

Tension, Fear, Injustice, Unhappiness, and the Use of Guilt

Every job, home, family, and group of any kind has its own peculiar sources of tension and fear. This discussion begins with the question: What irritated you most in the convent? Of the 65 who answered, six categories emerged: unkindness, put-downs, and better-than-thou attitudes by Superiors or older nuns, (20), having to do with Rules (14), lack of being treated as an individual (13), poor treatment specifically by Superiors (9), and things resulting from the dynamics of living in community (9). As in every subject and chapter of this book, there were overlaps, e.g., a Rule over-emphasized by a Superior to the point of totally squelching one's individuality, could be listed under any of the above categories.

My belief system conflicted with rules that didn't make sense. CONNIE

Rules that didn't make sense. Meaningless rituals. DIANE, GAYLE, CASEY

Too many restrictions. The complete lack of freedom—mental and physical. BEVERLY, DONNA, JULIA-2

So many ridiculous permissions which seemed like a perfect waste of time: changing one's underwear, cleaning one's clothes, taking a bath, throwing away an old toothbrush and asking for another, etc. Common sense seemed to have vanished forever. DOROTHY, KATE

Having incoming and outgoing mail opened and read. ANN

One might say, if the nuns didn't like the rules, why were they there---they shouldn't have entered in the first place. But the truth is that _no one_ who entered the convent in those days was *ever* told what they were getting into. Not even by a relative who was already a nun in the same Order. Nuns were forbidden to speak of such things with outsiders, and until one became a nun, one was an outsider. It seemed to be a perfect setup—once the candidate became a nun, she couldn't complain to anyone or stop anyone else from entering by telling. The nun herself stayed because she had a Vocation and to deny that could place her eternal happiness in jeopardy. Stories were told in the Novitiate of nuns who left and had terrible things befall them, or who were never happy again. These, like the scare stories about biting the Host in Communion, usually "happened" to someone whom no one in the present group personally knew. (For an exception, see Chapter XI: Leaving.) As quickly as the habit changes, though, once nuns in *your* class left and weren't obviously punished by God—in fact, seemed *happy*, more and more women left this life where they had become less important than the institution or its Rules.

Not being considered as, or treated as, an individual human being was at the heart of most dissatisfaction, regardless of how it was stated. For example, irritation at *seeing people hurt*, though listed under "unkindness", really is a result of poor treatment of the individual nun. Specific complaints against individual treatment mirror some of the greatest tensions:

WHAT LITTLE THINGS CAUSED TREMENDOUS TENSION?

Unfortunately, I do not see these things as little, although in the minds of some, they might have been. The schedule we were expected to follow was very stressful. Every minute was taken, so much so that I frequently could not find time to go to the bathroom. By the end of my Postulancy, I began to suffer physically. JULIANNE

I couldn't stand the constant humiliation, of being put down. ELIZABETH, OTTER, JEAN-3

It was hard trying to be good all the time, not having an outlet for normal anger, and not learning any skills to dissipate normal community-living frustrations. MARGARET, GAYLE

I disliked not being allowed to make my own decisions, being treated like a child, and having a   Superior have total control over my life. JAN, BEVERLY, DIANE, LORNA

These things caused tension: not being able to talk when I needed to share or get support, not being able to eat when I was hungry, not knowing where I would be working the next year, not being able to see (except rarely) nuns I wanted to have as friends. JEAN-2

Being given assignments I was not qualified for, had no training for. HELGA, EILEEN

Never being given enough time for what I was told to do. MERT, CAROL-2

Not being trusted. Criticisms. The checking on your private place/cell. ELEANOR, CAREN, DIANE, NANCY

Having to wear the headdress even when it caused ear infections. TRACE, DORIS

Being treated by parishioners as a non-person—put on a generic pedestal. JEAN-2

Unkindness to oneself (and to others) by convent women brought up sharp complaints:

I was irritated by fake people, sanctimonious old biddies. JULIA

By certain nuns who acted like superior beings and received extra privileges. GRACE

By unkindness to anyone. Seeing people hurt. Lack of charity. Bossiness. FRANCES, ELLEN, ROSE, LORENA

By jealousy, petty nonsense, unnecessary suffering. ELLEN-2, MURIEL, JAN-2, DOLORES, MARY-2

By Sisters who seemed jealous and were critical. In communal life you can't escape them. NELL

Pettiness, emphasis on Rule rather than the spirit, resistance to change. THERESE

Injustice, favoritism, unspoken expectations, lack of appreciation, thoughtlessness toward others, unwillingness to share the workload, unequal treatment of some. JULIANNE

Often, Superiors were the conduits by which nuns were irritated. Specific complaints about them:

Favoritism. GINA, JULIA, DORIS, MARY, JANN, THERESE, THERESA, MAE, HELGA

The uppity attitude of the Superiors. JANE

Superiors who spied on us or had favorites. Her dislike of me. JANN, JEAN-3

By the Superior's constant nagging, watching and judging. SARAH, THERESE-2

Superiors that humiliated me in front of lay persons, made bad decisions and insisted I abide by them, ordered me to do things that made me look dumb to the outside world. DORIS

By Superiors who put off or delayed requests. NELL

Then there were the usual hazards and expected irritations from human beings living together in a close situation: *perfectionists, personality conflicts, physical traits (like constantly clearing her throat that drove us nuts), noisiness and pettiness, dull conversationalists* (no practice), and other annoyances. *Meanness, jealousy,* and *using rank* as leverage was also present. In those days there was no training in anger management or assertiveness, let alone in living with difficult people. One simply made the best of it.

Some people seemed to get their way a lot because they did know how to manipulate. (See Chapter X: Peers.) *Everybody kind of tip-toed around them because they didn't know how to deal with that.* While these persons got what they wanted, some of us non-assertive persons (including myself) would be sent wherever we were needed, whether we wanted to be there or not. It caused very great tension to live with difficult people, not having the skills of knowing how to communicate that acceptably and work things out. So we lived with tremendous tension, being afraid to hurt someone's feelings or walk over somebody, and I, being the great enabler, would try to make everything right with the other people, in the meantime, feeling all of this stuff in my own self. Crying comes to mind as a tension-reliever, as did writing in my Dear Jesus Little Journal. MARGARET

There were some old cranky and ornery nuns—really bitchy. MARY

Some older nuns specialized in meanness and critical remarks. LILLA

Other nuns were always trying to order me around. JEAN-3

They could ask you to do something for them, but you couldn't ask them for help. ELEANOR

The non-assertive, non-elite nuns either *tried to ignore the tension*, or *pray it away*. For some, this resulted in *ulcers*, for others, more serious problems (see Chapter XI: Leaving). Some took refuge in their students, concentrating on them and enjoying them whilst pushing their own problems into the background. In the later years, nuns were allowed to speak to their friends, to go to their cells/rooms and rest, or to take a walk, but earlier, one either went to chapel, one's classroom,

Chapter IX: Liabilities

or the library. There was no privacy then, though that did not stop some from crying.

Of the 56 women who answered the question: WHAT WERE SOURCES OF FEAR? 3 said None, and 7 said they did not remember; 11 did not reply at all. Thirty said their fears were related to approval of their Superiors and/or not being accepted for vows. Two feared *having to spend the rest of my life in a convent*. One each mentioned *fear of dying, losing a friend, the implications of a PF, family problems, "stealing" food,* and worrying about the unknown *cold war status.* Three said they feared *being yelled at or scolded for something I didn't feel was wrong.* And eight feared an unknown future, such as:

Going unprepared into the classroom, keeping silence. JANN

I was always afraid, I'm not sure of what—probably of failure, but I don't know what. Afraid somebody was going to be mad at me or something. CAROL

Lack of confidence made me afraid that I didn't have the ability to do certain things. EILEEN

I was afraid of doing something wrong, having people think badly of me, of not being the perfect good little girl. And then in those early pre-Vatican II days, wanting to do whatever God wanted you to. I wasn't living. I don't remember specifically being afraid of going to hell, but I must have, because I really did think in those old ways. I feared the Superior. I never did anything in those pre-awareness days before I started questioning, but I was afraid of being in disfavor with the Superior or my parents. MARGARET

Criticism and what it produced: I came to the Novitiate with a fairly stable self-image. I was gifted, fairly intelligent, healthy, friendly, self-disciplined, and hardworking. Within the first few months I discovered that my gifts were not important. My grades slipped to average because of the study program, and I was relegated to Novitiate classes while others began college on campus. I developed the headaches, which were regarded as emotional, therefore, my responsibility. Having friends was held as suspect, and my self-discipline and hard work was expected as the norm. Add to this the constant watching in order to correct us for the slightest insignificant infractions—and I was placed in a constant state of fear. I had considered my mother a disciplinarian; she was an angel along side of what some Superiors put us through prior to Vatican II. Asking for what I needed—if I hadn't needed it, I wouldn't have asked, but there was the constant possibility that I would be refused for some "high religious motive", and then what would I have done? I frequently went without, rather than asking. It took me a long time to realize that I was not going to be refused, however, I resented being questioned about my reasons for asking in the first place—they seemed pretty self-evident to me. JULIANNE

One of the ways fear/guilt was used most often, had to do with loss of Vocation. Vocation was a considered a direct calling from God, no matter whether the candidate recognized it first, or whether a nun told her about it. To deny one's Vocation was serious, and it was not uncommon to be taught that this would lead to Hell. When a candidate entered the convent under this apprehension, being threatened with "You'll lose your Vocation" had great effect. Nearly everyone at one time or another, whether directly told or not, feared dismissal from the Order. It happened that a lot of very good women were dismissed unjustly from their Communities (see Introduction and other chapters).

When asked, WAS "YOU'LL LOSE YOUR VOCATION" EVER USED TO KEEP YOU IN LINE? 25 out of the 67 who answered, said definitely Yes. Forty-two said they were not told that.

Always. CASEY

We were told that if we didn't follow rules, for example if you didn't get up at the first sound of the bell, "You do not have a Vocation". SUZANNE

Oh yeah, they made us worry a lot about losing our Vocation. Now that I look back, I think it was a hilarious threat. CHERRY

When I associated with an outside, I was warned that I could lose my Vocation. CAREN

Chapter IX: Liabilities

If prayer and meditation were not performed daily. SARAH

When I wanted permission to go and do something extra. ELEANOR

It was a constant reminder to keep the rules, to remain detached from lay people, to strive for perfection, or I'd lose my Vocation. Of all the Sisters in final vows who left our Order, all (sic) were held up for ridicule as "having lost their Vocations" because they didn't keep the spirit of their vows, or became too friendly with lay people who lured them away. We were told that if we faithfully kept our Vocations until death, the Church Fathers claimed our families would be saved down to the 4th generation. We were told that if we lost our Vocation, we would have a terribly hard time saving our souls. I don't know if all my friends were told exactly the same thing, because we had different Novice Mistresses, and at times, different Superiors. However the loss of our Vocations by infidelity was stressed to each of us. Every Superior stressed it. LILLA

It was mentioned on a daily basis in the Novitiate. ELIZABETH

I was told that whenever I talked about secular life. ELLEN-2

Particularly in the Novitiate. ROSE

When I was not praying. MARIE

I'm not sure my Superior thought I had a Vocation. BEVERLY

I had already lost it, and the Superiors would not let me go. K.T.

WHAT WOULD HAPPEN IF ONE DID "LOSE ONE'S VOCATION? Of the 49 who answered, 20 said they would fail grievously or go to Hell. Twelve said they didn't think they'd lose their Vocations, so did not consider the consequences. Thirteen said merely, I'd leave; and 3 weren't sure what would happen. One said:

Nothing would happen, but they tried to make us believe that we had divorced Christ. MARY

I'm sure the fear of being dismissed because I did not measure up to the expectations, added to my stress level. JULIANNE

My folks would be devastated. JULIA

I would have failed at what God wanted me to do. SARAH

I wanted to leave as a postulant, but the Mistress told me a story of one who did leave and who had a life of unhappiness afterwards, implying that this might happen to me. JEAN-3

Before final vows we got lots of horror stories about nuns who were tormented the rest of their lived by losing their Vocations. I recall a real feat of not measuring up. JEAN-2

I thought of myself as an "un-nun", like uncola. JULIA

Nobody threatened me—I used to think Yes, I would like to leave, then I would daydream about somebody telling me, Well, we think you should leave the convent. Then I could leave without having a guilty conscience. So I didn't have a fear of being told—I wished I would be told. MARGARET.

Yes, I was threatened with leaving after the second time I was sent to the state hospital. The board there told me I would never be completely well unless I left the convent. They tried to make my leaving a condition for release from the hospital. But since I was technically self-committed, they could not enforce it. The Mother General told me that if I didn't straighten up and stop getting sick to my stomach that she would commit me for life. She actually did commit two others. She also ordered one Sister to undergo a lobotomy. She did and was never the same person afterwards. So I knew her threat was good. She used to keep me kneeling in her office for as long as an hour at a time while she lectured me and told me what a terrible sinner I was and how useless I was to the Community. I was forced to write to her once a week from mission and declare in writing that I was keeping the rule and had not vomited that week. LORENA

Personal Injustices, Dealing with Unhappiness

Injustices? I tried not to remember them. I want to forget the past and move on. ELIZABETH

Forty-eight out of the 66 women who answered the question, tell of personal injustices, especially some that still rankle. Eighteen women said No, they did not undergo any injustices.

I was put into a position other than teaching, and my Superior would not allow me to do the things I felt were necessary and important in order to do a good job. What bothered me the most was that students were involved, and I could not administer to them as I felt necessary. It was very unfair to the students as well as very frustrating to me. HELGA

When I asked to leave, I was assigned to work alone in the stacks for what turned out to be a whole year of complete separation from the Community, spent in complete silence and without communal recreation. They said later they had "lost" my papers. JAN

While ill and recuperating from the illness, I was given no consideration. GRACE

I did student teaching in the 7th grade with a nun who was mentally and physically ill, but she was well esteemed in the Order. She forced me to teach subjects she hated, which were the ones I knew nothing about. There were no textbooks and I had to write out word for word the entire lesson in, e.g., history. She forced me to teach math concepts I didn't understand. She left the classroom often and I couldn't handle the kids. I was scared to death. Finally, 2 weeks before the time ended, I got to work in 3rd grade and at least use a manual. I knew the nuns talked behind my back; I felt insecure and stupid for the next 3 years. I'd finish my school year, then have to finish the last 2 weeks for a nun who had a breakdown. Then I'd teach 2 weeks of vacation school, do 6 weeks of summer school, then wait anxiously every August 15th to see where I'd be sent the next year. JANN

Accusations of lesbianism ruined three of us, and there never was a way to right the wrong. MERT

Once when I was afraid to do the wrong thing, so I did nothing, my Superior said I "didn't have the brains of a cat". ROSE

I was a convert to Catholicism and there was a lot I didn't understand. My Novice Mistress put me through a lot to test my faith. ELLEN-2

Finally I can laugh at some incidents, but we were never supposed to explain or stick up for ourselves. Being accused unjustly and having to remain silent hurt deeply. LILLA

I was living in a convent for 6 months experience and denied recreation. CAREN

My health needs were delayed. JAN-2

I believe I was treated unjustly when I returned to secular life, in that I was not given the necessities for starting life over. My sister dyed some material for me and went with me to buy one pair of shoes—I don't remember having anything else, and don't believe any money was given me. It seems to me that justice, if not charity, would have indicated that more was needed. (See Chapter XI: Leaving.) TRACE

    I had lived with my great-aunt (whom I saw as my only grandmother) for 17 years. She died when I entered the convent, and as a Postulant, I was not allowed to attend her funeral. HOLLY

    While I was studying for my Masters Degree, I asked for permission to try for a scholarship for a PhD, but was told that I was "too old" (I was 31) to pay back the Community with my labor. It had taken me 10 years to earn my first degree— while I taught school. I felt I could have been given the chance. THERESE

    My Novice Mistress belittled me using erroneous statements, but because of her rank, was able to "put me in my place". I tried hard to make conversation with her in group situations, but nothing I ever said was right or adequate. SARAH

    Because I would not spy on the young Sister students, I was denied an M.A. LORENA

    The Mistress of Novices treated me and about 15 others like dirt. OTTER

    At one mission, as I first entered the door, the Superior said, What are you doing here? She had it in for me, putting me down constantly. JEAN-3

    My mentor had asked me to write an article, reminding me that in the spirit of the Order, it would be printed anonymously. She claimed the article as her own. (Other examples listed.) There were countless contrived snubs or humiliations set up to embarrass me. I felt a network of spies around me, and knew I wasn't mistaken when I'd be interrogated by my Superiors. DOROTHY

    After working in the Infirmary for a year, I was named as Infirmarian at the local mission to which I was assigned. There was one Sister in that large group who was known for being demanding and unbearable. One morning, when she was ill, I took a tray to her as I'd been told, but she threw me out, whereupon I went to the Superior and said I would not do anything more for that nun, that she was intolerable. My position as Infirmarian was given to someone else. The injustice was the fact that that nun controlled the situation and that nobody, especially the Superior, would do anything about it. JULIANNE

One particular incident involved the rule about contact with families. While I was a Postulant, we were not allowed to use the telephone at all. That year, my grandfather died. My mother called and really wanted to talk to me to tell me about it and to share her grief with me, but she was not allowed. I was not allowed to talk to her, and I felt that was particularly unjust because it affected the family in an unfair and harsh way. K.T.

The list of injustices done to me would fill a book. I used to wonder if there was something about me that attracted bad things. Someone who left the convent after I did, said the nuns were jealous of my talents, though I didn't see mine as being greater than anyone else's. I was criticized and judged, shunned and forbidden to speak to my friend, sent to teach without any training (like many other nuns), and had many other specifically cruel things perpetrated upon me—some of which are spoken of in the answers to other questions in this survey. It took years of therapy before I could accept myself as being of intrinsic worth. DORIS.

Being torn out of familiar and comforting surroundings so soon after my mother's death was unfair and insensitive to me. I can hardly think about it without a residue of anger, still. I had an exceptional class. At Christmas they got together and bought me a huge set of Waterford glasses, which I never got to see used—I knew that gifts belonged to the whole convent. What I enjoyed most about this great class was that they that sopped up all the knowledge I gave them about anything creative—classical music, art, poetry, role playing. I encouraged them a lot and they responded beyond what other classes had. Teaching in that town had made me feel closer to my mother's memory. JEAN-2

There definitely was a power structure although that was not a part of our philosophy, and everybody parroted that we were all living equally in this life. The power lineage came from the German lineage, and then there was the outsider group. In the 60s and 70s we started to see that and to accuse and openly name the injustices that occurred. But the independent living situations let individual freedom within the community become abusive for some people. Those with access to money or monied friends could act in certain coy ways to get money for their pet projects or for whatever they wished, and nuns who didn't have that skill, didn't get that. I was one of those people who didn't know how to manipulate the system enough to provide for my own set of social concerns. So finally I just woke up to the fact that it's the same within the convent as outside. MARGARET

Sixty-one women participants answered the question: IF YOU WERE UNHAPPY, WAS YOUR UNHAPPINESS EVIDENT TO THOSE YOU WORKED WITH? Thirty-two said Yes, including those who qualified: *only to closest friends, perhaps, probably,* and *sometimes.* One said, *I can't really say I was ever unhappy* (MAE). Twenty-five said No, including qualifiers: *don't think so,* and *not sure how people saw me.* The three main ways others discovered a nun's unhappiness were: 1) she told them, 2) she cried a lot, and 3) her *demeanor, facial expression, weight loss* and *illness.*

I do not know how many times someone has said to me, Smile! when I thought I was. Also, I am not sure that during this time even I thought about being unhappy. TRACE

The last years, I was either crying or on the verge of it most of the time. DORIS

I couldn't hide my unhappiness—I am one of those people who can't hide my real feelings or put on a false front, as far as being happy. MARGARET

In the early years, I was so very diligent about observing the Rule of Silence, custody of the eyes, arms in sleeves, etc., that I didn't smile much—we weren't supposed to. Then all of a sudden one day, the Superior made a point of telling me that I should smile more—was I sad? I didn't tell her how much I wanted to leave, so just thanked her and got on with trying to smile more. MARY-2

I worked as an assistant to a wonderful Sister once, and I told her how unhappy I was with the Superior and with the other Sisters whom I felt treated our girls harshly or unfairly. MARTHA

When I was trying to leave, 2 other nuns saw me walking in my sleep. DONNA

I noticed the unhappiness of others and I was very quiet. LILLA

All of us had a hard time with the Superiors. NELL

The Mother Superior saw that I cried a lot, refused to open up to her, and was becoming forgetful. BEVERLY

When they noticed I was unhappy, I was reprimanded and sent to the state hospital. LORENA

During the worst year, as I approached the door that was being held for me by a nun at school—we were the only two around, I wondered whether I dared say anything since I was dying for empathy and comforting, and she was a kind woman. I could not stop my eyes from filling with tears. But I knew there would be more trouble if I said anything because she was a nun of another Order, so I said nothing, though I could tell from the reflected hurt in her eyes as we passed, that she knew I was suffering and was sorry. That was one of the rare times I felt cared about that entire year. DORIS

DID YOU GET ALONG WITH MOST SUPERIORS? Fifty-seven out of 65 said Yes, though 11 qualified their answers with: *some, a few, half of them,* etc. Eight said No, they did not get along with most Superiors.

One said, *They were wonderful women.* (NELL) One called them *compassionate* and said they *listened.* (JULIA-2) Others explained their "getting along" by: *I was respectful,* obedient, cooperative, docile, I do not like conflict, I gave them no trouble, I was non-confrontive, subservient, agreeable, I didn't want them angry with me, I was conscientious, I was afraid of them, I conformed, I had vowed obedience, I was suitably humble, anxious to please them, I felt I had to, I was a "good" nun, I was malleable, and I kept anger inside.

I got along beautifully with my first Superior—she was a bright and cheerful woman. She was followed by a Superior who was mercurial and had manic depressive traits. We had a rocky relationship which found my lips to the floor quite often. MARTHA

I was told that I might become a Superior, and it frightened me because I knew I could never treat Sisters the way Superiors were expected to treat them. There was also a money contention between the Bishop and our Order--we had collected donations that exceeded our needs. Because I knew this, I was threatened by one of the Superiors to never tell anything about convent life, or my soul would be in peril. This sounds like a soap opera, I know, but maybe others have also been threatened about losing their souls if they told "convent secrets" and my telling will offer them a kind of support. LILLA

If you didn't go along with your Superior, you didn't get much help to get your work done. ELEANOR

I did not get along with my Superiors, but neither did I come into conflict with them. I kept my thoughts to myself (probably sometimes even from myself) and was externally conformist for the most part except on rare occasions when the stupidity of certain things was a last straw. I suspect that most Superiors knew I did not fully buy the program. ANNE

Two Sisters left the Order and the Superior spread such lies about them that we were aghast. One of them could not find a job and the Community had not succeeded in filling her high school position, so she came back to the convent to visit and to request her old job. She was told to get out of town because she was a scandal to the Community. We were very distressed about this since most of the Community had welcomed her back with open arms. That evening the "saintly

Superior" was praying at our Community house meeting, "O Christ, come to us and be with us, etc." I spoke up afterward and said, "How can you ask Christ to come to us, when He did come in the person of our former Sister and you told Him to get out of town because He was a scandal to us?" I was reported and had to go 7 times before higher Superiors to answer charges. Each time I was asked, "Did you say that? Did you mean that? Would you do it again?" I answered in the affirmative. LORENA

"Got along with"—yes. "Liked"—no. The few I had treated me like the bottom of the heap. There never was anyone lower, no matter if there were 12 persons on that mission. I felt like I had to shut up and take it to make up for having been sent away to study 2 years, like it was something I did wrong and now had to atone. Like no one in the Order had any motivation to like me or even treat me like a human being. Like I was lucky they even let me live there and work for them (for no pay, remember). I got very depressed on my last mission and used to cry in chapel. A couple of times the Superior used to "happen" to be there watching me while I struggled and strangled my sobs, trying not to shake visibly. When I walked out, it was still dark, so I didn't worry about her seeing my face. Once I went to her room thinking I might talk about it, but I started to cry. When I put my arms out for a hug, she pushed me away. I knew then that there was no hope for happiness there. Problem was, I thought I had to stay unless God Himself came and let me out. DORIS

I usually got along in those earlier years because I played deference to them. I was afraid, I needed to respect them and they demanded it. They were considered God's representative, and so of course I tried to get along with them. Years later I was going through a delayed adolescent growing spurt and I did hold Superiors, in my mind, as along with all Superiors through out the country, as being responsible, and I was critical of them. I did eventually become more confrontive, and I still am. MARGARET

I was a conformist for many years, but I had been trained to respect persons in authority. I also had a basic fear of them, which I did not start getting over until I was about 27. Some of the Superiors were wonderful women whom I respected

Chapter IX: Liabilities

and appreciated, and who treated me like an adult. The others, I lived around, did what I was told and avoided them except when necessary. JULIANNE

Mostly I tried very hard to be obedient and follow the rules. Towards the end of the time I was in the convent, they were closing down a local house and another nun had been sent to help pack, etc. She made friends in the community, and with an 8th grade boy who was too ill to attend school—she befriended and spent time with him. The Superior decided she did not want that nun to stay, and the nun came to me and cried in grief because that was the third convent she had been in that year. And so I took it upon myself to approach each of the other Sisters and the Superior and say, "Couldn't we in Christian charity allow her to stay, since she so much wanted to stay, and there was only 6 weeks left?" And they all said, No, we have to go along with the Superior. And the Superior said it was the Provincial's decision. It was one of those situations where everyone passes the buck and no was willing to take a stand. And I remember that as being one of the turning points around my decision to leave, although it was not the primary cause. For the rest of the year I refused to go to the chapel and pray with the Sisters because I felt it was such an injustice and unkindness to this one particular Sister, and I just didn't feel I could tolerate this kind of behavior or belong in this kind of Community anymore. K.T.

As was mentioned before, there was no convent training in the early years in community dynamics. The Rule of Silence sometimes made conflict resolution impossible. The Superior's absolute authority was another stumbling block—it wasn't like one had a choice to go in the other direction from her attacker. For the most part, dealing with "personality clashes" was like dealing with Superiors (above) in that many women gave short answers: *kept it quiet, ignored it (4), did more penance, stifled my feelings, avoided them as much as possible(18), withdrew, tried to live in peace with them, gave in every time because it was the Will of God, tried not to call attention to myself, etc.*

I remained closed. It resulted in my being dismissed. BEVERLY

They didn't exist—they were _denied_. HOLLY

I clashed, but good! MARY

Pretended they didn't exist, or got ill. JANN

In my pre-awareness days, I avoided them like crazy, and when I was confronted, I backed down or submitted or apologized for my wrong doing whether it was wrong or not. I was sweet and conforming and allowed those people to be verbally abusive to me without any retaliation. Eventually I learned how to deal with them a little more assertively. I am not the type of person to run away anymore. If something bothers me, I get close to myself, grow, and find my real self. I deal with the source of the trouble, or the person I'm having the trouble with, rather than avoid the conflict. MARGARET

I definitely had a clash with one in my class who was next (down) in rank to me. She truly tried to make me feel inept and not worthy of being first in rank. I couldn't have cared less about rank order. JEAN-2

I lived in larger groups most of the time, so it was easier to avoid these individuals. When I was younger, I covered up my feelings because it was the correct thing to do. As I grew up and gained more experience, I stopped hiding my true feelings, began to confront individuals, and risked the consequences. It saved me from ulcers, although I'm sure I did not gain them as friends. JULIANNE

When I attended high school (taught by this same Order), my favorite piano instructor was taken away from me and I was switched (over my protests) to Sr. Petunia, the head of the department, whom I despised. The woman was condescending, extremely conservative and formal, and tended to equate mistakes with "badness". Imagine my horror when, as a prospective member of the charter groups of Aspirants, I was told that this woman would be our Aspirant Mistress. When I informed the Mother General of our conflicts and suggested that I might not want to enter then, she told me that if I didn't enter at this time with this woman as our leader, I would not be welcome to enter at any time. The thought of having already announced my decision, having had a "trousseau shower" by my friends, and worst of all, of risking Hell for not following my Vocation made me say, Okay, I'll enter. I thought, How bad can it get? According to my letters home (in which we were not allowed to state feelings or internal secrets), this nun took the Aspirants (hungry teens, all) to the convent basement every Friday and let them cook candy and popcorn as a sort of bonding, a way to their hearts, of reeling in the kids. But the woman still rankled me.

When I taught music at the high school, she was made the head of my department. When I went on mission the next year, she was again my immediate Superior. Now I knew that this nun could see and hear everything I did and said (she was across the hall and I had to leave the door open) and that she was just waiting for me to make a mistake, so I was trying my hardest not to get upset at, e.g., students' not practicing their lessons—for which I would be personally judged. (By this time I was already burned out, exhausted, physically weak, and in a highly nervous state, and should not have been teaching. I'd also had no real vacation for years.) Sister Petunia would swish into the room where I was teaching and at random tell my students the opposite of whatever I had been saying, even if it was only an alternate fingering. This was particularly humiliating to me since I had been sent away to study music, but was not allowed to use anything I had learned, nor was I allowed to observe anyone in our Order teaching music. An older nun later told me that Sr. Petunia had been in the same class as the Mother Superior and had expected to be "sent away to study" instead of me. (Other parts of this story are related in answer to other questions.) DORIS

This story tells of a Superior that brightened one nun's life:

Had it not been for the students, especially the kindergarteners, I couldn't have survived. Then a high point was granted me: Our Superior General came from France in 1957. Before her election she had been Superior and Principal of a girls' school in Paris. The French government had prohibited nuns in the late 1800s from wearing their religious habits as teachers, even in their own schools. That was why so many had immigrated to other countries. Some complied with the government, as she had. In the dining room one of our nuns said, Oh, Reverend Mother, how you must have missed wearing your habit. Not at all, she answered, I became closer to the children I taught and to their parents--I learned too, that the garb does not make the religious. I wanted to cheer. She said so many other good things in the course of her visit. In addressing one of the nuns who had come up from New Orleans, she asked, How can you continue to separate your white students from black students and still claim to be followers of Jesus? When someone mentioned that a senior was pregnant and might give the baby up for adoption, the Superior said, This seems like a strange solution—in our country we do what we can to *not* separate a mother from her child; the family and the community do all they can to keep them together. I wanted to shout for joy. She believed in Christianity! Each Sister got to speak to her privately. I trembled a little at the thought, remembering that we had to kneel when we were in the presence of higher Superiors, especially the Mother General. I was surprised when I went in, but not afraid. Sit, she said. My God, she was humble, too! Most of the Superiors I met preached humility, but seldom lived it. She told me I was gifted. She said I would go to a certain college to work on a bachelor degree. She said, It's an injustice to have kept you here all these years without further formal education. She asked whether I'd had time to develop my artistic gifts. She complimented me on my French. You should teach French, she said, the Sister who teaches it pronounces it so badly. I had hopes again that it possibly all would change. On her trip South, her driver stopped at a gas station where my father happened to wait on them. My Superior pointed out to Reverend Mother that the man was my father. She got out and shook his hand. You have a very gifted daughter, she said, and you should be very proud of her. I am, he answered. He had waited all these years to hear this. DOROTHY

PEERS

social strata, gossip, rank
the convent elite
treatment in convent by peers
personal shunning

Social Strata, Gossip, Rank among Peers

The very superior-oriented structure of the religious community encouraged social stratification among peers. This was exacerbated by the pervasive system of ranking women according to their entrance (into the community) dates, or if several dates coincided, according to the whim or decision of the Council. For example, in a class of 50, the first girl/woman to enter would be given the very next rank number after the last person to enter before her. If she were #987, the rest of her class was given numbers from 988 through 1036, even though they all had the same official date of entrance. From sitting at table in the refectory, to kneeling in chapel, to deciding who went through the doorway first, nuns forever walked and moved in rank. Rank was not an optional thing, nor was it debated, protested, or ignored. If you were a nun, accepting your rank was part of the package. The existence of Rank generally produced no reaction to participants in this project, but the artificial ranks of social stratification were deemed hurtful.

As in any organization, in convents there were givers and users, the naive and the political, those who strictly observed the Rule, and those who took rules lightly. The latter, outside of some noticeable speaking during Silence times, operated mostly in private, drinking wine in their rooms with friends after Grande Silence had begun, visiting priests or friends at night, or having sex in out-of-the-way places. Some kept a round of secular clothing for these forays, while the naive slept obliviously in their beds.

At the same time, nuns were required to do things in groups. No pairings, however innocent, were sanctioned. "Three or more" was the norm everywhere (see VI Sexuality: Particular Friendships), especially before Vatican II. Normally, and in most cases, the mid-century religious woman went where she was told, with whomever she was told, and worked at the task she was told to do. This unquestioning obedience, engendered in the Novitiate, was referred to as "cadaver obedience" and considered the apex of vow observance. Individuality as we know it did not exist.

    I got in trouble for asking the Novice Mistress why we always had to walk in a "herd"—I actually used that term—like when we walked to the (convent) cannery to snap beans. And why we had to take a certain circuitous route through the sunroom down the basement and across the courtyard. I was warned that by questioning any order, I was "fomenting discord"—a dreaded phrase that often led to culpable loss of Vocation, and subsequently, hell. DORIS

Here are some of the comments received from the 73 about peer social strata in mid-century US convents—by those who lived through it:

    Social strata stopped what could have been nourishing friendships. There was an elite group, but I never really knew what it took to get into it. I suspected they were the Mother Superior's favorites. BEVERLY

    Yes, there was an elitist group, but I was not a member; I guess I didn't measure up to their standards. MAE

    Gossip played a huge role in our community. Though I felt "in" in my peer group, with older nuns I was seen as somewhat radical. You were important (in our community) according to the grade you taught (highest was better). A few nuns seemed to have an air of something being owed to them. We acquiesced. THERESE

    The social strata seemed to consist of those in authority on top, then "famous" nuns—those who performed music or other public tasks well, then the rest of us. We were not all equal, even though we pretended to be. SARAH

    Gossip in the order was pretty terrible sometimes. It was why I left. There was an elitist group, but I did not belong to it because I could not bring myself to exclude anyone from anything—I accepted everyone. Those whose families had money were privileged. LORENA

Chapter X: Peers

I was a fence-straddler and didn't belong to any cliques, but some of the older nuns had mysterious groups. It made me angry when I saw some of my peers ostracized. DENISE

I avoided gossips and accepted the social strata as a remnant of the court system of Europe. MARTHA

In my estimation, the community was rampant with gossip. "In" groups bred other "in" group. I did not belong to the strong controlling groups, and though I felt excluded, I really had no desire to be a part of them because of the way they behaved toward others. I felt the injustice of social strata—that is the exact opposite of how I treat people. I felt anger, rejection, resentment. I believe it was very influential in my decision to leave the community. And yes, some nuns ruled by intimidation, had means of getting others to do things for them and for getting what they wanted, whether within the Rule or not. JULIANNE

The strata needed to be changed. Who could explain their power to intimidate others? They didn't scare me any—I went nose to nose with a few of them. CONNIE

Some of the older sisters passed harsh judgment on us "youngies" who taught high school. I was not a member of the power structure and I especially hated the favors enjoyed by those who were buddies of the powerful people. It seemed also, that certain people could spend money for their projects without being questioned. JULIA

Social strata was very unfair. "They" always had some excuse when it came to physical labor. SHIRLEY

The "in" group did not want me—I wasn't perceived as a leader and did not "glad hand" well. I didn't care—I didn't want to be a superior, and there were some really good people not in that group. MERT

I participated in sort of an "in" group because they were talented and creative teachers and so was I. But I was concerned that superiors appointed those similar to themselves to positions that some of the outspoken members like myself were never given. NELL

I was a friend to most, but at best a fringe member of the "in" group which received more privileges, trips, and education than others. FRANCES

Gossip was the cancer that made our title ironic. In my own entrance group, I was "in", but never again. The only nuns I personally excluded were "tattle-tales". ELLEN

I steered clear of the "in" groups because I did not like the immaturity required to belong to them. In my first year of Novitiate, I was shocked at the favoritism shown to specific novices, one of whom was related to the Novice Mistress. Favoritism and "in" groups were a big problem. There also seemed to be a mother-daughter syndrome. Many of the favored were former students or relatives of superiors. GINA

There was an "in" group—I don't know why I wasn't a part of it, except that it seemed unfair. Keep in mind that at that time I was socially inept and inarticulate with very low self-esteem. I was more concerned with my own affairs, what I was told to do, and didn't bother anybody. MAXINE

Just as in any other group of humans, gossip was there. As a small community, everybody knew everyone's business in most ways whether we talked about it or not. No, I never felt a part of the "in" group. I felt angry that I wasn't a part of it even though I didn't want to do the games it took to fit in—that didn't feel natural to me. I would deliberately include everyone in whatever group I was with—I guess I could relate to those who are always on the fringes of community—I knew what it felt like to be on the outside. The top social layer of our community were those who came from the local German Catholic community in our diocese; the rest of us were the minority. As for the educational strata, at the bottom were the humble kitchen and outdoor crews. That kind of thing was very real to me. I saw and felt it was an injustice. MARGARET.

Gossip produced an undercurrent of mistrust in the community. The "in" group was overbearing—not people I felt comfortable with. With heavy authority at one end of the strata, I felt I was a peon and very insecure. CAREN

Nuns gossiped a lot. It was not only unjust, it was worse than living in the outside world. CHERRY

Gossip was used to try to get some control while in community. At one place I was "in"--a friend of the school principal, and went to movies and outings with the parish priest sub rosa. It bothered me only slightly that others did not have this privilege. After experiencing these privileges then having none at a different convent, I did feel there was an undesirable hypocrisy. When my contemporaries started getting more responsibilities and graduate studies, I noticed an "in" group. But I still took every benefit, e.g., beach trips, movies, concerts, that came my way and regretted not tapping into more of this on some level. It did not consume my thoughts, however—I didn't go out of my way to cultivate such privileges. JEAN-2

There was more gossip on the individual missions than in the Motherhouse. There was an elite group centered around the superior, but I was not included. I remember on mission, the group watching TV while I cried in my room. JEAN-3

It was extremely clear to me that I did not belong with the elite. Though I was given the (then rare, in our community) privilege of studying at a special college in a different state, I paid dearly for it by being shunned and harassed by certain members of the community. When I first entered at 15 years of age and noticed an "in" group, I naively thought that when I got to be in my 20s or 30s I would have moved up to join this crowd, but that wasn't the way it worked. DORIS

Gossip was a daily thing in the Motherhouse, but we tried to avoid nuns that talked a lot. I felt out of groups because I had no money or degree. As for the social strata, it made me sick and upset. Jesus wouldn't treat his disciples that way. Especially nuns who came into the order when they were older, or had money or land, or a degree—these women were treated special. ELEANOR

There were those who curried superiors' favor—not my way. I resented the social strata, but wouldn't pay the price. CASEY

Nine women said that there was either no "in" group in their community, or they did not notice one. And eight said they saw the situation, but went right on with their own lives without being bothered.

Above the Rule

Besides the "teflon elite", rules were broken by well-meaning nuns who made mistakes, as well as by more mature religious women who had a different sense of what was important than the naive individuals who had entered the convent as teenagers and who had (through no fault of their own) never grown up.

WAS IT GENERAL KNOWLEDGE THAT SPECIFIC NUNS DISOBEYED THE RULES OFTEN?

> Yes: 33
> No: 22
> Don't know: 4
> Didn't answer: 14

The rules in question were listed as mostly Silence, Poverty (Chapter II: Religious Life), and Particular Friendships (Chapter VII: Sexuality).

Silence was one. Accepting gifts from friends and family was another. Going to bed on time. Coming to prayer, meals, and other functions on time.
JULIANNE

It was not so much the act of disobedience that irritated the former nuns as the fact that, as in many parts of life, there was no reward for following the rules, and those who dared often found ways of gratifying themselves with impunity.

Once I became a friend of the assistant principal and as such, got invited to outings with one of the parish priests. This was done surreptitiously and made me aware for the first time that superiors had a different lifestyle from underlings. I noticed many evenings in other convents where superiors disappeared evenings without much explanation, and assumed that such special treats were usual. JEAN-2

These types of rule infractions were considered more serious before the Vatican II changes; in fact, elimination of daytime silence, plus the handling of money made the first two subjects into other issues completely.

Our group was one of the first to start to treat the breaking of discretions in a different way—I remember our Novice Mistress saying that. When we would talk about breaking the rules (during recreation time), we would laugh, make fun of them, tease each other about it. This was something new. MARGARET

In earlier days, retribution for disobeying rules (for those who were not the elite) often came in the form of "penances"—public humiliating acts done in the refectory during other people's meals. (Public penances are discussed in Chapter V: Refectory.)

I remember the penances we had to do if you broke silence all the time: you were seen out in the middle of the refectory floor holding a stick in your mouth, kneeling on the floor with your arms upraised, and saying prayers with the stick in your mouth. MARGARET

Later, penances given for anything were less public, e.g., apologies or prayers.

I never felt that Sisters were generally disobedient to the rules—I think the vast majority tried to live the spirit of the Rule. Punishment came in the form of reprimands. We weren't strong on punishment. JANET

Some shrugged off the fact that certain nuns evaded punishments. Others attributed it to their *"power"* (CONNIE), *"power status"* (THERESE) or their "special privileges" (MERT). "They were funny and got away with it," said MARY-2. Also: "I soon learned that there was strong favoritism practiced. I also know from experience that some individual Sisters were skilled at intimidation. No one dared correct them." JULIANNE "What could they do?" asked ANN. "It was overlooked." (DENISE) "Top dogs", SHIRLEY called the evaders. WERE THESE NUNS PUNISHED?

Yes: 14
No: 15
Not to my knowledge: 6
Don't know: 7
Didn't answer: 31

IF NOT, DID YOU SPECULATE AS TO WHY THEY WEREN'T?

Yes: 21
No: 13
Don't recall: 5
Didn't answer: 39

This quote is from a letter that one participant wrote and distributed among her Community as she left:

It appears to me that this is a Community of friends and cliques of friends. If your clique merges with a powerful one, you are "in the gravy" to use a very apt and current slang expression. And if you are an individual who has no gift or desire for politics or flattering the Superiors, then your enemies can accomplish anything they wish with a turn of a phrase here, a subtle insinuation there, or a perfectly harmless-seeming recommendation. If I did not see this, I would not say it. LORENA

❖❖❖

Peers: Shunning

Shunning is a seriously hurtful thing. To outsiders, shunning is "too bad", "a shame", and "painful". To the shunned, the act is a continuous violent earthquake in one's life which produces a depth of self-doubt and despair beyond explanation. When you are shunned, others do not speak to you or look at you. You say to yourself, I can handle this. I'll just get on with my life without them. In convents before the changes from Vatican II took hold (which is when these stories took place), there was no significant contact with family or friends on the outside. Those who were shunned in community had literally no one besides themselves and those who were doing the shunning. Shunning endangers one's sanity, confidence, and hope. The shunned nun begins to question who she is. The bravado of thinking that one can get through the seemingly endless shunning period (there is often no clue as to when or if it will end) wears thin. She becomes emotionally, psychologically, and sometimes physically fragile. Shunning can produce Post Traumatic Stress for years and is completely unnecessary and cruel.

In the questionnaire for this project, there was no mention of shunning, no questions about it. Who would guess that in a loving Christian community of Sisters shunning would occur? However, four women in four different cities brought their shunning experiences to discuss. Three of them (from three different states) happened to be incarcerated by a community in the same "hide-away" (as one of them calls it) at the same time, awaiting their official dispensation of vows so that they could leave their order. All were torn apart by shunning before they left. All survived and are wonderful women. But there was no excuse for anyone to treat them that badly. Here are their stories (see also details in other chapters):

MARY, a teacher in her 20th year as a nun, was treated unjustly and with bitterness by a Superior. She applied for a change of workplace and was turned down. When she shared her doubts with another nun, her school principal, she was surprised to learn that the principal was also considering leaving the convent. She was taken to a house in another town where she (and MERT and LILLA) waited with two nuns in charge, for their dispensations to come through. No one was talking to them. They were warned not to tell anyone that they were leaving, but when the superior refused to allow nuns to associate with her friend, Mary says she "got a bit nasty".

MERT, in her 6th convent year, was in her third year of temporary vows, right before she would be taking final (forever)vows, when she was falsely accused of being a lesbian. After "the shit hit the fan" (her own words), she decided to leave and told her mother, to prepare her for the homecoming. Her superior found out and a miserable time ensued. *I felt betrayed and very angry,* Mert said. *I was taken to a cabin with two other sisters who were also waiting for papers. At the end, they gave us clothes, we changed into them, and were taken to the airport. I was given $200, 3 changes of clothes, and a coat. I asked for advice, but was told nothing. I couldn't wait to leave because I had been shunned for about four weeks. I was too angry for several years to think of my friends left in the convent.*

About her tenth year as a nun, LILLA says, *I feared I was becoming internally like those I least admired. I told the Mother Provincial. I didn't want to lose my Vocation. I was transferred and given new challenges and goals for which to strive."* (She left the convent eight years later.)

It was in trying to help another nun with her doubts that Lilla, Mert, and Mary discovered that they had each been thinking of leaving. The nun they had been trying to help told the Provincial and *the results were terrible. We three were ostracized and that little sister transferred to the convent to which she wanted to go. It made it impossible for us to change our minds. Everyone was told. At our convent they were forbidden to speak to us except in dire emergency.*

My health began to fail. In 1963 (I think) I went from flu to pneumonia to asthma—severe, and allergies, to pleurisy. The asthma was quite severe, and in late 1964 a Catholic doctor told me that he had treated many nuns, that I need not tell him one thing about convent life, but that I was too sensitive a type person and did not belong in the convent. He said that he would give me 15 years at which time I would either walk out the door without a dispensation or I would be committed to a mental institution. I myself had watched 4 sisters grow to the point where they were considered mentally insane and were in various hospitals staffed by our Order.

And there were other nuns whom I did not know personally, but who were in our hospitals. Lack of charity on the part of other nuns was <u>definitely not</u> an acceptable reason (in those days) for a sister to leave the convent. A priest told me it was my call to martyrdom. If I was to become mentally ill, then it was my vocation to do so. I felt I could serve God better with all my faculties. Ah, but there was the problem! Was it my will versus God's will as spoken by a priest? All of those years of convent mental conditioning said, "Stay!" My intellect said, "Go!" And so began many years of doubt and anguish because I left. If I stayed, because the superiors now knew of my doubts, I knew I didn't have the courage to bear the scorn, the shunning I had seen happen to others, the years of being looked down upon by the others, the impossibility of ever being valued as a good member of our order, of ever being trusted. All of the Apostles save John doubted, but a trusted nun couldn't. They were forgiven their weakness and became pillars of the Church. But we couldn't. They were saints, but we had no hope of ever being such. We were unfaithful and lost our vocations.

    The sisters were forbidden to talk to me before I left. I was told by one of the superiors, At the risk of losing your soul, never tell anyone about the convent life. I was only allowed to tell my mother I was leaving, but I couldn't tell her when.

    We were told we were going to the Motherhouse one day and were taken there where Mother Provincial grilled each of us. I was shocked to realize that all of the sisters there knew about it. That meant no turning back. Then the Provincial said she would assign me to any convent I wanted, but I said no, I must go. She tried persuasion, testiness, sarcasm, etc., but I knew I could not turn back. I actually felt [by then that] I was being called out, but they would never have accepted that so I kept still.

    We were not allowed to tell our families anything except that we were coming home. The sisters were forbidden to talk to us. One morning—very early—we were awakened and driven to the order's summer house in a different town. The telephone was locked in a closet so that we couldn't use it. I was indignant and angry. After all those years of being faithful, and still being under vows, I would never have touched that phone. We waited there for our dispensations.

When the dispensations came through, the Provincial said she was sorry they couldn't give us more money but that they had had to buy us coats because it was winter. The money barely got me home to Mama.

They told this story about those days locked up in the cabin:

The nuns had bought them a few clothes, but had forgotten about shoes, so one morning they were picked up, driven to another town, and told to buy shoes. Never one to shirk, Mary led her friends (all in habits) into a shoestore and marched right up to the startled young male clerk, saying, *Probably this has never happened to you before, but we're nuns who are leaving the convent, and we need some shoes.*

By 1999, Mert was blocking some of the memories. After having disclosed the shunning, she was moving on. Mary and Lilla, too, were happier in their last interviews.

The next story is about DORIS, who entered the convent at age 15 and who was told by her Mother Superior the day she passed from the Novitiate to temporary vows that she would be going to college in another state. In that small community, few nuns had been sent "away" to study.

The next day at early "talking" lunch (for refectory readers like me, and other lunchtime workers), the few of us were all seated at the same table—4 or 5 final professed nuns (to whom we Juniors were forbidden to speak) and I. The older nuns were discussing the fact that "some young upstart" would be "studying away". One nun nudged the speaker, whispering that the upstart was at the same table, but that nun looked at me and said loudly that she couldn't care less if I heard her, and that I had no business studying there and shouldn't be going. At that time I had no idea that many of the final professed nuns had worked for years without obtaining college degrees, so red-facedly, I tried to be calm and eat my soup. Years *later after I'd left, I encountered that same nun again at a crowded retreat registration desk where she challenged me loudly (the woman had no soft voice), Well, how's your marriage going—is it any good? Like it was her business. Like she was waiting for me to fail again and again.*

That first year studying "away" was wonderful. The next year a larger group of us was sent back to that college. I was feeling somewhat edged out of the group, but considered that I might be imagining things. We nuns were each responsible for completing our own prayer schedule and we all took different classes, so did nothing together as a group besides eating. As usual for those days, we were not to speak to outsiders, though some in our group became good friends with some college students. We knew no one in that city. We were graciously housed in a section of the girls' dorms, courtesy of the religious teaching order whose members smiled at me while observing silence.

For a while, I tried to stay in denial that those from my own community were actually deliberately separating themselves from me. But the coincidences time after time of their being over there and my being here made me want to put this to a test. One day I had some news to share from the music department, and took the paper to where they were all gathered in one bedroom discussing something. From my first knock they were quiet. Hey, it's me, Sr. Cedrus, I said. No answer. I tried the door, but it was locked.. I knocked several times more before one nun broke the silence and asked what I wanted. I said I wanted to tell them something. Then tell through the door, they said. I said I wanted to show them the paper. They said they'd see it later. A wild thought flew through my head—anything but shunning: maybe they were planning a surprise for my feastday. Then I remembered that my feastday was months away. I paused, screwed up as much assertiveness as I could muster and asked what they were doing in there? No answer. Could I come in? No! Why not? There was a short buzz of voices, then the equivalent of "we don't want to talk about it, go away and don't bother us". From that moment there was no doubt that I wasn't imagining it—my sisters in community were rejecting me.

The reason was as elusive to me then as it is now, though I have re-examined the situation in detail and repeatedly asked those involved for an explanation or even a hint as to Why these sisters (which included my former mentor and idol as well as my high school good friend) so effectively excluded me from their lives.

Between the end of that term and the beginning of summer school, we were housed in an empty wing with the luxury of single rooms. No one, not even Sr.

Caladium who now claims that she alone was "neutral", spoke to me except to briefly answer if I asked a direct question in public. At meals in our own "guest sisters' dining room" I stared at the walls and at my food since I was unsuccessful at even rousing eye contact from anyone who sat across the table from me. I cried silently in chapel, and huge racking sobs under the covers at night. When summer school approached and we were asked to double up in rooms, no one wanted to room with me. It seemed an embarrassing (to me only) stalemate until Sr. Marigold said she would, but only on one condition---that I never spoke to her. How am I so awful? I wondered. One night when the spectacular lightning of the Midwest struck a flagpole on the lawn in front of our open window and the thunder seemed incredibly brutal, I whispered across the room to Marigold, "Did you see that?!" For a few seconds we stood side by side at the window, two barefoot young women dressed in cotton pioneer nightgowns with caps tied under our chins, and hope leapt from its cage again, but after one slip, Marigold put her fingers to her lips, got back into her bed, and turned away from me. The next day she complained to the others that I had violated the terms of our agreement.

I can still see myself sitting at the small light oak table/desk in the campus bedroom, writing home and trying not to splot telltale tears on the page. Besides the fact that whoever was in charge of any group of nuns was allowed to read incoming and outgoing mail, I definitely did not want my parents to see me as a failure, so I never complained. Hadn't I left home because I thought things were bad there? And sharing convent things with family was verboten anyway.

Mostly I followed the Rules. The one rule I was getting lax on was reciting the Office and the rosary every day. They were so long and repetitive, I felt nothing of my original fervor for the religious aspect of it, and I was often so weary from studying for extra credits that I would say part, then spend the night worrying whether I would go to Hell or be dismissed from the Order in even more disgrace if anyone found out that I hadn't said the whole thing every single day.

After completing one particular letter to my parents, I had set down my pen and was rereading my words when it dawned on me that I was _lying_ to everyone I wrote to. Not just like answering "fine" to "how are you", but in giving details to prove what a wonderful privilege this "away study" was and how much I loved it, though that part was true. The actual education gave me no grief. But was I happy? Not that anyone in those days ever asked or expected to hear such a personal comment, but it bothered me that over and over in my letters I was doing everything possible to give the impression that I was in Paradise. The truth was that I couldn't wait until shower time so that I could cry unlimited tears without being seen. Now it was clear that I was in essence lying to my parents. What kind of nun was I? I spent time reviewing my options on this occasion, and could not discover any way out. I would just have to resign myself to going around with one more sin weighing me down, one more imperfection for which I blamed myself.

At times I tried to embrace the shunning as celestial punishment. In the Catholic religion we shared sins—I prayed for yours and you prayed for mine and through willingly going through suffering, either of us could "make up for" the sins of whomever we chose. The goal of life was to die with as few sins on our souls as possible, so this wiping-off process was important. I thanked God who had sent me this means of clearing my soul-slate. I certainly did not hate my sisters who shunned me—it was one of the most deadly sins to be angry or hate anyone.

Though I tried to lock it all inside, the enormous, ubiquitous pressure of so much misery kept leaking out in tears that would fall on a text during class or run down my cheek when I was student teaching. I had to keep reminding myself to concentrate hard on each individual word and idea and musical phrase, so that thoughts of my abandonment could not surface and precipitate an incident of uncontrollable weeping. I feared greatly that one day I would simply not be able to hold it all together and I would shamefully explode in huge racking sobs and wails in some public situation, such as in the middle of a Bach string quartet. During the pauses in music dictation class, I carefully controlled each breath, lest a sobbing gulp escape and be noticed. Surreptitiously I wiped the tears that ran unannounced down my cheeks and if my instructors noticed, they said nothing. These were times that I was sorry we had recently adopted an abbreviated veil instead of the old large starched veil-support that came outside the shoulders, where no one behind or beside me could see my face.

That Christmas our whole group was invited by Sr. Geranium's relatives in town for a buffet dinner. [Sr. G was the head seamstress at the Motherhouse.] There was no question but that I had to attend, not only because one nun left alone was against the rules, but because there was the possibility of hurting the host family's feelings by refusing. The biggest reason, though unspoken, was that someone outside of the group might find out that something was seriously wrong with the group dynamics. It was dark by the time we reached the house and we entered the kitchen door since it was by the driveway. A large table of food filled the available *space, and after introductions, we each took a plate and made the rounds of the buffet. I was last in line; we had convinced the family to go first. When I followed with my plate to the family room down the hall I was surprised to find the door closed. I knocked timidly, then opened the door. The nuns, led by Sr. Kalanchoe, were sharing a handwritten copy of "The Little Drummer Boy" (a new song that year) and performing an original version in harmony. I stood by the door while they sang, the familiar "horror" feeling creeping over me as I realized how many times they must have met in secret to accomplish this. Every one of the nuns except me was involved. It was clearly not a case of their accidentally not telling me; they had deliberately excluded me again. Worse, in a few minutes all of this would dawn on the host family and they would know what a throwaway person I was. A part of me was amazed that, observant as I considered myself, I had not heard the nuns even a mention the title of this song, much less hum it. Here and there I had heard of the song from students, but I was under the impression that the nuns wouldn't be allowed to sing it because it wasn't a certified religious Christmas hymn.*

The song ended, the host family clapped, and Sr. Kalanchoe announced that that song was our gift to them. I was greatly embarrassed, even before I noted that there was no place left for me to sit or stand. The father made some move to give me his place, but I declined, by this time being too ashamed at the glaringly obvious fact that I had not been included in the preparations and therefore was the only one without a gift. I mumbled that I'd forgotten something in the other room, and closed the door again. I went back to the kitchen, the lump in my throat so large it hurt to swallow my own saliva, my eyes literally gushing tears. I tried desperately not to make any noise or draw any attention to myself, or to redden my eyes more than they already were, since sooner or later I would have to face the host family, even if just to say goodbye. The father had driven us here, so there was no car for me to hide in. At some point they would all come out of that room and I would see in the family's faces that they knew that I was an outcast, and they would most likely judge me as worthy of being one because that was the way things were. I feared that this would be the moment of my uncontrollable eruption of public grief, an act which would humiliate myself, the group of nuns, certainly the host family, and disgrace the community. And somehow I'd pay for this later, without a doubt.

At that moment an angel in the form of Sr. Geranium walked through the kitchen door. This was a complete surprise--she was supposed to be at the Motherhouse back in our home state. She had come alone by taxi from the airport. For some reason, the rest hadn't heard her arrival and we two stood alone in the kitchen. What I knew of Sr. Geranium was confined to the hours she had spent pinning new habits together on me before sewing them for my "away-study" wardrobe. She wasn't one to go about smiling at the young nuns, but in a talkable situation, was a kind soul, intelligent, with definite opinions of her own. I had felt a potential bond between us during those few days of fittings. I blew my nose, muttering something about a "cold", but I definitely did not look normal and Sr. G was not stupid. When she asked me how things were going, I answered too brightly, "Just fine! And how are you?" --trying to shift talk to affairs of another state. She walked over to me and put her arm over my shoulders, saying softly, "But how are you really?" and then the floodgates really opened. I clung to her and sobbed loudly, uncontrollably, barely aware of the sudden silence in the next room or of Sr. G asking those who drifted into the hall to go back, that she needed to talk to me alone. I remember using up all the napkins on the table. It was a long time before I was able to speak at all. Then I babbled about various incidents, ending with my not being included in the Drummer Boy performance. She repeated some things I had said to verify that she had heard correctly about my being excluded from the group. Yes, I blubbered, most definitely yes--and I couldn't figure out why. She gave me a hug and said she'd carry that message to the Mother General. That gave me enough hope to straighten up and stop crying long enough to say goodbye to the host family as the nuns had now decided to leave. Sr. G stayed to visit with her relatives and I don't remember ever having contact with her after that night. Certainly nothing changed on campus or within the group.

But we were sent notice soon afterwards from the Motherhouse that only Sr. Caladium would be finishing her degree there, the rest of us to be shipped home at the end of the school year for other teaching destinations. I felt extremely guilty, and while no one said anything to me, they shook their heads and shot blame from their eyes when our paths crossed. I felt somewhat relieved emotionally, but was greatly disappointed in the orders, as I had only a year left to graduation and this was the best music school someone of my talents could hope to attend.

I loved the music faculty, small groups of whom would drift into my practice room at night to hear my interpretation of Bernstein's "Seven Anniversaries" and to discuss the rationale for how I chose to play unmarked passages. (At first I had thought they were laughing at me and had come to ridicule me. Slowly I accepted that they were laughing in delight at the humor in the music, and were sincere in their wanting to know my opinions about the musical interpretation.) I woodenly went through the rest of the year, trying to suck as much goodness, comfort, and memories of beauty from the music courses as I could. At night when I went back to the group and my silent room, it was more bearable to me than before "the cry" though physically nothing had changed. I felt that I was in a waiting mode rather than in an endless pit, and that I could stand anything knowing it would eventually end.

    The other order of nuns knew something was wrong even before our Mother General wrote to Sr. Santolina, our piano instructor, to ask for her view. At no time did anyone of our group do or say anything quotable in front of the host community so basically, they knew no details. There was an L-turn at the very end of the hall going out of the music department and one day when Sr. Tithonia (the department head) was opening the exit door, she caught a glimpse of me about 20 steps behind her around the L. She stopped and held the door open until I got there. For some reason my eyes got tangled up with hers and I couldn't pull them away for those last very long strides. I remember being surprised at the sympathy in her face, and started walking faster, because from the moment I recognized that sympathy, tears had again begun to stream down my cheeks. I barely made it through the doors, mumbling "Fine" to her "Are you all right?" and with superhuman effort, recomposed myself enough to enter French lab with its individual cubicles where I would have time to do more than a quick pasteup job on my emotions. The thought of confiding in a sympathetic person appealed to me since at that time I had literally no one, and I was having a miserable time trying to field everything alone. But speaking confidentially even, to a member of another community would have been scandalous (not only wrong, but flagrantly wrong in a betrayal-of-the-Order sense) and most likely would earn myself immediate and irrevocable shunning from everyone left in the community at home. I was counting on most of the home Community's not knowing that I was a bad enough person—for whatever reason-- to have been shunned at "away-study". Since I couldn't count on my nun group or speak confidentially to other nun-students, couldn't discuss the same with the host order or write about it in letters to anyone <u>ever</u>, was forbidden under pain of sin to allow a suicidal thought to even flit across my mind—and then on top of this, lost even the ephemeral possibility that there might be someone left in the Community when I went home who wouldn't think I was the most awful nun they ever met—what was left? Why did I exist?

At no time did the new Superior General ever speak to me privately or bring up the subject, nor did anyone else, including those who had been involved. Once, the year I left the convent, the nun whom I had originally accompanied "away" sent a note to me saying that she wished to tell me why this had gone on. But by the time I raced over there, she had changed her mind, saying she would never tell me. Others in the group do not associate with me except for my old high school friend, who has apologized over and over, saying the problem was jealousy. I still do not understand it, have worked this out in therapy over and over, but will probably never be able to talk about this incident without tears until I can find out why it happened.

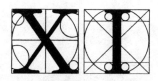

leaving

decision, process, consequences
silence, support, shunning
leaving in the 50s, 60s, 70s, 80s

Why I Don't Tell People I'm An Ex-Nun

This is what usually happens when someone finds out you're an ex-nun:

1) They don't hear another thing you say unless it relates to "convent secrets", so if you're in the middle of giving a lecture, forget it.

2) They want to know right now why you left, and only then,

3) Why you entered in the first place.

4) They tell stories about the nun who rapped their knuckles and start to be angry.

5) Forever afterwards they forget that you're an artist or doctor or somebody's mother or their friend's friend, and continually refer to you as "that ex-nun", inundating you with requests for scintillating details, such as: "Did you have to bathe with your clothes on?" *

*Yes, some.

Leaving The Convent

Leaving anything is generally difficult. For these women to leave convents where they had sunk their hopes and dreams, where they had thrown themselves into work and prayer and dedicated their lives because they believed that God had called them to a Religious Vocation—this was particularly difficult.

For that reason, and because they were loyal and had been taught that perpetual vows were just that, sometimes the start of their decision to leave came well before the actual leave-taking—31 years, in one case, even though not every nun in the 1950s believed that she would be sent to hell if she willingly disregarded her Vocation.

Back in the 50s, there was little convent endorsement for any woman leaving the community, though there was plenty of shame, silence, and demand for secrecy. Leaving the convent was not at all like today's adult taking on a new relationship, adventure, or job. Because of their vows and rules, nuns had lived quite dependent lives, knowing little of the outside world, making no significant decisions, and having to ask permission for every little thing. Fewer than 25% of the women in this project had ever held jobs outside of the family business, babysitting, and farm work before entering, and now they had to very publicly grow up, catch up, and get a life--all at once. And so they were basically alone. Religious women who had been forbidden for years to have close friends on the outside, were (most) now in their leaving, forbidden to speak to any friends back at the convent—some for a year, some longer. Most mid-century ex-nuns were simply cut off and, having never been salaried (or had anything paid into Social Security), had to begin their new lives with little but their wits.

The mid to late 60s were a mixed bag: some Communities had welcomed the suggestions of Vatican II, some adopted a few changes, and others held onto their old ways. By the end of the 70s, Vatican II changes had encouraged self-esteem, independence, and fraternization with the laity to the point where leaving the convent was a different and often supported experience. After 1970, more Orders had changed than not, although today there are still some communities who wear the habit, avoid communication with outsiders, and keep the Rule of Silence. With the new breath of air from the changes, transitions from the convent to the outside world were generally simpler—nuns were already out of habits, lived in apartments, and had jobs and friends outside of the Community. Yet, as in all the preceding stories, there were individual exceptions for everything.

No one in this project came and left in the same calendar year. In this chart, the entry year is counted, as is the leaving year, though there may be a discrepancy of some months.

Years spent in the convent:

> 1 to 5 -- 7 women
> 6 to 10 -- 14 women
> 11 to 15 -- 18 women
> 16 to 20 -- 16 women
> 21 to 25 -- 8 women
> 26 to 30 -- 6 women
> 31 to 35 -- 3 women
> 36 to 40 -- 1 woman

These women left convents between 1954 and 1985. The busiest years for leaving were 1969 (7 women left), 1972 (6), 1973 (6), 1965 (5), 1971 (5), and 1963 (4). (Also see Charts.)

Now for their stories:

Leaving in the 1950s

I taught 6 years in the same parish and the experience convinced me that I must move on. I had accomplished all I ever would or could as a nun. The Holy Spirit was not constrained to convents. So also did He brood in mothers and fathers and children, and I was being carried into another career. I had no specific destiny but personal freedom. When I told one of the older nuns I was leaving, she asked, "Where will you go? You've been our student for eleven years and our colleague for 20. I would understand if you had someone waiting for you." "I'll be free," I answered, "and responsible to my own conscience." Leaving was arduous to say the least. I sought counsel, but the nuns wanted more delay as though twenty years had not given me enough time to know my own mind, but I understand now that this was a compliment. I left on August 9, 1954, eight years before Vatican II. Girls were coming through the front door as I slipped out the back. 1934-1954 DOROTHY

As a postulant, I did not feel ready to commit. When I shared my doubts with nuns, I found out that others also were not happy. I told them I wanted to leave, but they tried to change my mind, telling me I would never be happy on the outside. I was given no money or goods, and was told by the Mistress of Novices that I was making a mistake. I followed the Rule in not telling anyone that I was about to leave, but felt guilty. I felt badly at facing all of the family, like a failure. It took 1-2 years to feel comfortable on the outside. I was not allowed to visit my friends in the convent at first; this made me feel of no personal worth. 1955-1956 LORNA

Two years after entering, the Mother Provincial told me she felt that I did not have a true Vocation. I was disappointed, but consoled by the knowledge that I had done God's will for me. I left two days later, since I had not yet taken vows. I simply went to a room that had my clothes, put the habit away, put the clothes on, received a blessing from Mother Provincial, and left. I was given back what I had

Chapter XI: Leaving

brought, as far as money and goods. I felt guilty about not being allowed to tell anyone I was leaving. Stayed with friends from my university days. I wasn't forbidden to visit my convent friends, but I knew that I'd never return there. 1955-1957 MAXINE

    I was still a postulant when I first thought of leaving. I told my superior, Mother Mistress, and she told me to stick around, that I shouldn't be homesick. I learned later that you had to go to her three times. Then I just called my parents to come and get me and bring some clothes. I wasn't given anything by the convent except they said, "If you ever want to come back, don't come back here." I was sad about not being allowed to tell others from my group. It didn't take long for me to adjust, since I'd only been in a short time. 1956-1957 KATHLEEN

    I never worried about "losing" my Vocation, but was threatened with dismissal from the Order. They said I was "too proud" and they kicked me out. I felt awful. They put me in an outside room to wait until someone in my family came to get me. I had to go without saying goodbye to anyone. They gave me no money, goods, or advice. I did not want to go; I loved it there. I didn't visit any of my friends afterwards, but many of them were dismissed, too. Being busy helped me adjust, though it took about a year. 1955-1957 JOSEPHINE

    I was denied final vows--told I was a square peg in a round hole, but given no other reasons. I felt not good enough and my life deteriorated. I was told at the end of May, but had to wait until August 5th (till my temporary vows expired) to leave. My parents were told I had no talent for teaching, nursing, or for anything else. Yet I had to remain in the convent for nearly 3 months until my vows were up. I was given no money or goods. One Council Member told me, "Have no regrets." Priests helped me adjust. I didn't visit the nuns again because I never wanted to. 1951-1958 NANCY

    Although I would have been glad to leave Seattle, it never occurred to me to leave the convent. I was surprised that I was refused final vows, but my reaction was also relief; I would be out of this terrifying city. The Superior General told me she felt it was better that I return to secular life. I asked her to tell the rest of the sisters while I was on phone duty. One dear old nun, while I was cutting her hair, told me tearfully that she thought they got the wrong person. My gentle principal stopped me in the hall and asked, "Why didn't you tell me?" –but there had been nothing to tell. I went to summer school as usual, already neither fish nor fowl. One day I was on my way over for Chapter of Faults, but met Mother Provincial on the way, who told me it wouldn't be necessary for me to come to Chapter this time. We were learning several beautiful songs for a feast day and I wasn't going to be there for the performance. Another day we were swimming in the college pool and I ended up walking back to the dorm alone. I just didn't seem to fit in anymore. I don't think they "cast me out" or tried to shun me, they just didn't know what to do with me. Then the thought of going didn't hurt so much. While I was still in Seattle, a superior said she wished they'd have assigned me to a small convent; I never had been. She thought that I'd never had a chance to discover what real community life was. One sister counseled me not to try to continue the schedule of prayers as a secular. I was told to leave during a particular part of meditation. I didn't know the why's, but this way I could talk with no one and no one could speak to me. But I'm sure the Sisters next to me in rank on either side of my place in chapel knew exactly where I was going and that they'd never see me again. I was driven to my sister's place in the city, still wearing my habit. I had not a cent. One of my first orders of business was to take apart my holy habit (nuns did this before washing the wool habits), so that it could be returned to the Provincial House. My sister saw to it that I got a permanent; the hairdresser knew immediately that I'd just been a nun. Soon after wearing new shoes, I could not walk; six years of wearing only same-height Cuban heels had shortened the muscles in the back of my legs so that even standing was painful. So I spent the better part of several days sitting on the davenport with my legs outstretched. I wrote my mother, but I think she was hurt about my coming home. Certainly she never understood, even after I told her the reason. It was at least a year, when I again was teaching, before I felt less uncomfortable on the outside. Time was probably the best healer. When I taught, as far as I knew, only the lady who'd recommended me knew that I'd been a Sister. I was the first secular to teach there, so it's probably just as well if I was still pretty "nunny"; at any rate, I felt at least so-so. I wasn't forbidden to visit my Sisters in the convent, but it would have been impractical because of distance. Physically, I felt better moving to the eastern part of the state—less mold spores, to which I'd become allergic. Family disapproval hurt. I believe that until the day she died, my mother never understood my return home. To her, it showed that I was a failure. That was the general feeling of the secular community of those who "couldn't stick it out." Now, I'm comfortable in my world; in the world in general, no. 1953-1959 TRACE

Leaving in the 1960s

Just before final vows, I thought about leaving. I began to think there would be more happiness elsewhere. But I had made a commitment, so I stayed. Sixteen years later, a doctor suggested I leave. I was nervous and put off the decision for a couple of years. Finally I wrote a letter to the Superior General. She was surprised and disappointed, but did not try to convince me otherwise. I was given $250 and an outfit to wear. I was happy and felt comfortable immediately. 1948-1960 GRACE

I was not accepted for final vows. On the morning of August 5, 1960 (the natural end of first vows) I dressed in street clothes and was driven to the airport with $25 and some clothes. I was not happy to leave. Though it took me years to feel comfortable on the outside, I went back to the college to finish an education degree. 1953-1960 DOLORES

Before final vows, I wanted out. I told a priest, who said it was only a temptation, and I should do penance and pray. By two years later, I felt terrible. I had applied twice for temporary vows. I waited one year and three months for my dispensation during which time I was isolated from all the others. When I left I was given $100 and my clothes, and not allowed to tell anyone I was leaving. I felt shameful, that I had disgraced my family. Meeting my future husband helped me feel comfortable. 1956-1961 JAN

During temporary vows I became dissatisfied in general—no specific reasons. At first, I told no one because I was afraid and felt guilty. Finally, I talked to my immediate superior, who had me write the reasons down, speak to the Mother Superior and a priest, write a letter to Rome requesting dispensation, and sneak away. Even though I only had temporary vows, I had to rewrite the request letter three times before it was sent. I was given no money or goods, and told not to tell anyone. I wasn't exactly happy to leave because I wasn't sure what would happen. I was told I shouldn't write or see the nuns back at the convent. I didn't like that. 1957-1962 SHIRLEY

In my sixth year, the Provincial had a talk with me about how she was made to suffer as a young sister and how it made her a better person. She said the problem with the younger sisters was that they didn't suffer enough. And she was going to remedy the situation. She told me that she wasn't at all certain I had a Vocation and that this test of being held back from final vows would be good for me. So I taught school as best I could two more years and got held back from vows again. By the end of my eighth year I finally gave up—I'd tried as hard as I could to suffer for God and to be faithful to my Vocation. I had prayed for God's guidance, but felt misunderstood. I wrote to the Provincial before I left and said I thought over her theory of suffering, and also the story of St. Bernadette. My conclusion was that the system that made St. Bernadette suffer so that she could be a saint, required other people to be awful. Surely there had to be a way to come up with a better system where everyone could be holy and no one had to be cruel. I told her that being treated cruelly had made her cruel, and that I didn't want to grow up and be like that. Sooo—goodbye. And to everyone's relief, I went to a convent in my home town, took off the habit, put on civies, and went home. They gave me several hundred dollars to start out with. I was not happy, but totally exhausted and sad. It took only a couple of months to acclimatize on the outside. 1955-1963 ELLEN

Way in the beginning I had spoken seriously of my doubts to my Postulant Mistress, who then told me to wait until the next week when the Order-favored Jesuit was coming for a visit. She insisted I talk to him, because he would "know" whether I should be staying or not. The first thing the priest asked me was, What is out there that you can't get here? I want to be a real person, I said. I want to travel and be Somebody. He laughed. Travel is highly overrated, and you can be Somebody right here, he said. That's not a good reason to leave. Is that all? He spoke enigmatically, saying that getting out wouldn't change things. (And the final seal:) He said that I must have a Vocation or I wouldn't have come to the convent in the first place, ergo (therefore—Jesuits were fond of inserting Latin into their conversations) it was wrong for me to leave. So I resigned myself to staying. The second time, I was a new Novice on the yearly 15-day Retreat. The topic for the last conference had been Hell, and I had asked to speak to the Retreatmaster privately. I wanted to leave, I told him, but didn't want to go to Hell. Then, because I was young (16) and believed the fire and brimstone theory, I asked if it were possible that if I went to Hell, I could be of some use instead of burning up, e.g., cooking meals for the devils. "I'm a good cook," I said miserably. I can still see his head jerk up and hear his harsh laugh as he told me that wouldn't work. He never said anything that led me to believe I could leave without going to Hell, so I went back to the Novitiate. The third time, I was a second-year Novice, the daily noontime reader in the Refectory. I was preparing the assigned readings, which were so-many-minutes of classical theology, followed by a few more minutes of contemporary theology, and then the Martyrology. In the contemporary theology book, I discovered the term "Temporary Vocation". According to the book, some people could feel called by God, and then later could leave the convent without damning their immortal souls. I hurried to the Novice Mistress and showed her the passage. See! I said, That's probably what I have—a temporary Vocation!" She said the book was dead wrong, then took it away from me, saying she would replace it later with another volume, and I was to skip the contemporary reading today. I was shaken. The day I graduated from the Novitiate, I was told I would be "sent away to study", a rare honor for anyone, and rarer for someone my age. I felt that not only was this a sign that I should stay, but that perhaps things would get better. I was wrong. I ended up taking temporary vows twice, and couldn't make up my mind about finals. I thought if I took finals, I'd be there the rest of my life, and I didn't know if I could take that. By this time I was quite depressed and I couldn't think clearly. Every night, after everyone else was asleep, I'd tiptoe over to the chapel (same building) and kneel there and weep. At one point when I turned to leave, I saw my superior sitting in the back. First I froze. She said absolutely nothing to me, but showed up for several nights until I quit coming. Then I decided I didn't care if they saw how miserable I was. If I just up and said, "I'm leaving," all by myself, it would be like throwing my Vocation away deliberately. Finally the Mother General told me that the Council had decided I should not take my final vows. Part of me was relieved, though I feared whatever life out there. I had been in the convent for 8 years, and didn't know anything about the outside world. I was assigned to teach a few weeks of summer school with an older nun in another city, then was allowed to leave immediately even though my temporary vows weren't up—they didn't want me around doing nothing during my class's rehearsals for the vow ceremony. (As it turned out, a man with whom I worked as a volunteer right after I left, asked me out right away, but since my vows weren't up at that time, I didn't go.) I was warned by my superiors not to tell anyone I was leaving, though I longed for some closure, or at least a Goodbye from someone after 8 years. The older nun I boarded with that summer was horrified that in the evenings I read secular classic novels from our host's library, but I didn't explain. That last morning, spirited away during meditation when nearly everyone was in chapel, I tried to signal to my favorite nun who had been my superior a few short months. I waved through the car window behind my other hand, then blew her a kiss. By her startled look, I was sure she understood. They drove me to another mission house. I had been allowed $100 (though I never personally handled the money) to buy material and patterns to make 2 dresses with, so there was hardly any cash left. I was given also a Virgin Mary nightlight and a laminated pious verse and that was it. At the mission house where I tried to get ready, I couldn't move well—it seemed as though I was under water or in a dream. My hair wouldn't separate from the curlers I'd tried to sleep on all night (worn under my coif) and everything seemed to be in slow motion. My mother was parked outside in front, the superior was knocking at the door constantly telling me to hurry up, and I felt like I was walking through molasses. Finally I got the dress and nylons on and my hair combed and I had a panic attack walking down the long hallway to the front door. What if I couldn't make it? "What if I changed my mind?" I whispered, but the nun, my former superior, pulled me inexorably even faster. down the hall by my elbow. "Nonsense," she said. I felt she was glad to get rid of me. I feared by then that no one would say goodbye to me, not even her. I tried to stop a moment and say, "Is this really what I should do?" but she hurried me on out the door, then disappeared back inside as we drove off. What did I feel like? No one in my family asked me any questions or comforted me. I cried in secret. I didn't

Chapter XI: Leaving

know who I was or where I was going. I felt abandoned and thrown back into a world that had metamorphed from one I'd previously rejected. I wondered if I'd still be treated as Mom and Dad's 15-year old daughter, like one of the "kids". The first day my mother got some material and patterns and my dad drove us to a faraway beach house where Mom sewed constantly until I had a wardrobe of sorts. We talked rarely. I was fighting tears, and surprised to see that sometimes she was, too. We hadn't been an emotion-sharing family before, and we weren't now. On the boardwalk to the restaurant (our cabin had no kitchen) I met one of my high school students with her mother (who knew Mom). "I know you," the student said loudly in the midst of the other tourists. Then it dawned on her who I was and she shouted on the boardwalk, "Migod, you look so different without your habit!" We met her every place we went. I was embarrassed—I hated to meet anyone I knew as a nun, because, like some divorced people, I felt I had failed. It took me a very long time to get used to the outside world, even though I was offered a teaching job immediately and the use of my parents' car. When I left the convent, nuns were still wearing the full habit, so I'd be going up the stairs or an escalator in a department store, and I'd reach for my non-existent long skirts to hold them away from the stairs. Or I'd nervously adjust a headgear that wasn't there. Once in a department store I met a nun who had been critical of me and she was bowled over: "You have taste!" she kept saying. Of course I did. But how could I have shown it in a black habit? I was shy and worried each day about meeting someone who would create a public scene by telling everyone around that I had been a nun. I was torn between feeling it wasn't anyone else's business, and concern that they'd make up worse reasons as to why I left. I was very lonely. My former friends in the "world" had moved on and away (it had been 8 years), and since we hadn't been allowed to write or visit anyone but family (and that was limited to once a year), all I had was my friends in the convent—whom I had been sternly warned not to contact for at least one year. It was like starting life over. I had to get a Social Security card and some identification. Once when I was very lonely, I called the Mother Superior to say "hello" and was told not to call back until the year was up. When I called the nun who had dictated our education courses to get some information I needed for state accreditation, I made the mistake of adding, "How are you?" and was again humiliated and rejected. 1956-1963 DORIS

When I decided to enter the convent, I knew I wasn't going to stay. I cut the amount of things on the trousseau list in half: if it asked for 20 pairs of socks, I cut it to 10. I knew that I wasn't going to stay very long, so why bother to buy all those things? I was very scattered when I entered. Instead of putting everything in a suitcase, I arrived with various small parcels and bags—very disorganized. I don't think that I ever made a firm commitment to stay, because I wanted children. I needed to try this, but I was sure it wasn't going to work. I told the Novice Mistress right way, in an attempt to be honest. She said I would be an asset to the community, but that it was my choice. I loved being in the convent environment and going to school. I had great friends. The problems would come when, at each point of our preparation (6 months or a year later) I would have to write a letter asking permission to continue. These were formal letters and I followed through on each one: the 6 mo. Postulancy, the end of the Novitiate, first vows of three years only--I figured I could deal with those. At the end of that three year period we were again to write a letter asking for a 1-year extension of vows, then at the end of that, another year. So that preparation period was seven years. Unfortunately, when we got to the end of that and I needed to write another letter asking permission to make final vows, I fell apart. My letter was not a form letter; it was a complete outpouring of my soul, my reservations, my fears, my longing for children of my own. The superiors had no choice but to deny my request to continue. I knew what the answer had to be, and yet I was devastated. I talked with the Provincial superior and she said that maybe I needed some distance, that if, after a year or two out in the world, I decided to return, she would work with me in every way possible. I had stayed seven years. I really wanted to believe that I was chosen to do something special and believed that religious life was the only way to fulfill that. After summer school, I was put into a small convent and every effort was made to make my transition back into the world as easy as possible. We practiced every way possible fixing my hair, shopped for a small wardrobe, and I was given money. Also, I was helped send resumes to various schools where I might be employed. I also received understanding, compassion, and love to make the transition easier. They gave me $500 and mixed feelings. I really didn't want anyone to know I was leaving, so I didn't tell many nuns. My mother came for me, and within ten days I left the state for a job. I had no problems adjusting. 1956-1963 JULIA-2

Chapter XI: Leaving

I spoke to the Mother Provincial my very first year about leaving—I wanted to make things clear, but she talked me into renewing my vows. Then I waited a year to fulfill my vows. I was happy to leave, and pretty disgusted with my Congregation by then. The process seemed simple: you decide not to renew, you leave upon expiration of the vows. But my leaving was excruciating—I was recalled from mission to the Provincial House and admonished by the Juniorate Mistress not to talk to anyone especially the other Juniorate sisters about my decision to leave, as she didn't want me influencing anyone. I told her that my decision was a personal one and not "catching". I said that each one of us was responsible for this decision on our own and that I would not "contaminate" anyone else. My Provincial, surprisingly, put me in as an Assistant Mistress with one of the classes and I resumed my work (which I loved). I was very comfortable with the Head Mistress. After about three weeks, Mother Provincial called me into her office and talked to me about my Vocation. She said that if I stayed I would probably be made a superior some day. I told her that I still planned to leave and that I had no ambitions to be a superior. She asked me what I thought my "poor dead father" would think if I left the convent (he had died 5 months before). I told her that he would have been thrilled to death because, while he supported my Vocation, he periodically would tell me that he would welcome me home. With that I was told to kiss the floor and pack my bags because I was being sent to the Order's house in Indianapolis. The Juniorate Mistress then told me that many ex-nuns had lost their souls; to which I replied that she had no canonical grounds to throw that lie around. (I again kissed the floor!) The Indianapolis stint wasn't bad because the Superior there was a marvelous sister who had been my first post-Novitiate superior. She immediately told me upon my arrival that she would exert no pressure on me. She was as good as her word (God rest her soul!). 1958-1963 MARTHA

Once I had been accepted for final vows, I had my first doubts, which proved to be my termination. At first I was devastated because they would not even consider a one-year waiting period, and I was thus "kicked out". Ironically, two years later they were allowing more time. I was troubled by the inequalities: certain nuns in favored positions, the constant checking up on us, what I read, whom I talked to. They would not pay for dental needs. I didn't tell anyone about my doubts, because I'd worked so hard to get that far, and if you left, you had to start rank all over again at the Postulancy level. There was no going back, even in thought. Just expressing the doubt to the Provincial—I was out! I felt hurt and sorry. Since I was going to take final vows, had already been accepted, I expressed the need for one more year, but was told to leave. After the retreat, the day before the ceremony, I was to turn in the habit and rule book, and leave without telling anyone. They gave me $200 and some clothes and told me to keep in touch. I wasn't happy. I felt naked and awkward without my habit. I was also forbidden to visit my friends in the convent for two years. A friend helped me get through the next year until I felt more comfortable. 1958-1965 CAREN

In my tenth year I considered leaving because I feared I was becoming internally like those I least admired. I didn't outright tell anyone, but strongly hinted about my doubts to Mother Provincial, who transferred me and gave me new interests and goals for which to strive. I actually only left eight years after that, when urged to by a doctor, because of my deteriorating physical condition. This Catholic doctor told me that he had treated many nuns, that I need not tell him one thing about convent life, but that I was too sensitive a person to belong in the convent. He said in 15 years I would either walk out the door without a dispensation, or I would be committed to a mental institution. I had watched four sisters grow to the point where they were considered mentally "insane" and were in various hospitals staffed by our Order. There were also other nuns whom I did not know personally, in our hospitals. . I consulted a priest, who assured me that lack of charity on the part of the community was <u>definitely not</u> an acceptable reason to leave the convent. He said it was my call to martyrdom. If I were to become mentally ill, then it was my Vocation to do so. I personally felt I could serve God better with all my faculties. Ah, but there was the problem! Was it <u>my will</u> versus <u>God's Will</u> as spoken by a priest? All of those years of convent mental conditioning said "stay!"; my intellect said "go". And so began many years of doubt and anguish because I left. Had I stayed, because the Superiors now knew of my doubts, I knew I wouldn't have the courage to bear the scorn and shunning that I had seen happen to others, the years of being looked down upon by others, the impossibility of ever being valued as a good member of our Order, or of ever being trusted. All of the Apostles save John doubted and were forgiven their weakness and became pillars of the Church. But we couldn't. A trusted Nun couldn't. They were saints, but we had no hope of ever being such. We were unfaithful by doubting, and so lost our Vocations. I had to write three copies of the petition to leave, and send it to the

Pope. One morning very early three of us were awakened and driven to another Order's summer home to wait for our dispensations. The one telephone was locked in a closet, which made me angry—if they had said not to use the phone, I wouldn't have used it, but they didn't have to lock it up. I was given $150-200 and a few bed linens and clothes. Then I was told sternly, "Never tell anyone about the convent life, at the risk of your soul." The sisters had been forbidden to speak to me before I left. I felt awful, wronged, betrayed—after years of fidelity. 1946-1965 LILLA

    It is hard to admit that entering the convent was a deal I made with God. I would give Him my life if He would cure my little brother of Muscular Dystrophy. I had been praying for his cure for years. We had relics and Lourdes Water and Rosaries blessed by the Pope. I went to daily Mass and Communion and prayed novenas and 30-day prayers and nothing worked. I was still in the convent trying to keep my end of the bargain when he died. I think this is a part of the reason why I accepted everything without question. It was several years after I left the convent before I learned that you can't make deals with God.

    The bad thing about being in the convent is that it was a time of no growth. I came out thinking like an 18-year old at 23. I have heard that this is the same thing that happens to prisoners. If I had stayed much longer, I think the adjustment to leaving would have been even more difficult.

    My third year of temporary vows, I and two other nuns were accused of being lesbians. I wrote of my Vocation doubts to my mother to prepare her for my homecoming, and she told my sister, and ex-nun, who wrote to the superiors, and the shit hit the fan! I left in a matter of months, after being grilled and shunned. I was taken to a place with other nuns who were waiting for dispensations, given some lay clothes and $200, and taken to the airport. I thought it would have been better if I had been able to tell members of my class. I had been shunned for about four weeks and was very angry. My father met the plane and told me I never should have gone to the convent in the first place. I didn't know if people thought I was a failure. I was uncertain. It was several years before I made contact with the convent again. 1959-1965 MERT

    From Day One I thought of leaving. I would tell my fears, but was told it was a temptation of the devil and not to heed it. Though I never stayed beyond the

Novitiate, I doubt I had a calling to that Order. I told my doubts to the Aspirant and Novice Mistresses because we were not allowed to talk to others; they lectured me. Then I was assigned to teaching, after being told I would never have to. I felt intimidated, then desperate. I was out the door in less than 48 hours after my decision to go. I was not allowed to tell any sisters, including my best friends. I was given the cold shoulder, and the door was slammed on me. I was given no money, goods, or advice—just warnings. I was broken hearted at not being able to say my goodbyes, but happy to leave. It seemed like forever before I felt comfortable on the outside. I was permanently forbidden to visit with my nun friends, which made me feel awful. 1963-1965 DONNA

When I was 18 years old, lonely and on mission as a cook (my first 3-years of Temporary Vows), I thought seriously about leaving and told my superior. She said, "You are a lovely person. Don't doubt your vocation." Ten years later I left. All that time I still believed they would let me go into nursing someday. If my parents had been able to pay the dowry, I believe I would have been allowed to become a nurse. I was sick. My sister had just died and the nuns had given me no sympathy, hugs, or understanding. One said, "Just the fact that she died at the age of 34 means it must have been the Will of God." Cold, to me. Another said that I was a nobody in the order, so why should they let me go on to nursing? So I blew my top and asked for my papers to leave the order. They said that since I had final vows, I would still have to stay on another nine months before I could get released from the Order. That maybe I wouldn't want to leave anymore then. I told them that I knew the Mother Superior could give me special permission to leave right away if I wanted to. Also, that if I didn't leave soon, they were going to have bigger problems on their hands. My papers from Rome were sent to me releasing me of my vows. They gave me a little money, two outfits to wear, and told me I couldn't date until my vows were up. The Rule was that we weren't allowed to tell anyone we were leaving, but I happily told three nuns. They were not happy with me. I couldn't wait to leave. I was sick of the way they had treated me. I was relieved to be out of the habit—I hate black clothes! . My sisters and brothers comforted me that first day, and held me in their arms. I was 27 years old, and when I put on the lay clothes and left, I felt like I was 14 again—very strange and upset for a few months. I didn't know how to act or talk with people in the world. I also needed surgery when they let me go, and I had to get a job and work 15 months before I *could get insurance for the surgery. It took a year to feel comfortable. Up-to-date clothes helped. I wasn't interested in visiting the nuns for quite a while until I had adjusted. 1952-1965 ELEANOR*

By my 20th year in the convent, I was thinking of leaving. I had been treated unjustly and with bitterness by a Superior, and was refused my request for a change. I confided in the school principal, who was contemplating the same thing. The Provincial wanted me to stay, but there was a several-months' mess of shunning and false accusations and grilling by Superiors. Then I was sent to a holding house with some other nuns to await dispensation papers. I was given $200 and the clothes on my back. When the superior refused to allow other nuns to associate with me, I got a bit nasty. I hated the discord, and was ultimately happy to leave. It took an overnight to stop feeling a little weird without the habit—people were friendly. The tension while waiting was a problem, but I tried to dismiss it all from my mind. I finally visited with a few nuns 13 years later. 1943-1965 MARY

I left the convent because the restricted life was having a negative effect on my mental health. I talked to no one except God about it—I wanted it to be God's decision, no mine. Then three months later, my Mother Superior asked me to leave. I felt relieved. I was to tell no one, pack my clothes, and leave on a bus. She told me that if I didn't open up, I'd never make it in life. Said I should go to college and get married. I was happy to leave, but disappointed and empty at not telling anyone. I went home to see my family, and my father unloaded his side of the divorce problem on me—it was overwhelming. I felt uncomfortable without the habit, because I didn't know how to move modestly. I was told not to visit with my friends in the convent, ever, which made me sad. 1964-1966 BEVERLY

After 7 years in the convent, I finally got psychological help to recognize myself as a person, and decided to leave. I didn't tell anyone right away, not even my priest psychologist—I didn't have the nerve to. I had reached Last Vows and realized that I did not want to go on because I knew by then that I only felt alive when I had a close friend to share with and love—and because I found the daily fear of teaching, of Superiors, of criticism by older nuns, of my own inadequacy, such a constant drain on my energy and vitality. Yet I was imprisoned by my conviction that, hate it as I did, this was "God's Will" for me. Also, never having held a job, I didn't know if I could make it in the world by myself. I'd been thinking seriously about leaving for a couple of years when I saw the movie "The Private Life of Walter Mitty" with Danny Kaye. I went up to my room that night and thought, "Here I am 44 years old, just like Walter Mitty, and I am day-dreaming my life away." I sat down that night and wrote my letter of intent to my Provincial. From that point I never looked back or regretted my decision. One experience tickled me when I thought about it later. For my interview with the Bishop, I looked great. My hair was attractive, my winter coat, gloves, purse, and high-heeled shoes were elegant. This Bishop had a reputation for treating nuns as second-class citizens, yet when I entered his office, he took one look at me and automatically rose to his feet! It was a very small moment of triumph, but for once I felt like a VIP. The biggest problem I had getting adjusted was that I had no 'history'. When I first left, I did not want to tell people about being a nun, so it was as though I was suddenly dropped on the planet without any background. I had been given $500, my dowry, but no other goods or advice. I was not supposed to tell anyone I was leaving, but I did because I felt I was letting down many of my friends and pupils who believed in me. I was happy to leave—I wanted to stretch my wings. I was always welcomed back to visit my friends, except for a few nuns who objected. There was no difficulty about the dispensation; I was given immediate exclaustration within a month of my first letter, because I made it known that I suffered from hypertension. 1944-1966 THERESE-2

In my eleventh year, I was physically worn out and felt guilty about a physical relationship. I told the new Mother General that I felt I could not go on. About nine weeks later, I left. When the dispensation came from Rome, I had to turn in my ring and habit. I was given no money or goods or advice. I left the state immediately. It took nearly seven years to feel comfortable on the outside. I had no problems with the dispensation. 1956-1967 ELIZABETH

I thought about leaving even as a postulant—didn't feel like I belonged. I didn't like what I saw especially the uncharitableness and selfishness. I told the Mistress of Novices that I wanted to leave, but she warned me that I would be unhappy. I stayed 21 years longer. The Provincial Superiors refused to let me go, so I clammed up into myself. When the appointments came for the next year, I was assigned to the Provincial House—we all knew why. My last superior, though,

Chapter XI: Leaving

listened to me and helped me go. I went home and after a year, wrote my final letter to the Mother General. I was given back my dowry plus $200, no goods or advice. I felt a bit strange without the habit and I was always hiding myself. I was glad to be living in the country. 1946-1967 JEAN-3

After first vows, I thought about leaving the convent—I realized that I wanted children very badly. In the beginning, I didn't tell anyone, but after a year, I talked to a priest who suggested I leave. I felt weird about it. I was told not to tell anyone, to leave in secret. I was given no money, no goods, and no advice. I told someone about my leaving, though, because I thought that rule about not telling was stupid. By then I was happy to leave and get on with my life, though it felt odd at first without the habit. Six months later, I was comfortable. 1963-1967 OTTER

Some time after final vows I was not happy and felt very frustrated. I shared my doubts with my friends because I needed to talk to someone. I was in the convent a year more, because I wanted to make sure it was the right decision. First the Juniorate superior suggested I leave. I felt devastated. The Superior General ruled against it. The community did not send for the dispensation—they wanted me to take exclaustration. I went to the Archdiocesan Chancery office and applied for my own dispensation. It took a couple years to feel comfortable. I left with $100 and no goods or advice. Left in 1968. HELGA

I left the convent after 28 years—I was disillusioned by 1965 and final vows seemed too restrictive. My first doubts had been 20 years ago. I stayed because I was happy—I had friends. But I was not fulfilled. I wanted freedom, peace, to get on with my life. I wrote a letter in October asking for dispensation, but offered to stay until the end of the school year. They gave me $250. I didn't need any advice. Most people were very supportive and friendly—it took no time to be comfortable. One thing that helped was that I had a job. I was encouraged to visit my friends in the convent. 1942-1968. FRANCES

I first started thinking about leaving the convent in my third year. I was depressed, my friend had just died, and I had no self-esteem, felt psychologically abused by my superior. I didn't tell anyone of my doubts, but decided to stay. I guess fear of the unknown was worse than the convent. It was twelve years later before I left. Meanwhile I grew up, learned to adapt. I was working with lay study/prayer groups and was very impressed with the spirituality of these people. Yet at the same time my own prayer life was failing; I was neglecting prayer obligations. I had to change—either live up to my commitment as a nun, or leave. At this time, I also met my husband, who first suggested I leave when he asked me to marry him. I was unsure. I explained things to my Provincial (who is still a good friend) and she asked me to wait a year—go somewhere else—do something else. Then see her again if I still wanted to go. My husband went to see her the next day. Neither of them ever told me what was said, but the Provincial then gave me her blessing. I was given $40 which I had paid for dowry. The Order changed to lay clothes about a year before I left, so it only took a few months to feel comfortable. I had never been in love before that. I stayed that summer with my family and wrote to Rome. I was told that if the request wasn't worded "strongly", it would be denied, so I cited my fiance as a reason. Papers came in September. We were married the next June. 1953-1968. ROSE

    Before final vows we got lots of horror stories about nuns who were tormented the rest of their lives by losing their Vocations. I recall a real fear that I would not measure up. I was not evidently unhappy even to myself, and did not allow myself to question the Order until about two years after my parents died. I was on retreat near Mt Hood where the five of us dressed in jeans since no one would see us. There was a blizzard and we were snowed in for a while, during which people brought us candles and blankets and we walked out to the store. I was treated like an ordinary person and liked it tremendously. After that I did begin questioning and started noticing inequities with the vows of obedience and poverty. It's tricky how the mind works. I had shut out a lot. It was long after final vows—my 12th year, that I left. I had stayed because I believed vows were a commitment forever, much as divorce was unthinkable at that time. It took me two months to think it through, and the dispensation arrived a few months after that, though I stayed on to finish one last class for my major in college. The last couple of months I thought a lot about my sexuality, and also began sneaking out to meet a friend who had left the year before. One of the first things I planned to do was to relinquish my virginity and become sexually active, but not married—I had a strong desire to become independent and didn't think marriage was the way to acquire that. I was told not to tell anyone and just to leave on a certain date, dressed in clothes from the second-hand store. Since my parents were dead and my stepfather didn't have much money, I asked the community for some. I was told that since I hadn't brought a dowry, the best they could do was to loan me $600—which I never repaid. I felt that being forbidden to tell any other nuns that I was leaving was unnecessarily painful. I had to get temp work right away, which did not leave me much adjustment time. I loved grocery shopping, walking around on my own, a million things that were a revelation to me. However, I did not have a placement file for teaching and had no counseling about any of this—it was a struggle for me, though I was able to do some substitute teaching. I joined a Catholic singles group which eased my way socially. I did not try to see friends in my former convent for a long while. When I left, I didn't really see anyone who knew me as a nun for some time. By then I had contact lenses and had dyed my grey hair (had it since I was 25). When one nun saw me, she said in a shocked voice that I was a knockout. It wasn't a matter of being cute or pretty, but of learning how to present myself with the help of haircut and makeup. It was fun discovering my physical self. It was longer than a year before I could relax and not monitor what I said in case it revealed my being out of touch for 12 years. By that time I was teaching in Australia and felt more comfortable even though I was 10 years older than the rest of the American exchange teachers. I regretted very much not seeing friends in the convent for years after leaving. More than that, I truly wanted to see other ex-nuns to share experiences. That first year was a joyous revelation to me—I could make choices! It was impossible to explain how wonderful all my discoveries were to people who had not been sequestered like this. 1957-1969 JEAN-2

After a series of emotional (not physical) attachments where I ended up hurt and rejected, one older nun told me that maybe the pattern of my relationships was telling me something. That set me on the journey of finally being able to acknowledge that I was not meant to be a celibate, and that I needed to leave. It was like I had been trying to force myself into a puzzle with all the pieces going one way, then one day I turned them all over and they made sense. When it was clear to me that I needed to leave, I told my highest superior. She was upset with me because I had been up until that time a fairly good nun. She said I was letting my head lead my heart, but I think she meant the opposite, though I was but following my inner wisdom which said it was time to leave. I also knew a very wonderful priest whose vision of God was much bigger and greater than the one I had, and he helped me to believe that God would love me no matter what I did. That freed me up so that I could begin the process of leaving. I had already made final vows, so the Provincial (Superior) sent me to a priest for spiritual direction. After the second session, he said, "It seems to me we are dealing with a fait accompli—you have already made your decision to leave. I don't see any point in further counseling." Originally, I signed papers for a leave of absence, then applied for dispensation. I was able to tell my friends—an act both painful and wonderful-- because the old rules (no telling) had been dropped and I was past the Novitiate. Many of them were saddened, and (I found out later) those who were thinking of leaving themselves found the decision more difficult now. I always felt that those who were secure in their own vocation were able to support me and allow me to leave with their blessings. When the dispensation actually arrived, I was going very seriously with my spouse-to-be, and he drove me to the convent and waited in the car while I signed. So that was kind of an interesting touch. It was not too difficult at that time to get a dispensation because many, many people were leaving during that period. 1961-1969 K.T.

After final vows, I started thinking of leaving. I was away full time studying for an MA and realized I could live happily without the community. I was in a Gestalt therapy group as a preparation for counseling young new members. The leader of the group reframed many of my ways of responding, and this began the process of reexamination. First I thought I would get a job to support myself and three others; then I realized I wanted to live alone. Studying for an MA in Religious Studies made me realize that much of Catholic Church law and practice was created by history and the male clergy that was in charge—it had nothing to do with the gospel or Christ. Religious life had lost its purpose. In leaving, the community gave me back my dowry—$400. I was eager to begin my new life. 1952-1969 THERESE

After 28 years I began to think of leaving the convent. I felt unfulfilled and the need to minister outside of the convent. I told a priest-psychologist and got good counsel. Three months later the dispensation arrived and I left. They gave me $200 and some clothes. Adjustment was easy. 1939-1969 YVONNE

It happened that I was constantly ill, so the Provincial superior gave me "permission" to consider leaving. Within an hour I had decided to leave. I wrote to

Rome, though the Superior General gave preliminary approval to my leaving. I told my friends and received much support from the under-30s group. Outside of a face-to-face meeting with the Archbishop (who scolded me), I had no difficulty with the dispensation. Soon, with my parents' help, I registered at the university and moved into shared student housing. 1957-1969 ANN

  I thought of leaving my very first night in the convent. I remember—as a postulant—standing by the dormitory, we were all there, and the Postulant Mistress said, "We're going to process to the chapel to say goodnight to Jesus," and I thought, What!? Here we had spent days, hours of days praying, and if Jesus is within you, then what was the point of going up to the chapel? I was really sick of it. I didn't tell anyone right away. I may have said What? but nobody said anything to me. I left after 14 years, my idea. I couldn't handle it anymore. For one thing, I kept falling in love with women, and it was way too hard on me. Also, it was obvious that the life that I was living was not realistic—it was awful. In order to leave, I needed to get a job, so I wrote to a friend of mine in Boston and asked her about New England. She suggested Connecticut, so I wrote to every place there that I could think of and got several answers and set up interviews. My superior didn't know about this. Nobody did. Nobody knew. I also had to get a Social Security number without anybody's knowing about it, had to learn to drive (again)—I'm not sure how I did it, but I did. Anyway, I asked for a leave of absence, got on a plane, flew to NY, went to Connecticut, got 3 interviews and was offered 3 jobs—I was so lucky. When my leave of absence for the year was up, I wrote for dispensation. I had taken final vows, but there didn't seem to be any problem. We did it all by mail, and nobody said anything to me or did anything or came to visit me, or anything. By that time we could tell people that we were leaving, but I didn't want to. I didn't want to have any attention drawn to me or have anybody noticing me—I just wanted to get out, to leave. The Provincial superior did know. The house superior didn't know, but she was curious and put a lot of pressure on me. In the middle of breakfast one day—this was during silence—she asked me what I was going to be doing next year, and put a lot of pressure on me to tell. I just said I was going to teach in Connecticut, nothing else. But that made me angry. However, for most of the time that I was in the convent, people were not allowed to tell. They would—this is simply awful—just disappear. There were 32 people in our set and in the end there were about nine left. Nine in the convent and all the others had gone. And nobody said goodbye. It was arranged somehow that they just disappeared. In the chapel and in line, their ranks were just filled in. And nobody said anything—it was terrible, as if they had never existed. It was pretty bad. I was very, very happy to go. No, I didn't meet any former students or anybody I knew the first day. It had taken me so long to see somebody without a habit that I didn't really care that they saw me. 1955-1969 CAROL

Between Juniorate and final vows, I first started thinking about leaving, though I wasn't sure why. I told a priest that I didn't know whether to go on, and he said doubts were normal. Two years later, things got intolerable. I told my superiors, who advised exclaustration. I refused, wrote to Rome, and waited until the school year was up to leave. I was given $200, no goods, and advised not to tell anyone about my leaving. The last year was intolerable, so I couldn't wait to leave. I felt strange without the habit, but visiting other ex-nuns helped. 1962-1969 CONNIE

Leaving in the 1970s

I thought about leaving at every stage of my convent life, but only seriously after final vows. I'd read an article in Sisters Today which indicated I was unsuited. I mentioned it right away, but didn't leave for 1-2 years because the concept took a while to work through. I did the counseling route, which was difficult. Also, I felt like a failure. I was given $200 and they paid for summer school. I was happy to leave because I'd been unhappy in the convent. We didn't wear the habit at school, so leaving without it made no difference. There was no problem with the dispensation. 1958-1970 JANN

Chapter XI: Leaving

I first thought of leaving before first vows, but finally left the summer of 1970 because I wanted children and a husband. When I told friends, they encouraged me and reminded me that first vows are not "forever". It had taken me 10 years to actually leave because I kept convincing myself that being in the convent was God's will and "children were my will". I was in graduate school then, and requested a leave of absence to begin a job search. I was interviewed by the superior, all the Provincial officers, and the bishop. My release came 5-6 months after I wrote to Rome. I was allowed to keep two outfits I'd bought in recent years, plus I was given $300. We were allowed to talk about leaving, and did. Because I had good friends and good memories of the convent, I was not overjoyed to leave, especially because contact with these nuns was not encouraged for several years. It took me about a year to feel comfortable on the "outside", even though I hadn't been wearing a habit to graduate school. 1959-1970 THERESA

Fifteen years into my convent experience I considered leaving, having realized that many sisters, especially higher Eastern Superiors, told lies and were not "real". I decided to keep it to myself, and I prayed not to judge others. I was convinced God wanted me to stay. I was there another six years. Then rumors began that I would not be at that convent the next year, although a new policy was in effect that if a sister was satisfied and doing a good job that she would not be changed unless she requested it, or unless she was needed for a definite position for which no one else could be found. So I called the new Provincial to ask where I would be the next year—should I prepare my trunk for shipment before leaving for two summer school teaching assignments in the country? She said she'd tell me in writing. When I returned, there was no letter, and my phone call was hung up on. I'd had permission to visit my sister in California, so I left. Every time I called the Provincial House the phone was hung up. My brother-in-law suggested that I write them and say that if I did not hear from them in ten days, to consider the letter a formal request for a leave of absence. My doctor told me to leave. There was no reply from the Motherhouse, so I made preparations to leave, but the superior came home and said she hadn't known anything about the situation (not true). I then told her I was prepared to go wherever she sent me and to do whatever work she wanted me to do, but she told me to go ahead and leave anyway. I felt torn. I asked for a leave of absence but was told to go, so I applied for a dispensation with my confessor's and a doctor's recommendations. Though we were not allowed to tell anyone, I wrote a letter to all of my friends explaining why I left. I wasn't particularly happy about leaving; I loved my sisters. I was given back the $300 dowry and told to buy clothes. The first day out I met a parent of one of my students who also bought me clothes. My brother drove up from CA to get me because I had no way to pay my fare home. Before I left I decided that my friends should know the cause of my leaving because it was always kept such a big secret, and so many lies were told about other sisters who had left. So I wrote a letter and sent a copy to the Reverend Mother and to each of my friends at other convents. That is probably why my name is still anathema after 23 years. I didn't look back, but it took me two years to feel comfortable on the outside. I was forbidden to visit with my friends in the convent for seven years. I felt no charity or forgiveness from the convent. I believed I had a Temporary Vocation and that God would give me grace and guidance on whatever path I found myself. It has proven to be true. I have so often found myself in the right place at the right time to be of great help to another. 1950-1971 LORENA

I was uneasy in the Novitiate as were some of my peers, and ended up in a special group of nuns whose superiors had qualms about them. Three years later, my superior suggested I leave. I cried for three days. I was told to call my parents, who took me shopping for $100 worth of "leaving clothes". I told everyone and wrote letters, since it was allowed to tell, but I was scared. It took years for me to feel comfortable on the outside. 1964-1971 DENISE

I was in love with a priest when I first considered leaving the convent. I told him right away because I could trust him. We both stayed for two more years until we were sure, then wrote for dispensations. Mine came in about 4 months, but I didn't sign it for another six months or so. I was given no money, but some clothes. I didn't tell anyone because I knew no one would understand. We moved immediately to another city. Being with someone helped me feel comfortable on the outside, and our nuns weren't wearing habits then, so it was easier than for some. 1959-1971 MURIEL

During prayer, I got the troubling thought that I should leave. I begged God to guide me, and He led me back home. This was fifteen years after my final vows.

Chapter XI: Leaving

I stayed 18 months longer because I wanted to get advice, and also to get a leave of absence to explore my feelings. When I left, I was given $600 and much encouragement and appreciation by my superiors and associates. Leaving was a big step, and I'd been very happy there, so I wasn't overjoyed to go. We weren't in habit then, yet it took a while to feel comfortable on the outside. Months later, I shared with other sister-friends. 1952-1971 EILEEN

I first thought about leaving the convent very late, and it took me two years to actually leave, because I had to figure life out. It seemed to me that community life was dissolving. I discussed it with the Mother General who suggested a leave of absence. Later, I simply signed out—no problem. I was given $1000, no goods, and no advice. In those days we could tell people we were going to leave. My first day out, I met lay people who were glad to see me, though the first time I went without a habit, I was embarrassed. The transition didn't take long, due to my friends' acceptance. 1933-1972   PRISCILLA

It was after final vows when my decision to leave began to evolve. I talked to my close friends in the community and found that many of them were also experiencing difficulty. My Provincial was newly appointed and I did not know her, so because I was far from my community physically (at school) I did not mention leaving to her at first. My reasons for leaving were many—some so hidden I don't think I really understand even today. I lived with a very backwards group of sisters in Boston during my first year in graduate school. They were poorly educated, yet ran an expensive private school for girls. They were good women, but very unprepared for what they were doing. They kept themselves separate from those of us who rented rooms in their building. I remember arriving after a long train ride to Montreal followed by a bus ride to Boston (Memorial Day weekend). I was starved and low on cash. I assumed that I would eat with them, but the sister who showed me to my room informed me that I was responsible for my own meals. Though I had a check to deposit in the bank, this was Saturday and everything was closed until Tuesday. Finally, she brought me an apple and some milk, bread, and cheese. I ate alone and watched them picnic in the back yard just below my window. They called us Sisters of the World! Later they offered eight of us a hotplate, and a refrigerator to store food in. There were no laundry facilities. We lugged dirty clothes and food 12 blocks in heavy snow, rain, or sun. No one ever *offered assistance. We had no common room. A priest friend gave us a TV and we set up folding chairs, trying to create a place where we could relax from our studies. The parish was served by an ancient Irish priest, and Mass in English was the only hint that Vatican II had happened. We were starving for something to feed our spiritual lives; there was no access to spiritual books. We tried to attend the monthly Archdiocesan retreats held downtown, but there was no semblance of silence or reflection. People walked in and out constantly. I tried the Newman Center, but sitting on the floor in front of a twanging guitar wasn't for me. We did attend the Paulist lectures where Eugene Kennedy and Hans Kung were among the speakers. Our host Order did not attend these because they did not go out at night. I remember going to Cambridge Cor Triduum and crying. The church was famous for their boys choir. I have not participated in a more beautiful liturgy to this day. The second year I spent teaching and living with my community in New York. With rules relaxed, everyone went her own way except for liturgy and meals. I really felt adrift. I began to feel more and more that the life offered me was not the life God had led me to and that I could live the life of a dedicated woman within the Church without living in the decaying shell of what had been a great religious order. The third year I returned to Boston knowing I would not return to my community, but buying time to make my future more secure with additional education. I was saddened—leaving was not a time to rejoice. I was given $500 and the Provincial brought the papers to my apartment to sign. 1960-1972 JANET*

I was at final vows before I thought of leaving, and shared my doubts with a friend who convinced me to stay. Two years later I told my superior, wrote the letter, left and went home. I was given no money or goods or advice. I was forbidden to visit with my friends in the convent for four years; this made me feel sad. 1962-1972 JANE

I left many years after final vows—felt I was being destroyed physically and emotionally (too much work, too little support). A doctor and a friend advised me to leave. The grassroots changes I had hoped for didn't happen, and I was overloaded with work, exhausted. I took a year's leave of absence and accepted a grant for graduate study, then realized I could not return to the convent. The community gave me $200, certainly not even enough for a month's rent. I wrote to the Provincial superior and suggested $100 for each year of service would be more appropriate. Of course, that was denied. A greater hardship was lack of Social Security. After I left there was some community arrangement with the SS office to get Sisters enrolled, but it was a one time deal, and I was never notified that I could have been covered. I found out too late. 1946-1972 JAN-2

My first year in the Novitiate, I was shocked by the favoritism shown to specific novices, one of whom was related to the Novice Mistress. One incident sticks in my mind: There were at least two of us who were old enough to be required to fast (see Glossary) during Lent. This Novice Mistress would make hot chocolate for her favorite during breaks, but not for the rest of us. At the end of the second year I was up for final vows. One day I found an envelope addressed to me on the mail rack. It was a very brief note informing me that I would not be allowed to make final vows as I was not "community minded." I was told I could renew my vows, however. Mother General never ever discussed this with me personally. It was obvious that their idea of community did not agree with mine and that my maturity and intelligence was a threat. However, instead of leaving, I took it as a challenge. I was finally allowed to go to college, then was told to teach older kids when I really wanted to teach younger ones. I was shifted from place to place, never allowed to stay more than one year at each, and required to teach high school classes without any college background. I did all this to show the community I could take what they dished out. When I was being shifted from here to there, sometimes in the middle of the year, I was being told by superiors that I was one that they thought they could change like that, but the gossip in the community was that I couldn't get along with people. This was absolutely false. It did serve, though, to make me hesitant to make friends and put down any roots. Then I was allowed to make final vows. Though I was probably more intelligent than most, I was not allowed to study for my Masters degree and was kept out to work at the convent while the rest of my class was allowed to go to college. This made me lonely. Leaving the convent was not a long, drawn-out process for me. I was on mission and had some surgery—quite traumatic for me, and the Mother General said that I could choose to leave that mission if I wished. Things were going on between the other two nuns and some priests that I wanted no part of. Then one of the priests spread around the Community that I had had a nervous breakdown. By that time the people knew what was going on and ignored him. I returned to the Motherhouse to recover from the surgery, and was offered a position as a religious education coordinator at another parish. I had already spent two years in WA in a similar program, and that freedom was like opening doors. I worked with Franciscan priests and a woman there, and finally found the community for which I had entered a "community" fifteen years before. When I first went there I had no idea I would be leaving, but I did arrange to get my own paycheck, take out my living expenses, and send the rest to the Motherhouse. As soon as I decided to leave, I kept all my salary so that I would not leave penniless. A friend had recommended a lay counselor connected to the parish. He helped me to see that the things laid on me were not my problems, but the stupidity of my Order. He was a marriage counselor who worked for the county and we found parallels between bad marriages and religious life and cults. I worked at that parish during the school year and the Franciscans allowed me to live there during the summer, even loaning me a car. I got a job and my own apartment by September. I did not sign the community papers until the following spring. The only reason I did sign them was because it was the only way to get back some money of mine that the community had—without interest, of course. They cashed in my US Bonds, which kept me from getting even that interest. 1955-1972 GINA

At some point, the convent no longer seemed a community to me, and I first thought of leaving. Things were changing in the world and I discussed it with my friends, but didn't leave for three years because I wanted to show that I could teach art full time. First I asked for a leave of absence. I was given the money from my art show. Though I wasn't sure if I was doing the right thing, I was generally happy to leave. Friends gave me money for the trip to CA—we were not wearing habits at that time anyway, so I felt comfortable right away. The dispensation came before I married. 1955-1972 JANET K

I didn't think about leaving the convent till the year before I actually left. I shared my doubts with a Sister who is now 91 years old. She was the one who helped me during my teaching years and who helped me think about different things that were happening in the convent and in the outside world. I used to think she was a terrible radical, but I owe her the most. I left on my own and told them after the fact. I said, By the way, I have left the convent. Here's the ring I was wearing. Send the papers to the local pastor here and he will notify me to come down and sign them. They informed me that they would send my $500 dowry.

Chapter XI: Leaving

Nothing else was given me, no advice, no nothing. I heard from friends later; some were really sorry. A few expressed concern. Others in my peer group accused me of having had sex, of being pregnant—now I can laugh at it, but at the time I didn't think it was funny. People that left before 1965 left in secret. They would disappear from the table—we just didn't know where they were. Superiors never wanted us to know they were gone. Or they would take us for a walk and we would find out somebody had left. They would never tell us directly. Someone would find out and say so-and-so left—that's how we would find out. That's why we went out for this long walk and were given candy bars and special treats. We were already wearing regular clothes, so transition was simple in 1973—except emotionally. The convent had left its scars. 1960-1973 CHERRY

We weren't allowed to tell anyone, but I did because I was loyal to my friends. I was happy to leave—I'd waited long enough for freedom! I felt great, like: I'm a person! We were forbidden to visit friends in the convent for years afterwards, but I did it anyway. Of course there was some insecurity and loneliness at first, but I don't look upon that as a disadvantage. 1960-1973 CASEY

I had taken final vows by the time I decided to leave. I just didn't fit; celibacy was hard. I talked about it with a friend, but it was four years (I'd been encouraged to wait and see) before I let the Provincial know. I left with love and warmth—signed papers three months later. I was happy to leave because I was in love, though it took me years to feel comfortable on the outside. 1959-1973 CAROL-2

I'd taken final vows, but wanted to get married. I woke up one morning knowing I'd move on. I asked for the papers and 5 months later signed them. I was given back my dowry and personal effects. Some persons who felt threatened gave me advice, but I was happy to move on. Sixteen years was a good time for one career. I felt comfortable right away and looked forward to life. 1947-1973 GAYLE

Though I ultimately remained ten years in the convent, by the end of the Juniorate I was thinking of leaving. I didn't fit the mold and disliked the politics, yet imposed upon myself pressure to stay. It took a long time to summon the courage to tell Mom and Dad & Mother General. I had to write a letter and make an appointment with the Mother General first. Then a letter to Rome stating my reasons and asking for dispensation. Wait for reply. I was given $300 upon leaving and told to remain quiet about it, but I told some people anyway. I was happy to leave because I knew it was the right thing to do. I had made my clothes. It didn't take long to feel comfortable on the outside; my folks accepted me. Maybe another reason to leave was seeing these embittered old prunes (Sisters) and not wanting to end up like that. I have a tendency to be hyper-critical and to see such problems, so it seemed to me that I really needed to get out of that environment. The issue was men. I found them quite attractive and that was incompatible with the vow of chastity. A third problem was the power structure and the "most favored sisters" who catered to them and vice-versa. It seemed quite in opposition to the whole notion of Community. 1963-1973 JULIA

Well after my final vows, the French Canadian majority of the convent rescinded some rule changes, and if we didn't accept the changes, we had to leave. I left within a year. I was sorry the rule was so inflexible and that Canada's majority was able to dictate my state's rules. I changed the wording on the old-fashioned dispensation form, and sent it to Rome. We wore no habits at the time, and were allowed to talk about leaving, so it was very open. I always felt comfortable on the outside. 1953-1973 NELL

Early on, within my first two years, I wanted to leave. What happened was that my younger sister was getting married, and I was so naïve as to assume I could go to her wedding since it was in a Catholic Church and would be at Mass. My mother had even written to the Provincial asking for me to come home for the wedding. I was told, "Sister, you know we don't go to weddings", so I went to Chapel and cried. A Sister asked me what was wrong, and I told her I was going to leave the convent. She said, "Well, the wedding is on Saturday—what will you do on Monday?" I hadn't thought about that—so I decided to stay because of my commitment to school and to God. I believed that it looked like God wanted me to stay. Then stories like: "Sister So-and-so left and two days later her mother was killed by a truck!!!"—these left a real impression on me and I was determined that none of my family would die because of me. I finally decided to leave after getting my Master's degree; by then, I had tried living in community for two years. It got so bad that I cried myself to sleep and dreaded going home at night to the convent.

Chapter XI: Leaving

Teaching 4th graders became my refuge from the unhappiness I felt in community. Finally I was able to say the words "I want to leave" and not feel the guilt I thought I would. I was free at last! The Provincial suggested I get an apartment in the small town over Christmas while I remained teaching at the school. I felt lucky that I could leave this way—I couldn't stand one more day of living with those sisters in the convent. They were not friendly to me after I left, but I didn't care. When the school year finished, I moved away. From January to June of that next year, two sisters came to visit me, trying to persuade me to stay. But by then I was confident that I could live on my own and found I would never return to that lifestyle. In leaving, I had found myself at 31 years of age, doing things that most 18-year olds are doing: getting a job, apartment, managing a car, paying insurance, etc. I felt like I was actually 10 years or more younger emotionally because I hadn't grown up in the convent—I had regressed! All these years since, this has still been an issue because I didn't have a lot of the experiences my contemporaries had. For me, for example, the 60's were "dead years". The Vietnam War meant nothing to me other than praying at daily Mass: "For all those who died in Vietnam, we pray to the Lord". We couldn't read newspapers, see TV or anything about the outside world. I feel like I lost ten years of my life, though I will always be grateful for my education and teaching degree. I was happy to leave, wanted freedom, but I was also scared. People on the outside were very supportive. When I saw my friends back in the convent, I was struck by the loneliness in their lives. Getting my dispensation was so easy, I wondered if they wanted me to leave. 1961-1974 MARY-2

When I could no longer find peace within myself, I told a counselor about my doubts. I was sent on retreat, then changed mission houses. To be really sure, I waited another five years. I really didn't want to go, but too many changes got to me. After making the decision, I was relieved, but sad. I wrote the proper letters, and was given my dowry back plus $750 and some medical goods. The superior said they were there to help, if I had any needs. I knew I would miss the life-security and my friends. The first time without a habit, I felt strange, out of place, but working on the outside helped make me comfortable. I never went back to see any nuns, although I was always welcome. 1957-1974 LILLA

After 15 years in the convent, I was becoming more and more detached from the Catholic Church and the Order, and wanted to leave. The first people I told

were sobered. I stayed long enough to finish my teaching contract. I was given $300 and the advice (by my Provincial) to keep reading. In those days we were allowed to tell that we would leave, but I felt I couldn't because then they wouldn't accept me. We had no habit at that time, so being comfortable on the outside was easier. The form letter we had to send to the Papal Nuncio asking for dispensation was demeaning and I detested it, but I did it to get things over with. 1959-1974
SUZANNE

I first thought about leaving the convent during the time I was sent to teach as a novice. The Superior had no idea how to handle a novice, and she left me with the impression that she would rather not have me. In fact, she told me that the following year when I was reassigned to her convent. The living situation was very difficult. I slept in the linen room. I had to practice the piano in the convent and there were several ill Sisters who could not be disturbed. Then I was scolded for not practicing enough. The Sisters in that group were not compatible. I taught at two schools and spent hours on a bus every day. Besides, I was not allowed to go off the school premises to walk, and I had to go to my room when they showed a movie. When I returned to the Novitiate for the last months before making vows, I told my Mistress of Novices that I really thought I could not live that way for the rest of my life. She was very understanding and helped me work through it during the summer. In the end I believed her, that this was not the usual living situation, and that she really thought I had a Vocation. I remained. However, I was reassigned to that same house the next year. At some point after Vatican II, a very subtle change began to surface in me. I finally got my degree in the early 60s and turned my attention towards a Master's Program. My schedule in teaching was more and more taxing. The tension was affecting my health. It was during this time that I became more cognizant of my limited role in the community. As I said, this was really subconscious. There were so many other things going on that took my full concentration that I did not recognize what was really happening. Also, I really did not want to leave. My Vocation was still vital in me. When the idea did surface, I still could not imagine my doing anything else except being a Sister. About 1974 I sought counseling from a secular priest who was assigned as the Spiritual Director for the Archdiocese. He and I had gone to school together, although he was at least one year behind me. I really went because of my problems with friendship, but other things surfaced. He was probably the first person to question my ever having

Chapter XI: Leaving

entered, and after that I began to look at it squarely. Naturally I was frightened. I had no idea what I would do. There was no place to go. My parents were dead and my family scattered. It was not an easy period. I kept going for counseling off and on until I left. But in 1976 My Provincial Superior told me very frankly that she really thought I should leave. We began the formal steps almost immediately. I was relieved to have it out, for I had not spoken to anyone other than the Spiritual Director. Even one of my best friends who had also decided to leave did not know any more than I knew about her decision. Of course, we were accused of deciding it together. The Provincial Superior had to appeal to Rome. When the dispensation arrived, I had a certain amount of time to sign the documents and arrange for my departure. It was solemn, but simple. I was given back my dowry, $500 and allowed to take my clothes and a few books. I particularly requested that I keep my crucifix and my ring which had been made from two family rings: my Dad's and my older brother's. No advice. However, the Provincial Superior was most encouraging, as were all the Sisters. They expressed great confidence in me that no matter where I went I would succeed. This was amazing to me. After 27 years with them I never suspected that they really thought of me in those terms. It was a relief to leave. On the other hand, I felt sad to be departing from a life style that had meant so much to me and to which I had given so much. One strong feeling in me was peace. I knew I had not made a decision impetuously or out of anger; it had taken a great deal of time and prayer and suffering. I flew directly to Chicago to my sister's and a job in a medical practice. I was not around people I knew for a long time. There was still some emotional rawness in me that had to heal. 1949-1976
JULIANNE

I suppose I thought about leaving all along—I always was daydreaming about leaving the convent. I didn't because I thought I had a Vocation, but I used to wish I didn't have one and could be just a normal person. I thought about leaving lots of times, every time somebody left. I didn't tell anybody about my doubts. I didn't doubt my Vocation, it was just that I didn't want to go through with it sometimes. It was a secret thing that I didn't talk about a whole lot, but I certainly thought about it a lot. Nobody suggested I leave. In fact, when I was a Novice, I remember asking to leave. Mother said, No, you shouldn't, you can't leave, you goofy little girl. She didn't take me seriously, and since I was so non-assertive and she'd said I had a Vocation, I suppressed it, never let myself take it seriously. I just would daydream, and eventually left after 20 years. The process of leaving in our order was that you would notify our Superior, and kept things very secretive before the Vatican II changes—people would just be gone and there would be a solemn announcement in the refectory that Sister so-and-so is no longer with us. She's left, but please pray for her. But we couldn't contact those who left. Then after the changes it was still kind of secretive until the last few years I was there. When I left, I decided three months before and I called the Mother Superior from the mission and told her I would finish out the school year. I was given $500 and allowed to take personal clothing and articles. I was happy to leave then, and was really looking forward to it, because by the time I left I had overstayed my welcome and had prepared for it, having already gotten a part-time job in the community, a place to live, and a boy friend. I stayed in the same town and had lots of lay friends who helped my leaving with a party, a housewarming, and by being friendly at church. I had taken final vows and had to wait a year for a leave of absence. At the end of that year I had to meet the nuns in a cafe and sign these weird papers in Latin from Rome, from the boys in Rome—I felt that I had nothing to do with them, and that part felt strange and cold. But my transition was very easy. 1958-1977 MARGARET

I first thought of leaving while I was still in the Juniorate—under first vows. Convent life seemed to run contrary to what I thought life should be like. My superior convinced me I had a vocation to stay. Nine years later, a psychologist suggested I leave; I was frightened. I'd always had the hope that things would get better, or that I'd grow up and things would fall into place. I couldn't leave until I felt I would not be a "failure" if I left. By the 14th year it seemed very clear to me that I would destroy myself if I continued to live the life of a nun. It became apparent that this life was no longer valid for me. In '76 I met with the Provincial Superior to tell her I wished to leave. She suggested I think it over and come back in three months, after which we started letters to the Mother General, etc. I was given $700 when I left, and a car loan for $3000. Some nun friends brought me used towels and sheets. We were allowed to tell anyone by then, but I only told close friends until 2-3 weeks before I left. I felt I was abandoning them. I also wondered why they could make it in the convent, but I couldn't. I was relieved to be leaving and eager to get on with my life, but very sad to leave my best friends and the security of what I knew. 1963-1977 SARAH

Chapter XI: Leaving

In my 25th year (I had taken perpetual vows) I met and fell in love with Ron. We worked together—he was the Superintendent and I was the Associate Superintendent. I immediately told my parents, my sister, and a friend, and we discussed pros and cons of my decision. They were supportive. I finished out the year (3 months) on my job, then left. It was my decision and I felt great, though apprehensive as I looked for housing, a job, etc. In order to leave, I had written to the President of the Order and asked that she apply to Rome for my dispensation. I was given $400, my own belongings, some miscellaneous goods, and lots of advice by the Council, and my friends and family. I wrote a letter to all my friends telling them of my changes in commitment. I had been independent in the community, and was invited for all community meetings. I was in love and couldn't wait for the actual day. We were already in contemporary dress, so there was no "habit" adjustment. Rome responded in two weeks. I still have strong community ties, and am happy. 1952-1977 MURIEL

I first thought of leaving 4 years before, at my 25th anniversary of vows. A priest first suggested it, and I felt devastated—the convent was a very meaningful part of my life. At some point I spoke to my sister friends about it, but waited for a year while I lived in an apartment. When I told the Provincial (there was no difficulty with the dispensation) and the papers came from the Vatican, I went to her house with my best Sister-friend and signed and had breakfast with them. I was given no goods, money, or advice, but was free to tell anyone that I was leaving, so I wrote a letter and sent it to each community member. We were out of habit already, so it wasn't visually as bad. I had been a faculty member with tenure at a college for many years, and that remained the same. Basically, I did not think of myself as leaving because I had permission from the Provincial to keep attending all the functions, including assemblies, which I did as an "Associate Member." 1957-1978. MARIETTA

About my fifth year I began to feel I didn't belong in the convent. I didn't tell anyone, and for the next 8 years kept trying to make sure I would make the right decision. Then I told my superiors, who didn't think I really wanted to leave. A year after that, I signed the papers and was given $2000. I was happy to leave. I felt a little uncomfortable—for an hour—the first time anyone saw me without a habit because they only knew me as a nun. It was the right decision. 1964-1978 JESSICA

I left 10 years after final vows because I realized I wanted to be in a relationship, not a community. If I had needed help I could have gotten some. As it was, my inheritance from my father's estate was turned over to me with a financial statement of expenditures made for my tuition, room and board, and some gifts to help out my sisters' families. The community kept the interest on my inheritance or I would have had twice as much. When I first asked the Provincial about leaving, she suggested a leave of absence, but I said no, so she initiated the dispensation papers. I taught the same high school class the next year, except I went from Sister to Ms. We weren't in habits then. 1960-1979 CAROLYN

I left when I left because the time was right. No one suggested I leave, or gave me any money. I could have told anyone. There was no difficulty about the dispensation. 1952-1979 ANNE

Leaving in the 1980s

I always feared that I'd get kicked out—if you were sent back to the world, you'd have failed. Community was important to me. I felt insecure about the strong attraction to a priest before his ordination, but didn't tell anyone else until later. By 12 years later, I was more secure (I'd been working with the farm workers in lay clothes) and didn't need the Order as much. When I left, I had no assurance that the priest would be there for me or that we would marry. I was given $1000 and a car. I was happy to leave. 1959-1981 JEAN

Chapter XI: Leaving

I left after final vows when I realized certain wrongs were being continued. My therapist was the first to know. I was in therapy for three years after I decided to leave, because I was determined I was not going to leave with anger/baggage. Even then, I was scared. It was like I heard a voice in the back seat of the car and I looked to see who said, "Leave". The Provincial was supportive. She cried and I cried. They gave me $500 and a car I made payments on. We already were in secular clothes and I kept my same job with lay people, so it didn't take long to feel comfortable as an ex-nun. 1954-1983 HOLLY

It was after final vows that I saw that I just didn't fit in the convent. I told no one at first, then only my lay friends. Within several years I left. They gave me $500 (my dowry) but no other goods. I didn't speak to the nuns about leaving because I just wanted to leave and close that part of my life forever; I also didn't visit the nuns afterwards. Leaving the habit behind made me feel naked, but I moved to another state and it only took about a year to feel comfortable. 1958-1981 MARY S

Twenty years after I said my vows, I fell in love and asked to leave. I was scared and excited all at once. Then I learned he wasn't the one for me, but perhaps someone else was. I needed to move on with my life. The leaving process for me was healthy and peaceful, taking 2-3 years in all. I was given no money, but received financial advice and was allowed to purchase a car from my Order with low financing. I was happy to leave—felt I was becoming my truest self. We had no habits then, and I came out so gradually—geographically away from home---that psychologically, it was not a jolt, though the dispensation took a few months longer than the Order had anticipated. 1960-1984 DIANE

After nineteen years, I realized I needed male companionship. I couldn't make up my mind right away, so I took a leave, came back and thought about it, then left. At that time it was mandatory that we have professional and spiritual counseling before leaving. Then I wrote a letter about leaving and sent it to the community as a whole. It was not as traumatic as it used to be—one kept in contact, had the same friends, had no habit to shed, etc. 1960-1985 CAROLYN

When I was a postulant, I got homesick and first thought of leaving. A priest-counselor encouraged me to stay. I believed God wanted me in the convent, so I stayed 31 years more. Then I began to be anxious and a counselor helped me work it through. I wrote a formal letter to the Superior General and to the Council. Wrote to Rome. Left to find a job and live alone. I was given $3000 plus some household items from the sisters. I was happy because I knew what I was doing was right for me. It took three months to get the dispensation. 1954-1985 LOUISE

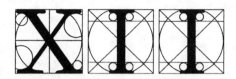

healing, dreams

Afterwards: healing, dreams
blocked/first memories
acceptance, support, strange reactions
looking back: letters, photos written in convent
re-contact with nuns, ex-nuns
early dating, relationships

Healing/Dreams

Child: I was writing this paper on how I wanted to be a nun, but then you left, so I'm thinking there must be something wrong with it.

There is no doubt that healing was necessary after being in the convent, especially in the pre–Vatican II years. Sixty-five out of the 73 participants were teenagers when they entered (the youngest was 14 years old). Imagine *not* growing up—spending the years that others date, listen to music, hang out in burger joints, go to college, and get that first job—in keeping silence, going through the convent boot camp, accepting one's subservience, not communicating with one's former friends, visiting one's family once a year, never handling money (or getting paid, or writing checks). And then suddenly, without preparation of any kind, being thrust back into this unfamiliar and very public world, losing one's nun-friends (for at least the first year), and being still saddled with the naivete and emotional maturity of a 15 year old. Such was the situation for many ex-nuns.

Their confusion and agony at trying to find themselves without help registered in their dreams and nightmares. It is normal to include pieces of our lives and concerns in dreams. It is not normal to have "trapped in the convent" dreams for up to 30 years.

I still occasionally dream I am trapped and cannot leave—it is upsetting. DONNA

I still have those dreams sometimes, about trying to get back in or about nuns who were good to me. Guilt may still be in my subconscious for not living my vows until death. I cared about my Sisters in religion and never knew how they felt or what happened to them. LILLA

Yes, when I'm very tired, I'm back there and wondering why!! FRANCES

In the dreams, I'm aware that I am a married woman, but I'm trapped in the convent trying to figure out how to get out. I don't know that the dreams will stop. JULIA

When I have the "trapped" dreams, I know my life is out of control at those times. JANN

Yes—two or three times I have had dreams that the Pope makes all of us return to convents. MERT

Yes, I have had confused "trapped" dreams about the convent. They tell me: take a look at your life. CAREN

Yes, I still have "trapped" and other dreams of the convent. MARY S

Yes, I dream constantly that I am going to leave the convent or I am returning to the convent. THERESE

Yes, "trapped" dreams and I'm trying to decide whether to leave. They are still a deep part of my life. OTTER

Yes—I have repeated dreams about wearing the habit and being ashamed of it. SUZANNE

Yes, I still have these dreams where I can't understand how I got back into the convent. I am so relieved upon awakening. JEAN-3

I often dream I am preparing to leave again. CASEY

For most of the ex-nuns in this project who started out with (sometimes years of) "trapped" and other anxiety-provoking convent dreams, time itself has been the healer. Some went to therapy. Some discussed their concerns with other ex-nuns, or healed by reading books about others' experiences. Though a number of them still have convent dreams, such dreams are no longer threatening. Twenty-five women claim they either never had convent dreams, or they do not remember them.

> After about 15 years after leaving, the dreams (about not finding my way out) stopped when I began accepting myself as is. CONNIE

> I had dreams until I was 50 years old. I think they were associated with feelings of guilt, and they stopped because I felt fulfilled. JAN

> For several years I dreamed about being in the convent and not being able to find my clothes so that I could get out. My convent dreams in general stopped after 6-7 years. HELGA

> I did have "trapped" dreams, but not any more. I think therapy helped. CAROL

> Some dreams stopped when I retired and led a more relaxed life. FRANCES

> There were some "trapped" dreams. Every once in a while I dream that I am in a convent and don't belong there. I haven't had any nightmares. I think my dreams are being resolved more, are not so confusing now that I am giving myself permission to be exactly who I am now. I am doing much work in journal writing, therapy, and by joining the women's spirituality movement. MARGARET

> I dreamed for years about being back; those dreams gradually changed from pain to acceptance. DOLORES

> The "trapped" dreams where I entered and couldn't leave—these lasted quite some time. JEAN-2

> No "trapped" dreams, but I often dream I'm leaving the convent. I have gone through several years of psychoanalysis and I now realize that leaving the convent for me symbolizes moving away from perfectionistic attitudes and strong self-judgments. I will probably always have these dreams, but they do not frighten me now that I understand they are symbolic. SARAH

Yes, I have "trapped" dreams—when my life is going poorly, I dream I'm in the convent. I'm anxious in many of the scenarios. Not nightmares, just uneasiness that still occurs, though at longer intervals. DENISE

The dreams stopped after years. I think they reinforced my sense of failure. NANCY

The convent dreams I did have stopped ages ago. I think they remind me that I hated Chapter. JOSEPHINE

It was over 30 years before the "trapped" dreams stopped. Sometimes night after night I would find myself in a convent with no idea how to get out. There was always some reason I couldn't leave. Sometimes the way out was through a labyrinth of tunnels and I would always get lost. Or I was being held prisoner in the convent. My first reaction in the dream when I caught a glimpse of my reflection, or saw the tip of a veil or habit out of the corner of my eye was, Oh, no! I'm in the convent again—how can I get out? I think the dreams and nightmares meant that I hadn't worked through all the misery I'd buried about the convent days. DORIS

Yes, I've had "trapped" dreams. Often I relived humiliating experiences, but I always knew my husband was waiting for me outside. The dreams meant I didn't belong there. They stopped years ago. THERESE-2

Not "trapped" dreams, but I do have recently, dreams that center in the Community. Usually these come after being with ex-nuns from my group or after receiving the Community newsletter. Sometimes the dreams are stressful, but usually they are dreams I can peacefully recall. The psyche has to bring daily or past experiences into the whole picture. The Community was a profound part of my past, and I am sure there are still some things that have not been resolved. In fact, since I have started this questionnaire, I have had had more "Community" dreams than before. It only seems natural to me. The period between the initial dreams and the recent ones could have been a blocking out of the past, but it could have been that I was so busy and did not have time to dwell on the past. JULIANNE

❖❖❖

Chapter XII: Healing, Dreams

What was the greatest advantage to your leaving?

Concentrating on the good memories, thinking of the best things in our lives, is often a good way to heal.

Of the 61 women who answered this question: WHAT WAS THE GREATEST ADVANTAGE TO YOUR LEAVING? five said that their greatest advantage now was *Peace*. Nine mentioned *Freedom* and *Independence*. Sixteen spoke of their *families*. And the remaining 31 gave answers related to personal growth.

After a number of years, I have begun to think independently. ELIZABETH

Freedom. I can remember my first day at work. At lunch time I went to a local coffee shop and sat there with the greatest feeling of elation and freedom I had ever had in my entire life. I loved it. I feel perfectly normal in the world and haven't thought about this convent stuff until you called me. CHERRY

Freedom to grow up. I feel comfortable now—no woman will ever dominate me again. ELEANOR

Return to life! I've gotten beyond the guilt. DONNA

I got into a real world. The Sisters had no idea of what lay people in the real world go through. They have absolutely no concept of not only the problems, but the fun, either. CAROL

That I was finally out of there, and yes, I'm having a helluva time. KATHLEEN

I didn't have to keep fitting into stupid rules of an Order. HOLLY

New lifestyle—I am comfortable and accepted by all. YVONNE

No one is holding me back. DORIS

I have been able to pursue my own interests and talents, and to focus my love more humanly, more humanely. MARTHA

I believe that my greatest advantage is the self-confidence I experience. I have been able to do something good with my education only because I was not under the constraints I felt in the Community. I know that I am helping make this town a better place to live—making an impact, building a legacy. And personally, the greatest thing that has happened to me is that my life is now in balance and no longer askew. JULIANNE

Apparently, they were right—I'm happy on the outside, too. JOSEPHINE

What was the greatest disadvantage to your leaving?

If there are advantages to everything, there are also disadvantages. Though nearly all ex-nuns left the convent to experience real poverty, 10 women in particular mentioned as disadvantages:

Lack of finances,
Lack of security,
Lack of jobs and *lodging.*

Sixteen said there were *no disadvantages*.

Eighteen mourned
> *loss,*
> *separation,*
> *lack of closure,*
> *abandoned friends,*
> *lack of preparation,* and
> *self-doubt.*

Two had families that did not accept them.

One was disturbed by *curiosity* and *invasive questions from the public*.

Two regretted less praying going on on the outside..

The greatest difficulty was finding my place in the Church. To some I appeared an outcast, a disobedient daughter, a rebel, a destructive influence. Former priests and religious are still not looked upon with comfort by many. JANET

Naivete—I was 27 years old when I left and I felt like 14 years old again, very strange and upset for a few months, not knowing how to act or talk with people in the world. ELEANOR

Insecurity and loneliness at first, but basically, none. CASEY

I was sorry to leave the elderly nuns. YVONNE

I felt like a failure. NANCY

Doubt. LORNA

I was alone. I did not know why my siblings seemed to resent me. My parents did not understand, never asked me why I left, and complained to relatives

that they knew nothing. On one memorable occasion they laughed at me while I wept. I think they were as confused as I. In those days there was no help from the convent or other places when you left. It was like being dunked in a cold water tank: sink or swim. And you were working double-time to understand the world and catch up in order to make a living—you couldn't take time off to heal, so everything got buried for years until it came out in depression or physical ailments. Do I feel comfortable now? Yes. I still hurt when I think about some things, but I'm working on it. It's only been 35 years. DORIS

Blocked Memories:

**ARE YOU CONSCIOUS OF HAVING BLOCKED OUT CONVENT MEMORIES?
FROM WHICH STAGE?
HAVE SOME BLOCKED MEMORIES NOW RETURNED?
ARE YOU CONSCIOUSLY TRYING TO BRING BACK CONVENT?
BY WHAT METHOD?
WHY OR WHY NOT?**

You don't have to be a War veteran, be beaten bloody, or be an incest survivor to have Post-Traumatic Stress. Any part of your life that was a shock to your system can result in temporary loss of memory--"blocked memories" which must be dealt with upon their return.

Women ex-religious in the mid-twentieth century were generally good people, loyal and close-mouthed about the convents they left. Although some were threatened by their communities upon leaving and some by the Church (fear of creating Scandal--see Glossary), some simply wanted to concentrate on their new lives and not remember their convent experience in detail. Regardless, memories were lost. Now, strong, intelligent women of today take care of themselves. They realize that blocked memories may surface and cause more problems, so they make decisions as to how to deal with those memories: completely bury them so deeply that they do not resurface (women who chose that option did not contact me, were not interviewed, and will not read this book), or they work out their problems in various forms of therapy. Did you block out convent memories?

YES: 20
NO: 47
POSSIBLY: 2

YES, I HAVE BLOCKED OUT MEMORIES:

It is the only way that I can survive. I need to look forward--I cannot change the past. Focussing on past hardships is a waste of my energy. NANCY

Yes--I deliberately wanted to avoid negative feelings and get on with living. I had to decide if I was going to gloss over those years and decide that it wasn't a total loss. I did realize that those years were not without their learning experience and good memories, but on balance, it was not a good choice to enter the convent. I have certainly forgiven myself, but I do wish the Peace Corps had been available at that time. JEAN-2.

The Postulancy period seems to be a blank. I'm not working at bringing back memories, but as I read and think about these questions, more memories surface. It's interesting to recall what I've been through, especially since that way of life is probably extinct as we knew it. TRACE

I don't remember the first 2 1/2 years completely, though I'd like to. I block out memories that have returned because hurt is difficult to deal with, especially when there was no good reason for it. CAREN

I have blocked out from final vows on. I still need to grow, but am not consciously trying to recall these memories. I see my group (in the convent) periodically, checking how I've matured and who hasn't. HOLLY

I have blocked out those years of teaching high school with older sisters. I went back to the city and I couldn't recognize the school--I had no physical memory. I am not trying to retrieve those memories, though I do work on analyzing my dreams. THERESE

Yes--from two specific years. It was necessary at the time, but now that the memories have returned, I sometimes discuss them with other ex-nuns or with my husband, and I can face it all better now. It is behind me. LORENA

Chapter XII: Healing, Dreams

In answering these questions, I realized that I have no memories of the early stage (1954-65). I don't mind having them blocked--I don't need to clutter my mind with more things. LOUISE

Yes, it's a part of life. I don't remember things from various years. Why relive the past and force the memories back? That's not healthy. JANET K

Yes, but answering these questions has brought things back, though as soon as I finish, I'll throw these thoughts away again. JEAN-3

Yes, but I don't dwell on the negative. JAN

Yes, I have blocked out some convent memories, but I don't want them back. CAROL

Earlier I did block some memories, and still cannot remember some things that other ex-nuns speak of. No, I am not drawing out those memories without purpose--I want to expose to the light of reason as many hard instances as come to mind so that I can lessen the pain and decrease the anxiety they still cause. The worst occasions are still slow-to-heal wounds. DORIS

Yes, from all stages, and that's fine with me. ELIZABETH

Yes, but I let it be. In answering some of these questions, things are coming back that I haven't thought about for years. HELGA

Starting the day I left, I blocked out convent memories--I just wanted to put it all out of my mind. Some memories have returned, but the negative experiences are best forgotten. I would only bring these memories back to write a book--the convent is a lifetime removed. DONNA

It's sad, but I have blocked out memories of the Novitiate, and they haven't come back. It was a defensive mechanism. When I meet former classmates, they remember more. JANN

I blocked out convent memories from 1950 on. This is perplexing--I once played the pipe organ and directed the choir, but to this day I cannot play a single note. Hearing about different sisters, and laughing about things has brought back a lot. JAN-2

I have blocked memories from different stages in the convent, though this paper has brought some of them back. LILLA

Yes, I've blocked out memories, but I'm not trying to get them back. ELEANOR

NO, I HAVEN'T BLOCKED OUT MEMORIES THAT I KNOW OF:

I'm not conscious of having blocked out convent memories, but I'd like to bring them all back so that I can write my autobiography. YVONNE

No. I do like to visit with my old Novice Mistress. JOSEPHINE

No to blocked memories, and I'm consciously trying to write my autobiography. THERESE-2

No, though it's hard to remember that life--it seems like it happened to someone else. DENISE

No, but I may try hypnosis if my present ill health persists; perhaps they never left interiorly. ANN

I remember most things clearly. ELLEN-2

No, and there is no need to bring them back. CAROL-2

No, but I am amazed how many memories this questionnaire has brought to the surface. I have learned to face situations as directly and as soon as possible, therefore, I do not tend to block out memories. I just simply forget some things. I refer to it as being "slow of head". JULIANNE

No, but I don't remember it all---may have blocked out some. KATE

No conscious blocking---I remember all but natural forgetting. ROSE

Time eventually heals; some stuff, I just forgot. I think I have worked on the important stuff. ELLEN

No---I had a good counselor of my own choosing, unbeknownst to the community. GINA

Memories that have returned are about crushes on other nuns. I see these as a natural though embarrassing development of my gayness. CONNIE

I am trying to bring back those memories so that I can answer this questionnaire better. SHIRLEY

There may be some unpleasant things I'd rather not deal with---again! JULIA

No need, and my memory is poor. FRANCES

I want nothing to do with bringing back blocked memories. MARY

No, and no reason to bring them back. KATHLEEN

MAYBE SOME MEMORIES ARE MISSING:

Either it's normal or blocking has occurred from the past. Or maybe a lot of this stuff has become non-important to me and that's why I forgot about it. CHERRY

As some memories return, I notice that back then, I didn't realize there was so little laughter in my life. MERT

When you are reminded of the convent, do you have bitter or sweet memories first? What are they?

The key word here is "first". Some women who answered "no" to the question *do* have bitter memories---they just do not come to mind *first*. Conversely, those who are *first* reminded of sad and harsh incidents/attitudes are not necessarily devoid of *happy* memories. Nuns were trained to be loyal, and ex-nuns do not go out of their way to make things seem bad, unless the situation is so intolerable that they just can't handle it anymore. So, then, why did we ask this question? To get some interesting answers. Read on:

DO YOU HAVE BITTER MEMORIES FIRST?

> YES: 16
> NO: 44
> SOMETIMES: 1
> OTHER COMMENTS: 5

"YES" ANSWERS:

The attempt to make and keep us in a childish state still rankles. CASEY

> I have a resentment against the woman who was Provincial Superior when I left. In earlier years there was a sharp division between the younger Superior with younger nuns, and a group of elder nuns who passed judgment on her every action. The Provincial went there supposedly to assess the situation, but she rejected my efforts at friendship and cozied up to the elder nuns. When later I faced her about her lack of support for the Superior, all she said was, I didn't want to get involved. THERESE-2

> I have memories of women supposed to be serving the Lord who pushed down other Brides of Christ so badly that they cracked under it all and became seriously ill. ELEANOR

> The "put-downs" by some superiors, favoritism shown to some nuns, permission needed for small things, my letters read, all gifts turned in…whatever, it's in the past, and I hold no grudges toward them now. I'm grateful that I had the education I had and met all the people I met along the way. MARY-2

> I feel we were exploited by the Church--we worked so hard and were given so little. The state of retired nuns and the financial state of communities of nuns is a disgrace to the Catholic Church. We are the ones who built the schools and hospitals, the priests just gave orders--orders they did not understand as they were not educators. THERESE

> Yes, e.g., my mother's death and my guilt in not seeing her for four months before while she was at home recuperating from a heart attack. She was 58 years old and I was about 27, and I could have been more assertive about visiting her at home after being denied that right. I had been allowed to see her once in the hospital. Likewise, I was allowed 3 days to see my father in the hospital in another state, but not allowed to stay a few hours longer to be at his death. JEAN-2

> Yes--authority oppression, dumb rules. HOLLY

> Unfortunately, the injustices of the novitiate and my first Superior have created strong indelible impressions on my memory. They have influenced my life

to this day. My husband and I understand my refusal to be dominated in this light, e.g., I would often refuse to watch "Star Trek" with him because I was forced to watch "Lawrence Welk" in the convent in silence for six years. It took me a while to figure this out. Sometimes I found myself treating my children the way my superior treated me, and didn't realize it until it was too late. So I think I was scarred by those experiences for life. Just within the last couple of years, I've begun to relate these current events to the past, which has helped me overcome my negative overreactions to things, though not completely. But when I see the nuns, I am reminded of the happy side--the friendliness and support I did get and still get from them. I recently connected with a friend I had lost track of for about 15 years. She reminded me of the day I told her I was leaving. I also saw my first superior about 10 years ago. After we had talked awhile, she said, "Well, Margaret, you've turned out to be quite a lovely woman. I really didn't think that would ever be possible." I responded as a "lovely woman" would. ROSE

Memories of the treatment of nuns, of being shunned, of the anger of our superior, of attempts to make me feel shame--these I remember first. Best of all, my own anger helped me leave with no longing for what should have been. After all the years of confessing anger, I finally accepted it as a freeing gift. MERT

My first memories produce anger at the disrespect for God's diversity in the precious people He creates; anger at the hurt done to nuns that taught, causing them to hurt people they worked with. ELLEN

When I finally "escaped", I was told never to darken their door. They made me feel like I was totally responsible for leaving, and that only I was killing a Vocation. Until 8 years ago, I always felt horrible about it and was in pain until I joined Renew where the facilitator was a nun. She invited me to her Silver Jubilee and there were a lot of other former nuns (my community) there. They never made any attempt to reach me, but I am turning everything into positiveness. I am okay now, having healed myself--but they have a long way to go. The way we were treated as non-entities--for example, each nun was given a nickel to go to the school store and buy candy--maddening! MARY

Chapter XII: Healing, Dreams

Yes, I felt there was no way to grow, mature, and become an adult woman. All decisions were made for me---education, work, recreation. HELGA

Yes, memories of being put down, of slave labor. MARY S

Yes. The main one is: Why I didn't have the guts to leave when I first wanted to. Only to be continually urged to stay in. It was getting so bad I used to wish I could be two persons---the one staying and the main one leaving the convent. JEAN-3

Yes. The rare good memories are triggered by specific things---they're not just hanging around in abundance. DORIS

"SOMETIMES" ANSWERS:

Our whole focus was only on teaching successfully. My last year when my teaching became better, I felt hated by my superior and she succeeded in sending me back to the Mother-house in March, where I could be anonymous and work in the Infirmary. NANCY

"NO", MY FIRST MEMORIES ARE NOT BAD:

I think it's hysterical. Now if someone were to say, Is it true that you were in the convent, I would have to do a double-take and say, Oh! Yeah, but it was so long ago, I've forgotten. CHERRY

Early days: happy, unfettered, somewhat strict and forbidding. Later on: happy, fulfilled, freer to be myself, give my opinions, share in visionary and leadership aspects. DIANE

I did have bitter memories for the first two years or so, but then I grew to respect that time, while at the same moment being happy that I had chosen this life instead. MARTHA

No. Well, the bitter memories are of the circumstances in which I entered. I didn't really want to go in before high school was over. I had a rough summer and my parents wouldn't let me buy a record player and I was very upset, so they locked me up in a mental institution for about a week. Then mother came over there and told them she was going to send me to a private school, and the private school was this convent, so they took me over there and signed me up for that and I didn't get to finish high school. Eventually I did get a diploma, but I didn't get to participate in graduation or anything. Those are bitter memories. Good memories are the good times I had with the kids. One little boy, a 4-year old, would say, Sister, how come you have ears and Sister Elizabeth doesn't have ears? And I'd say, Oh she has ears, they're just covered up. Ask her---she'll show you her ears. Then he came back over to me and he said, You have hair and Sr. E doesn't have hair. And I said, Well, she has hair, she just has it covered up. So he came back to me and he said, Just what kind of a sister are you anyway? And I said, Why don't you go home and ask your mother then you come back and tell me what your mother said. He came in the next day and he says, I know all about you, he says, you're not a sister---you're just learning how to be a sister. KATHLEEN

First reaction is of broad, rich experience. No, I don't think bitter comes first. TRACE

My memories of the first 10 years are beautiful. The last 5 were hard, because I was in turmoil with myself about certain aspects of convent changes. ELLEN-2

I have memories of great times teaching school. FRANCES

No. It was very difficult for me to leave a lifestyle that I had chosen freely. JULIANNE

My years in the community were not "bad" years---only some bad moments! The problems were mainly the power structure. But some people do really live up to the ideal. Unfortunately, their numbers are rather few. I think that may be another reason I'm no longer there---I'm idealistic, and that means I can't

Chapter XII: Healing, Dreams

say one thing and do another--which I saw happening. It seemed that what we looked like to the public was somehow more important than what we really were--I couldn't live like that. JULIA

I've buried so much so deeply--I feel the joy and happiness I once had, but there was also pain, hurt, sorrow, and anger at injustice. Making contact with a friend who left when I did and talking with a couple of sisters has put my mind at rest about many things. Before, I had no one with whom to talk for 25 years--no one who would understand. LILLA

No. I feel sorry for those who are bitter--maybe their experience was different from mine. I do feel badly in the sense that to live with bitterness does not seem good. The longer I see people holding onto whatever resentment--I guess I feel that at some point they have to DO something about it. Every way of life has injustices, drawbacks. JEAN

It was a fine place to go into an emotional holding pattern for a while and I needed that for personal development. I felt socially compelled to marry when I got out because I wanted children so badly. Marriage was a mistake. CONNIE

The years that I spent in the convent were for the most part enjoyable and rewarding. I had no problems with rules and regulations as I accepted my superior's role as leader. In those days I was very passive and naïve. SHIRLEY

My memories are: 1. struggle to learn and obey, 2. fun and laughter, 3. friends. CAREN

When I think of the days in the convent, I remember feeling trapped. JAN

No. I'm reminded of some wonderful women that were truly dedicated to God and to their students. Good people that I am blessed to have known. MARIE

I remember much music, reading, chores. A beautiful place. It's the institution in "Rain Man" where the mentally altered brother had been living. DENISE

COMMENTS:

I believe someone should have sent me on a vacation before I got too exhausted. ELIZABETH

Never bitter, just sadness. It was my first love, which one never forgets. DOLORES

I do have some bitter memories of unnecessary suffering and limitations on creative growth. I also have good memories of wonderful dedicated friends who have been very supportive. JAN-2

Not any more. In the beginning I was bitter because of the nature of my leaving. We had a change of superiors who were completely lacking in charity and truth. They could not brook any confrontation or criticism. LORENA

I have mixed memories. A part of me is angry with the Catholic Church and how I bought the religious orders' part in my life. I resent male patronage. I fee the order was producing "church workers", not developing individuals to be the best they could be--and thus helping the Church. SUZANNE

Did you get what you'd hoped for in the convent?

Suppose that one enters a relationship or career and later discovers it has absolutely no redeeming qualities (this is a hypothetical situation). After leaving such an experience, it would be very difficult to heal—one would be constantly reviewing one's actions that led to the connection, berating oneself for having been so stupid or naïve—and that whole process would greatly delay the development of new and better relationships or careers. The way to heal from any situation, regardless of the percentage of its positive and negative effects, is to learn from it. To say, Yes, I went there in good faith. This is what I learned.

Listing what they learned from being in the convent answers this question: DID YOU GET WHAT YOU'D HOPED FOR IN THE CONVENT? Of the 59 who answered the question, 28 said Yes, they had gotten good things or what they'd hoped for. Twenty-one said No, they had not. And 10 were non-committal or ambivalent.

Of the Yes and ambivalent answers, five categories of gifts from the convent are mentioned (a few mention more than one item):
- 14 – prayer, spiritual life, good moral background
- 8 – an education
- 8 – personal growth, discipline
- 5 – friendships
- 5 – happiness, joy

Yes. despite the external negatives already covered, I was blessed with the company, guidance, and friendship of some really wonderful mentors who cared about the interior life and who nurtured that in me. MARTHA

Yes, I got more than I ever dreamed. I discovered God in a deeper way. I learned the complete joy that accompanies the attempt to make a gift of oneself to God. I received real friendships that have endured and grown over the 23 years since I left. I had the great privilege of going to another culture and being loved and accepted there, and I learned to value that culture as unique members of the human family. My vision was broadened to the whole world and especially to its poor—because of shared conversations and experiences with intelligent and wonderful women. I received the wondrous gift of prayer, too. EILEEN

I got other than I'd hoped for. I learned to meditate and got most of the education I needed to begin a career. I didn't expect to be exposed to so much neat stuff and great people. TRACE

Yes and no. I had wonderful experiences, met some beautiful people, and grew up with a strong faith. At the same time, the thrust of my Vocation was really not fulfilled. My prayer life did not develop as I expected. I still feel somewhat hollow over that. JULIANNE

Of the 21 No answers (a few giving multiple reasons) to Did you get what you'd hoped for in the convent, five categories emerged:
- 10 – no personal growth, love, consideration
- 10 – lack of positive, supportive community
- 2 – I was too young to know what I was looking for
- 1 – too much pain, rejection
- 1 – never learned to pray

No, there was pettiness and squelching and limiting of self. JAN-2

No, the ambiance was materialistic, proud, and unloving. BEVERLY

No, "community" was a lie. MERT

No. I'd hoped to be supported, loved, and treated respectfully in a Christian way so that I could do good things for humanity. By the end, after having gone through the horrible year of shunning and its aftermath, I was ready to do anything rather than stay there. DORIS

Unequivocally, no. I wanted to feel I was helping humanity, and teaching was certainly something I could have done without vows. I did not get a sense of greater dedication because of my vow of virginity. I tried to figure out how this deprivation was supposed to help, but even without having experienced sex, it was not intuitive that I was more focussed than I would have been with a sex life. What I observed was real devotion to service, but I saw or guessed that it was present in the secular world also. I saw in the convent also, a childlike quality that I did not admire. JEAN-2

No, I don't think I helped people or did anything very well—there was always so much work and no real guidance to feel successful in it. It was not a growth experience for me. JANN

No, there was too much disillusionment. GRACE, DONNA

No, acceptance of uniqueness was missing. MARIETTA

No, there was too little support from the nuns I lived with. ROSE

Did your family save your letters written home?
How do they sound now?

YES: 18
NO: 39
DON'T KNOW: 7

Yes, my Mom saved them all and gave them to me a couple of years ago. It was so interesting to read them—I sounded like a little brainwashed woman that would parrot these pious little sayings by my parents—really weird. You know, I could just see how I could fit in the mold—I really did become that other person for a while. MARGARET

Of the YES answers, participants say the letters seem/sound:

immature – 2
pious, sanctimonious, holy – 4
silly, stupid, sappy – 3
good for my autogiography – 1
embarrassingly mushy – 1
corny, funny – 2
insipid, vacuous – 1

No, but I began to keep a journal in the years I had psychotherapy. Pretty weird in some instances—I can hardly recognize myself. THERESE-2

Early dating and relationships after leaving the convent

Rarely do we walk down the street and meet someone who becomes an instant friend. For women leaving the convent, especially in the first half of the 1900s, nun-friends that they had lived with for years in Community were no longer accessible for support (most often this ban lasted for a year—for some it was longer, and a few Orders did not have that rule). Having been allowed little contact over the years with one's former friends on the outside while she was in the convent, the newly emerged woman before Vatican II was quite alone. For some, family members rallied. A new job would mean new coworkers and potential friends. But the most instant way of obtaining one-to-one human contact was by dating. Here one could speak to another human being who would most likely listen, have a good dinner or dance or other entertainment, and observe the mores of the unfamiliar world without being conspicuously solitary. So it is not surprising that many women dated very soon after leaving their convents.

A number of nuns were released from the convent while still under vows. This means that they either had not yet received their dispensation papers (in the case of final/perpetual profession), or that the date for their temporary vows to be up was still in the future. Ex-nuns were cautioned not to date while still under vows, although technically, there is nothing in the vow itself that says one cannot date—it simply was not considered. What would happen if an ex-nun dated, or even had sex while under vows? Physically, nothing. The guilt and personal conscience of each individual dictated her actions. Nine nuns who left under vows, dated before their vows expired. One did not:

> *I was asked out right away, but declined ingenuously for the 15 days till my vows expired. I was still an obedient nun interiorly, and still did not even question what I had been told. DORIS*

Fifty of the 66 women who answered this question began dating during the first year—many *"immediately"*, *"soon"*, or within a few days or weeks. A few women were already in relationships before they left the convent; one was engaged as a nun. Thirteen married in a year or less (one within a week of leaving), and 21 more married by year 5. Thirteen women married between 6 and 10 years, and one each married at 16, 20, and 21 years after leaving. Eleven never married at all (see Chapter XV, Making It, for their comments on the single life).

I dated shortly after leaving and married too soon, but it lasted 21 years and produced 3 wonderful children. I did a lot of growing, so I feel that that was what I needed to do at the time. K.T.

I dated right away. My dispensation came through in June and we got married in October. CHERRY

My mother wouldn't let me date till 3 years out. KATHLEEN

I began dating at 2 years, married at 5 years to a man with two sons. We had a rocky 3-year relationship because of his drinking. Then I lived with a man for a year before we were married. After that, I allowed another to live with me for a year—this was back in the 70s. I've lived alone almost 20 years. CAREN

I began dating 3 years after I left, and in my naivete, married a teacher in the church who was a homosexual. The marriage was subsequently annulled both civilly and by the Church. I married my atheist husband in the Church 6 years after leaving the convent. LILLA

I dated soon after I left and had a long term relationship that ended when Bob was killed in a plane crash. To me, marriage meant giving up freedom and I had already done that for 17 years. GINA

I became reacquainted with my future husband (best man at my sister's wedding) when we began carpooling to work a month after I left the convent. We spent evenings and weekends correcting papers side by side and dated often. We married 11 months later. DORIS

I didn't wait very long, I'll tell you. I was so homophobic about possible lesbian sexuality that I latched onto a friend of a lay woman when I left the convent. He was a truck driver and would stay with me on weekends. I waited until I had birth control before having sex with him, then I married him a year later.
MARGARET

Nine women married priests/ex-priests. Some of these couples got to know each other well and began relationships while they worked together and the woman was still a nun.

Bob and I first knew each other in high school, and having known each other for such a long time, it gives a history together, and I think this is valuable. When I left or was considering leaving, there certainly was not an assurance that Bob would be there and that I would marry him. I remember coming to grips with the idea that if I wanted to be married, there might be anyone out there--that whole concept of building a relationship. Well, so much happened after Vatican II in the whole experience of going to Cal State LA—of having men for friends But then Bob and I began a relationship immediately and married in a year.. JEAN

We became good friends first. Love came later. We had common goals of being good people. We had served the Church for the best years of our lives and we wanted to spend the rest of our lives together. You meet future mates where you are, and we were both teaching on a high school faculty. He was still a priest. Falling in love was not against vows, because loving someone can't be bad. We still loved God and had served him for more years than most people do. KATE

He was still a priest when I left the convent and his dispensation/laicization took 9 months. Declaring my love was not against vows. One real hurt: after 9 years as principal of a Catholic schools, I was fired by the Archbishop because I'm married to a priest. He fired all who were in any way related to a married priest. MURIEL

Yes. I met him before I left, and afterwards, he pursued me. This was after 1965. He had left the January before I did. He's still a priest to this day, because the

only way he could get a dispensation was to prove that he was crazy or gay, and his bishop sent him to a psychiatrist—they ran a battery of tests on him—and since they couldn't prove that he was insane or gay, they never dispensed him. It came to the point of where it was so degrading that he didn't pursue it anymore. CHERRY

I met Jim. He was planning to leave once he had completed his Masters in Social Work. He was protecting his back to insure that he would get work. We both wanted to remain Catholic. We had similar interests and understood where the other was coming from. He was still a priest when I left. In my own heart, I knew that my commitment had changed direction from the convent and that declaring our love was not against vows. JANET

Yes, I married a priest. We each have the same value system and understand what each other went through. He was still a priest when I left the convent, and though we declared our love, we did not act on it, so I do not consider that against vows. SARAH

I married a priest who had a like background and values. He was still a priest when I left the convent. Declaring our love then was not against my vows, but part of a growth process. GAYLE

I did marry an ex-seminarian (Jesuit) who had been in the order for 10 years, and yes, this was and has been a boon to our relationship because we understand each other very well and respect those years spent in developing our inner lives. MARTHA

One participant commented about marrying priests: *No, I didn't marry a priest—I thought they were damaged individuals.* HOLLY

Another said: *At one time I considered marrying a Christian Brother—a friend from my convent days. This is why I came to Hawaii. It didn't work out. He later left the Order. Neither of us really knew what "being in love" meant. As far as declaring love while under vows, all time is present to God.* THERESE-2

❖ ❖ ❖

Reactions of family/friends/coworkers to the fact of one's having been a nun

Few people go through life truly not caring a whit about how they are perceived by others. Even when, intellectually, they have convinced themselves that what others say makes no difference, following some negative experience they will sometimes find themselves inexplicably "down", or depressed. Like everyone else on the planet, the ex-nun's emotional reactions are not in lock-step with her logical conclusions. Some things just hurt.

In the early days of adjustment to a new job and unfamiliar social skills, most ex-nuns are protective of revealing their past. It's not necessary, they say, so why do it? After the sometimes traumatic experience of leaving, why open oneself to possible further criticism? What good could it possibly do for anyone to know that I was a nun? Then years go by, careers and friends are established, and these women gain confidence. A few friends are told, and then a few more. Having children speeds up the process, because they talk about anything and their conversations with peers are not easily controllable. The ex-nun can either keep it all secret forever (inventing some plausible excuse for the gap in her CV), or get used to people knowing about her past. The latter is hardest for those ex-nuns who wish to blend into the population; believe me, letting out the fact of having been an ex-nun is not one way to do that.

Reactions by dates, friends, coworkers, etc. to one's having been a nun vary. Most people are titillated, curious, and ask endless superficial questions. Amazement is commonly expressed if the ex-nun has adjusted into society well. A rare few persons register gratitude at the former nun's dedication to serving humanity. Others will speak of it among themselves, but not so much directly to the ex-nun involved. Teasing is widespread. A good sense of humor is *de rigeur* for getting through the coming-out period. In the end, the woman involved is who she is regardless of public opinion, although it is not always easy to accept that, after she has worked so hard to build up her public *persona*, others will never think of her in the same way again.

There are more shocking revelations than mine—I would rather not discuss it. ELLEN

They wonder why, and think it's weird. It's okay with me that they talk about it. OTTER

For a long time I did not talk about it and requested that my sister not tell others. And I was right. I learned that most individuals could not handle that knowledge. They treated me as different. When I dated, it was even worse. Now I just play it by ear—if someone cannot handle it, I guess it is his/her problem. JULIANNE

We don't talk about it. It is not relevant to my life now. I think others accept me as I am now and don't question my previous life. KATE

They express surprise with many questions about why I left. It's best that they don't speak freely about it—that was another life, like I did my military experience without government benefits. CAREN

Amazement. They don't talk about it. ANNE

My coworkers don't know I've been in a convent. Years ago I found that others' knowing this seemed to change how they related to me, so I tell few, and none in the office. TRACE

I'd rather others didn't speak about it. It is a closed chapter of my life—I doubt they will interpret it correctly. BEVERLY

It's not an issue—they don't speak of it. I have closed that part of my life and I do not wish to re-visit it. MARY S

They are curious and speak freely about it. Over the years this has become less difficult for me. JANET

Coworkers don't know. I've been offered curiosity, support. I don't like it when others speak freely about it. I want to be known for me, not a "freak". HOLLY

People find it curious. In my profession in a Quaker college, it means a value on religious faith. Some people think it means you are a moral person. Some people wonder how you could possibly do it. I only tell people who are close. I used to be concerned about controlling who knew, but I am less so as I grow older. THERESE.

They thought it was fascinating, but weird. When they speak about it to others, I am embarrassed because I only want to tell someone after they already know me as normal. CONNIE

I have tried as much as possible to keep that part of my life private. If it does come up, I just tell people it's a part of my life of which I am not proud. I was idealistic and taken in by a cult, but glad I had the courage to get out of it. GINA

They think it is great. They speak about it and I am proud that it is a part of my life. NELL

I don't say much to anyone—only close friends. They don't speak about it freely, but it makes no difference—it's in the past and best left there. MARY

It's a curiosity—most are amazed. When they speak about it, I feel okay and not okay. Sometimes I feel people think I'm underdeveloped. JANN

Disbelief, laughter, husband doesn't care, children use it as shock humor or scare tactics. When they talk about it, I feel free. I never wanted it to be a secret shame. MERT

My husband knows better than to blurt out that I was a nun, but he teases me in front of friends who know. It's not a big deal to him. My children probably told everyone in sight from the beginning, and I knew I'd just have to live with it. What I don't like about telling, is that people get stuck on that subject and once they know you were in the convent, can't talk about anything else. DORIS

They show delight, interest, curiosity. I don't mind talking about it or having them talk about it. GAYLE

My child will say things like, Pretty unusual—I have a mother who was a nun and a father who was a priest. It doesn't embarrass me to know that she talks about it. One side of me knows how people create this whole curiosity around nuns. On the other hand, you hope somebody is comfortable enough with the truth and reality to put it into perspective. JEAN

Not everyone understands. I don't speak about my past with all coworkers because it is just too much to explain. I'm sure most of them know I'm an ex-nun even though I haven't told them personally. HELGA

My husband says the convent "saved" me for him. We don't advertise it, but if it fits the situation, we bring it in. Usually he lets me offer the information. ROSE

They are proud of me and speak freely about it. Sometimes it makes me uncomfortable because I want to be who I am now, not who I was. LOUISE

Laughter, disbelief. I was initially awkward about hearing others talk about it—I felt lost, not totally in the world, but it's fine now. DENISE

My children grew up knowing about both of us. I'm happy that they speak freely about it. No special reactions. Friends are always surprised that I was ever in the convent (particularly one with a rule of silence!). MARTHA

Chapter XII: Healing, Dreams

Fairly positive—they see it as one of the things that makes me unique. They don't speak much about it—it's happened a long time ago and it's not too relevant to their lives. K.T.

They show interest, pride, curiosity, and ask good questions. It's okay with me when they talk about it—my convent years were a positive part of who I am. THERESA

It's part of my life's journey and it brought me to who I am now. DIANE

Do/did you ever avoid other ex-nuns or nuns?
What have you learned about ex-nuns at gatherings?
Would you read/have you read a book about ex-nuns?

The reader may think it strange of ex-nuns to avoid other ex-nuns or nuns still in convents, but unhealed parts of our lives prompt us as human beings to do whatever it takes for our own preservation and peace of mind. A number of the ex-nuns in this project do have issues, and healed (worked out) or not, are not interested in associating with anyone who reminds them of those issues. Others who used to feel that way, have resolved the most prickly problems and have moved on. Few claim not to ever have had issues of any sort. Of the 69 participants who answered the first question above, 58 said they did not/do not avoid *ex-nuns*. Twenty-two said they did not avoid *nuns* still in convents. Fourteen more stated specifically that they *do* in fact avoid or used to avoid nuns. The rest left that question blank.

Yes, I do avoid ex-nuns because of the mutual pain. ELLEN

They avoid me. BEVERLY

I used to avoid nuns because of feelings of betrayal. MERT

Nuns are no threat to me. KATE

I do avoid nuns—it hurts. That was me. HOLLY

I used to avoid nuns, did not want to be judged by them. SARAH

I used to avoid nuns—they made me uncomfortable. NANCY, SUZANNE

I don't avoid them but don't seek them out, either. Nuns make me nervous—probably because they were so judgmental while I was still in. DORIS

I have avoided nuns because I can't stand snobs. ELEANOR

I used to avoid nuns because they rejected me. CAROL-2

Last summer, they invited all the ex-nuns of the Western Province to a gathering—except me. LORENA

Eight women say they are not greatly interested in reading any book about ex-nuns, in spite of the fact that they are contributing to one.

It isn't a topic I dwell on. NELL

I would read one if it thought it interesting and without bitterness. GRACE

I'd read a book about ex-nuns if it were not sensationalized. JOSEPHINE

I'd read one if it were honest. K.T.

Forty-six out of the 65 who answered said definitely Yes, they would read a book about ex-nuns. Reasons? *Interest. Curiosity. To compare experiences. To see what's in common. To learn something. To understand more. Because it's cathartic.*

I'd maybe read yours—I'm interested in the direction you're taking, not in a rehash. MERT

Organized Convent Reunions

Gatherings of ex-nuns alone get mixed reviews, although everyone learns something by visiting with women who were with them in convents. Sixteen (of 69 respondents) have never attended a gathering of ex-nuns. Those who have attended convent reunions, even reluctantly, came away having learned something, e.g., that:

Most ex-nuns have positive feelings about our Order. THERESA

Several have come out as lesbians since leaving the convent. CASEY

We are all well-rounded, happy people. MARIE

In spite of many of our horrible feelings at leaving, we have made adjustments back into the real world. SARAH

They are still the same people—and glad to see me. LORENA

They only wanted to talk about their husbands and children, not themselves. JEAN-2

I found out everyone hated the Mistress of Novices. OTTER

They're all good people. DENISE

I found out that some ex-nuns adapted well, and a few have neurotic problems. YVONNE

I realized how much we have in common, and that we are happier now than in the convent. JEAN-3

At an ex-nun gathering, I felt at odds with those who left voluntarily. It was a tough experience. NANCY

Some are still not happy. LORNA

Some have less favorable memories, and do not feel positive about the Community. CAROLYN

Ex-nuns are really great women doing wonderful things. GAYLE

It seemed that ex-nuns that married seem to be better off and happier—not so lonesome. ELEANOR

I learned that those still in the convent seemed bitter about the men in the Church. JOSEPHINE

I found out how little we really knew of each other's private sorrows and hardships. CAROL-2

I learned that we all have had life journeys of meaning and value. K.T.

Most ex-nuns are interested, talented people who share. JANN

That they are still dear to me and we share an unbreakable bond that few others could understand. ROSE

It was exciting; our friendship is not dependent on the "nun" part. MURIEL

I noticed that most were married without children. KATE

I learned that there are more ex-nuns than nuns in our Order! And that each one of us took a different path. ANN

Learned that we've grown worlds from those days—are far more independent. CAREN

I realized that I was very naïve before and during my convent experiences. Only later did I understand that the pain some were having was homosexuality. JULIA-2

I responded to an ad in the local lesbian publication that asked if any lesbian ex-nuns would like to get together and meet, to come to breakfast. There were only four of us. We had a very interesting meeting—all have very busy lives going in different directions. We have not contacted each other again. Some I feel are sort of stuck in some ways, and I sense that they haven't worked through some things in their lives. I enjoyed the book Lesbian Nuns Breaking Silence and would have liked to contribute to that because my agony was so—I really agonized over that. Most lesbian ex-nuns that I meet are not as open about the fact as I am. MARGARET

They had become more themselves, richer, more mature, and strong women. TRACE

I learned that these are basically good people with a one-sided view of the world. CONNIE

I discovered we still have an interest in each other. SHIRLEY

I went reluctantly to a small gathering of ex-nuns—and I had fun! JAN

I learned that most who left were the best and the brightest. JULIA

We may be all ex-nuns, but many of us no longer share the same faith experiences. LOUISE

I learned that I still enjoyed those who were my friends. EILEEN

I went to a gathering of ex-nuns—there were a lot of bitter women there. JESSICA

If somebody were to say, We are going to have a gathering of all ex-nuns, I'd probably go the other way, though it would be fun for me to go to a reunion of my Community and see people who were in my set (class) and see that they are doing. Or even a broader meeting if it were related to the question What is the role of nuns in the world today, in the Church, and how does it create diversity for the Church—I would go to something like that, but a group of ex-nuns who wanted to get together and share stories, I wouldn't. I suppose it has a lot to do with the feeling—I don't feel bitter about it, but I have this suspicion that an awful lot of people still have not gotten over some things. It's not one of the things in life that I choose to do. JEAN

On the subject of nun/ex-nun reunion gatherings: one woman's opinion

Lately, in the name of healing, some Communities have been staging reunions of former nuns at their Motherhouses and are including all current nuns in that Community who care to attend. So in one room, we have ex-nuns—some with issues which they may or may not feel courageous enough to bring up, the now-older nuns who were involved in the ex-nuns' lives and problems, and a whole lot of fresh new faces—religious women with no experiential or other real concept of what pre-Vatican II life in convents was like.

These reunions often do not work out as well on the individual level as they appear to on the surface, and sometimes end up functioning placidly only if ex-nuns keep their mouths shut and don't say anything that nuns in the convent don't want to hear—or to have the younger new members hear. This type of get-together has little to do with healing, and more to do with public relations for the convent.

Though a number of ex-nuns who attend these gatherings may be pleased with them and consider them a sort of homecoming, no one in this project wrote at length about the wonderfulness of the occasions.

Some of the problems in holding such a gathering are:

1) A number of still trauma-influenced ex-nuns will be too timid to attend for fear of meeting up with ghosts and real persons who rejected them in the past and who may reject them again.

2) Ex-nuns who do attend with the expectation of healing may find themselves not only disappointed, but squelched, and may go home even angrier or more upset than when they talked themselves into taking a chance in attending.

3) Any ex-nun daring to hint at an unacceptable topic or incident may be publicly or privately attacked by watchdog nuns.

4) The ex-nun becomes more convinced than ever that bland, blend, and not rocking the boat are still vital convent values.

5) No healing will have been accomplished, beyond the important fact that the ex-nun has forced herself to overcome her reluctance for going and take the risk---the result of which is now a feeling of having been duped once again. Being fooled is a big deal because it increases the sense of naivete which the ex-nun has worked hardest to overcome (and may have thought she succeeded in) since she entered the World.

6) Inastute nuns are convinced that all is well merely because of a lack of publicly mentioned subjects. It is interesting to note that of those attending a single same convocation, all of the nuns asked, said that things went well, as opposed to the lingering or increased uncomfortableness among many of the ex-nuns who attended the same convocation.

7) Contrary to many nuns' beliefs, a large number of ex-nuns no longer buy into the Catholic Church's or any organized religion's tenets, and for that reason, scheduling a Mass or any chapel prayers is alienating to some and should be elimated. Nuns can pray at their own Mass for ex-nuns' healing, or at any other time they wish.

At one of these reunion-gatherings, an ex-nun was attacked publicly (at the microphone) by two others who were little children when the situation alluded to had taken place, and who knew nothing about that decade. Then an older nun came over and impugned bad administrative behavior to the woman's daughter. This was followed by several nuns (who were aware of the involvement of Sister X in hurtful situation) grimly warning the ex-nun that she had better not speak at all to Sister X, because that nun was ill—taking for granted that the ex-nun would be so callous as to upset an ill person to justify her own means. At one point in the repast, all the nuns left the table where this ex-nun sat, to visit elsewhere. The woman sat alone for 10 minutes, during which she observed nuns at nearby tables speaking with heads together and watching her, though not waving back, returning her smiles, or even showing the kindness of introducing themselves. On her way out (the ex-nun did not choose to attend the Mass), another nun said several times how shocked and amazed she was that the ex-nun was now fat, and asked her what she intended to do about it. Then a nun followed her to her car and, when the ex-nun asked her why such-and-such a cruel incident (involving that nun) had been perpetrated upon her, The nun replied that she personally had not taken part—a direct denial, whether she now believed it or not. One could hardly call this a healing experience.

What do I want from them? Understanding. An apology. Reconciliation. Truth. Which are not available in a gathering where the prime purpose is to pretend nothing negative happened. Some things did happen. And I want it finished and over with. Done. DORIS

Some ex-nuns say that they have no issues, or that they do not wish to bring them up for discussion. And yet, many of these same ex-nuns from the mid 1900s have nothing ever again to do with their former convents. When asked, some said they don't know why they avoid reunion gatherings—they just don't want to be there. A psychologist gave this simile: if a person has a deep sliver, he/she can give it attention, dig it out, and let the wound heal. Or, if (providing there is no infection) he/she chooses to ignore it, it will grow a hard scar tissue over it—it will always be there, but just out of sight, not bothersome as long as the person doesn't think about it.

> *"The fear of a new attack in the psychology of victims is sustained by the following facts: First, the aggressors or their descendants have never acknowledged that the original act or acts of aggression were unjust. Second, the aggressors or their descendants have not expressed regret or remorse for the acts. Finally, they have never genuinely apologized or asked forgiveness of the victim group...for their aggression."* from "The Psychology of Reconciliation", Joseph V. Montville in Michael Henderson's book: <u>The Forgiveness Factor.</u>

> *"Explicit and sincere expressions of remorse or contrition by the aggressors can have a profound healing effect on the victim group. If such expressions are accompanied by a formal apology and request for forgiveness, the healing process will be under way."* from "The Healing Process", ibid.

The general apology and asking for forgiveness by the Pope for 2000 years of wrongs done by/in the name of the Church or individuals representing it, does not fulfill these conditions. The Holocaust victims and ex-nuns who gave much of their lives in service were particularly not mentioned in a healing manner. Healing can, however, be promoted on the local level if the attempt is made under calculated conditions.

The ideal mixed gathering (nuns and ex-nuns) would be one where ex-nuns can obtain closure. This, all but ignored in most convent-sponsored gatherings, cannot help but have a good effect on the remaining nuns, also. The gathering should be held on no one's turf, that is, neither in the convent of nuns nor in the home of an ex-nun, but in a neutral hall which is not open to any of the public, e.g., waiters. It should be carefully planned by a committee composed of an equal number of nuns and ex-nuns, with opportunity for pre-planning input from all nuns and ex-nuns who are not on that committee.

The conference itself should have specific rules, such as: Attendees will make every effort to practice creative listening (not just waiting for someone to finish talking)--this is of paramount importance. Attacking the person who speaks is not allowed. There would be a forum where ex-nuns (the brave ones!) could tell about things from their convent experience that still hurt them today. What they say would be accepted in the spirit in which it is given, and not defensively challenged, although there would be nothing to prevent nuns who have a different point of view of the same incident, from explaining their view calmly. After short statements, concern for the other party should be offered, but not superciliously or vindictively, as in: I'm sorry you have such a skewed outlook.

Ex-nuns are not whiny bitter women who love nothing better than to publicize their complaints—they are intelligent, good persons who have legitimate positive and negative things to say about their experiences. Ex-nuns tell their stories for the one great hope of both healing themselves and of helping other ex-nuns who are in need of healing--those who hesitate to share out of timidity or other circumstances.

It is possible that the hurtful Superior involved in their incidents is dead by now, or that the custom that caused a problem is no longer in use. That should not be an impediment to allowing ex-nuns to speak out. Then nuns who wish to understand their convent's history, promote their own growth, as well as help their sister women on the outside heal—these nuns, whether involved in the original incident or not, will welcome the chance to listen, to accept the ex-nun's statement, to say, I am truly sorry that this happened to you. In that case, both sides will be more likely to forgive and forget—to heal.

A very few convents have already apologized publicly at these gatherings for the pre-Vatican II treatment and for poor or even cruel management by some former Superiors. This is most admirable. Times have changed, most of the world has grown, and there is no reason to perpetuate hurt. Ex-nuns who were wounded want nothing more than understanding, healing, and above all, closure.

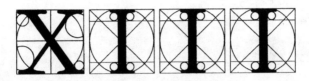

advice

to the Pope,
to potential nuns,
to Catholics in America

ADVICE TO THE POPE

Seventy-three women who cumulatively have spent well over 1000 years in one of the Roman Catholic Church's major institutions have earned the right to offer advice, even to the Pope, currently John Paul II. A few participants in this survey left the answer blank; the others are not shy about asserting their beliefs. In answer to: WHAT IS YOUR ADVICE TO THE POPE? They reply:

Be holy, be a spiritual leader, but butt out of running the US Church. Let women serve to capacity.

Allow priests to marry. Give equal status to women in the Church.

Listen. Resign.

Disband the College of Cardinals and retire. Ask all women for forgiveness for not valuing them in the Church or world.

I don't have any advice to the Pope, but I pray for him daily to serve others as Jesus did.

Get off your duff and look at the real world. Times have changed and the Church must change.

The pope is not infallible on sexual matters. "If you don't play the game, you can't make the rules." Get with it, give women leadership roles, stay out of the bedroom.

Get socially active and give the Church's wealth to the poor.

Step down, Pope John Paul II. Take your rest--you've earned it. Encourage equal participation in the running of the Church by all countries. Why do we need only one person--and a man at that--to lead, when it is impossible for one person to know everything? That's a big part of the problem today--you don't have the vaguest notion of the way things really are in America, for instance--except as an outsider looking in.

Continue to work with Jesus's teachings and not be pressured by individual groups against these teachings.

Priests should marry, and women be ordained.

Get a life! Allow women to be ministers in the full sense of the word. Encourage less reproduction.

Listen to the people, to youth. Change when necessary.

Open your ears to the Holy Spirit speaking in the Church. Be courageous. Get rid of Ratzinger!

Let priests marry and women be priests.

Allow birth control, then there will be no abortions. Couples do not mate just to have children!

Open yourself to hear the Spirit of God in the voice of your people asking for optional celibacy, women priests, conscientious use of modern birth control devices.

Allow no celibacy, and encourage artificial contraceptives to avoid worse problems.

Move over for a woman.

My immediate response was, Drop dead.

Chapter XIII: Advice

Get with it! Abortion is <u>not</u> ok, but birth control is sensible and necessary.

Allow our priests to marry if they want and need to. We're losing the best men.

Listen. Proceed carefully. Take small steps.

Ordain women, include the married priest as valid ministers, allow married nuns, priests.

Loosen up!

Consider that celibacy was not made a price for the priesthood until the 13th century. Abolish it. Make it a choice.

Get on with contraception.

In matters such as birth control, annulments of marriages--get real!

Preach Jesus.

Give women more authority.

Who is she? The Pope is only relevant to the RC church. He stands for an old institution unwilling to see the world as it is today, one which continues to perpetuate women's inequality.

Listen.

"Learn to suffer, to be humble, and to be obedient". (just kidding)

Get on with real life problems of birth control and sexual identity.

Lighten up. Work toward LOVE not LAW. Truth as you see it is not the same for everyone.

Whatever happened to the teaching of the Church on Freedom of Conscience? Why are Catholics denied this freedom? How can the Church determine when a conscience is able to function freely? The Church is refusing individuals the right to make their own choices, to make their own mistakes, and to accept the commensurate consequences. In the mind of the Church, are its members incapable of correct choice? If so, what is the Church doing about it? Is that really what Christ did with Judas or Peter? Are Catholics always going to be treated as uneducated children? Also, define for the Catholic what is extraordinary means as related to medical care. If I talk to you about the role of women in the clergy, you won't listen, so I won't go on.

Mary says that you are esp. chosen for this day and time and will be martyred. I say, Hold firm, Holy Father.

There is nothing I could say here that would not reek of sarcasm.

Don't dilute the faith.

Accept birth control and educate third world countries.

Loosen up. Join the 21st Century. Recognize that the Church needs to bless technology rather than fight it.

Rethink birth control and allow divorce. Two people can't make a marriage if one becomes unwilling. Why should the other one be deprived of marriage and sacraments?

Look at America---we're different from other countries. Women are professionals here and they should be allowed to be professionals in the church as well. They should be allowed to be ordained.

God would not allow science to advance as it has if we were not to use much of it. Look to Peter more than to Paul.

Make clerical celibacy optional and admit women to the priesthood

Rethink the role of women in the Church and the world. Church & clergy need to be more humane.

First join the 20th Century before we go into the 21st. Secondly, give people responsibility for their own lives.

Be strong in keeping all of our doctrines intact.

Get with it!

Open all the doors and allow the Holy Spirit to guide us. Continue inspiring our young people.

This is a different world and priests need to have an option to marry. Relationships are a good thing.

The Vatican does not have exclusive rights to the workings of the Holy Spirit. Be willing to take a risk.

Not printable.

Realize that there have been changes in the way people view life and the practice of their faith.

Allow marriage for priests and realize that a celibate vocation may be temporary. Get a better understanding of salvation. Allow contraception.

I won't bother giving the Pope any advice---he wouldn't listen to it anyway.

I don't keep up with his pronouncements, so have no particular advice for him.

Until you can trust the unique goodness, truth, and love of every human being, especially women--we will continue to leave the Church.

Get with it. Stop killing the Church.

Huh! It is he that should be with it. He should open his eyes up. He should allow women to help him run the Church. He should allow women to take over the Church. Then maybe there would be hope for Catholicism.

Advice to Catholics in America

O*ne of the best qualities of Catholicism in America is its demonstration of charity to the poor and disadvantaged-- keep it alive.* SUZANNE

Follow your conscience. HOLLY

Keep in touch with a community someplace; faith cannot flame of itself or by itself for very long. MARIE

Live according to your own conscience. Don't shop around to find a priest who will say what you want to hear. Many priests are hypocrites, untrained, unknowledgeable, incapable of giving advice. ROSE

Chapter XIII: Advice

Start over. MERT

Listen to your heart--answer to God for your choices. MARY

Accept Jesus as your personal Savior. OTTER

Be loyal, be Church, be people of prayer, of faith.

Live the gospel, be courageous. EILEEN

Use the sacraments. Give time to God. Act justly and fairly--keep the Golden Rule. LOUISE

Try to adjust to changes, but keep the basic beliefs. GRACE

Don't swallow everything hook line and sinker. Support your local parish with money and time and service. Become involved in the liturgy as readers, singers, etc. JULIA

Take what good you can get from Church teaching and leave the edicts to personal discretion. CONNIE

Comment: "Like sheep you are led." "Religion is the opiate of the people." ELIZABETH

Follow the teachings of the Church. SHIRLEY

Don't sit back, continue to demand change in the Church. HELGA

Be involved in Catholicism and enjoy if it is part of your heart and it is doing what you want it to do. Otherwise there are other alternatives. I have no desire to top other people from being involved in whatever faith they're involved in as long as it is positive. MARGARET

Get real. JEAN

Let Catholics follow their own conscience as regard to sexual practices. But do something about the poor and homeless. I predict that within 25 years there will be an American Catholic Church, especially as this Pope gets more repressive. FRANCES

Learn to trust your own wisdom and use what the Church offers you for your own growth without giving up your ability to choose what's best for you. K.T.

Keep the faith and have strong families. NELL

Don't let priests and Church think for you. CAROL-2

Stand firm! DONNA

Think, study, and risk---don't just follow someone who's loud. JANN

All people must feed the hungry, shelter the poor. All peoples, styles, must be respected. DENISE

Form a new real Community of Faith based on equality, diversity. THERESE

Be careful. There are many false prophets who could lead you astray. Do not leave the protection of the Roman Church. Christ promised to be with us in it! LORENA

There isn't experience of Pope & priests to make them much of an authority. Keep doing and thinking for yourselves with God's help. MARY-2

Stress good communications between Rome and us. Place women in administrative positions. YVONNE

Chapter XIII: Advice

Follow your heart. DIANE

Don't let religion-church get in the way of your spiritual growth/journey. Don't stop searching, don't close any doors. JULIA-2

Be patient. We are in the most exciting era since the Reformation. Change is coming—work for it. JANET

Stand up for your beliefs. JANE

Follow your conscience. Learn to pray. Get yourself a support system for your spiritual needs. Notice the age and number of religious and priests--whose children do you think are going to replace them? I'd like to see children presented with holiness as their goal from day one. It will take different forms, since everyone has a different vocation, but strive for that--don't just follow the aimless crowd. TRACE

Don't compromise with the world. Know your faith and ground it in the Bible. Don't put your hope in Mary or the Church. There is only one intercessor between God and man: Jesus. Avoid Teilhard de Chardin and the higher criticism. BEVERLY

Do what you want. Forget about the institutional church. CHERRY

Read. Follow your conscience. PRISCILLA

Look at other faiths, study the "good old boys club" and see people for what they are. Pray as you know how from your heart and ask God for her/his blessings. CAREN

Broaden your horizons. JAN-2

Take responsibility for your lives and actions, but live quietly so that the Church Fathers have no more control as well as no publicity. DOLORES

Don't be wishy-washy Catholics. Go along with the changes approved by the Vatican. JEAN-3

Learn to live your faith even though we keep losing our priests. God will never leave us or forsake us. His love will help us carry on. NANCY

Be patient. Take from the Church what you can apply to your life. LORNA

Live as your values dictate. MURIEL

Be broadminded—understand other religions, not only Catholicism. Live to be a Christian, not just while in church and receiving the Sacraments, but in dealing with others. ELLEN-2

Live according to your conscience. KATE

Chin up, is all I've got to say. If you stay with the church, maybe it'll change from within. KATHLEEN

Keep your faith. Follow your conscience. The Church needs an overhauling or tune up, but don't abandon your faith because of the upheaval. Look for the good seed. LILLA

Send your children to Catholic schools. ANN

Take what good you can from Church teaching and leave the edicts to personal discretion. CONNIE

Be true to yourself and look to friends and Church with a global view. JANET K

Get on your knees and pray for humility—Christ's Church is not a democracy. THERESE-2

Follow the Ten Commandments always and pray always for all Faiths to unite together in serving God's people. ELEANOR

Do your own thing---break away from "Rome". MARTHA

Renew interest in religion. Rededicate self and Church to the Lord. Reevaluate such things as married priests and birth control. THERESA

Live what Christ taught---love your neighbor as yourself and do not judge. Address problems of abuse, crime, and poverty. CAROLYN

Think, question, make up your own minds, read, learn, love. GAYLE

Examine your own beliefs and live up to them. Be true to your inner selves---trust what you know is right. Don't wait for someone to write it down and call it a "rule". Be a self starter. Go to God twice as fast under your own power than you would if you were being ordered to. DORIS

Be true to your conscience and do not do anything foolish. JULIANNE

Love. JAN

Don't dilute the faith. JOSEPHINE

Women priests, conscientious use of modern birth control devices. MARIETTA

Don't build another church without keeping title to property registered to people of the parish. And hire from the hedgerows. ELLEN

Live your life the best you know how. The Church has not cornered the market on sanctity. MAXINE

❖ ❖ ❖

Advice to those wishing to enter a convent

By now you know that convent life was an individual experience: some nuns had an easier life, others were treated badly. Ex-nuns who seem bitter have a right to be--not all the details of their miserable years have been listed here. Regardless, there is not a single participant of this survey who does *not* wish anyone else a good life. Here is advice for the prospective Candidate, advice which respects her decision, yet gives some pretty good tips.

Volunteer in a nursing home and get gerontology experience. ELLEN

Live there for a while. Talk to and listen to members & ex-members of all ages. DIANE

Persevere, be prayerful, have a well rounded holistic lifestyle now. YVONNE

Accept Jesus as your Personal Savior. OTTER

Go to college, work, have relationships so you know what you're getting into. MARY-2

Study all spiritualities first, then decide. DENISE

Don't go until you have worked a while and know what life is about. It's no picnic. LORENA

Go for it if that is what you want. SARAH

Don't. THERESE

Chapter XIII: Advice

Short commitment period---3 years? HOLLY

Give everything you have---the rewards are great. JANET

Make sure you can go it alone---today's communities do not have a strong support system. MARIE

Do it for the right reasons. grow up first. ROSE

Think about what you want to do in the convent. Get the education or training to do it. Live by yourself and work for a while before you go into a convent. MERT

It's a good place if you want to spend your life being socially involved. 1 JANN

Go for it if it meets your needs and no one is pressuring you unfairly. DONNA

Don't! MARY

Follow your star. NELL

Get lots of advice, especially from non-bitter people who were once in. Pray---look into the order very carefully. EILEEN

Good luck. It should be a free choice. FRANCES

Be "older", first experience life fully in all its aspects. LOUISE

Get a life! Get counseling! Volunteer elsewhere. CONNIE

Check it out carefully. HELGA

Pray, ask for guidance, enjoy. SHIRLEY

Think carefully about the commitment and your reasons for making this life decision. JULIA

Be sure as you can. Get real experience. GRACE

Know your options & if dedicated to helping others as a religious, go for it. CAROLYN

Carefully check out your reasons. GAYLE

Don't, unless you find an Order that lets you commit on a short term basis. Everything there can be duplicated "in the real world" with more besides. Keep your dream of saving the world, but don't do it in a way that puts out the fire in your soul. DORIS

Do not enter too young, know what you are about, really be sure the decision is your own and that you have a fairly clear understanding of what this life style is all about. Pray. JULIANNE

One should not enter without first experiencing life, dating, and the responsibility of holding a job. THERESE-2

Make sure you check out 3-4 orders and visit them for some time before trying any of them. ELEANOR

My first response was, "don't do it!" but I had the opportunity, so should everyone else. MARTHA

Be careful to put God first and not earthly power or desires. JOSEPHINE

Don't. CAROL-2

Chapter XIII: Advice

Enter with full information, full self-knowledge. Do it for you--no one else. THERESA

Talk to someone who has been there. CASEY

Keep a quarter with you at all times and in the novitiate, if you wish to leave and that's your only way out, use it for the telephone. JEAN-3

Go for it if you are led in that way. NANCY

There are many ways to serve The Lord.   LORNA

Don't. K.T.

Psyche out all aspects of the particular order you wish to enter. MURIEL

If you believe this is right for you then go for it! ELLEN-2

Try it! Might be good to go to college first & have some life experience. KATE

Things are much better today. I wish you all the luck in the world. KATHLEEN

Check out the rule of the order and its philosophy as best you can. Be sure of what you want. LILLA

Don't ANN

What are your reasons--don't go if you want to escape life and its problems. JANET K

Find out everything possible about the order first. JAN-2

Ask to see how they live, ask your own purpose in doing so, and ask what secrets they have. CAREN

I It's as good as any other choice: just don't put up with anything not required in any other way of life. DOLORES

Be prepared MAXINE

Think about other options JANE

If a friend felt called to community life today, I'd encourage her to get some good spiritual direction and perhaps some psychological testing--not necessarily in that order. Then if she still felt community life was her calling, do it. If it just "seemed like a good idea at the time," then no. I'd not encourage anyone to enter a community of sisters today. TRACE

Don't, many false teachings are being propagated. It is just too dangerous. BEVERLY

I see no need for anybody to enter. CHERRY

Don't. MARY-S

Read, read, read. PRISCILLA

Comment: I have to laugh when I see the Catholic Church condemning cults--sleep deprivation, stupid clothing, cut off from friends & relatives, communication with outside world cut off, guilt, overwork, no material resources, obedience to a head person--all of these we knew in the convent, and are a part of cults. GINA

❖❖❖

Would you encourage your child or friend to enter a convent today?

Women who strongly liked or disliked their convent experience may still wish a new and better experience to anyone else who wants to enter--if they think it is possible to have one. But as women who have been there-- would we *encourage* anyone else to enter?

YES: 3
NO: 52
I THINK SO, PERHAPS: 10
NO ANSWER: 7

Only a few explanations were offered (none in the "Yes" category):

NO:

Never! HOLLY, MARY, ELLEN

Not a Roman Catholic Order. CAROLYN

No encouragement, for I would not want to be the reason for her entering. The strongest support I could give would be to try to help her to be sure she knows what she is about to do, and to make sure the decision is really her very own. JULIANNE

No. I wouldn't say anything unless asked, but I certainly wouldn't encourage entrance. If it were my child, I'd fight for a better life for her. DORIS

No, but kids will do what they want to do. CHERRY

No. I don't encourage anyone in choices. JAN

No, but I would encourage them to fulfill their potential--whatever they decide. ELIZABETH

PERHAPS:

If the Lord wanted them to. OTTER

I might, cautiously. THERESA

It would depend on the order. DONNA, MURIEL

It would depend on her motives. DIANE

Only if this is a sincere desire. ELLEN-2

Why not? MAXINE

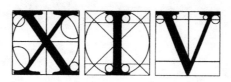

TODAY'S EX-NUN AND THE CHURCH

treatment of ex-nuns by the Church
practicing varieties of Catholicism
holding with the Pope's authority
the role of women in Church
relative value of the religious Vocation
sacraments, sacramentals, saints, venerables

Today's Catholic Ex-Nun

Today's ex-nun is as individual as any other woman who never "left the World". Generally speaking, however, former woman religious found their relationships with pastors, the public, and themselves underwent great and sometimes startling change upon their leaving the convent.

For example:

When we were dating, my future spouse and I knew that we couldn't be married in a Catholic Church ceremony because *he* had been divorced, and was not Catholic. He, however, found it incomprehensible that I could not be married by a priest in the Church because of *him*! We decided not to try and "find" a priest to marry us (which usually means some money trades hands under the table!), but rather to accept it and get married in the Episcopal Church in which he had been baptized, but was not practicing (nor has he practiced there since). Before accepting the Episcopal Church route, I did call three priests, and here are their responses: Priest #1 said he couldn't marry us in the Church, BUT if it "looked like it was a good marriage", in 3 months he could "fix" our marriage in the Church. (Our response: we just laughed to ourselves--in 3 months you're hardly out of bed--who knows if it's "good" or not?!) Priest #2 said that even though my husband wasn't a Catholic, if he had been baptized in another religion then he could not marry us. And priest #3 told me to talk to my parish priest (who was #1) or my parish priest from my hometown--#2! How do you figure??? My husband couldn't believe that after 14 years of faithful service to the community and the Church (no affairs or flagrant flouting of rules), I was denied the one thing that would have meant the most to me.

My parents were also devastated. They didn't understand either how someone could serve the Church for as long as I did and be denied a Church wedding. We got married at Christmas time and my mom and dad told the parish priest that they wouldn't make their usual generous donation because of my situation---that is how strongly they felt. They think the world of my husband and have a wonderful relationship with him. This situation shed a new light of their view of the Church. They remain very active in their parish, though, and loyal to the Church.

The IRONY of all this is: of my four sisters, three were pregnant (showing) when they got married. But they got married in the Catholic Church complete with a priest, white bridal gowns, and all the blessings of the Church. I am glad they had this support, but it was sad that the Church was not there for me when I needed it. There seems to be no rhyme or reason as to why the rules are what they are! That is why I sometimes honestly believe that God and the Church are two separate entities.

I believe God understood my situation and was looking after me. My husband is a wonderful husband, friend and father to our children. We've been married 17 years and still attend Church (in fact, I played the organ/piano for 7 years and served as Chairperson of the Pastoral Council). Our children are active in the Church. I receive the sacraments now--after all, what did I do that was so horrible? No, we have never pursued the paper trail to have our marriage "fixed up" in the Church. What is to fix? In my heart of hearts I know that God has given me so much and I am truly grateful and feel very blessed. He gave me back my life, and I never cease to feel that I want to give back as much as I can. MARY-2

Do you currently practice Catholicism?

Thirty-six former women religious (out of 73) responded "Yes", twenty-one said "No", eight did not answer that question directly, and eight more qualified their responses.

Being American and individual, each person considered "practicing Catholicism" to mean something slightly different from the others. Some said "Yes", then told how they are *not* practicing; others said "No" while remaining Catholic in name. What is "practicing" and what is today's Catholicism in America? Read this section in conjunction with the next few to get the whole picture.

Yes, I am very active in parish life. THERESA

Yes, in every way. JOSEPHINE

Yes, I go to church and take Communion to the sick. ELEANOR

Yes, I practice Catholicism fully since my reconversion (after 20 years away). I was much more liberal in my thinking after I returned to the Church through my saintly uncle's intercession. Then I read Vassula Ryden's "True Life in God" and went to Medjugorje. Through these influences I became a much more devoted Christian, and I hold fast to the teachings of the Church. THERESE-2

Yes, but I currently am not practicing because of the situation here where I live. Having lived through Vatican II in the community, having experienced what the Church could be, I found only two parishes in the years after my leaving the convent, where theology was current, and where being active in the Church was more than teaching catechetics or being a member of the Alter Society. My town is in the heart of fundamentalist religions. Catholicism is silent and invisible. My experience with the church here was a repeat of some of the parishes I tried in

Chicago. I would leave Sunday Mass either angry, feeling excluded, or completely at odds. It would be worse here. However, I have not lost my faith. JULIANNE

Yes, but not the 50s Catholicism. I believe in using anything that will help me go to God, whether it's a Lutheran sermon or a nature walk. I do not believe that some of the piddly rules are on God's wish list---they're made by man. For example, not eating meat on Friday---it comes and goes. God's rules are consistent with love for mankind and the durability of the universe. DORIS

Yes, choir, prayer group, Mass. NANCY

Yes, regular Mass, Cantor at Mass. YVONNE

Yes---I am a Charismatic Catholic, belong to a prayer group, go to Mass and Bible study. OTTER

I attend Mass, CCD, and belong to the Pastoral Council. MARY-2

I attend Mass when I feel the need for the ritual. I go to Mass and pray to the Goddess and use non-gender specific language during the prayers. THERESE

Yes. My husband and I are registered members of our parish. Our daughter attended Catholic schools and presently attends a Catholic college. I'm a member of the Liturgy Commission and Director of Environment for the parish, where I design and make vestments, banners, etc. I also sub at the piano for Music Ministry. JANET

Some. I attend Mass occasionally. MARY S

Some. I figure the church's structure is a dying institution, and I would like to see it die like it has in Germany and other countries, then see what grows out of that death. From the ashes something will come, but it won't be anything we know today as being a church. CHERRY

Chapter XIV: Today's Ex-nun and the Church

Yes. At this time I am questioning everything. I feel that the Catholic Church as we know it now will change. It needs to change. And I'm not sure that it's really going to change, because I'm wondering if you can repair it or if we need to look for a total restructuring. JULIA-2

Yes. Not institutional---I live in a remote rural area. JAN-2

I am not a Catholic at all. MARGARET

Yes, I attend Mass now and then. CAREN

Yes as it is in a contemporary California parish. JANET K

No. I am Catholic in name only. ANN

Yes. I have faith, I pray and attend Holy Mass as well as receive the sacraments. LILLA

Some, in a superficial way. I'm a lector in my church. I'm very liberal. KATHLEEN

Yes. I attend Mass occasionally. KATE

Yes. I am active in Journey Catholic Community. MURIEL

Yes. I pray a lot through the days, but don't go to church. ROSE

Yes, I practice Catholicism, but in an intentional community. JANN

Yes---I am an active, progressive Catholic DONNA

Yes. I go to church every Sunday and follow my conscience. I served on our pastoral council and contribute to my parish. Once in a while I serve as lector. I don't practice devotions. I do have religious pictures and statues in my apartment and I do some uplifting, if not specifically religious reading. I am making retreats *again after many years, and liking it. None of the above sounds specifically Catholic to me, though, more like just a healthy way of life.* TRACE

Yes. prayer, mindful of traditions. ELLEN

Yes, I practice Catholicism in every way--both my husband and I do. LOUISE

Yes, I go to Sunday Mass and am a church song leader. JULIA

Yes. I attend Church and raise my children Catholic SHIRLEY

Yes, on a regular basis. JEAN

Yes. I attend Sunday and sometimes daily Mass, say centering prayers. EILEEN

Yes, I attend a usual Catholic parish. NELL

Yes, I go to daily Mass and do centering prayer MARIETTA

Yes. At Mass on Sunday, I still lead the choir. MARIE

Yes--I went to church three times last year. HOLLY
Yes. I teach in a Catholic school, attend Mass, have my daughter in Catholic school. LORENA

Sort of. I sing in the choir two times a month. DENISE

Yes. I fulfill my weekly obligations and accompany the singing. JEAN-3

❖❖❖

How do you categorize yourself as a Catholic?

Even some participants who said they didn't "practice" their religion were willing to categorize their roles.

Twelve said they considered themselves Conservative Catholics.

Ten saw themselves as Radical Catholics, and five more as Semi-Radical.

Eighteen called themselves American Catholics, though one qualified her answer with an "I guess".

One wrote "mixed", and one was unsure if she belonged in any category. Four said they belonged in the "other" category, but left no explanation.

Others made up their own colorful titles or added explanations without categorizing at all:

Recovering Catholic. CAROLYN

I am a Roman Catholic in America. I choose to work on change from the inside. I believe the Church is in transition, guided by the Holy Spirit. It will come slowly. The Church is ancient and deserves great respect., but it also needs to move into the 21st century. JANET

I try to learn and conserve the essentials of religion, be loyal to the Spirit. JANN

I am a Modern Catholic. JANET K

Cultural Catholic DIANE, DORIS

An a la carte Catholic MARTHA

An Open Catholic. EILEEN

I am a Feminist Catholic. ELLEN, JULIA-2

I am a Disbelieving Catholic. MERT

I am Catholic in name only. ANN

I am my own brand of Catholic. TRACE

I am Far-out Catholic, but don't attend church. CHERRY

I am part of the women's spirituality movement, those many women of today who are spiritual leaders in recognizing the earth-based religion and God as mythology. MARGARET

I consider myself a Transitional Catholic, more liberal than radical, perhaps more conservative than what I understand the American style to be. I do not think Vatican II ever really finished its work; I also think that the results of Vatican II were primarily for the priests and religious of the Church. Only incidentally were the laity included. I saw that in the lay Church after I left the convent--they had little idea of what Vatican II was all about. If I were practicing today, I envision that I would find the Church upsetting, and swing to the far liberal side. JULIANNE

To what degree do you hold with the Pope's authority?

Of the 66 women who answered this question:

14 said the Pope's authority was high, especially in matters of faith

9 put it on a medium level

26 rated it low or barely there

17 said he had none, zip, zero

HIGH:

I rate his authority 100%.

In matters of faith, yes.

Very high. The Pope holds up the ideals for all of us to see, whether it is in sexuality or whatever. I can respect that. I do not have to jump up and down with joy for everything he says. He is infallible in matters of dogma, that is all!

His authority is equal with that of the Bible.

I hold with the Pope's authority entirely, except about married priests.

The Pope's authority is ultimate.

I accept his ex cathedra pronouncements. He is advisory, otherwise.

I still believe in the authority of the Pope ex cathedra. However, in so many issues the teachings really appear to me as lacking the gentleness and understanding that Jesus Christ tried so hard to pass on to his followers. I understand the dichotomy between theology and science, but I sometimes question whether the Church is really trying to resolve the tension.

I believe fully since I went to Medjugorje.

MEDIUM:

The Pope may be a good man, but he's human. God is what counts. The concept of infallibility was made up by men some centuries after Jesus died, as a means of keeping Church members in line.

Not 100% like I used to—I think money and politics talk.

Pretty much, but I think he is outdated.

He is a godly man, wise, but not infallible.

He is the Church leader, but I follow my conscience.

He needs new ideas.

LOW:

Very little—he is only the ceremonial head of the Church.

I challenge the Pope's authority.

Not in most matters

He has set himself up as sole authority, which I believe is in error.

He is supposed to run a CHRISTIAN organization.

His authority is man-made.

Little—I see the Pope as a symbol.

He doesn't know American Catholics.

I don't hold with his authority very much. I feel that he's a misguided man whose advisors are all a bunch of old Italian men who don't know what's going on in the world. They don't understand family relationships. I just think he's put there for the other people in the world who believe that he's next to God. I don't like what he has to say about women. I don't like what he has to say about quite a few other things.

That's self-explanatory. I have no problem with totally ignoring the Pope.

What is your opinion as to the role of women in the Church today?

Females have always been secondary in the Church, yet women (lay and formally religious) have been its backbone in charity work, organization of volunteer groups, Catholic education, etc. Many women of the 21st century no longer accept their "traditional place" in the Church. Opinions follow:

From what I can see from the outside, they're still wrongly second-class.

Women have more roles than formerly, and should have even more. I support women priests.

Women continue to be doing a larger part of the work with a smaller part of the recognition.

Women are too concerned about power and not concerned about God's will enough.

Women still need to stay home and take care of their children until they are of age, pray always, and later step out and have a vocation to others.

I do not believe in women priests; assistant pastors are okay.

The role of women in the Church today is constrained by the hierarchy. This does not diminish the work they are doing, but it does diminish the breadth of work of which they are capable. Women religious are doing outstanding work in a variety of fields, but they are still excluded from the ministry. That is sad, especially when vocations to the priesthood are still very few.

Chapter XIV: Today's Ex-nun and the Church

There are some mighty women out there, wise and patient and exuding peace. Some we have more access to than others--ordaining women would help. I believe there are many women who could make a greater difference for good in this world, were they not hampered by rules of the Catholic Church.

It's useless--the Church is too male-dominated and controlling to accomplish change.

It is getting better. We need a married clergy and women priests.

I want them to be active and in all the chief positions--but not become priests.

Equality with men in all aspects of ministry is the ideal.

The Pope and bishops always bypass the needs of church women.

Women should be given more opportunities to serve (readers, liturgical ministers).

Women have talents that are gifts for any institution. Women are undervalued in the Church.

The women in the Church are exploited and voiceless. The antiquated stand on birth control is an excellent symbol of how little the concerns of women mean to the Church hierarchy. There will be no progress until women are ordained.

Women should be ordained, since women in the early Church were.

We are beginning to find our place. We are beginning to see that.. Women have a very important role; the time will come when we can do what we want--priesthood--whatever.

I don't follow the arguments.

Women are very put down.

I do not believe a woman should lead a congregation as a priest, or teach men, because men need other men or they will give over the Church to women and there will be no godly leadership in the home.

Evolving...

No opinion--churches do not interest me now, however, I did attend an evangelical church for ten years.

They should be priests if they want to. They do more than the priests anyway.

Their gifts are not being fully utilized and won't be under the present pope. I favor their ordination.

I do not agree that they should be priests. I do believe they should know their faith's teachings better so that they will be the backbone of God's Church on earth, either by training their children, or contributing their talents as they can.

I believe that women can do a lot more and there are quite a few women out there who are qualified to be ordained priests today, but because they are women, they can't be. I think that women should be at least able to be deacons.

I personally do not want to participate more fully, but there is a wealth of talent among some who do. What a waste!

Women should be able to have a more active role in the Church. They should be able to be priests.

Changing, but priests must change first. "Old fashioned" priests have old ideas.

Chapter XIV: Today's Ex-nun and the Church

There is no role for women. I have accepted the Church's refusal of women--no longer work for it or care.

Let's go for women priests. Women are active and doing a great job.

I'd sure like to hear the real opinion of Jesus.

Okay, but I really don't care to see them become priests.

They should be equal and be priests and bishops.

Getting a bit better, but still not good--we have a LONG way to go. They're beginning to hear us.

Women are suppressed by Catholic teaching.

I'm beginning to question whether women can truly have more than a token role under the present patriarchal structure.

I feel that women are depressed and deprived in the church.

Women have found acceptance in lay roles, but I object to women priests.

I am an active participant. I hope women will be priests.

They are badly treated.

Women should be priests. The Church has improved over 40 years, but it has a long way to go.

Women are meant to be strong, helping, non-nun persons now.

Women should be treated equal to men.

It's good that those who wish have more opportunities.

What role? As long as the Old Birds are still in power, there is little progress possible.

Women are undermined in our sexist Church. I want women priests and a married priesthood.

With all women's education today, they should be priests, but then men wouldn't do anything.

I deal with involved women and ignore the "no's" of the Church.

We need more women in roles in the Church; the Church does not understand women.

The Church needs to validate the tremendous resource of women, not treat them as secondary persons.

I don't know what the role of women is in the Church today. With the present Pope and the direction he seems to be going, I would not want to be part of the Church. I didn't want to part of a church where women couldn't be priests, where there was only token recognition of women still in the Church, and which issued anti-women directives like not allowing them to use contraception. I just can't belong to a church like that. And women who do—I don't quite understand why they are still there, because I think they are going down with a sinking ship. I guess that is their privilege. I would just not have the patience.

Guess it's the same as our government—fledgling but coming to age.

I believe the Church will never allow women an equal role in the Church.

Women are taking nuns' role in leadership. But until the structure of the Church hierarchy changes, women will fall into the same devil traps men do as priests (that's if women become priests).

I am supportive of women spiritual leaders who set an example. Many are gifted in counseling. I don't want women priests in my lifetime. I don't think the world is ready for them.

Women don't have a real role.

Be women of God---stop worrying about "rights".

For those who want to "hang in there", I encourage every move toward equality and respect.

Still not realistic. Women should be ordained.

It is demeaning--no better than 1958, except that women think more highly of themselves now.

It's not enough.

Do you still believe that a Religious Vocation is more valuable than any other vocation?

S till believe" was used in the question, because in the pre-Vatican II days, a religious Vocation was so important that it was spelled with a capital "V"; other vocations were not. Moreover, other vocations were mostly referred to as "jobs" and "line of work". When a Catholic woman said, "I have a Vocation," there was no doubt that she was going into the convent. Marriage and celibate single life were next in line as vocations; no one spoke about any other categories in the Church.

Two participants still today hold Religious Vocations as more valuable than any other kind, one did not answer, and 70 ex-nuns answered that every vocation has the same relative value. Here are some of their explanations:

A Religious Vocation is still more valuable than any other vocation because a total giving of self is a proper sacrifice.

Religious Vocations are most valuable because the Church needs dedicated celibate women.

No, every phase or aspect of life has its own value.

A total giving of self is a proper sacrifice, no matter which vocation is involved.

The personal relationship with God is direct. Any life can either enhance or hamper it.

Chapter XIV: Today's Ex-nun and the Church

God is universal; people are complex. For man to believe in God, to reach any eternal goal, there has to be a variety of paths for individuals to follow. And after living in community for so many years, I know that the religious vocation is not so different from the family community, or the community of singles. There are just different emphases.

No way is the Religious Life more important. In the 50s we were taught that first there was the clergy, and farther down the line was the celibate single life, and beyond that, marriage. Marriage was less in rank because in marriage, the partners gave in to their baser desires (sex) and did not have the self-control or blessings of being a religious. In my first year on mission (in a parish) I had my eyes opened when I saw how much lay Church members worked like we did, PLUS they raised families, held jobs, paid mortgages, etc. Besides that, they were always available to drive us here and there like princesses--and they made no complaint. I more highly respected all married persons after that. Now I think it's not what you do in life that's important, but whether you are fulfilling your inner needs, being good to others, and benefiting mankind universally. I am of the opinion that God couldn't care less if you are the pope or a pipe-fitter. It's what you do, how you do it, and why you are doing it that counts, not the title of your occupation. I think that "going to God" is another way of saying "being in harmony with the universe, with the way things are". That's when we are happiest.

It is valuable along with other vocations.

I never did believe a religious Vocation was more valuable than any other.

I now realize how important the laity is and how hard they work for Church.

Whatever people feel they are called to is fine with me. If a woman feels she can best respond to God's call by being a nun--so be it.

It is one vocation; we all have vocations to serve.

We can serve God in many ways, all valuable to serving his kingdom.

Truthfully, in one sense, we all have a religious vocation. And no, I do not believe that one is better or more valuable than the other.

Each person must live whatever commitment God asks of us.

As I'm becoming aware of today's nun's role, there seems to be little community life. Holiness can be achieved without a religious Vocation, God's word can be lived and spread, His work done.

I believe a religious vocation is valuable to those who wish it.. I also believe secular life can be just as rewarding to others.

Being a good parent is the most valuable thing a person can do.

No way---my present vocation is just as important.

I am not sure I ever believed that--it was just my Vocation, but that didn't make me better.

I NEVER thought a Religious Vocation was more valuable than others.

No, to be the person you are and develop--that is the highest vocation.

Vocation to love God is flame in the candle of all we do.

God has a hand in all vocations!

The Religious Vocation is just another way of life.

I have never considered the Religious Vocation more important.

My marriage is a vocation, and I have had a far more positive influence there than being in the convent.

I believe the Religious Life is just one of the vocations. Everyone has a vocation. Mine is to be single.

One can serve God and fellows in all vocations.

I never did believe that. When I was in the convent, a high school teacher told us that the married state was more valuable than a religious vocation. A religious vocation was for those who didn't want to get married and that you should not be a single person, but I ended up single anyway.

Priests and religious deserve our respect, but every vocation is sacred.

I have met many prayerful, charitable, and holy Catholic lay women.

What is your present attitude toward the sacraments and sacramentals?

There are seven Catholic sacraments: Baptism, Confirmation, Holy Eucharist (Communion), Penance (now Reconciliation), Extreme Unction (now Healing), Holy Orders, and Matrimony. A *sacramental* in mid-century Catholicism was any item used as an aid to Mass, prayer, or religious ceremony, e.g., the holy water contained in the entrance font of a church (one dips center fingertips into it and crosses oneself before entering the pew). The Rosary is also a sacramental. Church statues, votive candles, Missal (prayer-book), the priest's vestments, incense, and banners are all sacramentals. The sacrament of the Eucharist as well as sacramentals are used in the Holy Mass.

Responses to the above question:

They are the center of my life.

I think most everything can be a sacrament: a sign of God's life and love.

I believe that sacraments and sacramentals are ceremonies/talismans that unite communities and were meant to remind us to be united to God in our lives. Other cultures and religions have other ceremonies, no doubt as valid, cosmically speaking. I reject the notion that if you don't go to confession during Easter Time you will have a mortal sin on your soul, or if you are not in the pew on Sunday, God in displeased. If God is the Master of all that is, then whoever goes against living creation by murder, rape, cheating on taxes or child support, or snobbing the kid in the next block, is the one who commits sin.

Have to avoid idolatry. Symbols are for focussing on the God connection. God is more present within persons than without.

I would like to go to daily Mass except I live in the country a distance from the Church.

Great---I respect all of them.

Since I have a personal relationship with Jesus, I look to Him and I see the sacraments as helpful if they are spirit filled.

My family participates at Mass each Sunday. My children are involved and I'm on the Pastoral Council.

They are valuable aids to living a good Christian life. I would not last long (I believe) if I abandoned them. I could not do that.

Whatever people feel they are called to is fine.

I use the sacraments as vehicles to meditate on human events, rites of passage, meanings in life.

I am an agnostic, and have no feelings about them.

They are rituals which I respect.

I believe the sacraments and sacramentals are now being restored through the women's spirituality movement. Like we do many ceremonies and rituals, celebrate menstruation of the moon, and seasons of the year. Sacramentals are things like rocks and trees and--that's on and on for me.

My beliefs on transubstantiation tend more toward Greek Orthodox, although I consider myself an Evangelical Christian. I respect tradition, but am not bound by it.

I do admit that sacraments hold me in a way that's very special, although my definition of sacraments may be different than the church's definition. Still, I do not feel uncomfortable remaining in the Church and yet disagreeing or having a different definition. For instance, the Sacrament of Reconciliation--I truly feel as Monica Helwig says, that reconciliation can take place between anyone, even at the kitchen table.

I have no interest in them--they seem to be just another way to instill guilt and/or dependency in otherwise sensible people.

They are good for the need of ceremonial and ritual.

Sacraments are a means to help one strive to be a better person and in this day and age we need all the help we can get.

I don't hold them as venerable as before.

I receive Communion when I go to Church. Not confession. We raised our daughter in the Church.

I am not familiar with today's Church teachings as I am not a practicing Catholic, but I would guess I'd feel the same reverence as I did while in the convent.

They should be available for those who need them.

Sacraments are good/necessary if you believe they are. They are an aid to faith. Sacramentals have no value for me now.

I never pray the Rosary; I go to confession 1-2 times a year. I guess I just see it all as part of the total package of being Catholic.

I value the sacraments, especially baptism and eucharist; I go to penance services in Advent and Lent; I love sacrament of the sick. On sacramentals—really don't consider or think about them.

Sacraments are important acts of the faith community. Sacramentals are reminders.

When women are healers as well as sinners, sacraments are valid and licit.

I receive the sacraments. Don't care for holy water (unsanitary) nor relics, not sentimental piety.

I believe the sacraments are my life's blood in growing as a God- and other-centered person

I value the sacraments--forget sacramentals.

They're great for those who benefit from them.

I don't care and don't believe. (2)

Chapter XIV: Today's Ex-nun and the Church

Sacraments are not all necessary for salvation. If sacramentals help one to become a better person, ok, but they don't do anything for me.

I believe the same as I did growing up.

I will not go to confession.

I guess I have suspended belief, if I go to Mass and receive communion, but I don't go often. I let confession go years ago. I have not figured out how to replace ritual. When I think of dying, I wonder what I would want. Extreme Unction and Catholic burial offer closure. One of the few things the Church does well is celebrate beginnings and endings. Sacramentals no longer have any meaning---they're on a par with a four-leafed clover or rabbit's foot.

They are still good symbols if people think and understand them. Most sacramentals are decorative.

I receive Eucharist regularly, but don't use other sacraments. Use holy water out of habit upon entering or leaving church.

I participate and have a good attitude.

Sacraments: believe in them. Sacramentals: not so valuable.

I believe in their importance now as always. The sacraments hold more value than sacramentals.

The same as it was. I'd like to participate more, but am completely alienated by our priest and still gun-shy. I was away from the Church for 20 years.

I receive communion at least every week. I have a blessed palm in my kitchen, religious pictures and statues in my living room, and a rosary by my bed. Often I have something religious on my bulletin board in my private office.

I go to communion if I'm at a Catholic wedding or funeral, otherwise...

I have faith, but do not avail myself of sacraments, sacramentals.

I hold them in high regard.

Sacraments, yes. Sacramentals, some.

When I first left the convent, I was put (by the pastor) in charge of the religious adult education. He taught the people advanced theology I could agree with. I don't even know what's been happening in the last 10 years in the Catholic Church, and that's okay with me.

I guess liturgy is my main source of prayer. A musician tends to go that way. I think the sacraments are good "hand-holders".

They are part of Catholic tradition. Society needs some tradition to hold it together. Religion is an important basis of society.

I no longer find them necessary or even important in my life.

Their history, meaning, etc., have been lost on most Catholics. Sacraments and sacramentals all have their place, but I don't need them in my life. I have other "sacraments" and "sacramentals".

I honor them, I enjoy Baptisms, Confirmation, I receive Holy Communion, participate in the Sacrament of Reconciliation. I feel privileged.

I love the Mass.

I miss the sacraments, except for confession. During my community experience, I had enough of confessional-type functions, such as Chapter of Faults. When I get the chance, I intend to discuss this with a competent priest-confessor.

Sacramentals are important in that people really need mythology in their lives. However, in our day and age, I think the Church needs to rethink this part.

I hold fully with the teaching of the Church. I attend daily Mass when possible and always receive Communion at Mass.

They have always helped me to see the good in even sinners of this world. Sacramentals remind me of the spiritual life.

I love Eucharist—I never hold with "Reconciliation". I think the rest of the sacraments are nice rituals, but unnecessary. I like some sacramentals.

I partake as fits the occasion.

They are beautiful rituals for society.

Do you still hold the same views on Hell, God, angels, sin, Mary, and Immaculate Conception as you did when you were in the convent?

Forty-six of the former women religious in this survey said their views had changed since their days in the convent. Twelve said theirs had not, one said she held "basically" the same views, and five others who explained their answers gave a mixed response.

When asked, Why or why not are you holding the same views? they replied:

I really believe that I belonged to a very enlightened, well-educated community.

I'm not convinced that God exists, but if god does, then he is not vindictive and there is no eternal punishment.

My whole spiritual-life journey has evolved to the point that few of these concepts are relevant--mostly my beliefs center on "God is everywhere in everything".

They are archaic.

Perhaps I am somewhat more intellectual in my belief foundations.

I now think and pray and trust my relationship to God, and so respond in a loving way to That Voice.

I am not so afraid of having ever committed a serious sin in my life, because that is the reason Jesus came--we are forgiven always when we repent.

I was out of the Church for 20 years and for a time didn't believe in God. My reconversion through my sister-friend, through Fr. Solanus Casey, my uncle, through Vassula Ryden and Medjugorje have convinced me otherwise.

No, in fact, some of these had changed during Vatican II. For example, I really believe we live out hell and purgatory during our lives with a final choice at the moment of death. My thinking on this came from reading the German theologian, Goldbrunner. God in very personal to me, I have not questioned angels, and I still have a lot of guilt feelings about the way I have handled things in my life, so I guess my concept of sin needs some rethinking. Mary is very personal to me also, but she has certainly been placed in a different position since Vatican II in the Church. I don't what to make of that. I still believe in the doctrines of the Church.

Chapter XIV: Today's Ex-nun and the Church

Not at all. Even as a young nun when I spoke to a priest as if HELL were fire and brimstone and devils in flaming suits, then saw the disbelief in his eyes, it occurred to me that I ought to reinvestigate what I had been taught about hell. I think hell as we knew it, doesn't exist. GOD is the Highest there is, Pure Love, neither male nor female. When we are functioning in line with the universe, i.e., not polluting the air and water, helping each other out, developing good things in communities, etc., we are in line with what God is, and so we are what we call "being good". The detailed rules that were invented with regard to religions are mostly restrictive, and the ones that go farther than guidelines were meant to make it easier for those in control to handle the members. (I did not come to these conclusions in the convent.) ANGELS: I doubt they have wings, but yes, I think there are spiritual parts of us that do not die, and that sometimes these spirit-beings make themselves known to us and help us. MARY: Of course she was the historical mother of Jesus. I believe she is powerful (as a spirit-entity) and cares about those of us on earth, but I'm not convinced that she physically comes to alleged visionaries. If I'm wrong, I apologize. In any case, I don't think it's appropriate to pray to Mary or God for a parking space, for example. You can pray about it, but parking spaces isn't what God and Mary are about. Maybe you needed to pray at that time for your own sake--the effort isn't lost. Neither do we see some other car being lifted away into the heavens as you drive up in front of the building. The parking space is either there or it isn't. IMMACULATE CONCEPTION: was considered a big deal when virginity was considered more holy than marriage. Not to be flippant, but who cares? Would we love Jesus less if Mary had had vaginal penetration to conceive Him, or love Mary less if she had not "conceived of the Holy Ghost"--I think not. It just doesn't matter anymore.

All these are man-made concepts.

I believe God is a more forgiving God.

I am continually growing and well more on God's relationship with me in a more comfortable way than before.

I was taught those views. I feel that if I lighten up on some of them, I might chip away on other fundamental doctrines.

I never took them too seriously and realize now that my spirituality is more "creation-centered" rather than "redemption-centered".

I met Jesus personally and was Baptized in the Spirit---Jesus is my focus.

I think God is a kinder God than what we were taught.

I received very excellent counseling by a Jesuit spiritual director and two priest friends who gave me a solid foundation in faith and self-image. I rely on that formation.

I'm still struggling with some of these. God is more "within" than before as a nun. Sin is not quite so cut and dried. Mary---some. Immaculate Conception is more symbolic to me.

I've grown and developed.

Always was liberal---doesn't bother me of Mary was married or not. God's love is always with us as is His power.

My education in Theology was very solid. The biggest change has been my sense of Woman and the role of the layperson.

I have read myself out of all that.

I totally do not believe in hell. I do not believe in a personal male God. I believe in a form of angels, or spirits, or spirit guides. I do not believe in sin. I believe that Mary is a strong holdover from goddesses. She was one of the allowed images of the goddess. She really represented the goddess to the early Christians and she still represents that even to this day to a lot of the other cultures in one way or another. The Immaculate Conception---no, I don't think I ever believed in that since the years I started to grow, because why does she have to---it implies that having sex is wrong, that Mary had her great son without getting dirty form of sex. Sexuality in the women's spirituality movement is greatly revered.

I believe that most of these concepts are used only to control people.

I don't have a lot of strong attitudes about hell, God, etc. I still believe in God though I feel that a lot of the other things that we learned in the 50s were just things that were preached to people as a form of control. I tend to agree with Oprah Winfrey who says it's important to have a deep spirituality, but not necessarily a religion. I'm not looking for any religion. I believe I'm still a very spiritual and deep, thoughtful person---maybe too much. But I don't worry about all those religious things anymore like the Immaculate Conception and so forth.

I read the Bible. Primarily my beliefs changed on Mary & sin & salvation. I now believe that Mary was honored among women and led an exemplary life, but is not an intercessor as Catholics perceive it.

I think all my views are gentler now. It may not be possible, but I think it would be nice if all the persons in Hell eventually were allowed Heaven. God hasn't changed, but my understanding of Him expanded in every way. Angels are neat; they've work to do and are active. Sin is a broader, more personal field, not so much specific things, but an attitude.

I have ceased to believe. I think I'm more a Buddhist.

I can't think of any one of these where I haven't changed my view on them. I'm not sure that I believe in hell anymore. I believe in a Supreme Being, or a supreme life force. My idea of angels has changed. My idea of sin is different. Mary is still my friend, but I have questions there. I even have questions about who Christ is. So you see I really cannot answer this question dogmatically, because I am at a point in my life where the definitions of these things are in flux.

I have broadened my views. Living in San Francisco, we see lots of lifestyles and the people are good people. Christ lived among all types in his day.

They are all just ways to control people, thought up by fearful men needing power.

I try to live a good committed life.

I was young, idealistic, naïve, and extremely needy of love and security.

Views have changed with growth and experience.

I'm softer on Hell and in disagreement with Church law as being as sacred as God's law. I have some serious doubts about faith in our Church's speaking absolutely for God.

First of all, I don't believe in hell. If I believe in hell, it's here on earth. God exists. I don't know about angels. Sin is when you hurt someone. Mary, Immaculate Conception--they're all just stories, I guess.

Mostly I see God as a loving God. I don't think He keeps a tally. He rewards us for doing our best and loving Him and our fellow man.

Other than Mary and the Immaculate Conception, all the views I grew up with and believed in then, I still do.

I believe heaven/hell is what you create for yourself--you will be as happy/unhappy in the next life as you have prepared yourself for in this life.

Those views don't ring true to my present experience and understanding.

They were pretty pre-modern concepts back then, for instance, nowhere did we ever see Christ in the poor as today. Service was secondary to rules.

All my views, my grasp of religion, are changing. I read, listen, and reach new feelings, conclusions.

I have matured, read, been to workshops, etc.

The Church has changed, and I have changed with it.

I believe there is a hell, but I don't feel God will send us to hell for insignificant things. He is a loving God. I believe in angels, Mary, and the Immaculate Conception.

God is more loving than I ever dreamed.

I don't believe in hell. Rather like angels. I do not think the Immaculate Conception is all that necessary.

I believe God is a God of Love and Understanding.

I continue to believe in my Catholic faith and its obligations. I teach my beliefs also.

Vatican II has urged me to read and study more, especially so-called "radical" writers.

The belief systems of the Church seem antiquated

It wasn't long after I left the order that I left the Church completely. Part of that had to do with some very uncharitable things that were said and done to me and other people by priests. These were not sexual in nature.

I relate to God as father/creator and pretty much, but don't think about the other stuff--except I rely on my Guardian angel to keep me straight.

Why? Because when I left the convent my views were solid and well-formed, and they still are.

The Immaculate Conception is a putdown on human sexuality and Mary. I think we make our own hell if we can't love or help make changes. Never had a link with angels---believed what the Church said. The God I believe in now is not nearly so well defined, but much more personal. I think God must be relieved to know "He" doesn't have to be an accountant counting days in purgatory, prayers said, sins committed, etc. I think this same God is glad He no longer has to be aware of each act of intercourse and to make an active decision of ensoulment at that time. I have freed God and God has freed me. Sin has also gone through a great change. I no longer worry about what the Church calls sin--laundry lists have no meaning. My personal beliefs of right and wrong are still a part of my life, but I don't think much in terms of sin.

I do not support in any way, organized religion. I think it does damage to people and it takes advantage of people who are poor. One of the reasons that I'm not Catholic or don't practice organized religion is: When I left the convent I was still practicing for a little while. It was hard, but I was getting more and more disgruntled, then I went to church one day and heard the priest ask for $3000 to repave the parking lot. And this was at the time when people were starving in Bangladesh--I couldn't believe it. I never went back--well, I did. I tried to go back once for somebody's friend's 25th wedding anniversary, and I had to get up and leave, even then, because the priest was talking about faithful marriages and--I just couldn't believe it--it made me so angry that somebody would have the--somebody who had never been married, never been through it, had no idea--he was just standing up there saying these things. I couldn't believe it. I'm a person who when I left, marched on Washington and went to the trial of the Berrigan brothers in Harrisburg, and so forth. I guess I consider myself kind of radicalized, but anyway....

I never really took it all totally seriously.

making it

on being a woman
on being an ex-nun
on having worked the Questionnaire
on being successful

Chapter XV: Making It

Current Statistics on Participants

At the time they answered the Questionnaire, the 73 participants:

- ❖ lived in 9 states and Canada.
- ❖ had worked (during their convent days) in 26 states plus the Philippines, Canada, and France.
- ❖ had been women religious in 21 different Communities,
- ❖ spent from 2 to 40 years* each in the convent, averaging 15 years and nearly 9 months

Of those women who declared their ages, TWO women were only 14 at their time of entrance to the convent.
  THREE were 15.
    FIVE were 16.
      TWELVE were 17.
        THIRTY-FIVE were 18.
          SEVEN were 19.
            ONE each were 20, 22, 23, 24, 27, 28, and 30.

At the time of answering this Questionnaire, the marital status of participants who answered that question was:
    single: 21
    married: 35
    widowed: 6
    living with partner: 4

Thirty-three had children, mostly grown up by now.

*We know the first and last years of this stay: the actual number of years spent in the convent may or may not be off by a number of months, because we count both the first and last years. If we did not, we would be off some months in the other direction. Six of one....

Two women had spent just two years in the convent.
　　　Four had each been there for 3 years, and one for 5 years.
　　　　　Three each spent 6 years in the convent; two spent 7 years.
　　　　Seven were there for 8 years
Two women spent 9 years there; two spent 11 years; and two, 12 years.
　　　Six women were in the convent for 13 years each.
　　　　　Four women were there for 14 years and four women for 15 years.
　　　　　　Three women spent 16 years there; two spent 17 years.
Five women were in their convents for 18 years each.
　　　Four were nuns for 20 years; two for 21 years; three for 22 years; two for 23 years; two for 24; three spent 27 years there; and one each spent 25, 26, 28, 30, 31, 32, 34, and 40 years in a United States convent as a nun.

As they answered the Questionnaire, these women ranged in age from 44 to 85.
　　　One each were 44, 46, 60, 67, 69, 71, 77, and 82 years old.
　　　Two each were 47, 61, 62, 64, 65, and 72 years of age.
　　　Three each were 48, 49, 50, 51, 57, 58, and 70.
　　　　　Five women were 53 and five were 59 years old.
　　　Seven were 52 years of age.
　　　　　Eight were 54 years old, and eight were 59 years old.

　　　Fifty-one of the women still worked at a job/career. Thirty-two were involved in education, 18 in business, and 11 in the medical field. Those in education listed themselves as being in one of 13 areas, e.g., college professor, research, media specialist. Three categories were listed besides the fields of education, business, and medicine: artist (1), homemaker (5), and child care (1). Only one participant was unemployed.

　　　Of their husbands/partners, only 5 (total) were involved in education. Thirty-three other categories of occupations were listed here by the participants, e.g., weather forecaster, engineer, dentist, commercial fisherman. The women had been with the same partners/husbands for 1 to 37 years. One partner was unemployed at that time.

Of those who answered question #6, i.e., ARE YOU COMFORTABLE BEING SINGLE IN THE 90S? only one said No:

I do not like living alone, have bouts of extreme loneliness, sometimes depression, but tradeoffs of independence seem to outweigh complications of relationship/marriage. Have had many "failed" relationships.

Reasons most often given for liking being single in the 90s had to do with:

freedom	independence
quiet, calmness	social life, sharing talents
broadened life view	suitedness to the single life

One reminded us that she missed her husband.

And one ex-nun stated: *I like being over the hill.*

What are your thoughts on having been a woman in the convent?

In the late 1900s and in the 21st century, being a former woman religious was a totally different experience compared to having been one in the first half of the century. There was far less contrast between the world and the convent as we drew near to the millenium, than there had been earlier.

I felt asexual in the convent. I had gone in as a virgin with practically zero dating experience. We were so isolated and insulated from others that in five years, my only exposure to males was to decrepit priests and little altar boys—hardly anything to have "thoughts" about. So I became a woman after I left the convent. I was still very prudish for years afterwards. MARTHA

It was a chance to get to know myself, to mature and to organize my spiritual life. JOSEPHINE

I love being a woman who had convent experience. It taught me order, grace, refinement. I still enjoy women's groups. CAREN

Subjugation in the convent prepared me for marriage to a Greek man. DENISE

Nothing comes to mind here. ANN

I'm glad I did it, it was kind of a fun place to go, you know--I had some good times. I was very young, inexperienced, and it was quite interesting. Now I know what it's like. KATHLEEN

Things have changed so much, the convents are so out of touch, there shouldn't even be convents. I see them as a thing of the past, a thing that's dying.

Chapter XV: Making It

They served a purpose when there was no one to teach children or take care of people in the hospitals. Now, for better or for worse, we have an education system in this country and we have hospital services. Convents are dying and they need to die. There is more uncharitableness and destroying of people who are in convents, by the mentally unstable, that the convent is a place nobody should be in. CHERRY

It was okay and a good place for me to be then. It gave me a chance to grow up and be sheltered for a while. MARY-2

I'm glad I had the experience because it did help me--obtained a BA degree and 7 years of teaching experience. Developed me in love of art and music and in some areas of etiquette (how to set a beautiful buffet table--silver, linen, etc.) I enjoyed the theology and stimulation of living with very intelligent, highly educated women. I wish I'd been more assertive in the convent. That is something I've tried to learn since leaving. SARAH

The convent holds women back from becoming full adults with autonomy and power. It keeps those in it childlike and dependent. There are the feminist issues also. I witnessed many scenes where nuns subjugated themselves before parish priests, one at least who was drunk at the time. Many times, competent well-educated women deferred to the judgements of parish priests on school matters or running the convent when the men were out of their field of expertise. I saw these men patronizing nuns while ostensibly respecting them. JEAN-2

Since I did not have a normal childhood and was totally naïve about men, it was probably better that I was 45 before bouncing around in the world of men. THERESE-2

I feel it was very enriching--able to deal with all kinds of people, my education was encouraged, and I was supported. MARIE

I learned "refinement"; I was a good scholar and admired for that; little was done to help my sexual feelings. CAROL-2

I feel that I wasted 17 years of the best years of my life. What a stupid way to live. People have urged me to write a book about this, but I closed that door a long time ago and moved into the future. GINA

I think religious women are undervalued, especially by the Church. In my experience I met strong, intelligent women capable of making a powerful positive impact. JULIA-2

The Sisters made me feel independent and worthwhile as a woman. My friends in and out are doing exciting and worthwhile activities. JANET K

I think I never would have become a woman in the convent. I was a girlchild, and leaving exposed me to fears, challenges, and decisions that promoted tremendous growth. MERT

It was a wonderful, difficult experience that gave me discipline and a place. MAXINE

I feel it made me a better woman. I had great role models, both in the convent and the many mothers with whom I came in contact. LORENA

I am glad I am now a mature woman outside of the convent. The combination of teenage growing-up and the rigidity of the convent's rules was bad. It has taken me a very long time to get over the hurt and pain of some of the unjustified convent experiences, and I suspect some of that will linger the rest of my life. There were some good things---singing in the choir is what comes to mind, but when anything triggers a memory of those years, most of the time it is negative. A convent is like any other institution: there are the very good, the very bad, and lots of levels in between. I happened to experience more of the bad element. DORIS

The convent did not prevent growing up, but it certainly slowed the process. For me, those years in the community were essential for me as a woman. They were hard, but I learned so much, and really came into my own. I like being a woman; I like me. And I appreciate all the experiences I had. They not only rubbed off some of the edges, but they enabled me to stand up and be recognized.

Chapter XV: Making It

Community life prepared me to be a professional woman who can be comfortable and productive in many situations. JULIANNE

I'm glad my life's been as it has. I wouldn't trade my convent experiences for anything. It has made my life very rich, given it more depth. TRACE

I don't regret my time in the convent, but it was a sterile, selfish experience. I learned to be more giving and loving in marriage. KATE

I had some great modeling on how to be a mature capable woman not under male domination. GAYLE

My experience was one of maturing emotionally, socially, and professionally. I'm much better for my years in the community. MURIEL

We had women superiors, but ultimately men were in charge back then somehow. We were always serving priests one way or another. JANN

I have not thought as much about "being a woman and my experience in the convent" as I have about convent/religious life. I feel strongly that institutional, professional, structured religious life is coming to an end. I think the Holy Spirit is leading the Church into a new era, if we would listen--into new ways of witnessing to the reality of God through Jesus Christ. The great exodus of women and men from convents, monasteries, and the priesthood is not just happenstance, or even a revolution. For me it was and is, the work of the Spirit--a voice with strong messages. As for being a woman in the convent, I think it is difficult to live, to mature in a normal healthy way in that setting. It can be done, I suppose. I survived, but could have used a bit more self-knowledge. I was older. I think the very young would have had more difficulties. There were some repressed, un-whole, mentally unhealthy women in our convents. I believe that I learned to be at home in and enjoy the friendship of men while still being comfortable with my vow of chastity---celibacy. EILEEN

I was/am happy to be a woman both in and out of the convent. I feel richer for having served--those were some of the most beautiful years of my life. ELLEN-2

I find myself terribly annoyed at Church law and the clergy's attitudes. Many believe that nuns leave at about the age I did because their biological motherhood clocks are ticking---rubbish! That's not why I left. And if they'd relax birth control restrictions, they wouldn't have to worry about abortion. LILLA

It was a good experience in some ways, but not my Vocation. JAN

The convent gave me an excellent education and allowed me to become a strong woman. NELL

It was a pretty mindless time, and we did all these things that came along. It was absolutely crazy when I think of a lot of things, not growing, their keeping you immature and not competent, putting you in a classroom when I didn't feel competent--poor kids. Those are the things I feel bad about. JEAN

Perhaps it helped me in my teaching career. SHIRLEY

I'm glad I was there--it helped me develop strong bonds with other good women. Though I am better for having been there, it was a must that I leave. CONNIE

Would a man have put up with it? ELIZABETH

I am proud to be a woman, but I don't think being in the convent enhances any of my womanly attributes. HELGA

I thought I wanted that life---found out that life changes. GRACE

I think I gained a great deal by being in the Community, particularly my education. And there are some truly wonderful people there---Sr. Ermelinda particularly. JULIA

The convent [lacerated] our bodies and stagnated our minds. MARY S

My experience in the convent was good for me professionally—I learned how to teach. Personally, it guaranteed that I would not have children, although my desire to have them was not strong. I think it arrested my psychological development—I have spent much time and money in therapy to uncover the repression and develop my emotional life. I liked living with other women. THERESE

It was a growing period for me; I learned much. LOUISE

I don't feel we were treated like women with minds and desires to have minds of our own. MARY

I was happy as a teacher and psychologist, and I retain many friendships with nuns and ex-nuns. FRANCES

Nuns were subdued by the Church—priests were authoritative. YVONNE

I was happy to give the privilege of motherhood to God for the opportunity to serve Him. I feel honored that He later chose me to have 4 godly children and a husband that is a committed Christian. BEVERLY

I experienced a feeling of "drying up" as a woman. MARIETTA

I enjoy being a woman of God, and I know my convent experiences helped me to who I am today. OTTER

I feel the Church downs women. HOLLY

Women nowadays are taught/told to think for themselves, be independent, and live life to the fullest. This is opposite to everything I experienced in the convent. DONNA

I was in the convent at a time when women were beginning to come of age. I am well-educated, I still teach, I am independent, I respect my community and its members. I'm happy to be me. THERESA

The convent promoted prolonged immaturity and pettiness. Convent methods were cult-like in early years. I knew many who were damaged psychologically and physically. JAN-2

I enjoy the conversations and ideals of lay people who are involved in charitable works. JEAN-3

To this day I trust men a lot more than I do other women. NANCY

The institution tried to depersonalize and de-feminize me and make me dependent---but they didn't succeed! CASEY

Would you still be in the convent if things had been different?

Hindsight is easy--there's no penalty attached. We can always say, Well I could have.... But the fact is, we live in the present. We only do what we do now. Which doesn't stop us from speculating on what would have happened if things *had* been different. Would we likely still be there?

YES: 11
NO: 32
MAYBE: 19
NO ANSWER: 11

Chapter XV: Making It

What things would have had to change for us to remain nuns?

YES, I'D STILL BE IN THE CONVENT IF:

If God had not pushed me out in the big exodus. EILEEN

If the convent had modernized. CONNIE

If there had not been the pressures, judgmental attitudes, and lack of charity. LILLA

If my parents had paid the $500 dowry that they wanted so that they would have let me go into nursing. ELEANOR

If I hadn't met Ron. MURIEL

If there had been changes. ELLEN-2

If we had kept abreast with the Formation Movement and had been truer to our Founder's spirit---But as I look back on it, I probably would have found the spirit of obedience a very difficult vow to keep. As I became more aware of how less talented and less well-intentioned Sisters ran their classes and treated the girls in charge, I became very disillusioned, and would have eventually left. MARTHA

If the Rules had been different. CAREN

If I'd taken vows. JOSEPHINE

If there had been more humanity, and kept promises of Vatican II. JAN-2

NO, EVEN HAD THINGS BEEN DIFFERENT, I WOULDN'T STILL BE IN THE CONVENT BECAUSE:

The convent wasn't the problem---I was. THERESA

It would have been too late. JEAN-3

If there had been more recognition, if there had been less negative supervision, if there had been allowances made for friendship, if the schedule had been more reasonable, if more care had been taken in the development of spirituality--it would still not take into consideration that I had to grow up. JULIANNE

I think the things that happened to me at the end, that caused me to leave, were for my greater good. It allowed me to go out into the world and find a job, make a living, fall in love, experience a love that I'd never experienced from my family--I was really very fortunate. Things happened to me in the convent which, at the time, I thought terrible, but I was lucky that other things happened. Someone was watching out for me that I would have a happy life. CHERRY

The immediate answer in my mind was NO. That intrigues me, because I don't think that while I was there it had ever occurred to me to think of leaving. Yet when I was told I could not stay, I was relieved. So, No, I don't think I'd still be there no matter what had been different. TRACE

There was not acknowledgement of our self-worth. LORNA

I have a better life than my nun-friends, and I don't have to apologize for a thing. They had 15 years of my best efforts, for nothing but room and board. I did nothing against them at any time, before-during-after, and when we have extra money, I send it to them. ROSE

Because I didn't have a Vocation. JANN

No, I don't think I'd still be in the convent even had things been different. I went in too young, and I still wanted to get out there and explore--you know, check out the world. If I'd entered later though, I might still be there. KATHLEEN

I DON'T KNOW, PERHAPS I WOULD STILL BE A NUN:

If I had not been shunned, if I had not been squelched for humility's sake, if I had been encouraged to develop, if I had been allowed friends, if we had been able to speak, if there had not been so many unreasonable rules--well, it would have been a different world. But then, I would probably have joined the Peace Corps, had there been one. DORIS

Maybe, if I hadn't gotten into music where I simply could not make it. I have a good mind, was an A student, and have a talent for writing. I needed to succeed because I am a perfectionist. THERESE-2

Maybe---I enjoyed the peace, the Office, the singing. DENISE

Possibly, if the rules hadn't changed. LORENA

If Vatican II had not happened, I might still be in the convent. With Vatican II I realized that it was not necessary to be separate from the world. If I hadn't gone for graduate study, the leaving probably would have been a longer process. THERESE

Probably--but who's to say? JANET

I am content with my choices. BEVERLY

If I had been a social worker. FRANCES

If the convent I returned to would have been a "normal" situation, I probably would have never left. MARIE

If our state had been allowed to progress without Canada's restrictions. NELL

If I hadn't been ordered to teach against my will. DONNA

If I had been more personally committed. JULIA-2

If community life had been different. PRISCILLA

Probably not. DIANE

Yet: Are you glad that you were a nun?

>
> YES: 46
> NO: 10
> BOTH: 4
> DON'T KNOW: 5
> NO ANSWER: 8

Nuns, even more than lay Catholics, were trained to see the good in everything, to believe that all was sent from God and should be accepted as a gift. Sunshine was a gift, as was suffering. The times were right for this—when the term "pollyanna" was born, it was considered a positive thing: let's not look on the dark side, but find something good in everything. The sarcasm for the pollyanna's pretending all is well, for ignoring the reality of misery, did not emerge until after mid-century. So it would be strange if these participants, as Catholics, as former women religious, and as products of the 50s, did *not* try to salvage the best out of any experience—especially from their convent years which were a dead serious contract between themselves and the Church, that same Church that preached hellfire and brimstone for sinners. One did not simply or lightly discard one's Vocation. To leave the convent in those early days took great personal and religious risk. One did not simply or lightly discard one's Vocation. To leave the convent took great personal and religious risk.

On the other hand, up to 45 years have passed for these brave hearts--time to forgive in the sense of moving on with one's life. If they were too close to see the good things before, they can see them now, and realize that noticing the positives doesn't negate the fact that, for many, there were hurtful things also.

Therefore, no one participant in this survey is completely glad or not glad about anything. When she answers "no" to this question (Are you glad that you were a nun?) it does not automatically mean that she has *no* good memories or thinks the time was totally without value. Although it might. In the same way, when she answers "yes", it does not mean that every single experience was pure joy. Read beyond the tallies.

YES, I'M GLAD THAT I WAS A NUN:

Yes---it brought me ahead on life's path. DIANE

Yes. I made good friends; also, it was too early for me to be with men. HOLLY

Yes. I answered that call, and I still respond to God's call in my life. NANCY

Yes--I am enjoying the aftermath from disciplined life. YVONNE

Yes, I met wonderful women. JEAN

Yes, I am glad that I was a nun because I learned a lot. It forged my character in many ways; it forced me to grow. My teaching career was definitely my avenue of growth during that 20-year period of my life, and it has made me who I am: a quilt of all the experiences I've ever had. I own the experience of having been a nun, and I tell people that I was. MARGARET

I loved it. OTTER

Yes--it kept me from marrying young and having a huge family. DENISE

Yes. I met wonderful, intelligent women. THERESA

Yes, it deepened my contemplative spirit. JULIANNE

Yes. It made me a better person. LORENA

Yes. That is who I am--that experience is unique to me. HOLLY

Yes. It made me a fighter for what the church can be. JANET

The experience was second to none. DOLORES

Yes. They're a great bunch of people. MARIE

Yes. It was very enriching. BEVERLY

Yes--lots of growth. GAYLE

Yes, I'm glad I had those years. I got what I needed for my life now: an excellent education, exposure to culture I'd never have gotten as a secular, experience in living in community with the consideration for others that it requires, and I've the acquaintance and friendship of many good people. TRACE

It helped me grow and mature. JANE

Yes. It saved me from marrying and having 5 or 6 children. I received an excellent education and found a very fulfilling career. SUZANNE

It is a unique experience. MAXINE

Yes. I gave 10 years of my life to serve others. ELEANOR

Chapter XV: Making It

I learned self-discipline. LORNA

It was right at the time. JANET K

A real asset to gracious living. CAREN

I served God in a special way, and met my husband. KATE

It made a great woman out of me. MURIEL

Yes. The first 10 years were happy ones. Got a free college education also. ANN

I learned so much about people and myself and I loved teaching. ELLEN-2

It was a solid, nurturing time. Perhaps I would have done better personally by going to college on the outside, but I'll never know that. I get together with several ex-nuns from my group who live close. They are dear to me--we share an unbreakable bond that few others could understand. ROSE

Yes--for as long as I was there. JOSEPHINE

Yes. MAE, MARTHA, THERESE-2

I'm glad I was there because I view many things in life quite differently than I would have otherwise. I am spiritually a richer person for having been a nun. I can empathize with others because of it. I still feel special and blessed by God. LILLA

I have good memories of some wonderful people. JULIA

It provided experiences I needed and enriched me as a person. LOUISE

It gave me discipline, depth, and wonderful friends. NELL

I met many committed women. MARIETTA

It makes a good conversation topic. Sometimes I think it was a good safe place to be during a time I probably would have rebelled if I had stayed home. Leaving the convent was my declaration of independence both there and with my family. It took me a few more years to really claim control of my life. There were times when I wanted to get back at my mother for her control. I thought I could really embarrass her by having a baby without being married. I was finally maturing enough to understand that it wouldn't be fair to a child, and I would have more problems than just my mother. The bad thing about being in the convent is that it was a time of no growth. I came out thinking like an 18-year old at 23. I have heard that this is the same thing that happens to prisoners. If I had stayed much longer, I think the adjustment of leaving would have been more difficult. MERT

I'm glad for the experience of having been a nun, very glad for the experience. I wouldn't do it again today. And I wish that I had left sooner so that I could have gotten on with it, but I didn't. I seem to be the eternal optimist, and think that things are going to get better. I did that with my husband, too. We were married for 7 years. I knew it was not okay, that it was wrong from the beginning, but I hung in there for 7 years. CAROL

Yes. I lived my commitment until it became destructive to my life and health. JAN-2

Yes, I'm better for it, though it was a must that I leave. CONNIE

Yes. I grew up, had strong role models, have good memories. I came out with a more adult faith. Had I not been exposed to theology education, I most certainly would have become scrupulous and narrow. JULIA-2

NO, I AM NOT GLAD THAT I WAS A NUN:

No. JEAN-2, MARY

Chapter XV: Making It

It was a time of suspended animation. ELLEN

No---it took away the years I could have had children. JEAN-3

No. I could have lived nicely without the hurt, thank you. Not that I didn't have any good moments or learn anything, but the whole experience was a mistake. Not the least of which was that 23, I was still emotionally a 15-year-old trying to be an adult. DORIS

No. It was a waste of my life. GINA

It was basically a waste of a part of my life. DONNA

No, I missed having children. CAROL-2

No, but I wish not to dwell on that. MARY S

Yes and no. Yes, because it was a place for me to grow and figure out what I was about. I thought the Sisters at two places were really loving and caring. I wanted to belong to a "family". I met some great women, happy, professional, powerful. I got to be a part of a community that was respected and that did good work. CAROLYN

I don't know if I'm glad for having been a nun. ELIZABETH, SHIRLEY

So-so. Yes and no. JAN

I liked the grounding it gave me, and I didn't like the stunting of my development. THERESE

There are some things I think being in the convent did for me. I learned to live with others and get along with others. I acquired an honest and healthy work ethic. HELGA

It was okay—I gave a lot and gained a lot. GRACE

Most of it was so good—such wonderful people and opportunities and adventures and growth in loving God. I do not mean to sound like my years in the convent were one long heavenly honeymoon. Life is not like that. The Novitiate was pretty awful and I knew real anguish at times. I barely handled it or acknowledged it, and ended up being "held back" for 6 months while the rest of my class went on for profession of vows. It was humiliating and not helpful to growth in any way. I now realize the novice mistress was about the same age as I, and was not equipped to offer insights or assistance. After making vows, I got into work that I liked and was comfortable with, but I always had problems with authority, with being forthright. One also has to deal with Sisters who were boring or difficult—that too is life. I never felt really free in the convent setting, to have close personal friends. For those subscribing to a communal life—it seemed to be perceived as not quite right. I also had resentment towards some who lived closer to home. For a long time, I was 3,000 miles from my family and got to visit them only after a lapse of 10 years. Those are some of the "bad" things—but even now they seem to pale when I think of the blessings, the gifts I received. And still receive. EILEEN

I'm resigned to having had the experience, but it was non-productive. I did make some good friends though, I had regular meals and sleep, and I didn't get divorced. JANN

I have mixed feelings, and often wonder how my life would have gone. MARY-2

Chapter XV: Making It

Are you happier now than you were in the convent?

YES: 55
NO: 5
OTHER: 8

Other than the question: Would you encourage anyone to enter the convent? this question polarized the most answers.

YES, I AM HAPPIER BECAUSE:

I experience more freedom of choice. JEAN-3

Yes, because I don't have to have another woman standing over judging every action of mine. ELEANOT

I feel more fulfilled, though somewhat more distracted. I feel that there are many more possibilities in life for me than there were in the convent. THERESE

I love my family. JOSEPHINE

I'm married, I'm in a career I enjoy, and feel proud of the fact that after I left I taught for 3 more years, then went back to school for a Masters degree and changed careers. And I enjoy my work as a dietitian in private nutrition counseling. SARAH

I lead a normal life now. MARY-2

I have a loving relationship now. CAROL-2

I am freer, less stressful. My health is much better. I laugh more and I appreciate myself as a person. JULIANNE

I have matured. LORENA

I am just myself now, and that's okay. NANCY

I am happier with my husband and family. ANN

I'm fulfilled in my marriage and in my life. DIANE

I have a fuller relationship with family and friends. KATE

I'm in love with David. JAN

I have independence now. MAE

My family gives me great joy. MERT

People care about me. JANN

I am very happily married. LORNA

I'm more fulfilled. CAROLYN, DONNA

Freedom! GINA, FRANCES, ELLEN, KATHLEEN, DORIS

I can be myself. CONNIE

I have freedom to make my own decisions. HELGA, JESSICA

My husband and I are well-matched. JULIA

Chapter XV: Making It

I am my own person. GRACE, CAREN, THERESE-2

I have less stress and a meaningful relationship. LOUISE

I have more control and can help my family. NELL

I like being single and living in a small apartment with a job to go to. TRACE

No tension---I think for myself. MARY

I have found a soulmate. MARIETTA

Of course I'm happier! CHERRY

I am in control now. ROSE

I am fully functional now. JAN-2

I am free and responsible to my own conscience. DOROTHY

Yes in some ways. At times I felt oppressed in the convent. BEVERLY

I can be me. HOLLY

I enjoy life. DENISE

Yes, even though life is harder now financially. SUZANNE

The main reason is that for all the struggles economically and emotionally to function in this world, at least I have the final say on the direction I want to go. Too much of my convent life I did not fit the mold they expected of me. JEAN-2

I am definitely happier now than when I was in the convent because I've grown to the point in my life where I have begun to pick up all the pieces and seen

myself as an integrated whole. I feel like one of these late bloomers; I am doing what I want in life with a wonderful partner, and I feel in charge more and more as the years go on. I am happy with myself; I love myself. MARGARET

NO, I AM NOT HAPPIER NOW, BECAUSE:

    Happiness is relative. JANET

    It's a different life stage. GAYLE

    Not happier, but also not as stressed. ELIZABETH

    I am still not at peace. ELLEN-2

    In the convent you had security--all the decisions were made for you so you knew you were doing the right thing. I was happy in the convent for many years. It was the tension, the magnification of little things into huge crises, the constant unkindness and immense pressure that led to a physical breakdown--that caused me grief. I'm happy now, too. I've always been a happy person, I guess. But now I'm not all tied up in knots, and when I'm ill, I can be ill in peace. I love my freedom and independence. I guess you could say I'm happier now, but in a different way. All the guilt has not yet passed, but it is getting less all the time now. LILLA

OTHER COMMENTS ABOUT HAPPINESS THEN/NOW:

    I am happy in both lives. MURIEL

    I'm comfortable that I'm where I belong now. THERESA

    There are two stages in my life--each is different. SHIRLEY

    That is difficult to answer. PRISCILLA

My happiness now is different. Loving well in marriage is a big job--a full time one. It is wonderful to love and to be loved in this very special way. It is pure gift to have someone love you in spite of your worst self showing now and then. It helps me believe how constant and tremendous is God's love for us. Marriage is far more concentrated and individual-oriented than the convent. I am more free of rules and restrictions than while in the convent, yet there is a responsibility in marriage that may balance that. I do know that on the day I made final vows 32 years ago, I knew a gratitude and peace that was not of this world. I'll never forget that joy. I also recall the ultra-joy of my wedding day 17 years ago. EILEEN

Happier? I am more secure. MARIE

Conclusion? It's hard to compare two sets of happiness. Or draw your own.

What values taught to you in the convent do you espouse today? Could you have learned these elsewhere? Where?

None. *I saw much pettiness and greed in the convent.* MARY S

Positive convent values were not much different from the way I was raised as a child. Some negative "values" I would NOT pass on are: putting others down, equating humility with humiliation, selective

shunning, maintaining a special circle of privileged persons, not treating anyone as an individual, and insisting on no personal worth. DORIS

Spiritual life, prayer, enjoyment. I could have learned those in parish life. MARY-2

I learned a work ethic there, which would also have come to me by keeping a home. THERESE-2

Meditation---not likely to be learned elsewhere at the time. MARTHA

The community did not give me a different set of values than the ones I had learned and espoused at home: prayer, respect for the individual, honesty, integrity, satisfaction in work well done, development of personal gifts and talents, joy in living, education. JULIANNE

Economy, simplicity, the 'zen of living'---I'm not sure about learning these elsewhere. DIANE

Strong faith, unconditional love. I could have learned these from my husband. LORENA

I believed in altruism before the convent, though the convent reinforced my commitment to giving to others. One value I learned there was concentration in solitude in research or study---which I could have learned in graduate school. JEAN-2

Most of the same values I'd learned at home. THERESA

Teaching and service to others; I could have learned these at home. CAROL-2

Spiritual values, simplicity. I doubt I'd have learned these any other place. YVONNE

Spirituality, service, the importance of teaching. However, if I had married after college, I would have spent my life raising children and probably would not have pursued my education. THERESE

I think I got a good education and the experience especially with the Sister who is now 91 years old, that opened my mind to become a more liberal and creative person. I can't see that having happened anywhere else, because in the convent we were kept very educated, we were the top educators and constantly going to conferences and meetings and staying on top of our field. I know that now when I meet people who married and had a lot of children in my regular college class, I can see that they're not very aware of what's going on in the world—they're not very openminded. And a lot of it was from taking so much time to raise those kids, I'm sure. They didn't have time to go study and learn and open their mind. CHERRY

Love for Jesus. BEVERLY

I still value meditation and quiet actions. Silence of action is more an attitude of mind; I don't think it would have been gained elsewhere. I think one must soak it in. Meditation could te taught outside a convent, but back then I didn't know that. Certainly I think it was more easily taught in a community where everyone was meditating together twice a day. TRACE

The importance of my faith. JANE

Perhaps I could have learned these values elsewhere. The biggest thing I learned is to question, to continually look for and search for truth. At that time we had fine teachers, theology teachers—and of course this is what I was thirsty for, hungered for. I could not have received it at home, and I truly believe that had I not entered, I would not have had the funds to continue my education anyplace else. I did not enter to be educated—I really did enter because of a spiritual need, but the gains of receiving a well-rounded education impacted my life in a way that I'll never be able to give back. So truly, I feel that my time there was a gift. JULIA-2

Honesty, discipline, prayer. I don't think I would have learned these elsewhere. MAXINE

I realized through the convent that education never stops, though I could have learned this elsewhere. CAREN

Conscientiousness. I would also have learned that through education. JAN-2

Using my talents--as I'd learned to do at home and school. CASEY

Thrift, low interest in hair/clothes/TV/food. I could have learned especially thrift, at home. ANN

Honesty, a deep abiding faith, trust in God, compassion for others, acceptance of others without judging, etc. LILLA

Friendship, responsibility. My Mom has these values--I probably could have learned them through experience or in my family. MURIEL

Kindness, consideration---you can learn these in any loving atmosphere. KATE

My values were instilled before the convent. MERT

Giving, loving unselfishly--though I was brought up with these values. ROSE

The value of "community". CAROL

I learned sharing; I could have learned that anywhere. DENISE

Not many. I don't even pray the rosary. DONNA

Love, charity, dedication--though these were also in my family. ELLEN-2

Honesty, trust, and the value of prayer. I might have learned these in a loving home, also. JANN

Love of God and others is primary--who knows if I would have learned this elsewhere? MARIETTA

None--I learned values on the outside. MARY

All of them. I hope I would have learned these in daily life anyway. NELL

Value of silence, prayer, friendship--I don't know if I could/would have learned these elsewhere. EILEEN

Service to others, being non-judgmental. FRANCES

Conscientiousness, honesty, justice--though I could have learned these with family or as a single person with friends. LOUISE

Keeping my Sunday obligations and accompanying activities. Elsewhere? Yes. JEAN-3

Honesty. GRACE

The same values I learned in my family. HOLLY

I practiced honesty and integrity, though I learned these from my family. JULIA

Morality, faith--but I learned those from the Catholic Church. SHIRLEY

Work hard. yes. one's own goals. JAN

Maybe learned same values elsewhere, but it would have been lots more work. JEAN

Care for those in need—I might have learned that in the Peace Corps. CONNIE

Discipline, but could have learned it in the military. LORNA

I could have learned all values in a small Christian family. ELEANOR

Practice of the presence of God—there was too much distraction for me to have learned it any other place. JOSEPHINE

I think none. ELIZABETH

I learned to live with others and get along with them. Also a healthy work ethic. HELGA

To seek God in prayer—I couldn't have learned this as well elsewhere. ELLEN

Poverty—I get along quite well with less now, and don't have a lot of money. I've learned to enjoy what I have. I might have learned this elsewhere, but I don't know where. KATHLEEN

Confrontation, getting along—maybe I could have learned these elsewhere. MARIE

Values I learned in the convent:
1. A great thirst for God.
2. A deep commitment to work for the church as it struggles through the difficult years of transition.
3. Discipline.
4. A healthy respect for authority.
5. A sense of what is essential to being a Catholic. JANET

Self-discipline, though I could have learned it in the military. MAE

Following Jesus. I could have learned that elsewhere, though. OTTER

Kindness towards all, actions prove spiritual values--I couldn't have learned them to this degree elsewhere. SUZANNE

Productive use of time and dedication--I could have learned these at home. NANCY

Values that were taught to me in the convent were a continuation of those I learned from my family. I value these strongly even today: the friendship/networking of women, continuing education, spiritual searching and priorities. I learned things in that kind of medieval lifetime that will never be that way again. It's kind of a unique experience to have been able to wear the habit as it used to be. That's not values, but I learned a lot of self discipline. Because we lived in groups, I learned to be respectful of other people, and to appreciate simplicity in my life. Creativity was valued, especially (after Vatican II) being able to create liturgy and prayer sessions together. I still carry that into my women's circle. MARGARET

Can you recognize an ex-nun on the street? How?

YES: 13
NO: 38
NOT SURE: 13

Once, in the days of this author's being absolutely certain of some things, she was chatting with a fellow retreatant before the opening conference. The woman was dressed like a typical ex-nun--even to the medallion around her neck. Her beliefs and thoughts meshed with those of the old convent days. The author wondered to which Order the woman had belonged, so she asked her. Turned out she was not a nun and had never been one. So much for infallibility and instinct.

On the other hand, when people (accidentally) find out some of us were nuns, they spend the next fifteen minutes with their mouths open, every once in a while saying, "You?! You were a nun?! You don't look like one."

So what does an ex-nun look like? No one knows for sure, but we never cease to hope that we do. Question: CAN YOU PICK OUT AN EX-NUN?

YES:

Ha! JAN

Sometimes I guess, but I don't really know. EILEEN

Sure, by their stature, expression, and demeanor. MURIEL

Most ex-nuns dress in drab colors and their hair needs design. MARIE

Chapter XV: Making It

    They wear little or no makeup and jewelry and are missing a sense of style. ANN

    They're something special. YVONNE

    I recognize them by their clothes, manner, and eyes. JANET K

    I can tell by their demeanor. JAN-2

    Many are conservatively dressed. SARAH

    They're dingy, naive, and good people. HOLLY

    I'm not sure how---it's a special quality---eyes, smile, demeanor. JULIA-2

    They have a certain peacefulness. THERESE-2

NO---I DON'T RECOGNIZE THEM:

    ---no habits! MARY-2

    No, but sometimes I think so---they dress kind of off-beat. MARY

    Not all plain women are nuns. ELLEN

    Some look "nunish" but may not be! FRANCES

    Not really, though it all has to do with posture and carriage. JULIA

I RECOGNIZE SOME OF THEM:

    To a certain degree---they're the dowdy type. MAE

Occasionally--by their plainness. THERESE

Some, by their confidence and carriage. THERESA

By their bad haircuts, little makeup, and polyester. JESSICA

Especially the over-sixty nun. I recognize her by her attire, general grooming, and comportment. TRACE

Not on the street, but if I talk to them I usually can tell. ROSE

Sometimes--by their looks, their walk. CAREN

Sometimes--by their unsophistication. CASEY

I usually recognize (habitless) nuns, not ex-nuns. DIANE

It's harder now that so many New Age women have adopted what used to be the outer signs of nuns and ex-nuns: let their hair go grey, keep it short, wear little makeup. Ex-nuns used to wear conservative simple clothing—lots of polyester, especially plaid jackets, sometimes a cross on a neck-chain. DORIS

I have in the past, but I'm not sure I can do it now. Total strangers, even now, ask me if I were ever a Sister. My sister tells me it's my carriage. I think it has more to do with an objectivity I can maintain while dealing with people. I am certainly no threat. Maybe I convey that. I would like to think it is an element of simplicity. Who knows? JULIANNE

❖❖❖

Do you consider yourself a Successful Person at this point in your life?*

Yes! Because I am happy and at peace and I'm retired! And I'm ever so grateful for life. EILEEN

Yes. I have been happy and had rich experiences in the convent and in teaching, as a single person and a married person, and I've had a rewarding career as a lawyer. I have been able to help others who have been less fortunate. NELL

Yes. After 20 years in the convent and still no B.A. degree (college only in summer) I completed my Bachelor's and got my Master's Degree as well, then continued to teach until 1979 when I retired with great benefits. Also, I am now a happy person. MARY

Yes. I've made enough money to have time for beauty, knowledge, and creativity. I have family and friends to love. I am free to skip the damaging aspects of the Church and my past. ELLEN

Yes. I am a tenured faculty member at a college and married to a wonderful man with whom I share a ministry to Chinese visiting scholars. MARIETTA

So-so. I have never had any confidence in myself, plus I have always had problems making decisions. I figure it is so ingrained in me to be obedient and do what others tell me that I'll always have problems to some extent. DONNA

*Unfortunately, the first 13 test-questionnaires did not include this question.

Yes. I have a wonderful family, other people like me, and I care about people. JANN

Yes. I think I give the children I take care of a safe, loving place to grow and learn. My children are caring adults and my husband and I have a good relationship. There is joy and laughter and love in our lives, and I had a part in making that happen. MERT

No. CAROL

Yes. We have relative financial stability, our children are coming along fine (fingers are crossed!) and we are happy with each other. ROSE

Yes. I'm successful both in my marriage and my profession. MURIEL

Yes. I have had two good jobs from which I am receiving retirement and also receiving Social Security. I am happy in my own way. Success is not always what you accomplish outside, but rather how you are and feel inside. ELLEN-2

Yes. I am happy, employed, and a good mother. The hardest thing at this point is missing my husband, but it's getting better. KATE

Yes, I don't make much money, but yes, I think I'm successful. I'm quite happy, thanks. KATHLEEN

Yes. I have had a happy, full life. I continue to grow. While I was not practicing my faith (I was married to an Atheist) I did not feel separated from God and I still had a deep faith in God, living as I believed but not going to church (as we consider "practicing" to be. My husband was able to let know before he died that he believed in God. That was a miracle in itself. LILLA

Yes. I have raised five physically handicapped and mentally ill grade school step-children to adulthood, and I am now financially secure. ANN

Chapter XV: Making It

Yes. I am thankful for all that I have received and done and I see God's hand and guidance in my life. I am very happy and lucky. The convent was like building blocks that I needed in life. I found a great job as an art supervisor. I quit after marriage and now have my own studio and two homes. I travel and have a marvelous husband who loves me and lets me do my own thing. JANET K

Yes. I'm a tenured teacher and make a comfortable living. CAREN

Yes. I have been highly successful as an educator and trainer of teachers, was president of our state's Council of Teachers of English and Local Director of Teacher Corps for five years. I have a 19 year loving marriage and have been foster parent/legal guardian of two abused boys. JAN-2

Although it has been a struggle materially, I feel much wealthier since my years of struggling with the real World from the convent. Although I value my friends who are still in religious life, I am amazed at how differently we see reality. ANNE

Yes. I am dealing with issues of age from a point of inner strength and do not feel that I have to follow any leader or superior or priest to find my happiness. DOLORES

Yes. You'll realize that I'm really in a questioning phase in my life. Successful? I've raised 3 beautiful children, I've been a successful businesswoman, I've continued in the Catholic Church both to teach and to be active. The last 5 years I have gone back to school with the idea of getting a Masters in Theology. What is success? Looking back, I can say yes, I have accomplished things that I wanted to do, but there is a great fear, a great longing to do even more. I said "fear" because at times I wonder what it is I am yet to do. Longing to find a new way here. What is success? When I was a child, if somebody would have asked me what I want to be when I grew up, without any hesitation I would have said, I want to be a saint---as we defined it in those days: a close friend to God. I'm not sure that that little girl has changed her mind. She's gotten older, she's just not sure where the next direction will take her. I have a great spiritual hunger and when that is satisfied, then I can honestly say, yes, I feel successful. JULIA-2

Yes. I live the best way I know how. I am 70--have good health and a wonderful partner, am part of the lesbian community in my city. I do volunteer work, travel, and I have learned to accept. In short, I am happier now than I've ever been. When my time comes to die, I shall have no regrets because I will have had a long life and I will have had it all, i.e., all that matters in this world, including a modest income, my neat car, and three cats. MAXINE

Yes. I have achieved many of my life's goals. MAE

Yes. Sure I think I'm successful. I'm happy. What more can you want? TRACE

Yes. I have good happy relationships and am maturing in my walk with Christ. I have been allowed to serve others in many capacities. I write books and articles, am involved in politics and in my church. Our children are happy, well adjusted, and serve Christ. I feel very blessed. BEVERLY

At this point in my life, yes, very successful. Had the world been in a different state, I would have considered staying and teaching, but I still had a very successful career, was able to retire early with a pension and medical benefits at 65, and now I have so much time and the ability to volunteer or do other paid work if I want. I don't call it a retirement, I call it a change of careers. CHERRY

Yes. I have my PhD and a good job, plus an excellent marriage. Although when I die--I may go straight to hell. However, I have decided that I'll have good company in hell! MARY S

Yes. I am still using my education--voluntary teaching, president of organizations, etc. I also wrote a book about my life. PRISCILLA

Yes. I love my husband, my work which deals with people all the time, our beautiful home, and the fact that we share so many common interests. My life is full with many friends. MARIE

Yes. I am a wife and mother and I am a successful piano teacher. I am still growing spiritually. JANET

Yes. I have completed my Master's and am licensed to do therapy--marriage, family, child therapy. I direct a homeless shelter of men, women, children---a 40-bed facility, and I feel that I help people get out of the homeless rut. I can effect change! HOLLY

I feel unsuccessful at making a stable, good income and establishing an intimate relationship, but very successful in learning about myself and becoming happy and independent. I feel like I am constantly growing. I have taken risks and challenges. JEAN-2

Yes. I'm happy in my marriage and in my profession. I also I continue to pursue self answers. SARAH

Yes. I know that I am a good teacher. I know myself, my faults and my good points. I have a successful marriage, I love my husband, and I consider myself a good mother. LORENA

Yes. I feel I've coped as well as I can considering I got a late start. I feel very grateful for all my experiences. MARY-2

Yes. I am following the Lord, happy in watching Him work wonderful relationships with my husband and 4 neat daughters. The Lord uses me continually in His work--drawing people to Him, healing them, loving them, guiding them. It's exciting! OTTER

Yes. At civic and community events, people seem intrigued by my 30 years of dedication. [flyer enclosed] YVONNE

Yes. I participate in my world and continue to grow individually and help to improve what is around me. SUZANNE

Yes. I have come to a stage of self-acceptance, and am still growing and learning in so many areas of life. I'm open to the adventure of life, and so far, life has been an adventure for me. DIANE

Yes. I am a retired school teacher and I continue to give harp lessons. I am asked to play my harp for many functions. I'm married and live in a lovely home (own two more) and enjoy my church. JEAN-3

Yes. Even though I don't earn a lot, I have lots of diversified skills. I do aerobics 3-4 times a week. I live alone and enjoy it. My children enjoy my company. NANCY

Yes. I teach, I touch a lot of kids, I'm special. I have always had the idea that things happen because they are meant to be. I was meant to be in the Novitiate. I left a better person. LORNA

Yes. I live with a wonderful woman, co-parent two sons, am successful in my profession, live a comfortable life-style, have a positive outlook, enjoy life, and am looking forward to future travel. I have a supportive family and friends. CAROLYN

Yes. Success is learning, growing, and loving. GAYLE

Personally, I've advanced a great deal since I left the convent. I am happy with my life, or I change things so that I'm happier. Financially successful I never will be---not because I don't like money, but aiming for it exclusively doesn't fit into my life. As the world sees me, I am somewhat successful. I've been in plays, had art shows, published books, raised fine children, volunteered all over the place, taught high school, still teach adults and lecture on the topic of my last book, as well as play with visual arts and gardening. In each area of my life I've had some successes and some failures. I continue to grow, to learn, to be happier. DORIS

Absolutely. I've come out of it all alive, well, and happy. Seriously, I am comfortable with the fact that I have used my talents and education in a constructive way. I still believe in God and lean heavily on the Holy Spirit. Oh, there are things I still want to do. I look forward to the day I can get back to writing. Maybe when I have my first short story published, I will really feel accomplished. But who knows what lied ahead. I'm sure there will be other challenges to face. JULIANNE

Yes. I own my own home with a reasonable retirement income. I held a good job as an accountant/office manager for 10 years. I loved and was loved by a beautiful man for 21 years. THERESE-2

Yes, because my three children are going forward in serving others and going to school, and I am still with my husband working to help the elderly be happy and comfortable before they die. Life is good because, unlike the convent, someone isn't standing over you all the time telling you that you cannot do this or that. In other words, you can be yourself. ELEANOR

Yes, because I am at peace within myself and with those whom I love, those with whom I interact. MARTHA

You bet---long marriage, good kids, own business, and I look fantastic for my age. Also, God still loves me. JOSEPHINE

Yes. I'm happy, in a successful marriage, and I enjoy teaching. CAROL-2

Yes, because I am finally where I want to be in a relationship that supports and challenges me to live my full potential as a woman. K.T.

Yes. I'm a good teacher and a good Mom. My students have done well. THERESA

Yes. I'm successful in my career, financially okay, at peace with myself, in a great relationship, challenged, and growing daily. CASEY

❖❖❖

Comments about working the questionnaire

Answering 212+ questions that probe into some of the most sensitive issues in your life is not an easy task. Here and there on the Questionnaire or in separate papers, the participants wrote notes about how it felt to summon up the answers. They also sent letters during the 9 years the book was being written, mostly after the author had sent out a newsletter. If anyone regretted answering these questions, they did not say so.

· MARTHA (wrote in 1996) My Mistress of Novices had a favorite saying: "Where there are a lot of humans, there is a lot of human nature: So when I read that you have found yourself in a virtual crossfire of strong opinions, you can be certain that you have opened the doors to a lot of repressed emotions exploding outward and inward in the hearts, minds, and psyche of most of us "veterans" of the convent. For my part, I found the questionnaire blessedly complete and very therapeutic. For once in my life I could review those years that still count so much to me (in spite of the pain/pleasure that the memories evoked). Of course I want you to publish your book and reap the rewards of your conscientious hard work. But for my part, you have already gifted me. Thanks.

NELL:(93) It was about midnight when I finished this. It made me sick to think that there could be Communities that could possibly answer Yes to questions about racism and punishment and other questions. No human organization is perfect, but my convent experience was a blessing.

THERESE-2: (94) Here it is...I still have oceans of indecision, but I'll trust you. There are many things in the questionnaire I've never told anyone. The reason I want to write my story is to share with others that even a quaking bowl of Jello® can learn to make decisions to bring about change. Much success to you. With love and aloha.

LORNA (94): I really had some reservations about filling out your request. I had mixed feelings about my experience there. I received some requests in the past, but I don't think that anyone is doing a research project similar to yours, though I do think that there is a real intent to heal any hurts incurred along the way. When I decided to leave, I was allowed to tell my parents who met me at the front door. I could not tell anyone of my decision, but left after the evening meal. The Mistress of Novices left me with these parting words: You will not be happy anywhere but here. These words stayed with me during trials in college, indecision in a career choice, and even a subsequent marriage. I have been blessed in so many ways---- great husband, wonderful kids, and now 4 very loved grandchildren. And yet, there still hangs over my head—when is this happiness going to come to an end? My friend, a nun for 23 years, and I visited the Motherhouse this last June and the whole system seemed to have crumbled and held no fear or wonder for us. We found older nuns living in the past and truly in love with the Lord. They had little conception of today's world and problems. But in their own way had served the Lord. The women in my set were among the most talented that I have ever met. Yet their real talents were often put on the back burner while they learned to conform to the standards set by others. They had to subject their true talents to the wishes of others. We were the student leaders, the members of the Honor Role, the top athletes, and for the most part, talented in many ways. Portray us well, because we deserve it. Good luck in your work

JAN (94): They treated us like dirt—crucified us. Wouldn't let us have friends because they were afraid of Lesbianism and they wouldn't even tell us why. We're healing ourselves by telling our stories. Even though we were very naïve, we were more knowledgeable than those who were trying to mold us. Rather than sit around and feel sorry for myself, I set goals and went for them. In strength and ideas, I'm a rich woman. Go to plan B has been my lifesaver. I've seen so many ex-nuns that were broken. If you carry that stuff all through your life with you, it just doesn't work out. You only go through this life once.

DOROTHY: (93) We were idealistic, right out of high school, and honestly believed the convent was the way to be a saint. I had a hard time, and the Church strikes me as being completely oblivious to us.

ELEANOR: (93): I was going through the questionnaire answering things, and it was too much—I had to put it down for a while. It's like opening a damn can of worms.

MERT: My sister who wasn't in the convent read the questionnaire and thought it astute, complete, and good.

JULIA: (93) This questionnaire has revived many memories, not all of them pleasant. I've heard stories of others' departures, some of which are nearly incomprehensibly sad when one thinks about them. Christian? Not at all. Some people were very badly treated when they left. This is a pretty exhaustive questionnaire. Some things made me uncomfortable. My years in the community were not bad years, only some bad moments.

ROSE: (93) Of all the kind, good Superiors, somehow it was the Will of God that I was in that situation at that time. Maybe writing it down for you (the Q) has been therapeutic for me, too. Good luck.

PRISCILLA (94): My 35+ convent years were happy, but now that I've been out some 15 years I realize how far from reality those convent years were. It seems, or at least I feel that they kept me from being myself, from even finding out who I am.

MURIEL: (93) From some of your questions, it sounds like I sailed through unscathed where others were injured. Good luck with your book.

LILLA (93): The questionnaire was a real catharsis. I have hurt so very much for so very long and am only now truly facing things I have buried deeply for many years. Although I actually told you very little, there was a tremendous burden which is now faced and lifted, especially guilt for not having remained a nun. There are timid and bruised souls out there who are all locked up within themselves--how well I understand that!

ANN: (93) Your questions seem to expect negative answers. I was well-treated in the convent and the experience was a positive one except for the basic unnaturalness of the life.

ELLEN (94) The questionnaire made me realize what old business—finished business, the convent is for me now.

JAN-2 (93): In retrospect I would say that many in the convent were incompetent for the positions they held. Many Superiors did not have concern for the individual. My own education came not from Community support, but because a good friend who believed in me got me to apply for grants. Almost everything I accomplished was in spite of the Community, not because of Community support. A greater hardship (than only being given $200 when I left) was the lack of Social Security. After I left, there was some Community arrangement with the SS office to get Sisters enrolled—but it was a one time deal and I was never notified that I could have been covered. I found out too late.

DOLORES (93): Reading through the questionnaire certainly did bring back a flood of memories. But I am pleased to have an opportunity to look at those years and tell someone. Thank you for asking me. I admire your courage in undertaking such an enormous project.

JULIA-2 (93): The questionnaire has taken me longer than I thought because it's brought forth a lot of memories, and it's forced me to examine where I am now. I sincerely pray for the success of your project. Thank you for letting me be a part of it.

TRACE (93): Last weekend I made a retreat, and the director, whom I've known since he was in the seminary with my brother, remarked that answering the questionnaire must have been good for me, and I think he's right. My prayers for your work.

MARIE (93): Maybe I'm one of few, but my 25 years in the convent (1960-85) were for the most part, very happy and enriching. The women (even my Superiors) were good women who were fair and trying to be good to the Sisters.

Maybe it was my Community, maybe the time, but the "horror stories" were not in my life. Good luck on your project.

JEAN-2 (94): This questionnaire has stirred up a lot of old emotions and feelings. I think I would recall more in a group discussion if you felt inclined to get information this way. Thanks for a thoughtful retrospective.

DENISE (93): The convent was not a truly spiritual experience for me, except perhaps in some of the music.

MARY-2 (94): I hope what I have to say is helpful to you. I am eager to read the book when it is published. This is such a foreign way of life to many people that it's difficult to relate it to their normal lives. In fact, when I left, that was the hardest part—no one understood what I had been through. Many are in disbelief that anyone could or would allow herself to be in such a situation. I could have used some support groups or more supportive people. Thanks again for reading this. It is good to talk about these things to someone who understands. Good luck on this project and thank you for doing it.

DIANE: (93): Thank you for the privilege of participating in this questionnaire.

JULIANNE (94): This has been a hard experience; but great. Thank you. I find that I am now having positive dreams about the Community, especially about some Sisters with whom I had differences. I want to make contact with them and eradicate any tension. I also discovered areas of anger that I had not realized were still with me. This has been a catharsis. At some point, I wager that all of that will be very unimportant. I feel better for having shared all of this with you, even though I do not know you. Good luck!

K.T. (93): I thank you for doing this. It has been of use to me and I hope it is of use to other people also.

HOLLY (93): I had to stop at question 59 and "lick my wounds" for three weeks. It really surprised me to know the questionnaire would affect me so. Love and thanks.

KATE (94): Five of us got together for a delightful time using your questionnaire as a springboard for the many things we'd forgotten. We learned so much about each other, why we entered and about our lives since. There was much acceptance. We hope to do it again.

LORENA (94): I think I laid many things to rest once and for all.

YVONNE (94): The questionnaire made me realize more the spiritual and educational benefits reaped in 30 convent years.

MARTHA (99): I want you to know how cleansing filling out the questionnaire was, and how important it was "to be counted". It was one of the most therapeutic things I've ever done for myself, and I thank you for that opportunity. I don't think that you will ever know how much healing you have created within each of us.

As the author, I also have been moved by the stories told here. There have been days when I wept as I typed, and ones where I had the strong urge to hop on a plane and go hug these women. The questionnaire also brought back blocked memories of my own, and gave me the opportunity to deal with hurts through therapy, talks with friends, and just the companionable feeling of working with the women participants in this project. I used to wonder why God had let me waste all those years in the convent when I could have been growing. Now I feel that (though, given the choice, I would not do it over again) this book is of such value to me, to the participatory women, and to future readers, that the fact of writing it alone gives worth to those years. Without having spent those years in a convent, I would not—we would not—be where we are.

❖❖❖

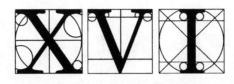

GLOSSARY

brief explanations of terms
according to mid-1900s thinking

Glossary

Brief explanations which pertain to Roman Catholic convent life in pre-Vatican II era. No two convents were exactly the same, though they all functioned in a like manner and used roughly the same terms.

ALCOVES: refers to the cell, or small curtained area given for use of the nun, especially in her formative years. In mid-century and before, permission of the superior was required for a nun to enter her alcove outside of official sleep-times. The alcove usually had a small bed, nightstand or drawers, and a wooden chair.

ALTAR SOCIETY: the women who met to clean and beautify the church.

ANNULMENT (of marriage): sometimes referred to as "Catholic divorce". It was and is (1999) insisted upon before a Catholic remarries in the Church. Basically, it seeks to prove the first marriage was not valid.

ASPIRANCY: (a relatively new concept, not utilized in all orders) refers to the first stage of "nun-ness" as well as to the physical space in which Aspirants lived under the direction of a nun Superior for a period of months.

ASPIRANT MISTRESS: the (final professed) nun who taught and shepherded the aspirants, instructing them on how to pray, behave, etc.

ASPIRANT: the girl who was "trying out a convent" and was being "checked out" by convent personnel for suitability.

ASSOCIATE MEMBER: of a community is a lay person who has been allowed access to community prayer and ceremonies and who often supports the community financially.

BENEDICTION: blessing. Refers to the ceremony/prayers in connection with the blessing of the congregation by the Host in a gold monstrance.

BENEFACTOR: a member of the (mostly unseen by the average nun) group of persons outside the convent that contributed monies and favors on a particular community.

BRACELET: a circlet for the upper arm, having prickly parts to it. Some communities wore this under their habits for short times as a penance.

BRIDE OF CHRIST: term used to indicate the close relationship between the nun and Christ; specifically a nun-Candidate dressed in a bridal gown for the convent's entrance ceremony.

CADAVER OBEDIENCE: term used to indicate that there should be no resistance to or questioning of authority at all. Nuns strove to have "cadaver obedience".

CALLED BY GOD: same as Vocation to the religious life. It was commonly accepted that God did the choosing, gave various "signs".

CANDIDATE: a girl or woman being considered as a possible Sister/Nun.

CANONICAL YEAR: the first full year of the Novitiate after the veil ceremony; the year during which most restrictions were applied in order to form the Candidate into a nun.

CANTOR: the main singer during the Holy Office, or the lead singer in Litanies or other church ceremonies.

CAP: the white cotton headpiece which tied under the chin and was used to cover the hair (modestly) at night.

CATECHETICS: lists of questions and answers about the Catholic Faith. In mid-century it was customary to memorize a few at a time from a book called the Baltimore Catechism.

CCD: Confraternity of Christian Doctrine. This was religion class for those who attended public schools.

CELL: same as alcove. Also used to refer to one's private or semi-private room.

CHANT: Gregorian plainsong; also recitation on a single note with endings variations, as in the chanting of the Holy Office.

CHAPTER OF FAULTS: the otherwise silent gathering of a convent group for the purpose of public confession, the giving out of penances, and sometimes public accusation and humiliation.

CHAPTER: the general community meeting held every few years to re-elect major superiors and announce new regulations. "Chapter" was also short for Chapter of Faults

CHEMISE: oversized unbleached cotton (not knit) shortsleeved pullover shirt worn over the bra (if bras were worn) and under the habit. It functioned as a washable buffer between the body and the wool habit, the latter of which was only spot cleaned except once a year when it was ripped at the seams, washed by hand, and resewn by each nun. The chemise as a modesty garment was also worn during doctor exams and bathing.

CHURCH: with a capital "C" refers to the Roman Catholic Church, especially the institution and its administration. With a lowercase "c", church may mean the building for worship, Catholics in the Church, or refer to all Christians.

CLERICAL DISCOUNTS: dollar reductions , e.g., in transportation, given to religious by airlines, etc.

COIF: (varied with each order) the daytime white cotton headpiece or cap that covered the hair (often extending under the chin), usually safety-pinned in back under the veil. Some coifs were sewn with a face-hole and a gusset under the chin. Coifs were worn every day, also in situations of partial undress such as hospitals or visits to the doctor.

COLLAR: worn below and around the neck or shoulders; usually heavily starched cotton or linen; in later years, made of a type of heavy (plastic-like) celluloid.

COMMUNION (HOLY): believed to be the body of Christ; also the receiving of the Eucharist, especially during Mass. There was a ceremony for the first time, and children dressed in white (shirts, veils, dresses).

COMMUNITY (with a capital C): Order, or Congregation of Religious Women.

CONVENT: in general, refers to the order or community, i.e., "she entered the convent". Also refers to the building where nuns live, either on mission or at the Motherhouse.

COUNCIL (The): The (usually) elected nuns at the top of the hierarchy who assist the Mother Superior in her decisions.

CUSTODY OF THE EYES: a convent phrase for "keep your eyes down and don't look at anybody/anything unless you're about to trip over it". The given purpose was so that each nun could remain in the state of contemplation, undistracted by the World.

DEVOTIONS: any prescribed set of prayers that nuns said usually together in chapel.

DINNER ON THE FLOOR: the practice of kneeling or sitting solo on the floor during a meal. This was considered either a voluntary public penance, or an assigned humiliation. Generally, one did not explain one's assigned or voluntary penances to others.

DIOCESAN COMMUNITY/ORDER: an order whose immediate authority was the local bishop.

DISCIPLINE (THE): the knotted cord whip used in flagellation.

DISCRETIONS: minor infractions of traditional customs in a specific Community not major enough to be listed in the Rule Book, but meriting penances all the same.

DISPENSATION: In this book, refers to the official permission from Rome or the Bishop (depending on the status of the Religious Order) for a nun to forego her final vows and leave the convent in good standing.

DOGMA: an official pronouncement by the Pope on faith or morals, which Catholics are required to believe; believed to be an infallible statement.

DOWRY: a sometimes flexible amount of money which the Candidate brought with her to the convent, money which usually went into the general fund.

EDICT: a pronouncement by the Pope for all Catholics in good standing to believe and abide by.

EDIFY: the goal of all one's actions—to edify others, that is, to give them good example, to inspire by one's goodness.

EJACULATIONS: see SPIRITUAL BOUQUET.

ENTRANCE CEREMONY: the religious ceremony preceding entry into the Novitiate. Candidates dressed in white bridal gowns (owned and recycled by the convent) to receive their stack of clothing, then exited as a group and donned their garb before returning for the rest of the ceremony.

EUCHARIST (THE HOLY): Jesus Christ present in the Host (as Catholics believe). See Transubstantiation.

EXAMEN: an examination of conscience for sin; also, the small form or booklet used to jog the memory in this examination.

EXAMINE: the term used when a formation candidate is checked out verbally by the Council and major Superiors to see if she ought to be admitted to vows, e.g., I was "examined" on Tuesday and took my first vows three weeks later.

EX CATHEDRA: literally, "from /out of the Church". When the Pope speaks *ex cathedra*, he is speaking officially, e.g., issuing a dogma.

EXCLAUSTRATION: Permission from the powers that be for a nun to live outside the community without giving up her "nun" status.

FASTING: technically, one main meal was allowed, no snacks, and the other two meals must not equal the main meal in quantity. Dispensation from fasting was gotten from a priest. Every Roman Catholic between 21 and 65 years of age was expected to fast on the Fast Days listed on the Church calendar.

FEASTDAY: the Catholic Church's designated day to honor the saint after which a candidate might be named. Also called "Namesday". These were celebrated instead of birthdays, with holycards as gifts.

FINAL PROFESSED: a nun who has taken final vows.

FINAL PROFESSION, FINAL VOWS: same as Perpetual Vows—solemn promises to God of poverty, chastity, and obedience for the rest of one's life. Dispensation from these vows was a serious matter.

"FIX" (MARRIAGE): to go through all the red tape required for an annulment of marriage.

FLAGELLATION: the communal (or sometimes private) self-whipping of the back and shoulders with a knotted cord or leather. Rarely, the whip had metal tips. E.g., after the general "lights out", on certain days, all nuns would remain standing and commence to whip themselves in silence until another bell/buzzer signaled cessation.

FOMENTING DISCORD: stirring up trouble. Sometimes a single word or glance could be interpreted as "fomenting discord" and merit public punishment. Keeping the "fomenting" under control was key to keeping the troups in line.

FORMATION: the years of pre- and Novitiate, also Juniorate, during which the Candidate was formed into the nun mold.

GENERAL COUNCIL: a special group of nuns, the hierarchy of an order, that decided about issues or people in the convent. The General Council would decide who was accepted for final vows, choose a new nun's name, and function as an internal Board of Directors, for example. They also met with elected lay Advisors and other financial Boards. The Council was key during "Chapter" which included the whole community in reelections of the highest superiors.

GENERAL SILENCE: same as Great Silence, Grand(e) Silence.

GLIDE (THE): the sometimes taught, sometimes emulated walk of nuns whereby they kept their bodies so still that they seemed to be floating. (More effective with long habits.)

GRAND(E) SILENCE, GREAT SILENCE: usually from after dinner-recreation until after breakfast the following morning, nuns especially did not speak or look at each other. One superior said we could "break Great Silence" if we needed a firetruck.

GREETING: the official community phrases uttered upon passing any other nun every non-public time, e.g., first nun says, "Praised be the Lord." Second nun replies, "Now and forever." If you met ten nuns one after another, you said it ten times.

HABIT: the whole outfit worn by nuns, but especially the "dress" part of it. Pre-Vatican II habits were usually wool, with yards of skirting and long sleeves.

HAIRSHIRT: an itchy vest-type undergarment worn more in contemplative orders as a penance. Some nuns made their own out of burlap.

HEADDRESS: whatever was worn on the head, e.g., wimple, coif, veil, headband, etc.

HEAVEN: the place of perfect happiness with God that (Catholics teach) is available to all good baptized persons after they die.

HELL: a place of damnation, utter hopelessness and despair after death. Also, in the 50s, fire and brimstone and devils. Catholics believed that anyone who died with an unforgiven mortal sin on their soul would be sentenced to eternal deprivation of God and happiness, i.e., Hell.

HOLYCARDS: sometimes compared to baseball cards, had pictures of Jesus, Mary, Joseph, or the saints on them and were traded among the nuns as well as given as gifts on feastdays or Christmas. After Vatican II, though not necessarily because of it, popularity of the "sweet" effeminate Jesus with tilted head and sad eyes, and the "Sacred Heart" series with dripping blood, declined. Woodcuts and faux woodcuts with aphoristic or biblical texts in red or black were printed on no-longer-gilt-edged cards. Today, text cards are common, as are additions of flowers and new colors such as violet. Your best bet to find the original picture holycards is to look at Christian supply stores and funeral parlors. The latter print the deceased's name, year of death, and a prayer on the back of the holycard, presumably for use as a bookmark/reminder to pray for the person who died.

HOLY FATHER: the Pope.

IMPRIMATUR: the official permission by a Cardinal or designated Bishop for a Catholic to read a particular book. If the book said "Imprimatur" inside the front, it was okay to believe anything written there.

INDISCRETIONS: minor infractions.

Chapter XVI: Glossary

INDULGENCES: though sold by the Church in earlier centuries, the invisible indulgences were "won" in the 1900s by saying certain prayers. At the bottom of a written prayer on a holycard, the number of days of indulgences was listed. E.g., if you said prayer #1, you might get 100 days indulgence. Prayer #2 might give 200 days. An indulgence paid your way out of purgatory.

INFALLIBILITY: of the Pope. Between the time of Jesus and now, Church authorities came up with this rule, that if the Pope makes an official pronouncement on faith or morals, he is infallibly correct and must be believed by all Roman Catholics.

INTENTIONAL COMMUNITY: The Living Enrichment Center, an international non-denominational group of Christian ethicists for new global thought. "We examine issues without guilt or fear; we help and assist."

INTERCESSION: what Mary or any saint did to plead our cause before Jesus/God. Prayer: "Mary, intercede for me."

JESUS THE BRIDEGROOM: using Jesus in the "Bride of Christ" theme which was especially preached to beginning nuns about to enter the Novitiate. Sometimes this was considered symbolic, but other times it was treated as entirely real, e.g., "You are truly marrying Christ in this ceremony."

JUNIOR(ATE) MISTRESS: a final professed nun who was in charge of those in the Juniorate.

JUNIOR: a Sister/Nun from the Juniorate. Not all convents had Juniorates.

JUNIORATE: the place in the convent where Juniorate members lived when they were not asleep in their dorms. Also, the years (often three) between the Novitiate and final profession. To enter the Juniorate, nuns took temporary (sometimes renewable) vows.

LAY PERSON: anyone who was not a nun, priest, monk, etc. Same as Secular.

LAY SISTER: in some communities, the term given to nun housekeepers, gardeners, etc.

LITANY: a specific recited or sung list of saints and intentions, each line answered by "Pray for us" or "Hear our prayer" etc.

LITURGY: religious ceremonies, especially the celebration of the Mass. After Vatican II, Liturgical Committees of lay persons gave input as to how the liturgy should be performed, e.g., banners? dancing? singing?

MARTYR: one who was killed for his/her religious beliefs.

MARTYROLOGY: the (often gory) stories of the saints who had allegedly been martyed, i.e., killed because they were Christian, on a particular day. The Martyrology was usually read in silent dining rooms after other readings, toward the end of the meal. Public penances were often performed during the martyrology, hence the phrase: "to do Martyrology".

MARY: when used without qualification, "Mary" refers to the mother of Jesus.

MASS: the main Catholic religious ceremony, required each Sunday. The Mass was said in Latin and the priest had his back to the people. It was not uncommon for Catholics to say their Rosary during Mass, though they were supposed to be paying attention.

MASS CARD: the card whereupon a the celebration of a Mass (religious ceremony) performed with a person's wishes in mind, was recorded. It listed the celebrant (the officiating priest), date, and sometimes the time. Having a Mass said for someone was said to have greater value than anyone's personal prayers. Nuns were given Mass Cards as presents by those <u>outside</u> the convent (since obtaining a Mass Card involved giving the priest a "donation", and nuns had no money).

MEDITATION: thinking of God/Jesus/Mary, or reading from the New Testament and pondering the words. Meditation was usually done silently for an hour before dawn in chapel *en masse.*

MENTAL RESERVATION: fancy exculpatory word for a lie. If a superior wished a nun to tell an untruth about a situation, she would say, Make a mental reservation. This was not considered sinful like lying.

MISSAL: the prayerbook containing variations for each day's specific Mass prayers. Missals were sometimes in Latin and English, although the author used one in French.

MISSION: 1. the purpose of a community, e.g., the mission of this group is to teach children. 2. any house away from the Motherhouse. Small groups of nuns were stationed at various missions for most of the year. 3. The parish rally once or twice a year when a "Missionary" (guest) priest preached dramatically, often of fire and brimstone.

MONASTERY: usually, a place where (male) monks reside, though a few orders of nuns referred to their convents as monasteries.

MONEY: the lack of which was significant. Outside of being in charge (that would be the eldest in rank) on a group excursion, no nun was to handle money, let alone own any. Their salaries were paid by the parish in lump sum, e.g., $68 a week for five teachers (in addition to use of a house, utilities, and food). A percentage was sent to the Motherhouse.

MORTAL SIN: any formally-unforgiven grevious sin (there were lists), the commission of which would damn a soul to Hell.

MORTIFICATION: literally, "dying to the flesh". Mortifications were actions that one did to humiliate/humble oneself in order to attain control over the body by the soul.

MOTHER GENERAL: the nun who was at the top of the heirarchy in an order. Whereas other nuns were called "Sister", the Mother General was called "Mother", as in "Mother Mary Jacob. Like the rest of the community, Mothers General used their "nun names" rather than their birth names.

MOTHER MISTRESS: the direct form of address for the Novice Mistress, e.g., may I please leave the room, Mother Mistress?

NOVICE MISTRESS: the nun in charge of the novices--both years. Sometimes the Postulancy was also under her care.

NOVICE: after the Aspirancy (about 6 months) and the Postulancy (another 6 months), came the Novitiate. First-year- and Second-year-novices were usually housed together with a Novice Mistress for their instruction.

NOVITIATE: the section of the Motherhouse where Novices (and often Postulants) studied and remained apart from the community (except for prayers). Also refers to the years between the Postulancy and the Juniorate.

NUN NAME: Each Candidate had 2-3 choices of a new name (given names were not acceptable), but the Council made the final decision. Some nuns took names of family members (often male). Many orders insisted on the inclusion of "Mary" in some form. E.g., Sister Mary John, or Sister John Marietta, etc. Nun names were generally as far from given names as possible, to signify starting a new life. Mature nuns were known to give each other nicknames, or refer to each other by the name without the "Sister" part, but formally this was frowned upon.

NUN: in this book, synonymous with "Sister". Technically, there are differences. Both refer to girls/women who take vows in promise to God with regard to the service of humanity.

OBLIGATION: as in "I did my obligations", referring to attending Sunday Mass, and sometimes following other rules, such as going to confession at least once during Easter Time.

OFFICE: 1. The room where you met your Superior for conference. Or, 2. The "Hours" (Matins, Vespers, etc.) of specific prayers which one read alone or, on certain days, sang in community, especially in chapel. A nun was expected to "say her Office" every day.

ORDER: for purposes of this book, interchangeable with Community. Here it refers to any specific group of Sisters/Nuns operating under specific rules in the Catholic Church.

PAPAL COMMUNITY/ORDER: an order whose ultimate authority was the Pope. He decided issues, gave dispensations from vows, etc.

PAPAL NUNCIO: The Pope's representative in a certain country, e.g., the United States.

PARISH: a definite geographical area around a church; also, the Catholics who were to attend a specific church, and that church only.

PARTICULAR FRIENDSHIPS (PFs): a mystery to the youngest Candidates and frequently preached about vaguely in the Novitiate, appearing to like one person more than another was called "having a Particular Friendship". The word "lesbianism" was never mentioned. One would be rebuked for sitting next to the same person two days in a row during "recreation", for example. However, nuns in the elite social class often had PFs with impunity.

PASTOR: the male priest who ran the parish.

PASTORAL COUNCIL: encouraged by Vatican II, some pastors allowed lay persons to give them advice in specific parish-related areas. Some priests still to this day will not have a Pastoral Council in their parishes.

PEW: Church bench, kneeler and place to sit.

POSTULANCY: the period of time (6 mo. or more) between Aspirancy and the Novitiate. Also refers to the place where postulants hung out with their Superior (in silence, for the most part).

POSTULANT MISTRESS: often the same person as the Novice Mistress. She guided Postulants.

POSTULANT: In religious communities without Aspirancies, this name was given to the beginning Candidate for nunhood.

PRIDE: in those days, pride in oneself was not allowed or spoken of. The only mention of pride was negative. Women were dismissed from convents for being "too proud".

PROFESSED (THE): nuns who had made their final profession of vows.

PRACTICING CATHOLIC: one who attended Mass every Sunday, received Communion and the other sacraments as appropriate, and who followed Church rules.

PROVINCIAL HOUSE: larger communities had not one Motherhouse-type building, but several, e.g., at least one in each state. These were called Provincial Houses and functioned as Motherhouses did in smaller communities. Provincial Houses had Provincial Superiors instead of Mothers General.

PURGATORY: a holding place in Catholic afterlife teaching, a place to work off negativity. Miserable and still with fire and brimstone, purgatory was not eternal.

RANK: a numbered system (used in most Orders until the 1970s or later) whereby each nun was listed according to when she entered the convent. The lowest in rank were the newest candidates, though even in a single class, each person had a different rank number. Nearly everything was determined by rank—where one sat in chapel or the refectory, who walked through the doorway first, etc.

RECREATION: often took place in convents during the half hour after dinner, before night prayer and Grande Silence. During recreation in the 50s, nuns were to stay in the recreation room knitting, playing board games, or darning their socks. Playing tennis or taking a walk was considered "exclusive", though permission was given to certain nuns now and then.

REFECTORY: the large dining room of the Motherhouse. This was mostly a place for listening to readings during silent eating, and for performing public penances. Generally, one was not allowed to speak in the refectory, except during "talking" meals on certain feastdays. Otherwise, e.g., if the sister who mopped the floor wished to ask her superior, a passer-through, for more soap, they would both step outside the refectory door into the hallway before speaking.

RELIGIOUS COMMUNITY: a group of women under one constitution or set of rules, who had either the local bishop or the pope as their ultimate head, and who lived in one or more convents pursuing the work of the order according to its written rules.

RELIGIOUS ORDER: (for this book's purpose) interchangeable with Religious Community

RELIGIOUS: especially a nun or sister, sometimes a brother, monk, or "order" priest (i.e., Franciscan, Jesuit, etc.).

RETREAT: extreme silence and prayer with conferences given by a Retreatmaster (priest) over a period of 1, 3, 7, 15, or 30 days.

ROSARY (BEADS): little stones or beads made of any material, linked together by chain or cord, the purpose of which was to count the specific "Hail Marys", "Our Fathers", and "Glory Be's" that made up the set called "the Rosary".

RULE OF SILENCE: in general, meant that unless one had something emergency-like to say, or it was a "free" day (special feastday), one kept one's eyes cast down and one's mouth shut.

SACRAMENTALS: any item or thing (even a ceremony) that aided in the ceremonies of the Catholic religion.

SACRAMENTS: these only: Baptism, Confirmation, Holy Eucharist, Penance, Extreme Unction, Holy Orders, and Matrimony.

SACRISTAN: the person assigned to take care of Mass vestments and vessels, prepare the altar, flowers, etc.

SCANDAL: a major sin, accomplished by telling about something bad that went on in the Church or in the convent. The witness/teller was then accused of Scandal, a sin always greater than whatever had been done in the first place. "Causing scandal" was grounds for dismissal.

SECULAR: lay; non-religious. A secular priest does not belong to an Order, e.g., Franciscans, but works in the diocese under the Archbishop.

SISTER: see "NUN".

SPIRITUAL BOUQUET: another gift given among Catholics, especially nuns, that did not involve money. It involved recording how many times one said certain prayers with the intention of the recipient in mind. E.g., for Sr. James's feastday (St. James's Day on the Catholic calendar), you bought a card preprinted with Spiritual Bouquet prayers and blanks for the number said. Or you made one:
    5 Our Fathers (say the Lord's Prayer 5 x)
    5 Hail Marys
    10 Glory Be's (they were shorter)
    1 Rosary, and
    100 Ejaculations
Ejaculations, before the days when you could say the word "sex" in front of your mother, were short bursts of prayer, like: "Jesus, Mercy!" or "St. James, pray for us!" Like the word "gay", the old meaning of "ejaculation" fell out of favor as it became used publicly (often) in a sexual connotation.

STATIONS (OF THE CROSS): fourteen pauses in a ceremonial procession which remembered Jesus's agony and death. These "stops" are marked by pictures or plaques in churches.

SUBLIMATE: same as "offer it up". The solution to bad times was to sublimate, that is, to remind oneself that this suffering could release a soul from purgatory, or be saved like points for one's own salvation.

SUFFERING: miserableness that one endured/performed to wipe away one's own or others' sins in order to attain Heaven after death.

SUITABLE CANDIDATE: a girl or woman who was intelligent, virginal (or now celibate), most likely to obey rules, and had talents to contribute to a particular religious order.

SUPERIOR GENERAL: see MOTHER GENERAL..

TALENT: in the 50s, you either had it or you didn't. None of this studying-for-skills. Like any self-effacing woman, nuns were to deflect compliments by either denying or denigrating the project complimented---and certainly their part in it.

TIME: in 50s Catholic religion, though before the scientific theory of time/space wormholes, Time was said not to exist after death. The belief was held that praying for something that happened earlier was logical because there was no chronological time in Heaven.

TEMPORARY VOWS: vows of usually 3 years, taken after the Novitiate and before becoming Professed (with final, perpetual vows). The vows were the same (Poverty, Chastity, and Obedience); the nuances and duration varied. Temporary vows were sometimes renewable, that is, one could add another year, or rarely, two. This was done either by request of the Candidate-Nun and approval of the Council, or by order of the Mother Superior or Council directly.

THE RULE (THE HOLY RULE): all the regulations written down in the Rulebook from the beginning of the community. Rules had been voted upon by the hierarchy/congregation and approved by the bishop or pope, then studied in the Novitiate, and supposedly were adhered to by everyone. Rules could be repealed. There were also unwritten rules specific to certain convents or administration, e.g., no lying down or entering one's bed space during the daytime.

THEOLOGY: the study of God in all aspects.

UNIVERSAL TRUTH: a truth inherent in all humans regardless of organized religion. E.g., that there is a power greater than we are, or that it is good to respect the dignity of man/women- kind—these exist outside of any religion's rules and are therefore referred to as Universal Truths.

VATICAN II: the Catholic Church Council convened in Rome by Pope John XXIII, in which decisions were made that loosened the restrictions in the Church and conservatism in convents. Theoretically, because of Vatican II, the Church would meet the World as it truly was. In practice, some Communities put off the changes for years. The Church's urgency to introduce humanistic changes lessened after that Pope's death, though assertive women in convents everywhere continued to promote the new era.

VEIL: the flowing (usually black) cloth attached to a nun's headpiece. Often veils were sewn every week by the nun to her newly super-starched veil-support, breaking many needles and pricking fingers in the process. "Taking the veil" was a phrase that meant "entering the convent".

VENIAL SIN: still an offense against God, but not as horrible as mortal sin. A venial sin might be: yelling at your brother (depending on circumstances and motive).

VISITATION: The time of year (or once every two years) when the Mother General visited individual missions and met individually with each Sister, purportedly for the purpose of hearing each side of each story and to offer moral support. Practically, it didn't always work that way; some nuns were afraid of retribution after the Mother General had left, so said nothing about problems that should have been aired.

VOCATION: ---with a capital "V", the call from God to enter the religious life. One did not refuse, under pain of mortal sin. How did one know that she had a Vocation? Various signs. See Chapter I: Beginnings.

VOWS: the most serious unbreakable promises to God in the categories of Poverty, Chastity, and Obedience. Examples of Poverty in the 50s: a nun could not own anything, especially money. Every present she received was turned over to the community. Obedience: All the Rules in the Rule Book were to be obeyed, as well as anything one's Superior ordered; obedience was to be immediate and without complaint.

WEEKLY OBLIGATION: to attend Sunday Mass.

WIMPLE: same as a coif.

WORLD (THE): everything/everybody non-religious. Usually used as a negative word, the World was the opposite of the convent, and referred to riches and lust and all the good stuff.

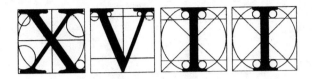

notes

the original Questionnaire, Methodology

charts, tables, other statistics

About the Author

Epilogue, Acknowledgments

Questionnaire
(personal identification, pseudonyms, release, etc. not listed here)

A. General Information

1. Marital status(es) since you left the convent:_____
2. If you have children, what are their ages?_____
3. How old are you now? _____
4. What is your occupation?_____ Husband/partner's?_____ Are you retired?___
5. How many years have you been married? _____ Living with same partner?_____
6. Are you comfortable being single in the '90s?__ Like/dislike best about it?_____

B. Before You Entered the Convent

7. What religion were you when you decided to enter the convent?_____
8. Family's religion?_____ What religion are they now?_____ Practicing?___
9. How old were your brothers when you entered?_____ Sisters?_____
10. On a scale of 10, 1 being nothing, what role did religion play in your home life?_____
11. Did you pray the rosary as a family?___ Pray for vocations?__ Attend Sunday Mass?__
12. What did you think Religious Vocation meant?_____
13. Did you live with both birth parents? If No, explain._____
14. What grades did you attend parochial school?_____
15. Was there any one nun you admired/loved most?____ Did you enter that order?_____
16. How did you come to know the order you entered?_____

C. Entering the Convent

17. How old were you when you began the first stage of convent life?_____
18. How many years did you spend in the aspirancy?_Postulancy?__Novitiate?_ Juniorate?_
19. What did you think "Bride of Christ" meant?_____
20. Did anyone persuade you to enter?_Who?__How?_Why?_What made you believe them?
21. What did you hope to find in convent life?_____
22. Were you sexually active at the time of entering?__Did that make it difficult to enter?____
23. Did the order have rules about non-virgins?____ Did you lie about your status?_____
24. Were you in love with anyone before you entered the convent?__How many persons?___
25. Were you aware of same-sex attractions before entering?__Had you acted on them?____
26. What job(s) for pay had you held before entering?_ How long?__ Salary range?_____

27. What was your last level of schooling before entering the convent?_____
28. What career interested you most before entering?_____ After entering?_____
29. How did you feel during the entrance ceremony? ___ Do you remember your thoughts?__
30. How did your parents/siblings feel about your entering?_____
31. Were parents/siblings allowed at the entrance ceremony?____ Did they come?_____
32. How many were in your class/set?___ In the entire community (approx.)?_____
33. Did you pay a dowry to the convent?____ How much?_____ Used for:_____

D.   Convent Life

34. Describe the habit you wore. How did wearing it make you feel?__ Were you treated differently when you wore the habit?_____
35. List any health problems you developed as a direct result of wearing the habit:_____
36. Did the habit go through any modernization before 1965?____ What/when?_____
37. Did you ever discuss wanting changes in the habit w/ superiors?_Lay friends?__Nuns?__
38. Who cut your hair?_____ How short?_____ Did you have a choice as to length?_____ How did you feel about that?_____
39. What did you wear to bed at night?_____ Was this regulation?____
40. What was worn for underwear?_____ Sanitary needs?_____
41. Were you ever embarrassed by your clothes at a medical appointment or hospital?_____ What happened?_____
42. Did your parents pay for your schooling while you were in the convent? Did you know?__
43. How many theology credits/courses (not for your degree) did you take in the convent?___
44. Did you attend college?_Over how many years?__Graduate?__What degrees?_____
45. Were you allowed to choose your college major? Other subjects?_ Did you like that?____
46. Were you allowed to buy your own school supplies?___ Did your parents buy them?____
47. If the order bought supplies and did not deliver on time, what excuse did you give in class? _____ What happened?_____
48. What foreign language(s) did you learn while in the convent? As your   minor?_____ How/why did you learn them? _____
49. Were you given time enough to study while you were attending college?_ Why?_____
50. Were you allowed to study in groups/partners at the convent? _____
51. Were you forbidden to speak to other students on campus outside of emergencies?___ How did you feel about that at the time?_____
52. What was your order's greeting phrase?_____
53. What were daytime silence stipulations?_____Evening?_____
54. How did you feel about the Rule of Silence?_____
55. Were you allowed to converse with lay people at work outside of emergencies?_____ Did you want to?_____ What happened if you were caught/reported?_____

56. Was it general knowledge that specific nuns disobeyed the rules often?____ Which rules?
57. Were they punished?____ If not, did you speculate then why they weren't?_____
58. List some of the smallest things you were required to ask permission for. Did you always ask, or just do it?___ How did that make you feel?_____
59. Did you ever protest a rule to authorities?___ Which rule?___ Why?____ What happened?___ What stage of vows were you then? Did you ever protest again?___ Why?_____ Did they change? _____
60. If they did not change, did you continue to follow the rule?___ How did you feel?_____
61. Did your order have mandatory meditation in the morning?___ What time?_____ How did you feel about meditating every day?_____ How did meditation improve you?_____
62. Were you required to say the Rosary daily?_ Did you?_ How many years?__ Did you feel guilty when you stopped?__ Did you ever lie about it?_ Were you punished for not saying it?_
63. Were you required to pray the Office daily?___ Did you?___ How many years?___ Did you feel guilty when you abbreviated/stopped it?___ Did you ever lie about not saying the Office?___ Were you punished for not saying it?___ How?_____ How did you feel?_____
64. Did you sing in the choir?_____ Why?_____ What did you like most about choir? _____ Dislike?_____
65. Did you study a musical instrument?____ In connection w/ your degree?____ Were you later allowed access to the instrument?____ To your music?__ How did you feel then?____
66. Did the order practice flagellation?____ How often?____ For which nuns?_____
67. Was flagellation in community?___ Private?____ Where?___ Regulated?___ Optional?_
68. Did you ever speak of flagellation among members?____ Outsiders?____ Why?_____
69. How did you feel about flagellation?_____
70. What were funny incidents involving this?_____
71. Did you have Chapter of Faults?___ Describe the ritual:_____
72. How did you feel participating in Chapter?_____
73. Did you have chains?___ Describe:_____ Optional? ____ How often?___ Hairshirts?_____ Optional?_____ How often used?___
74. Did the order use other instruments of self-torture? Describe. How often used? Optional?
75. Were you a reader/lector in the refectory? How did this make you feel?_____
76. Who chose the material for refectory reading?_____ Did you have a say?_____
77. Did the theology in the reading material ever conflict with what you were told by superiors?_____ Then what happened?_____
78. Was the Martyrology used? Whole or in part? Daily?__ How did you feel about hearing it?
79. Did you ever get the giggles in the refectory? Over what?_ Then what happened?_____
80. Was there other public humiliation connected to the refectory? Describe it:_____
81. How did one merit this punishment?_____ Was performance of it ever voluntary?_____ Did nuns know who <u>volunteered</u>?_____
82. Did you ever go through the punishment? How did you feel during it?_____ Afterwards?

83. What quality was the food in general?_____ Were there regular dishes on certain days?___Was quality consistent?___ Who did food preparation?_____
84. Was there different/special food for guests?____ Superiors?___How did you feel about that?____ Did guests eat in the refectory with the nuns?___ Resident priests?____
85. Was there a general silence rule in the refectory?_____ Punishment for clinking a dish, etc?___ What was the punishment?_____ How did you feel about it?_____
86. What hobbies were you encouraged to develop?____ Where did you get materials? When did you practice these hobbies?_____
87. How much leisure time did you usually have per week? How did you occupy yourself during that time?____ Was there silence, then?____ Rules for recreation?___
88. What games, athletics, activities did you do on special feastdays?_____
89. Did your family pay for your medical bills while you were in the convent? Did you know?
90. By what process did you obtain a medical appointment?_____
91. What made you cry in the convent?_____
92. What made you happiest?_____
93. What irritated you most?_____
94. What little things caused tremendous tension? Why? How did you relieve tension?
95. What were sources of fear?_____
96. Were there known mentally ill nuns at your convent?____ How were they treated?_____ How did they act?_____ Were you afraid of them?_____
97. What things made you feel guilty in the convent that did not make people on the outside feel guilty? _____
98. Was counseling by a psychologist/psychiatrist available to you?___ Easy to get?__ How?
99. Was there gossip/speculation about those who saw counselors?___ Did that deter you personally from seeing one?_ Did you ask for professional counseling?__ Did you receive it?
100. Was the counseling satisfactory?_____ Why?_____
101. What years were you the happiest?_____ Least happy?_____
102. If you were unhappy, was your unhappiness evident to those you worked with?____ How?_____ Describe any incidents that resulted from their noticing:_____
103. To what degree/how did you feel valuable in your convent years?_____ Did you ever want more control over your own life?_____
104. Were you encouraged to suffer silently for Jesus' sake?___ Did you agree that suffering was a good thing?_ Did you go out of your way to suffer?_ Was that considered virtuous?___
105. Were you ever told that Jesus was all and you were nothing? How did this make you feel?
106. Did you feel you were being brainwashed?____ Did that frighten you?____ Were you told that you deserved to suffer?_____ Did you believe it?____ Why?_____
107. Was convent humor very different from outside humor? How?__ Example:_____
108. Did you laugh a lot in the convent?___ More during which years?_____
109. Did your superiors often have a sense of humor?____ Explain:_____

110. Did you undergo injustices that still rankle you?____ Describe:_____
111. Did you notice racism in the order? ____ How did you feel about it?_____
What did you do about it?_____ Then what happened?_____
112. What kinds of prejudice were considered "okay" in your order?_____ Did you agree?____ Practice them?___ How did you feel about it?_____
113. Did you get along with most superiors?___ Why?_____
114. How did you deal with "personality clashes"?_____
115. Were you ever a superior?____ What rank?_____
116. Were you encouraged to develop friends in the community? Specifically discouraged? What was the reason given? ----------------------What rule(s) in the community discouraged individual friendships? --
117. Were you ever accused of having a Particular Friendship?____ What happened?_____
118. What role did gossip play in the order?_____
119. Were you aware of an "in" group?_____ Did you belong to it?____ Why/why not?_____
120. Did you ever exclude another nun(s) from the "in" group?____ How?_____
121. How did you feel about the social strata that existed in the community?_____
122. Were there certain nuns who did nothing and were served by everyone?___ Explain:___
123. Did you have recurring dreams/nightmares in the convent?___ Describe:_____
124. What did you think the dreams meant?_____
125. Did you often sleep during meditation?___ How did you feel then?_____
126. What were the sleeping arrangements for nuns?_____
127. Did you complain about insomnia often?___ What was done?_____
128. During your youth, were you encouraged to think of the teen Jesus as an idol and to fall in love with Him?___ Did that seem right?___ Why/why not?____   How did that work out?___
129. Did you feel sexually attracted to any other nun?___ Why, do you think?_____ What did you do about it?_____ Why did you think you felt this way?_____
130. Were you attracted to any priest or lay person while a nun?____ What did you do?_____
131. Did you have sex with anyone while you were still in the convent?___ Did anyone else find out? How did you feel afterwards?_____ What happened as a result?
132. Did you ever want to have sex with anyone while you were still a nun?___ Who?_____ What stopped you?_____
133. Did you know what the sex act involved when you entered the convent?_____ How did you find out?_____
134. Did your relationships with your parents or siblings change after you entered the convent? In what way?___ Why did you think this happened?___ Did you discuss it at the time?
135. How much about religious life did you tell your family?_____
136. Were there outside advisors to the order?___ In what areas? _____
Were they effective?____ Radical?___ Conservative?___

137. Were you allowed to read newspapers?____ Watch/listen to news? _____ Read news magazines?___
138. Did you vote?___ Was the list of recommended candidates posted?___ Who recommended them? _____Did the fact of the list bother you?____ Why?_____
139. Were you allowed to read books or magazines not assigned in class?____ Did you read them anyway?___ What kinds?_____ Where did you get them?_____
140. Did you watch any recreational television in the convent?___ What times?___ How much/wk.?_____ What shows?_____ Were shows your choice?_____
141. Was television of equal access to all levels of nuns?___ What were the rules?_____
142. How often did you have movies?_____ Did you like them?_____
Did you talk about the movies afterwards?_____
143. What were your jobs/chores in the years before first year Novitiate? _____ Between Novitiate and Juniorate?_____
144. Did you work at a boarding school?_____ hospital?_____ Other?_____
145. Did you work in the kitchen?____ Tell about the work/ relationships._____
146. Was there a social strata for unpleasant jobs?___ Were they shared equally?_____
147. What was the chore you liked best?_____ Least? _____
148. Was "You'll lose your Vocation" ever used to keep you in line?___ When?_____
149. What did you think would happen if you lost your Vocation?_____
150. Did you ever think/fear you'd be dismissed from the order?___ Did anyone ever threaten to dismiss you? Why?_____
151. What did you feel as you moved on to each new stage of vows?_____ How binding were you told they were?_____ Did you believe it?_____

E. Leaving the Convent

152. At what stage of vows did you first think about leaving the convent? For what reason(s)?
153. Did you tell anyone of your doubts right away?___ Who?__ Why?___ What happened?
154. Did you leave shortly after your first doubts?__ How many years later?__ Why so long?_
155. Whose first suggested that you leave? How did you feel?____ Then what happened?__
156. Describe the process of leaving in your order._____
157. Were you given money upon leaving? ___ How much?_____ Other goods?____ What?_____ Advice?_____ By whom?_____
158. Were you allowed to tell anyone you were leaving?____ Did you? ____ How did you feel about not telling? _____
159. Were you happy to leave?___ Couldn't wait?____ Why?_____
160. Your first day out, did you meet any former students/lay people you knew?___ What happened? ___
161. How did you feel the first time they saw you without a habit?_____ Why?____

162. How long did it take to feel comfortable on the outside?____ What helped?_____
163. How long after leaving were you forbidden to visit with your friends in the convent?_____
How did this make you feel?_____
164. If you had taken final vows, was there any difficulty about the dispensation?___ Explain.

F. Afterwards: Looking Back

165. What was the greatest advantage to your leaving?_____ Disadvantage?
_____ Do you feel comfortable in the World?___ Why?_____
166. How soon after you left did you date? ____ Were you still under vows?__ How soon did you begin a relationship?____ Marry?_____
167. Did you become pregnant while in the convent?___ What was said/done?_____
168. Are you lesbian?___ Did you know that in the convent?_____ Did you have relationships with other gay nuns then?_____ Do you now?____ Are you now openly gay?
169. Tell about special problems for the lesbian nun:_____
170. Do you now feel that having a crush on a nun precipitated your entering?_____
171. Did you marry a priest?_____ What do you think is the connection between marrying a priest and your having been in the convent?_____
172. Was he still a priest when you left the convent?____ Do you think declaring your love then was against your vows?___ Why/why not?_____
173. What are your husband's/children's/coworkers/reactions to your having been in the convent?_____
174. Do they speak freely with others about it?____ How does that make you feel?__ Why?
175. Looking back, do you feel any one reason caused you to enter the convent more than any other?
176. Do you ever wish you were back in the convent of those days?___
177. Do you ever think about re-entering a convent of today? Consider it?_ Plan to someday?
178. If you were young today, would you enter a convent?___ Stay there your entire life?___ Why/why not?_____
179. Did you get what you'd hoped for in the convent?____ Explain:_____
180. Do you ever have "being trapped in the convent" dreams?____ Explain:_____
181. Since leaving, did you ever have nightmares/dreams about other aspects of the convent? ____ Do you still have these dreams? ___ What do you think they mean? _____
182. When did the dreams stop?___ What do you think caused them to stop?_____
183. Are some then-tragic or -solemn incidents now funny?___ Tell about them:_____
184. What are your thoughts on being a woman and your experience in the convent?_____
185. Are you glad that you were a nun?___ Why?_____
186. Would you encourage your child/friend/ to enter a community today?___
187. Can you recognize an ex-nun on the street?___ How?_____

188. Are you happier now than when you were in the convent?___ Why?_____
189. Are you conscious of having blocked out convent memories?___ From which stage?_____ How do you feel about that?_____ Did you block out memories that have now returned?___ Explain:_____
190. Are you consciously trying to bring back these memories?___ By what method?_____ Why/why not?_____
191. Would you still be in the convent if things had been different?___ What things?_____
192. What values taught to you in the convent do you espouse today?_____ Could you have learned these elsewhere?____ Where?_____
193. Did your family save your letters written home?___ How do they sound now?_____
194. Would you be willing to enclose copies of parts of the letters (list approximate year)?
195. Do you go out of your way to avoid other ex-nuns?_ Nuns?__Did you ever?___ Why?
196. When you are reminded of the convent, do you have bitter memories first?____ What are they? Do you have good memories first?___ Of what?_____
197. Do you have strong non-sexual friendships now with any nuns?____ From the same order?___ With ex-nuns?____ Why?_____
198. Do you currently practice Catholicism?____ In what ways?_____
199. Do you consider yourself a conservative Catholic?___ Radical?___ American style?____ Other:____
200. What is your opinion on the role of women in the Church today?_____
201. To what degree do you hold with the pope's authority?_____
202. Do you still believe that the religious vocation is more valuable than any other vocation?___ In what way?_____
203. What is your present attitude towards the sacraments, sacramentals?_____
204. Do you still hold the same views on Hell, God, angels, sin, Mary, Immaculate Conception, as you did when you were in the convent?____ Why or why not?_____
205. What is your advice to the Pope?_____
206. Advice to Catholics in America:_____
207. Advice to those wishing to enter a convent:_____
208. Have you ever been to a gathering of ex-nuns?___ Did you initiate it?___Go reluctantly?
209. What things about yourself and other ex-nuns did you learn at this gathering?_____
210. Would you read a book about ex-nuns?____ Why/why not?_____ How many books do you generally read a month?_____
211. Have you had cancer since leaving the convent?____ What kind?_____ Other stress-related disease?___ Name of disease:_____
212. Do you consider yourself a successful person at this point in your life?___ Why?_____

Methodology

    This book was conceived in July, 1993 in Powell's City of Books at the magazine rack. I had bought and read *Feminine Broadcast Quarterly* and was touched by the simple telling of women's heart/soul stories, by the unwavering expectation by each author that those who read those stories would understand and empathize, thus enabling the writer to heal and grow and bond with this gigantic network of (mostly) women. I thought, in contrast, about the convent in the 50s where, for eight years I was denied growth, encouragement, self-esteem; where bonding with other women was punished, and where even desiring good-job recognition was considered sinful pride. The real Sisterhood leapt off the magazine pages at me, and I thought, What a waste—I could have spent those years learning the wonderfulness of adult relationships, how to interact with others in a way that we both grow and love living. Would that not have been more God-like than living side by side like silent sardines?

    Several months later, after having read books and articles, having discussed pertinent issues with women and men in person and over the phone, I was convinced of three things:

1. There was a wide range (positive to negative) of experiences among those women who were in US convents in the 50s before Vatican II and afterwards.
2. Some women who were especially scarred from the experience were still trying to bury it, to wish it out of existence.
3. Those women who had made the transition back into the world successfully could help heal those who were still struggling.

    Not for nothing was I born poor and Catholic of volunteering folk, and spent time in a convent—I know a cause when I see one. The first problem was locating ex-nuns, then convincing them to speak out. Catholicism, and the convent in particular, are bastions of secrecy. To tell is often considered worse than what the original dastardly deed you are telling about, was.

    There is no national registry for women who have left religious institutions. Besides that, most women who leave convents do not care to have their coworkers or new friends know that they are former nuns—some because they do not wish to be reminded of that part of their lives, but most because they do not want to be treated "differently", e.g., "Oh, sorry I said 'damn!'" "Did you ladies wear underwear?" "Hey, I thought nuns didn't make mistakes." And on and on. Or just looks—no small talk or confidences or easy warm humor anymore. We, ex-nuns of America, have all experienced this. It is each woman's right to decide when and to whom she communicates the fact that she was a member of a religious Community. One respondent said that I was the first she had told in the 30 years since she left the convent. Her parents had disowned her when she entered, and when she left, she had moved to another state to start over.

There was a marked difference in attitudes and replies between women who left the convent before the early 1960s and those who left later: the latter had more humane, positive experiences to relate. This led me to do more research on the 50s in America, on changes in institutions and religions and particularly the Roman Catholic Church. In the first couple of years, I read nearly 300 books, from the earliest popular books (reissued last year— the *Six Months in a Convent* and Maria Monk stories) and Josephine Bunkley's 1855 tome, *The Escaped Nun*, to today's works. I pored over references to ex-nuns in contemporary theological commentary, in sociology, and history, and skimmed a goodly amount of fiction. I became an admirer of Karen Armstrong, Joan Chittister, Tim Unsworth, Lillana Kopp, and others, and even increased my great respect (I'd not thought that possible) for the work of sociologist Father Andrew Greeley.

Among the articles read (several written by men who had not interviewed any actual ex-nuns), the theories as to why women left the convent varied, yet none seemed to apply to more than a handful of women. Of course, no one conclusion fits all, but most of the authors seemed *not* to understand the essential situation and ritual of "leaving"; neither did the families of the ex-nuns. Then in Greeley's *The Catholic Myth*, in a lengthy footnote, I found what was the closest to an answer that far: it had to do with what the institution (convent) had become, how what should have been social support had become social control over the individual nun.

Universities across the United States posted flyers (asking for participants in this work) for me, and some of the many newspapers I wrote to did articles or printed my request for participants. Many women called and wrote me, having been apprised by word-of-mouth. Some heard the topic mentioned on a radio talk show, or at a lecture. The *Umbrella Group* (married priests and ex-nuns—though not so many of the latter) printed a notice in their newsletter and invited me to speak at their holiday dinner. I had unrealistically made plans to interview several hundred ex-nuns when the incoming requests for questionnaires began to slow considerably.

Normally I am polite, but I went into the Post Office for the express purpose of making a scene. After waiting my turn, I asked to see the Postmaster, who was not available, so I spoke to the next-in-line. I held up a letter with my address on it (which at that time it was a box in a local mail place a few miles away from town.) Would this letter belong here? I asked. Of course not, the woman said. Can't you see that it's a different street and doesn't even go to this building. Exactly! my voice rose. Then can you explain to me why all my incoming mail for the past 4 weeks has been delivered to this other woman's PO box in *this* building, then sent back UNKNOWN to sender? They had no answer. I ranted on about losing a month's research contacts and of defaming the name of my survey. The next day the Postmaster made a point of speaking to the workers and apologizing to me, though there was no way to undo the damage. I might not have even found out that they were rejecting my mail, if the woman who rented the PO box where the mail was landing, did not get tired of turning my mail in every time and had written me a letter telling me so. There is no way of knowing how many contacts we lost that first month, or how many women, receiving UNKNOWN stamped on their returned letters, thought the project a fake.

At any rate, when it came time to call a halt to the incoming data, we had 72 good women in the project. They had worked in 26 states and several countries. The oldest was in her 80s (see ChapterXV: Making It: Current statistics on Participants) and they had spent an average of 15 ½ years in the convent.

The first version of this book was written incorporating many quotes and incidents from the background/historical books, as well as from three interviews: with Lillana Kopp (founder of the democratic international order of religious women, Sisters for Christian Community); Jack Hall, a non-Catholic pastor who, with Bert Griffin, had been asked by the Archbishop to counsel nuns who were leaving the convents in the latter part of the century; and Father Bertram Griffin himself, longtime friend, canon lawyer, and internationally known speaker. After a few false starts, I realized that unless the book were to be well over 1000 pages, there would be no way to include *everything*. I decided to eliminate all the reference books and the three outside interviews. After all, it was the stories of the women that were important. I also bit the bullet and added my own story to the group, though this took even more time since it seemed best to work through some things with a good therapist.

By then, two things slowed the project: 1) I had acquired a decent computer and had what they call a "learning curve" (frustrating months when I tried to figure out how to use the machine efficiently) and 2) a series of illnesses overtook me and it was nearly two years before these were diagnosed and management programs set up for each.

Tabulating all the material--not to mention transcribing the many tapes (I have no office staff and am not sponsored by anyone with money), was a far more dauntingly enormous task than I had envisioned as I naively penned the original questionnaire. So this nice guy (who happens to be my husband) spent hours doing data entry, and in the process, understanding more about my former life and that of other women in the same situation. A neighbor suggested he be named "honorary ex-nun", but we never got around to that.

Each respondent was taken at her word. An experience is what truly happens to us, regardless of how it registers on another person nearby. We each come to a situation with different backgrounds, expectations, visions, etc. and thus take away different impressions. E.g., in the same Order, crossing the same years, one ex-nun stated there was no official greeting in her Community, and others said there was (they listed it). Since this is not a scientific survey involving all of the Communities in the United States or a balanced representation thereof, what is important here is that for that ex-nun, there was no greeting--either it was discontinued in later years and she forgot the earlier greeting, or her experiences truly do not include reciting a Community greeting. There is no way to control individual response to an experience, and in this project, I truly wanted each person's story as she saw it. That was the whole point of the work.

All participants were:
1. nuns in Roman Catholic United States convents in the mid-1900s
2. practicing Catholics at some point
3. certain they'd had a "call from God" that could not be ignored

Among the small number of those who were approached and refused the offer to participate in this project, some gave reasons:

It is my private past and I don't wish to remember it.

Chapter XVII: Notes

I cannot see any good that will come out of bringing things up again.

I do not have access to the type of counseling I know would be needed as a result of digging through so many varied memories. After a breakdown where the Lord healed me, I feel I am better off leaving that chapter of my life alone at this time.

I'm finished with that convent experience and I don't want any more to do with it.

I'm a very private person and I don't want to share this part of my life with strangers. I trust that you will understand. Best of luck with your work.

I am interested in the project, but would prefer not completing the questionnaire for several reasons. It has been nearly 20 years since I withdrew from the Community and I would rather cherish the good memories and allow the bad ones to fade and disappear as most have. It's just too overwhelming to undertake, and be completely honest and straightforward about, at this point in time.

Two ex-nuns wrote that, after reading the questionnaire, they did *not* anticipate any good coming out of the project. Nearly all the others who declined to participate wished us luck and most asked to be told when the book would be available. *I shall be most eager to read it,* said one. One of the above persons claimed that the questionnaire was a "flawed instrument", and that the material would be "episodic" and therefore invalid.

The points I wish to make most clear are:
1. Though I requested responses from each state, not each state is represented here. Those who are, are not represented equally. This is not a scientific study, but statistics from volunteers.
2. We <u>want</u> episodic material, since this is a book of stories. Think of this material as conversations with ex-nuns. No national conclusions are drawn from it.

3. ("Why do you have to include sex?") Sexuality is a part of ex-nuns as human beings, as are various emotions and learning experiences. Questions about the whole person give a better picture of who we are.
4. ("Why are there so many negative questions?") The test questionnaire showed that it is just as possible and easy to answer each question with positive answers as it is with negative answers. The first 13 who responded suggested including additional areas of discussion which led to the complete questionnaire as you see it.

A great many respondents wrote that they were grateful for the opportunity to share their experiences, that this made them feel *"validated."* *"Those experiences were formative and vitally important to me. It has been a great experience to be able to share in such a full manner."*

Chapter XVII: Notes

Charts, Tables, Other Statistics

SIZE OF COMMUNITY	# OF WOMEN ENTERED
over 1000 members	19
500-1000 members	5
250-500 members	12
fewer than 250 members	12

CLASS SIZES were almost always proportionate:
    Small Communities had classes of up to 12 members.
    250-500-member Communities had classes of 4-37 members.
    500-1000-member Communities had classes of 13-41 members
    1000+ Communities had classes of 21-80 members.

20 participants had forgotten/never knew their number of Community members.
6 did not remember how many were in their particular class.

MONEY/GOODS GIVEN TO WOMEN AS THEY LEFT THE CONVENT:

1 received –0–; one said "little".   1 each received $25 and $40.
3 received $100 each; 9 received $200; 2 received $250; 5 received $300.
9 received $500; 1 received $600; 1 received $700.
3 received $1000; 1 received $2000; and 1 received $3000
7 received the unspecified amount they had paid for dowry.
2 were given cars, one of these in lieu of money.
1 received back her inheritance (unspecified $) and one a loan.
1 kept her last years' salary as a hedge against total poverty.
21 were given additional goods ranging from the clothes they wore to some household goods. And 21 declined to answer the question. ❖❖❖

UNCONVENTIONAL WOMEN

What jobs for pay had you held before entering? How long? What was your salary range?

EX-NUN	AGE	COMMERCIAL JOB(S) BEFORE ENTERING	TIME HELD	SALARY	DOMESTIC/FARM JOBS
1	18	none			
2	18	county hosp., waitressing, typing for college prof.		min. wage	
3	16				babysitting
4	18	catalog clerk	1 yr		
5	17				babysitting
6	16		2 yrs		domestic work
7	22	bank, farm	4 yrs		
8	18				babysitting
9	19	office, hospital			
10	16				sum't cannery (nite)
11	16				babysitting, berrypicking
12	28	clerical, bookkeeper	7 yrs	$3000	
13	18	parttime in hospitals & businesses		min. wage	
14	18	none			
15	18				babysitting
16	23	registered nurse	1 ½ yrs	low	
17	18				babysitting
18	14	none			
19	17	summers: drive-in	3 sum.	.65/hr	babysitting
20	18	parents' store; they cashed my checks	sum/nt	$25 chks	
21	17				babysitting, hsekpg.
22	17	bakery	2-3 mo	min. wage	babysitting
23	18		5 yrs		babysitting
24	27	USAF active duty Korean War camp counselor, real estate	3 yrs	$2.50/hr	
25	18	cannery	3 mo su		
26	16	store, library		min. wage	
27	18	AT&T (needed job permit)	3 mo su		
28	18				sum'rs in beanfields
29	17	at jeweler's		$2/hr	
30	15				babysitting
31	18	PN in nursing home	3.5 yrs	$1.10/hr	
32	19	Safeway, Western Gear Works	5y+sum	$1.05/hr	
33	18	store sale			domestic
34	18	clerk at BonMarche, theatre usher			babysitting

Chapter XVII: Notes

#	Age	Job	Duration	Pay	Other
35	19	classifieds for hometown newspaper	1 yr	$180/mo	
36	30	law office	5-6 yrs	entry level	
37	17	none			
38	18	school custodian	3 yrs	$40/mo	hired girl, babysitting
39	18	packer at warehse, strawboss/fam. orchard		min.	
40	20				farm jobs, berrypicking
41	18				family farm jobs
42	21	secretary	4 yrs		
43	18	cannery			farm crop jobs
44	24	dept. store, taught school	2 yrs	$3000/yr	
45	18	cleaners (summer job)		min.	
46	18	hospital kitchen (sum), insurance office	1 yr		
47	17	parttime playing piano in dance studio			
48	19	bookkeeper in bank	1 1/2 yrs		
49	18	(wkd each hs summer0		min.	
50	19	drugstore	4 yrs		babysitting
51	14	none			
52	18				babysitting
53	18	none			
54	18	camp KP	8 wks	$40(1938)	
55	18	drugstore soda jerk		$2.50/hr	babysitting, berrypkg
56	17	sales in dime store		low	babysitting
57	18	fish cannery, sales in dept store	6mo T	.90, .45/hr	
58	18	none			
59	18	summer jobs			babysitting
60	19	summer camp counselor (went to college)			
61	18?				
62	17				babysitting fr. age 12
63	15	maid/b'sitter to 5 in town			b'sitting, farmwk.
64	18	paper routes, carhop, canneries		good	b'sit., farm, lawns
65	17	none			
66	14	cleaning homes			babysitting
67	18	wkg. for parks/recreation, clerking			babysitting
68	18				
69	18	summer jobs only			
70	17				b'sitting, berrypicking
71	18				babysitting
72	18	camp counselor, dept.st.clerk, newspaper			picking fruit
73	15	newspaper: customer service	2 yrs	min.	

496 UNCONVENTIONAL WOMEN

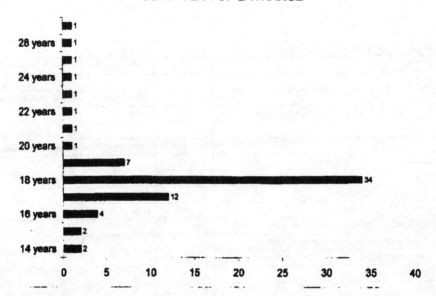

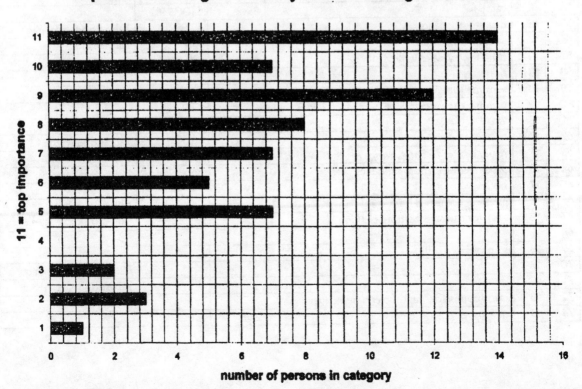

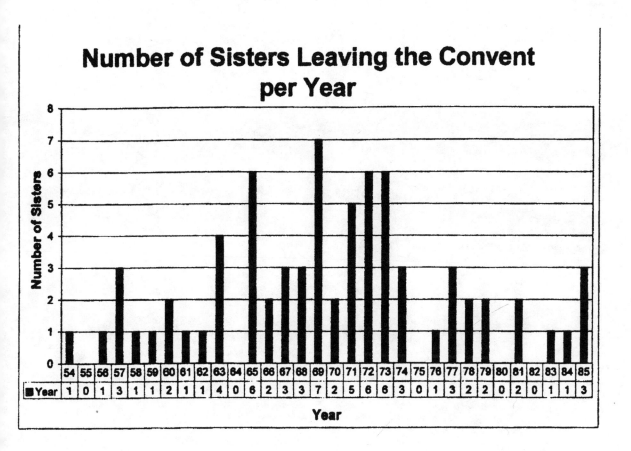

Epilogue

The world is changing at a greater rate than ever before, and we are changing with it. The thoughts and feelings of the 73 participants of this project may be slightly different after ten years, just as the readers of this book have changed and grown. But this project has done what it set out to do, i.e., set down for posterity the original thoughts and reactions of a large group of ex-nuns concerning their mid-century convent experiences.

Acknowledgments

Some of the best persons this author has met in a lifetime contributed to this book. They may reveal their names to you in private, or may participate in a book signing in your town, but it is not our place to list their real names here. These women have been most generous with their recollections, and are heroines of history, both for what they experienced, and for their honesty and bravery in sharing so that others may learn and understand. It has also been our hope from the beginning that the book might serve as an instrument of healing for other ex-nuns from that period (especially those who hesitate to share), by their reading and experiencing vicariously what these 73 women went through.

Gratitude goes to the Reverends Bertram Griffin, Jack Hall, Andrew Greeley, and other priests for their historical, sociological, and canon law perspectives. Thanks go also to Dr. Franklin Weingarten for psychological advice. Special thanks to authors Tim Unsworth and Lillana Kopp for their good words, and to the latter for writing a superb Introduction. Thank you to Joseph Montville and Michael Henderson for permission to quote from *The Forgiveness Factor*, and to Will Liebo for allowing the use of his school essay. Deep gratitude goes to many friends and colleagues who inspired, advised, and encouraged the author during this lengthy and difficult process.

About the Author

    Marie Therese Gass was born in Regina, Saskatchewan, Canada, in 1939, the eldest of six living children. After her family moved to the United States, she entered a Roman Catholic religious order of nuns. Since leaving the convent, Ms. Gass has been a teacher of music, art, writing, and basic high school subjects. She has worked with mentally challenged adults, at-risk older students, college adults, and senior citizens. Ms. Gass's most recent book is *Heritage Writing: Short and simple ways to hand down your story* (Sieben Hill). She currently resides in Oregon with her husband.

TO ORDER BOOKS FROM SIEBEN HILL
send the following information with your check:

PLEASE PRINT LEGIBLY:

NAME_____

STREET ADDRESS, APT.#, ETC._____

CITY_____ STATE_____ COUNTRY_____ ZIP_____

TELEPHONE_____-_____-_____ E-MAIL:_____

(LIST NUMBER OF COPIES AND TITLES ORDERED)

MAKE CHECK OR MONEY ORDER TO:

SIEBEN HILL
PO Box 243
Clackamas OR 97015-0243

CURRENTLY AVAILABLE:

heritage writing: *Short and simple ways to hand down your story*
$14.95 including shipping

unCONVENTional WOMEN
$25 plus $5 shipping